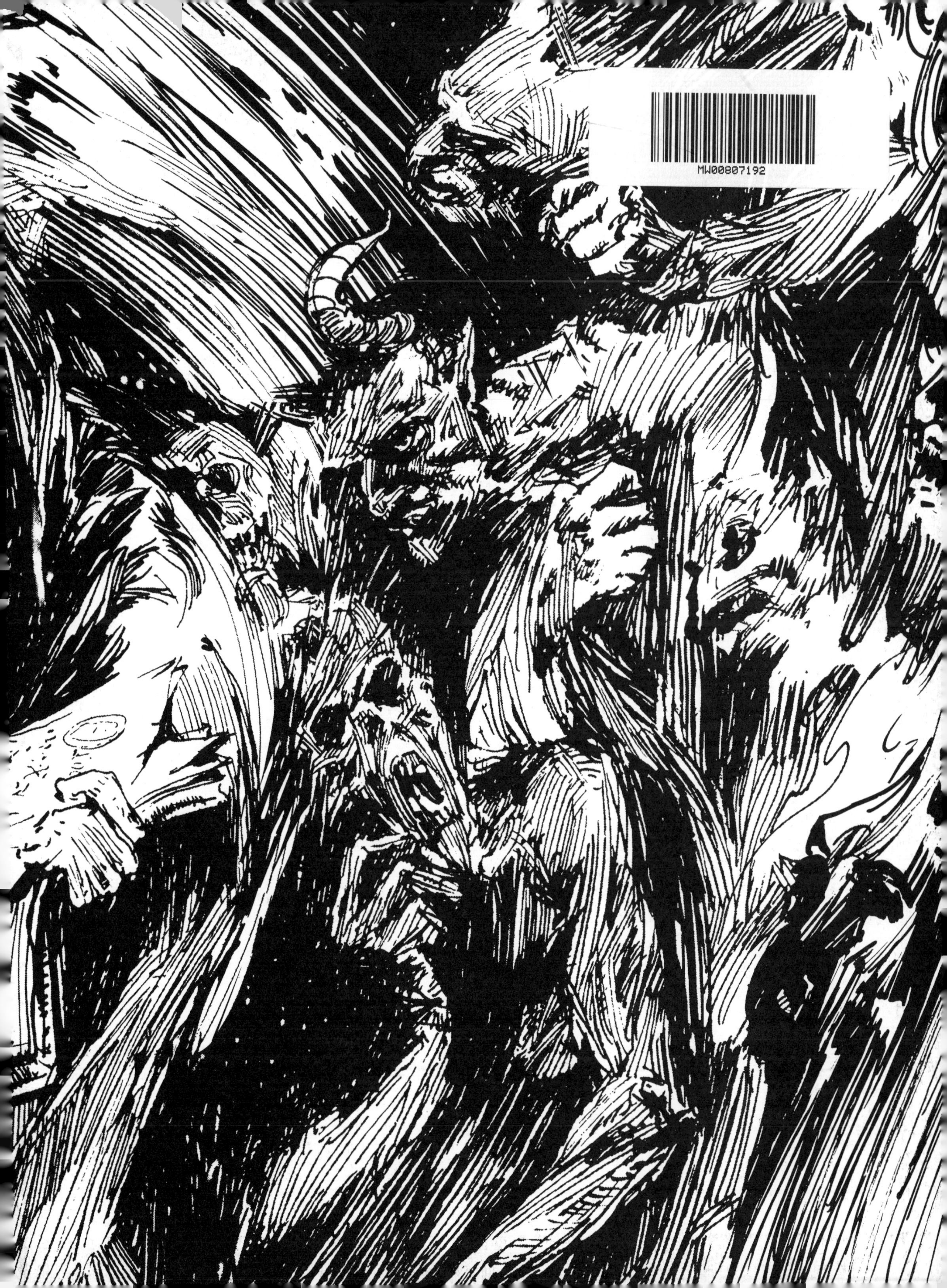

Gary Gianni's
M⊙NSTERMEN™
and Other Scary Stories

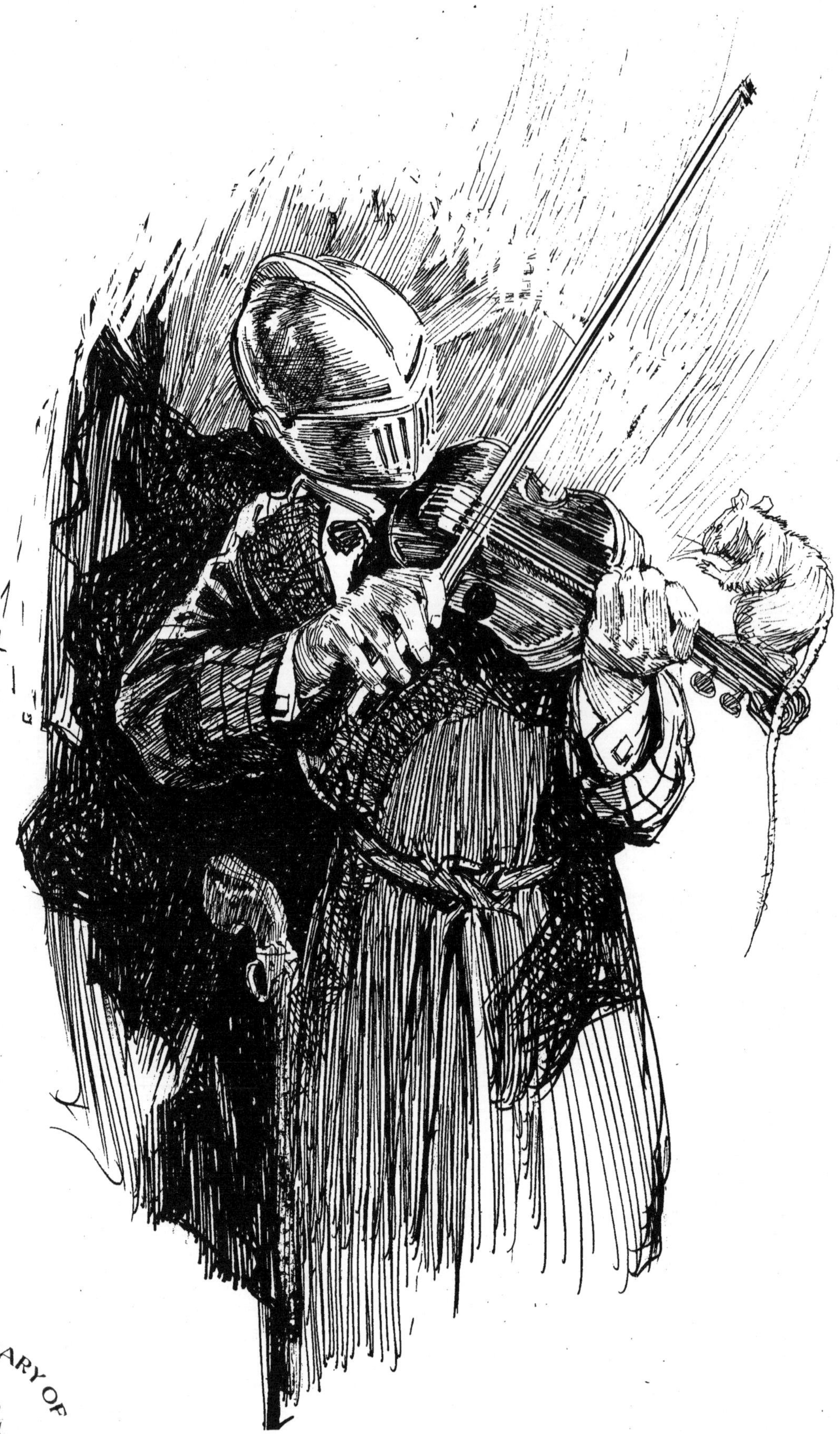

Gary Gianni's
MONSTERMEN™
and
Other Scary Stories

written and illustrated by

GARY GIANNI
with other authors

DARK HORSE BOOKS®

Gary Gianni's MonsterMen and Other Scary Stories
Written and Illustrated by Gary Gianni

Letters by Sean Konot, Todd Klein, and Clem Robins
Logo Design by Todd Klein

Editor, Scott Allie
Assistant Editor, Daniel Chabon
Collection Designers, Jim & Ruth Keegan

Special thanks to Cary Grazzini, Samantha Robertson, and Matt Dryer

This volume collects stories from *Hellboy: Wake the Devil, Hellboy Christmas Special, Hellboy: The Wild Hunt #5–#6, Hellboy: Almost Colossus, The Dark Horse Book of Monsters, The Dark Horse Book of the Dead, The Dark Horse Book of Hauntings, The Dark Horse Book of Witchcraft,* and the one-shot *The MonsterMen: The Skull and the Snowman.*

Published by Dark Horse Books
A division of Dark Horse Comics, Inc.
10956 SE Main Street
Milwaukie, OR 97222

DarkHorse.com

First edition: March 2012
ISBN 978-1-59582-829-3

1 3 5 7 9 10 8 6 4 2

Printed by 1010 Printing International, Ltd., Guangdong Province, China.

Mike Richardson, President and Publisher · Neil Hankerson, Executive Vice President · Tom Weddle, Chief Financial Officer · Randy Stradley, Vice President of Publishing · Michael Martens, Vice President of Book Trade Sales · Anita Nelson, Vice President of Business Affairs · Micha Hershman, Vice President of Marketing · David Scroggy, Vice President of Product Development · Dale LaFountain, Vice President of Information Technology · Darlene Vogel, Senior Director of Print, Design, and Production · Ken Lizzi, General Counsel · Davey Estrada, Editorial Director · Scott Allie, Senior Managing Editor · Chris Warner, Senior Books Editor · Diana Schutz, Executive Editor · Cary Grazzini, Director of Print and Development · Lia Ribacchi, Art Director · Cara Niece, Director of Scheduling

CONTENTS

Foreword by Gary Gianni
Introduction by Michael Chabon

THE MONSTERMEN
by Gary Gianni

OTHER SCARY STORIES
Illustrated by Gary Gianni

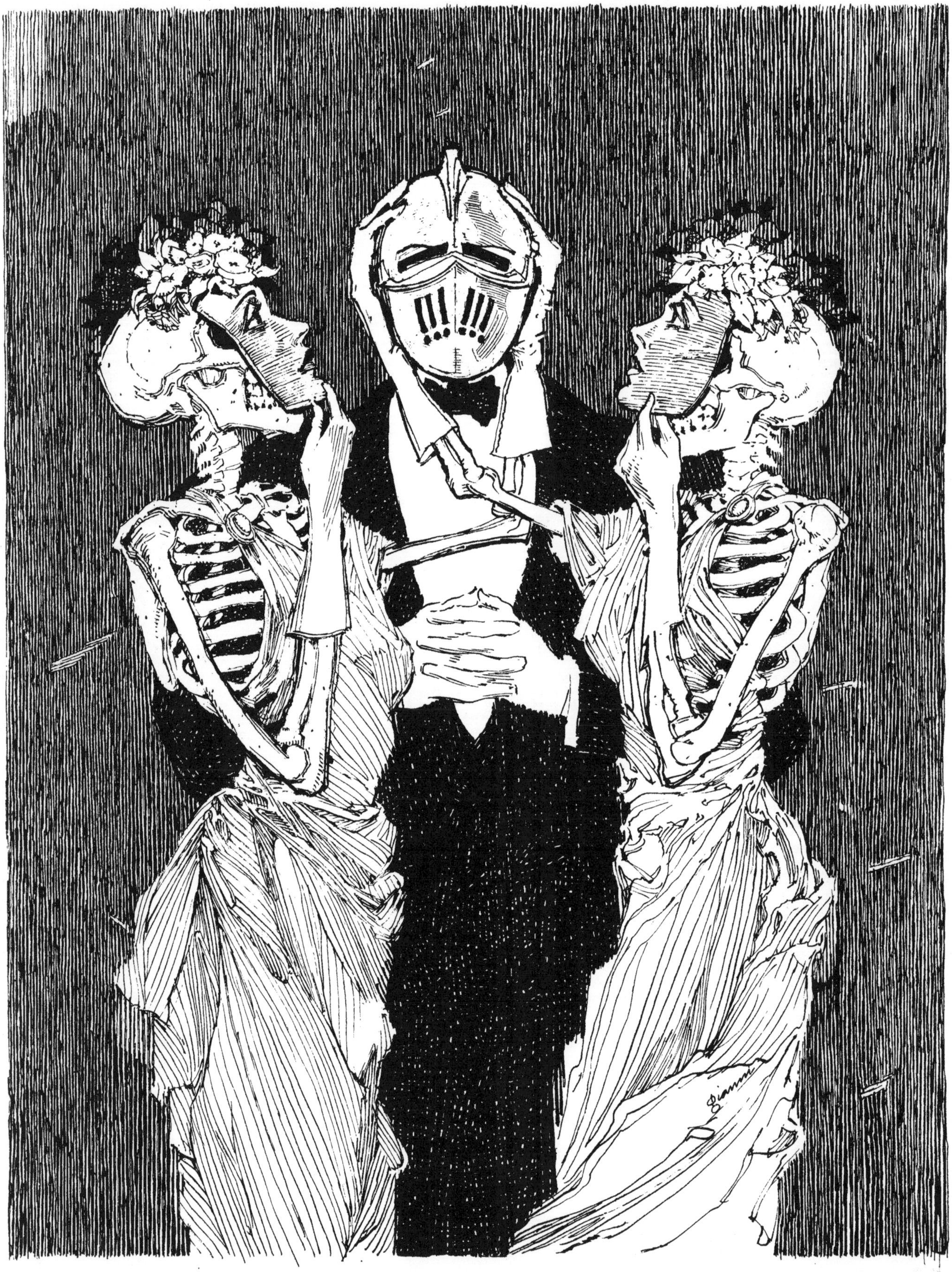

FOREWORD

HAVING CONTRACTED A SEVERE CASE of brain fever while studying at the University of Prague, I was forced to recuperate at the home of an aged cleric who knew of my interest in myth and legend.

My host was an engaging soul and the only fellow I have ever met with the peculiar habit of taking snuff. He spent a lifetime collecting oddities, not the least of which was a glass vessel containing the two heads of John the Baptist.

"Allow me to direct your attention to the fourteenth-century illuminated manuscript," he sniffed and motioned to a sturdy wooden pedestal. "You have, no doubt, heard of the order of the Corpus Monstrum?"

"Some sort of medieval guild founded to protect mankind from the powers of darkness, wasn't it?" said I.

My new friend nodded. "Aye, and the sole remaining member of that group still wanders through the ages. Benedictus. I imagine you're aware of him as well."

Before I could answer, the cleric was on his feet, rolling the lectern with the massive tome upon it over to where I lay. I propped myself up and examined the book. It was decorated throughout with consecutive panel illustrations similar in style to the glass windows of Chartres Cathedral.

"Because of your penchant for comic strips, you'll find this of interest," the old gentleman beamed. Indeed, with the text, written beneath each illustrated panel, the overall design was reminiscent of a comic page. The pictures were extraordinary but the Latin was difficult to follow.

The cleric translated a passage:

> *Benedictus entered a house where he found a spectre possessing a man. He commanded the demon to leave the body. Instead of going out (of the place) it entered the body of another man in the same dwelling and began to attack and bite those who were there. Benedictus put his fingers in the man's mouth, and defied him to bite. The demoniac retreated, as if a bar of hot iron had been placed in his mouth, and at last, the demon went out of the possessed body, not by the mouth which was barred, but through the behind.*

My host continued to read accounts of ghosts and demons and the beings who fought against them. The text seemed to suggest that darkness was greater than light. Evil more resilient than goodness. Only constant vigilance kept mankind from falling into the abyss. What sort of ancient scholars would author such ideas?

It was all too much for me. At length, I suffered a relapse of my prior condition and in my delirium was whisked back to England for treatment. During a stay in the hospital, word reached me that my host had disappeared and his home burnt to the ground in a mysterious fire.

Could this tragedy be linked to our indiscreet conversation concerning the powers of darkness? I wonder. Perhaps stories surrounding such things should never be whispered—much less adapted into comic-book form! And now that I have selected a group of supernatural tales to be published, my life might be in danger.

Wait—I hear something—dreadful noises from the cellar below.

What could be making those wet, flopping sounds on the stairs? Some horrible thing shambles closer. I continue pounding on the keyboard. Mankind must be warned! Heaven help me, now the doorknob turns! The door is opening . . .

Pray tha—

(*Editor's note: Numerous attempts to contact the author, Gary Gianni, have failed. The publisher has decided to print the above text in its unfinished state.*)

INTRODUCTION

WE WHO HAVE CREWED ABOARD Captain Nemo's *Nautilus* have been left by the experience—in all its antique and tempestuous splendor—with a certain look. We recognize one another, even across great distances and gulfs of years. I remember first encountering the work of my fellow Nautilusard Gary Gianni in the illustrations he did for the marvelous Wandering Star editions of the works of Robert E. Howard. I knew him at once: a sailor of the deeps of popular art and literature, a mapper of submerged, half-forgotten kingdoms with names like Valusia and Atlantis and the Misty Isles. And yet never—or never merely—a diver to the benthos and bathos of nostalgia. Our ship, remember, is state of the art—at once the *premier* and *dernier cri* of the modernity that Jules Verne arguably invented. The first gesture of modernity is to explode the past and sweep away its fragments. The second is to use those very fragments to construct new art in the landscape and language of brokenness. I saw in Gianni's classic pen-and-ink style, in the panache of his cross-hatching, in his mastery of black, in the dynamic flow of his composition and figures, in the evident breadth of Gianni's familiarity with the history of adventure illustration, a third gesture: the modernity of the *Nautilus*. We do not seek to rise to the surface of history like a sleeper surfacing from a nightmare. We do not dangle our little lines from cobbled boats, fishing up the bits and pieces. The sea is our home. We swim through it, in the state-of-the-art, electric-powered submarine of our imaginations, drawing freely upon it for everything we need. We are practical modernists. Where others become entangled in vast kelp beds of history, we roll cigars. I was not at all surprised to discover, shortly after that first encounter with Gianni, that he had (studiously, gloriously, and with his customary *élan*) adapted *20,000 Leagues Under the Sea* as a graphic novel.

If that book, and some of the other work that Gary Gianni has done in comics, like the weekly *Prince Valiant* page, exhibits a certain stateliness, an air of pageantry—if it never quite abandoned the illustrative tradition of which Gianni is a master—*The MonsterMen* leaves no doubt: the dude knows how to rock a comic-book page. In addition to all his usual swash and shadow, the easy grace of his figures, the depth and dynamism of his layouts, in these pages you will find Gianni putting on a clinic in the art of page layout, showing the degree to which he has pragmatically absorbed the lessons of layout saboteurs like Eisner and Chaykin and Miller—the Captain Nemos, romantic destroyers of the comics page—and married them to the Gianni style, nourished and enriched by the past as the crew of *Nautilus* by the bounty of the deep. Add to this a reinvention of the figure of the Occult Detective, steeped like everything Gianni does in a grasp of its history from Carnacki to Hellboy, and the result is thrilling, almost disturbing, and it brings us, out of the sea bottom of the past, as all art must, something new.

Michael Chabon
Berkeley, California
September 26, 2011

SILENT AS THE GRAVE

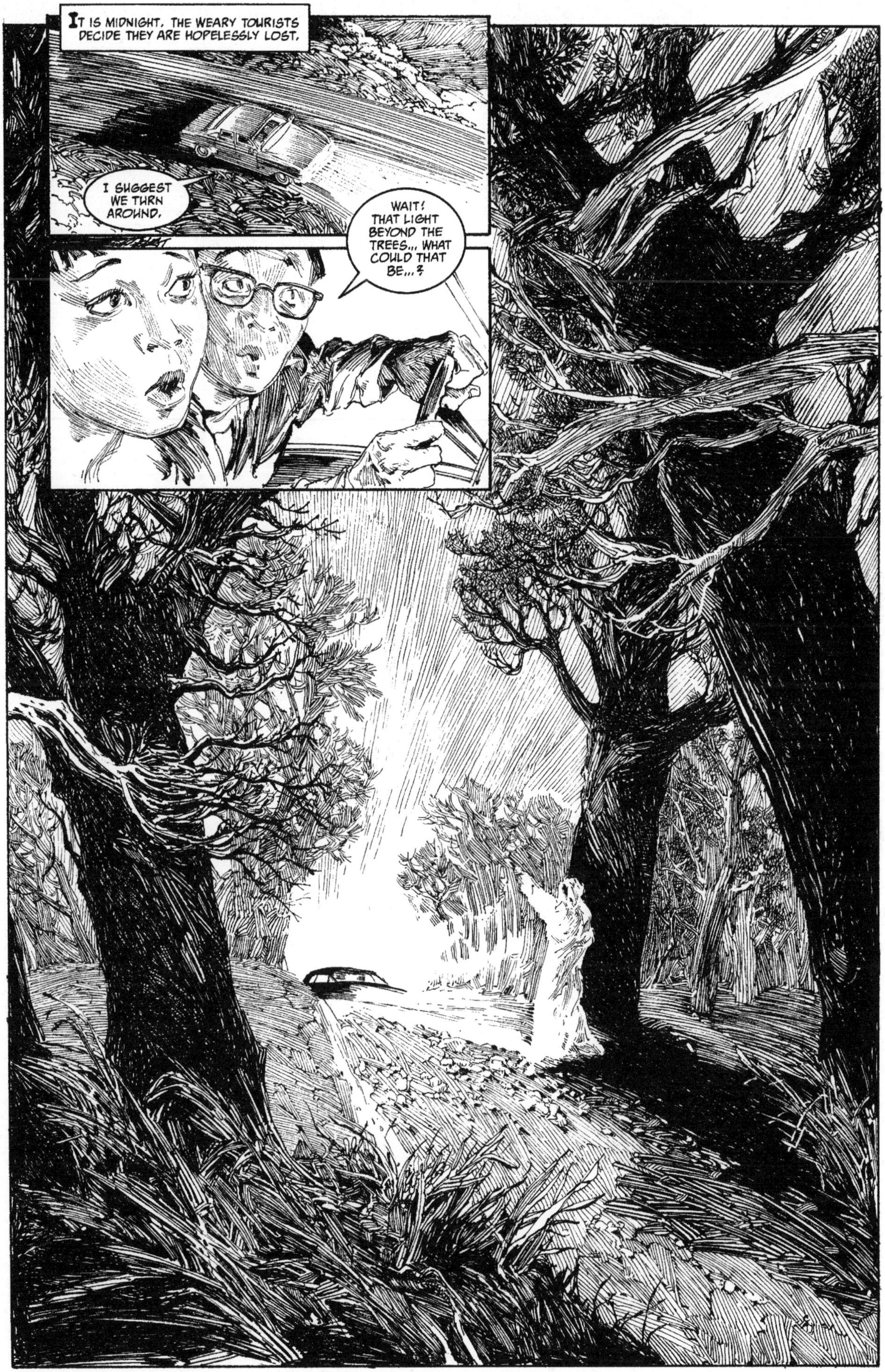
IT IS MIDNIGHT. THE WEARY TOURISTS DECIDE THEY ARE HOPELESSLY LOST.
I SUGGEST WE TURN AROUND.
WAIT! THAT LIGHT BEYOND THE TREES... WHAT COULD THAT BE...?

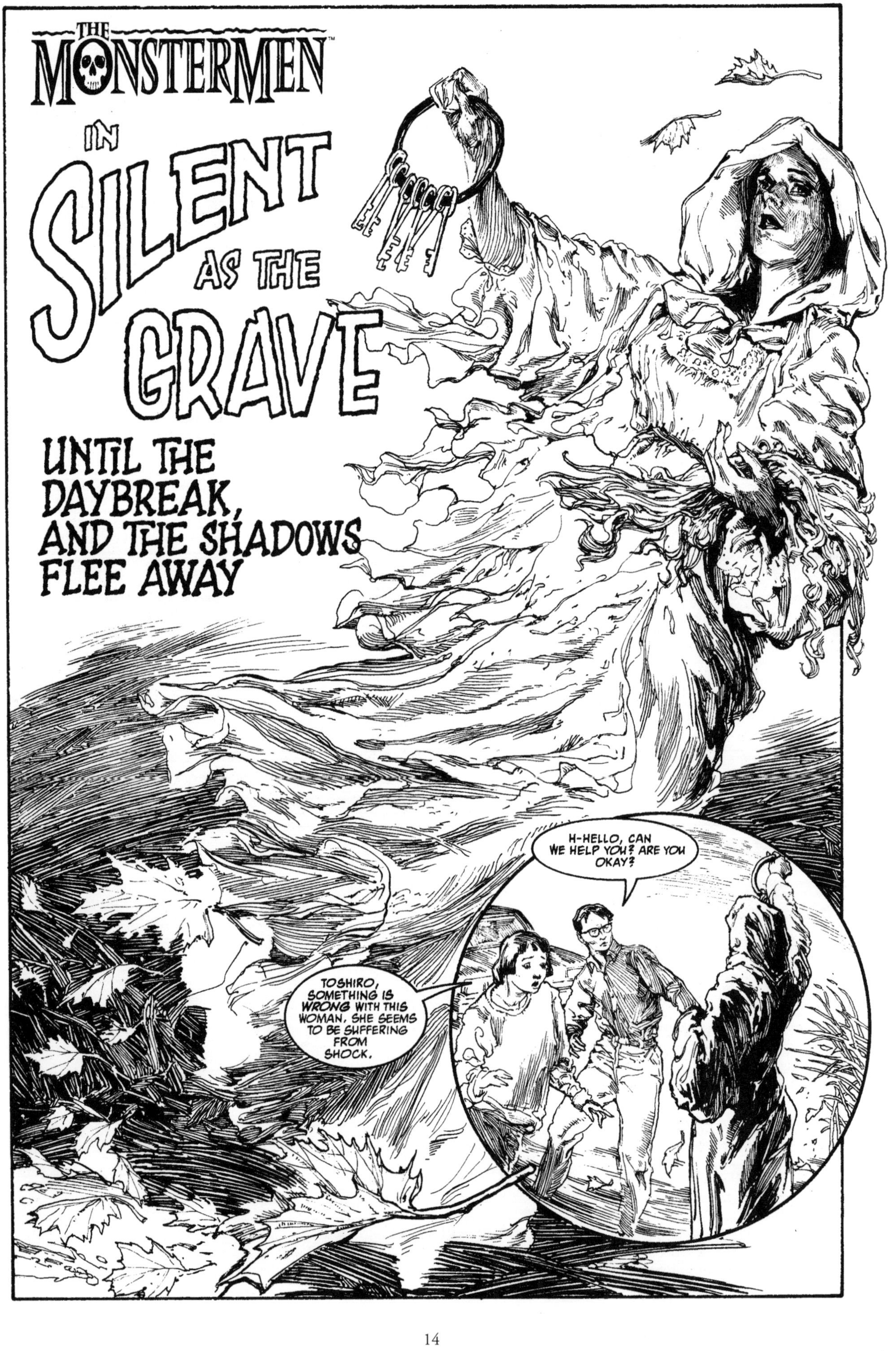
THE MONSTERMEN
IN
SILENT AS THE GRAVE
UNTIL THE DAYBREAK, AND THE SHADOWS FLEE AWAY
H-HELLO, CAN WE HELP YOU? ARE YOU OKAY?
TOSHIRO, SOMETHING IS WRONG WITH THIS WOMAN. SHE SEEMS TO BE SUFFERING FROM SHOCK.

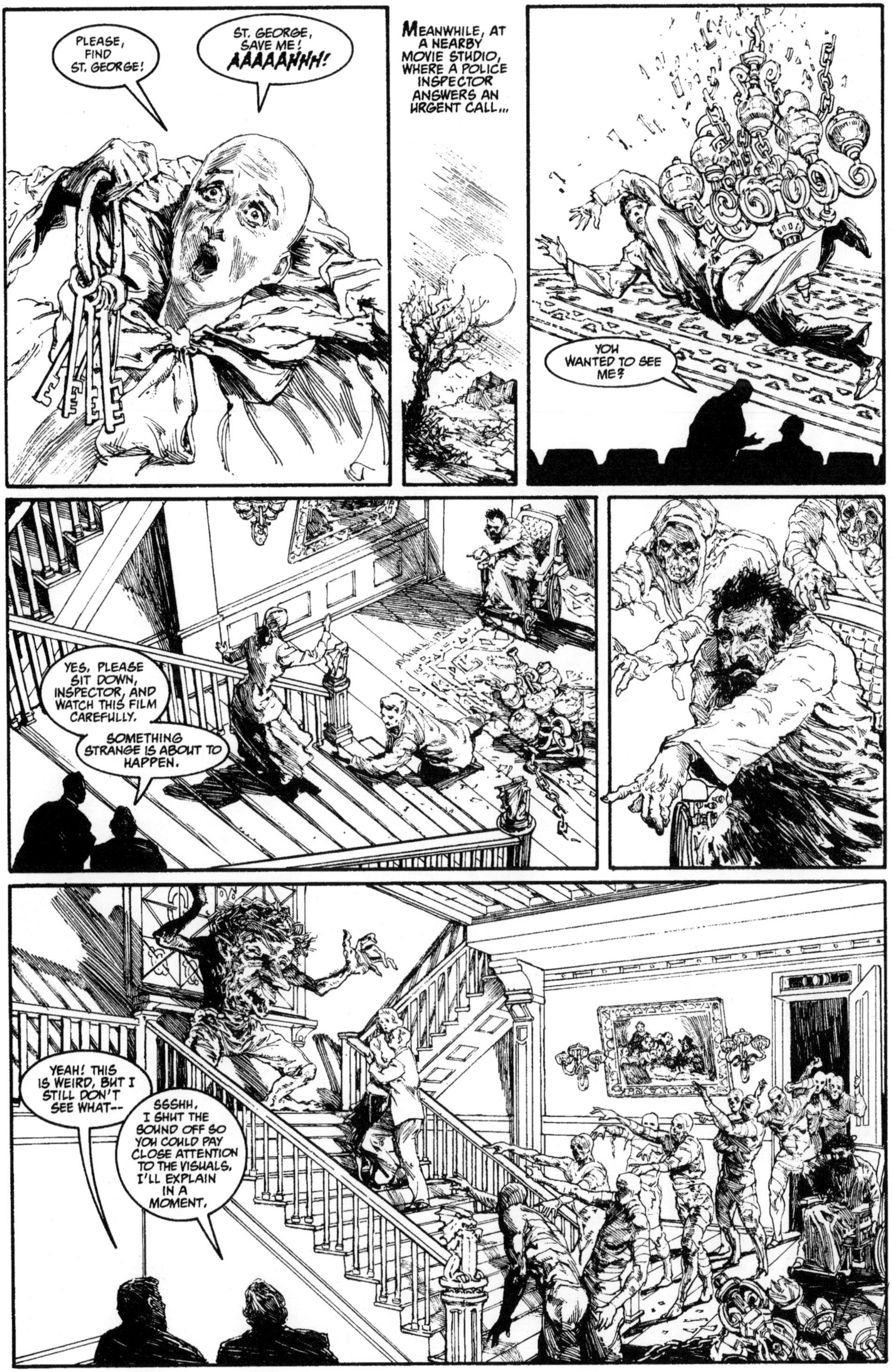

PLEASE, FIND ST. GEORGE!
ST. GEORGE, SAVE ME! AAAAAHHH!
MEANWHILE, AT A NEARBY MOVIE STUDIO, WHERE A POLICE INSPECTOR ANSWERS AN URGENT CALL...
YOU WANTED TO SEE ME?
YES. PLEASE SIT DOWN, INSPECTOR, AND WATCH THIS FILM CAREFULLY.
SOMETHING STRANGE IS ABOUT TO HAPPEN.
YEAH! THIS IS WEIRD, BUT I STILL DON'T SEE WHAT--
SSSHH, I SHUT THE SOUND OFF SO YOU COULD PAY CLOSE ATTENTION TO THE VISUALS. I'LL EXPLAIN IN A MOMENT.

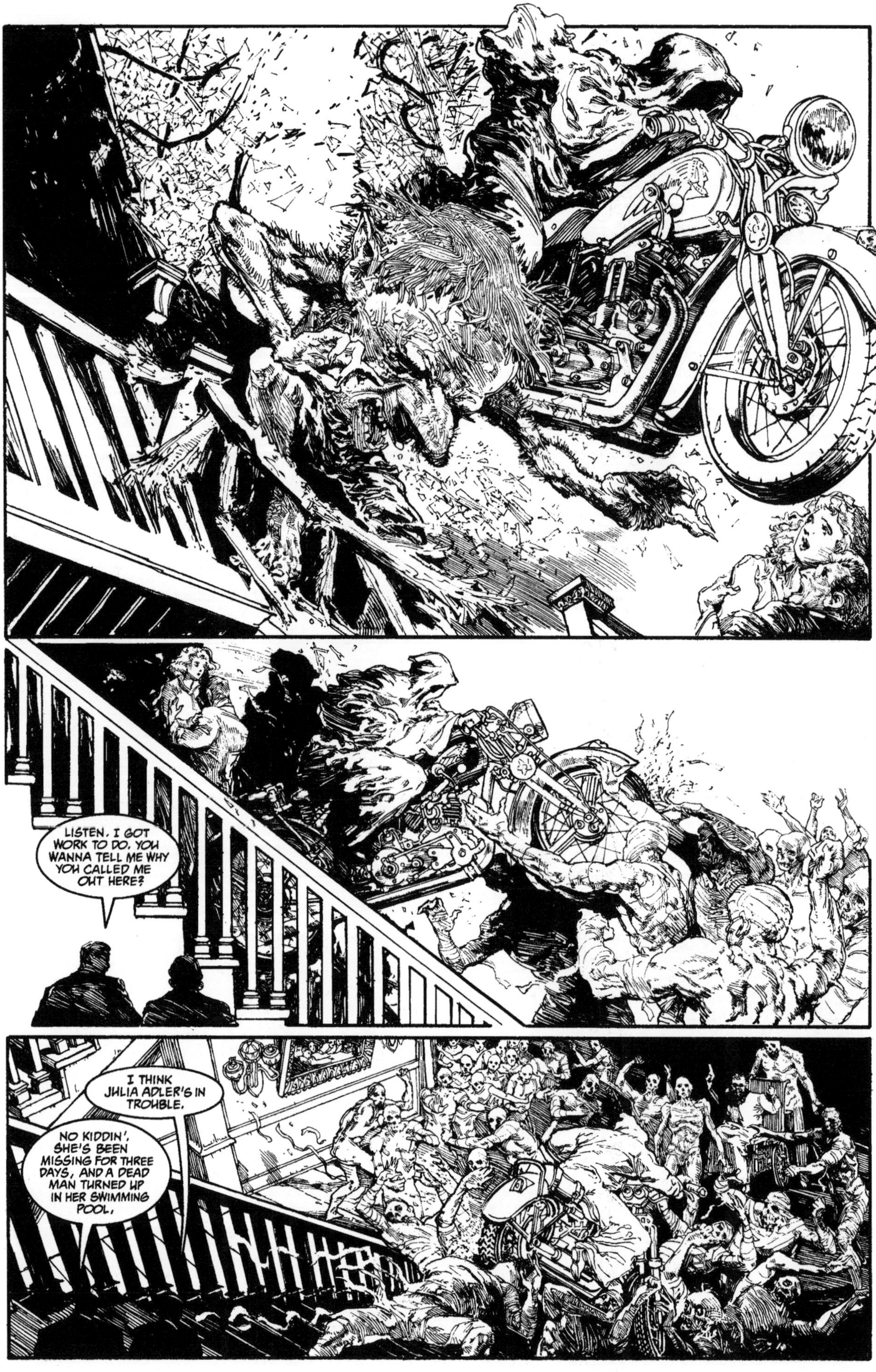
LISTEN. I GOT WORK TO DO. YOU WANNA TELL ME WHY YOU CALLED ME OUT HERE?
I THINK JULIA ADLER'S IN TROUBLE.
NO KIDDIN', SHE'S BEEN MISSING FOR THREE DAYS, AND A DEAD MAN TURNED UP IN HER SWIMMING POOL.

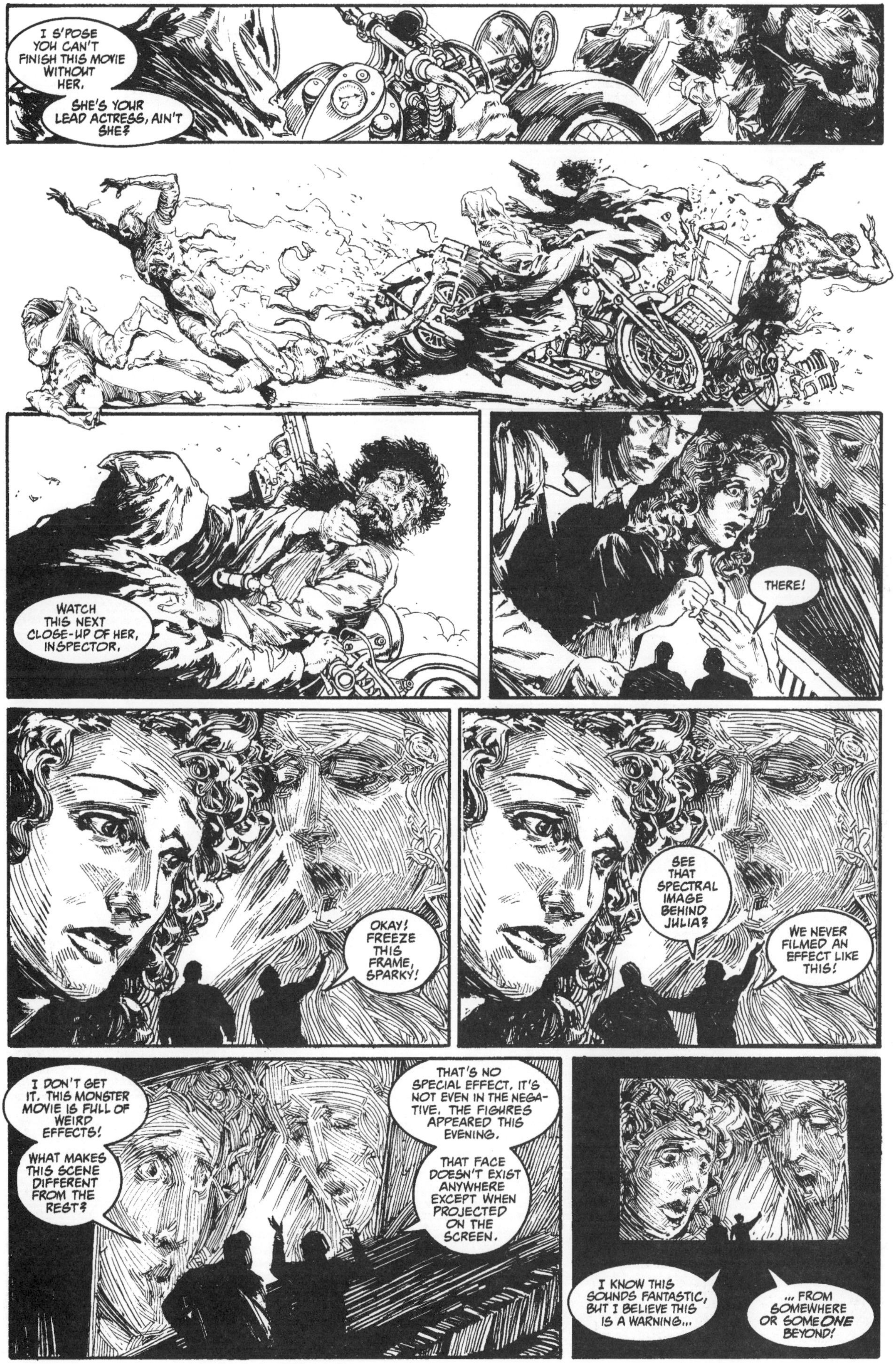
I S'POSE YOU CAN'T FINISH THIS MOVIE WITHOUT HER.
SHE'S YOUR LEAD ACTRESS, AIN'T SHE?
WATCH THIS NEXT CLOSE-UP OF HER, INSPECTOR.
THERE!
OKAY! FREEZE THIS FRAME, SPARKY!
SEE THAT SPECTRAL IMAGE BEHIND JULIA?
WE NEVER FILMED AN EFFECT LIKE THIS!
I DON'T GET IT. THIS MONSTER MOVIE IS FULL OF WEIRD EFFECTS!
WHAT MAKES THIS SCENE DIFFERENT FROM THE REST?
THAT'S NO SPECIAL EFFECT. IT'S NOT EVEN IN THE NEGA-TIVE. THE FIGURES APPEARED THIS EVENING.
THAT FACE DOESN'T EXIST ANYWHERE EXCEPT WHEN PROJECTED ON THE SCREEN.
I KNOW THIS SOUNDS FANTASTIC, BUT I BELIEVE THIS IS A WARNING...
... FROM SOMEWHERE OR SOMEONE BEYOND!

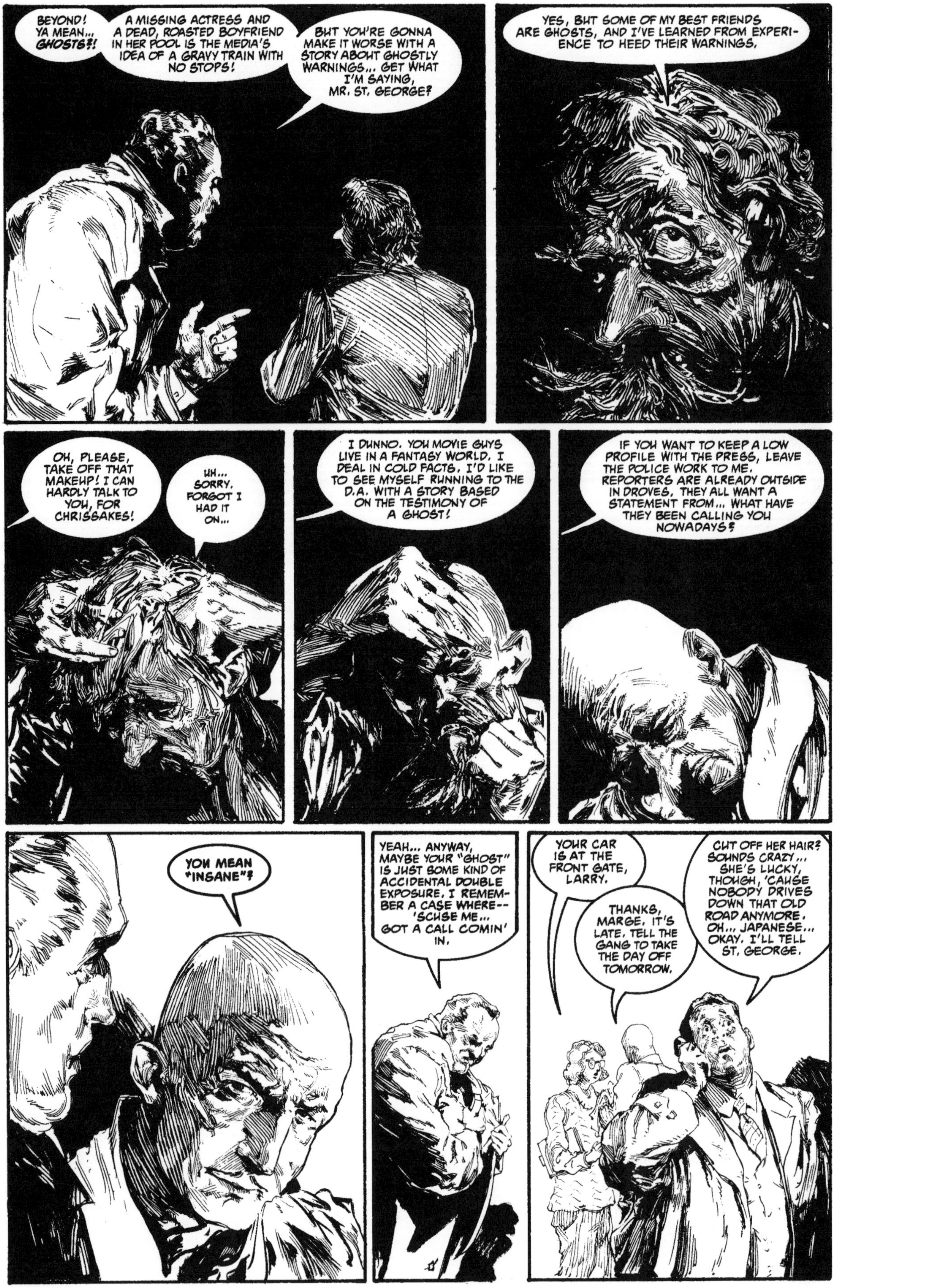
BEYOND! YA MEAN... GHOSTS?!
A MISSING ACTRESS AND A DEAD, ROASTED BOYFRIEND IN HER POOL IS THE MEDIA'S IDEA OF A GRAVY TRAIN WITH NO STOPS!
BUT YOU'RE GONNA MAKE IT WORSE WITH A STORY ABOUT GHOSTLY WARNINGS... GET WHAT I'M SAYING, MR. ST. GEORGE?
YES, BUT SOME OF MY BEST FRIENDS ARE GHOSTS, AND I'VE LEARNED FROM EXPERIENCE TO HEED THEIR WARNINGS.
OH, PLEASE, TAKE OFF THAT MAKEUP! I CAN HARDLY TALK TO YOU, FOR CHRISSAKES!
UH... SORRY. FORGOT I HAD IT ON...
I DUNNO. YOU MOVIE GUYS LIVE IN A FANTASY WORLD. I DEAL IN COLD FACTS. I'D LIKE TO SEE MYSELF RUNNING TO THE D.A. WITH A STORY BASED ON THE TESTIMONY OF A GHOST!
IF YOU WANT TO KEEP A LOW PROFILE WITH THE PRESS, LEAVE THE POLICE WORK TO ME. REPORTERS ARE ALREADY OUTSIDE IN DROVES. THEY ALL WANT A STATEMENT FROM... WHAT HAVE THEY BEEN CALLING YOU NOWADAYS?
YOU MEAN "INSANE"?
YEAH... ANYWAY, MAYBE YOUR "GHOST" IS JUST SOME KIND OF ACCIDENTAL DOUBLE EXPOSURE. I REMEMBER A CASE WHERE-- 'SCUSE ME... GOT A CALL COMIN' IN.
YOUR CAR IS AT THE FRONT GATE, LARRY.
THANKS, MARGE. IT'S LATE. TELL THE GANG TO TAKE THE DAY OFF TOMORROW.
CUT OFF HER HAIR? SOUNDS CRAZY... SHE'S LUCKY, THOUGH, 'CAUSE NOBODY DRIVES DOWN THAT OLD ROAD ANYMORE. OH... JAPANESE... OKAY. I'LL TELL ST. GEORGE.

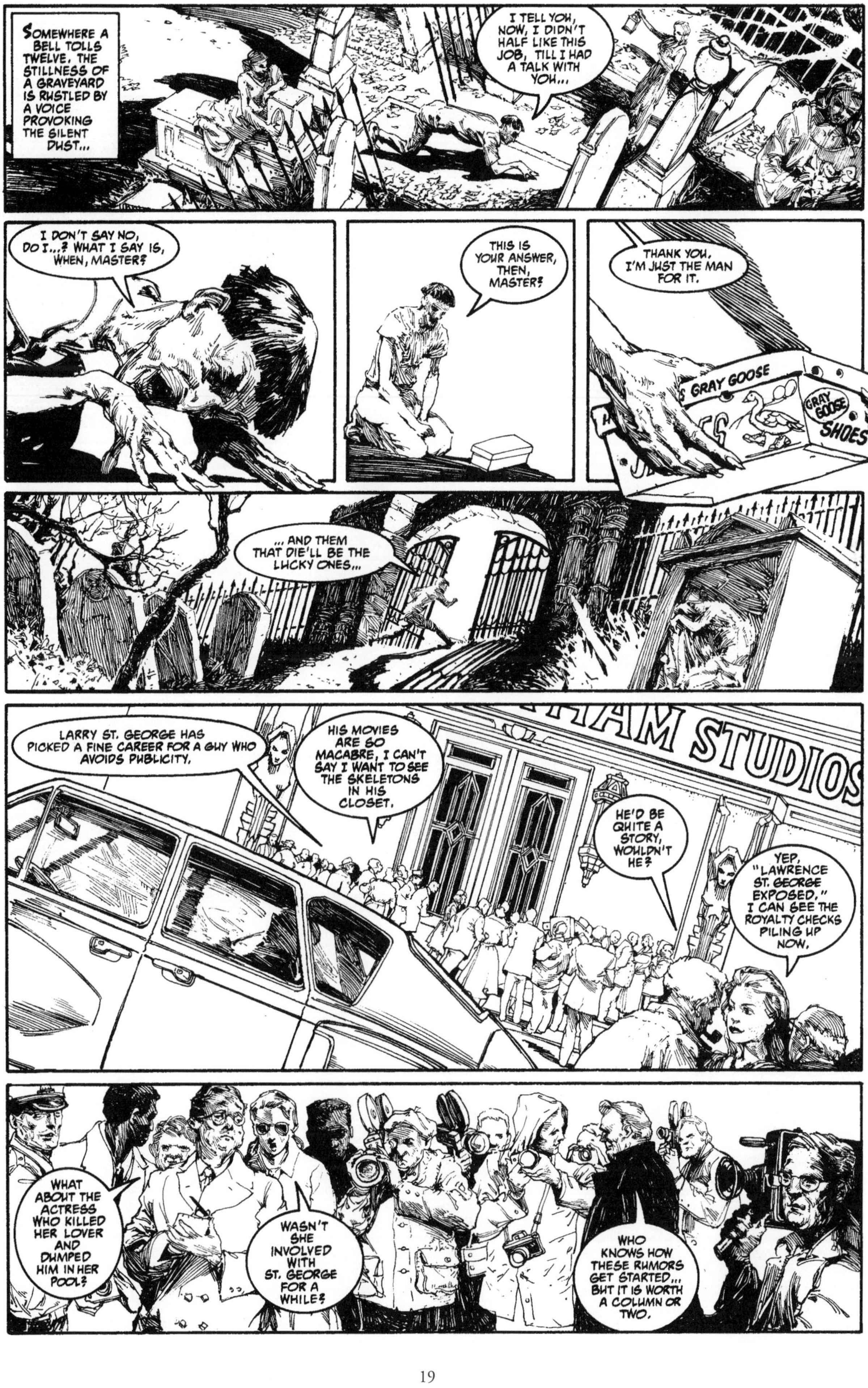
SOMEWHERE A BELL TOLLS TWELVE. THE STILLNESS OF A GRAVEYARD IS RUSTLED BY A VOICE PROVOKING THE SILENT DUST...
I TELL YOU, NOW, I DIDN'T HALF LIKE THIS JOB, TILL I HAD A TALK WITH YOU...
I DON'T SAY NO, DO I...? WHAT I SAY IS, WHEN, MASTER?
THIS IS YOUR ANSWER, THEN, MASTER?
THANK YOU. I'M JUST THE MAN FOR IT.
GRAY GOOSE
GRAY GOOSE SHOES
...AND THEM THAT DIE'LL BE THE LUCKY ONES...
HAM STUDIOS
LARRY ST. GEORGE HAS PICKED A FINE CAREER FOR A GUY WHO AVOIDS PUBLICITY.
HIS MOVIES ARE SO MACABRE, I CAN'T SAY I WANT TO SEE THE SKELETONS IN HIS CLOSET.
HE'D BE QUITE A STORY, WOULDN'T HE?
YEP, "LAWRENCE ST. GEORGE EXPOSED." I CAN SEE THE ROYALTY CHECKS PILING UP NOW.
WHAT ABOUT THE ACTRESS WHO KILLED HER LOVER AND DUMPED HIM IN HER POOL?
WASN'T SHE INVOLVED WITH ST. GEORGE FOR A WHILE?
WHO KNOWS HOW THESE RUMORS GET STARTED... BUT IT IS WORTH A COLUMN OR TWO.

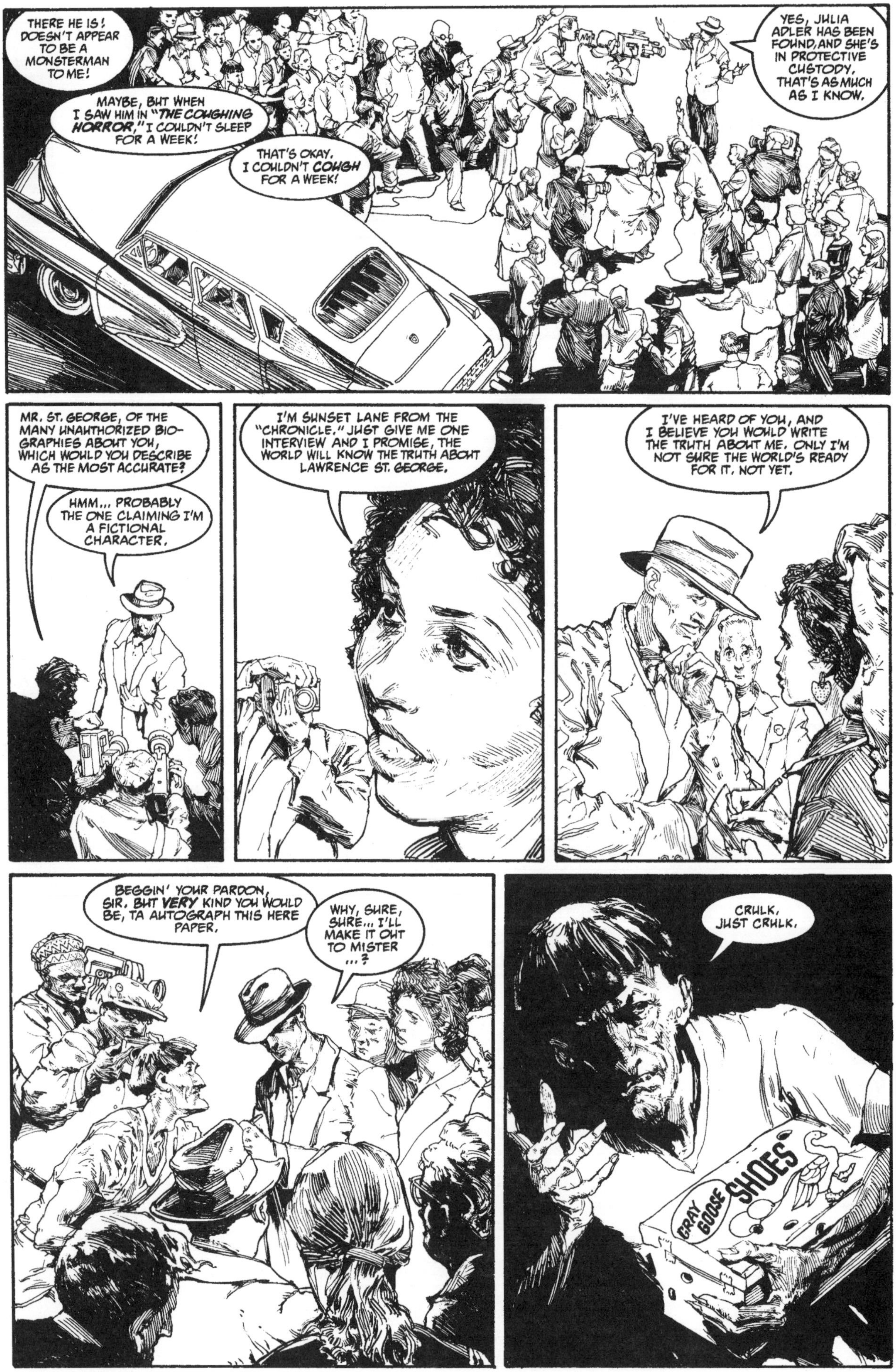
THERE HE IS! DOESN'T APPEAR TO BE A MONSTERMAN TO ME!
MAYBE, BUT WHEN I SAW HIM IN "THE COUGHING HORROR," I COULDN'T SLEEP FOR A WEEK!
THAT'S OKAY. I COULDN'T COUGH FOR A WEEK!
YES, JULIA ADLER HAS BEEN FOUND, AND SHE'S IN PROTECTIVE CUSTODY. THAT'S AS MUCH AS I KNOW.
MR. ST. GEORGE, OF THE MANY UNAUTHORIZED BIOGRAPHIES ABOUT YOU, WHICH WOULD YOU DESCRIBE AS THE MOST ACCURATE?
HMM... PROBABLY THE ONE CLAIMING I'M A FICTIONAL CHARACTER.
I'M SUNSET LANE FROM THE "CHRONICLE." JUST GIVE ME ONE INTERVIEW AND I PROMISE, THE WORLD WILL KNOW THE TRUTH ABOUT LAWRENCE ST. GEORGE.
I'VE HEARD OF YOU, AND I BELIEVE YOU WOULD WRITE THE TRUTH ABOUT ME. ONLY I'M NOT SURE THE WORLD'S READY FOR IT. NOT YET.
BEGGIN' YOUR PARDON, SIR. BUT VERY KIND YOU WOULD BE, TA AUTOGRAPH THIS HERE PAPER.
WHY, SURE, SURE... I'LL MAKE IT OUT TO MISTER ...?
CRULK, JUST CRULK.
GRAY GOOSE SHOES

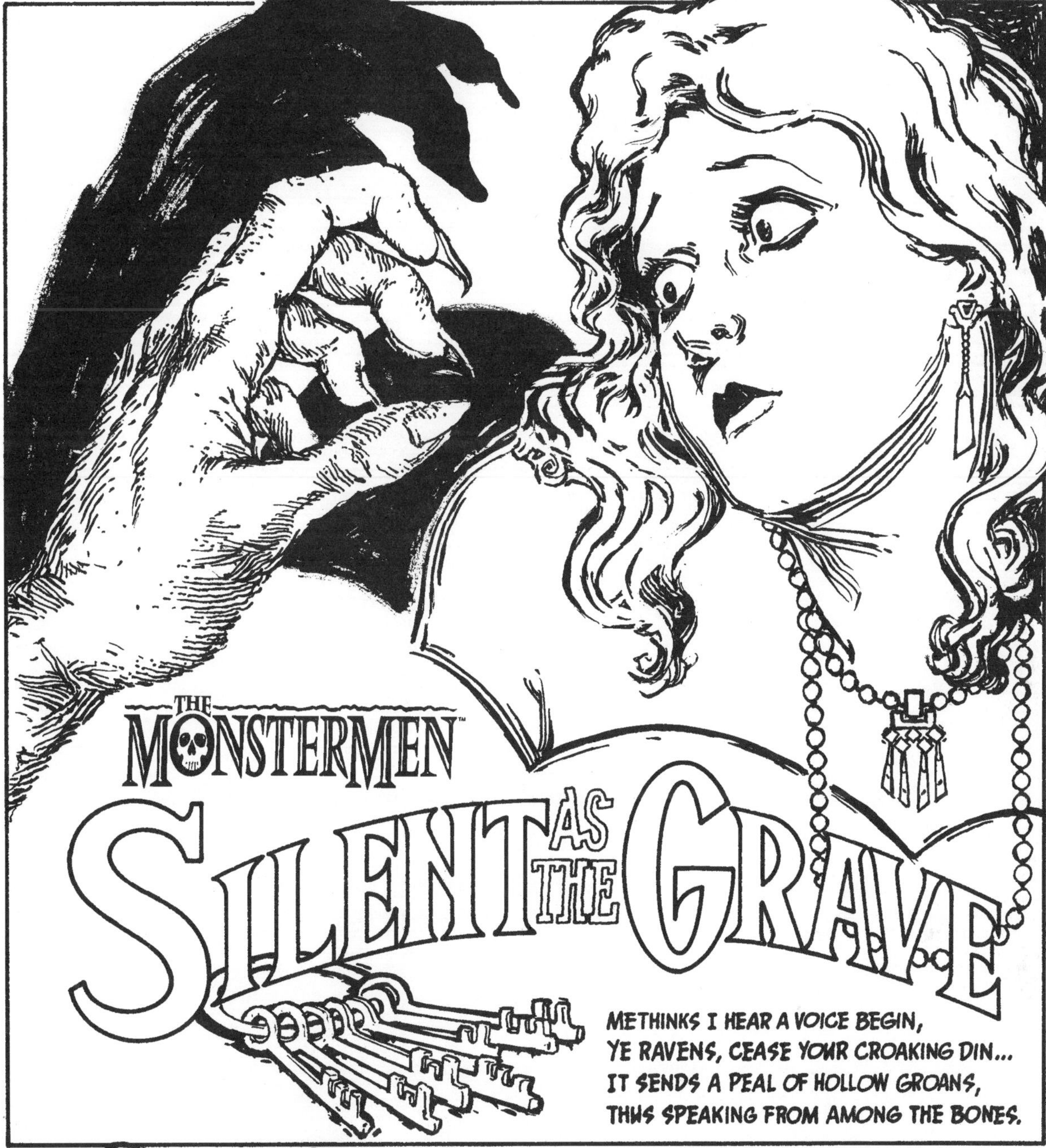
THE MONSTERMEN™
SILENT AS THE GRAVE
METHINKS I HEAR A VOICE BEGIN,
YE RAVENS, CEASE YOUR CROAKING DIN...
IT SENDS A PEAL OF HOLLOW GROANS,
THUS SPEAKING FROM AMONG THE BONES.

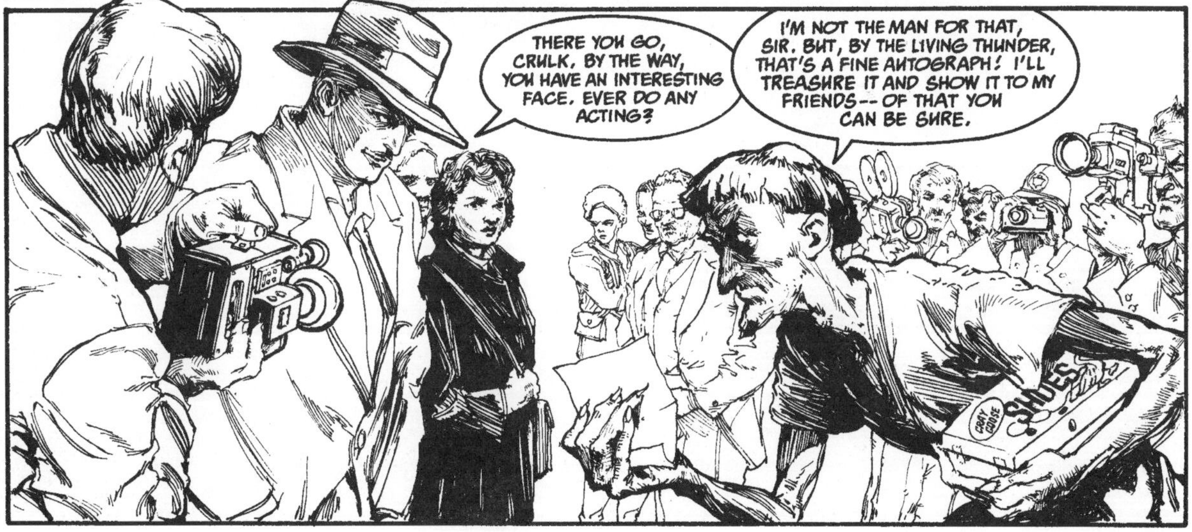
THERE YOU GO, CRULK. BY THE WAY, YOU HAVE AN INTERESTING FACE. EVER DO ANY ACTING?
I'M NOT THE MAN FOR THAT, SIR. BUT, BY THE LIVING THUNDER, THAT'S A FINE AUTOGRAPH! I'LL TREASURE IT AND SHOW IT TO MY FRIENDS-- OF THAT YOU CAN BE SURE.
SHOES

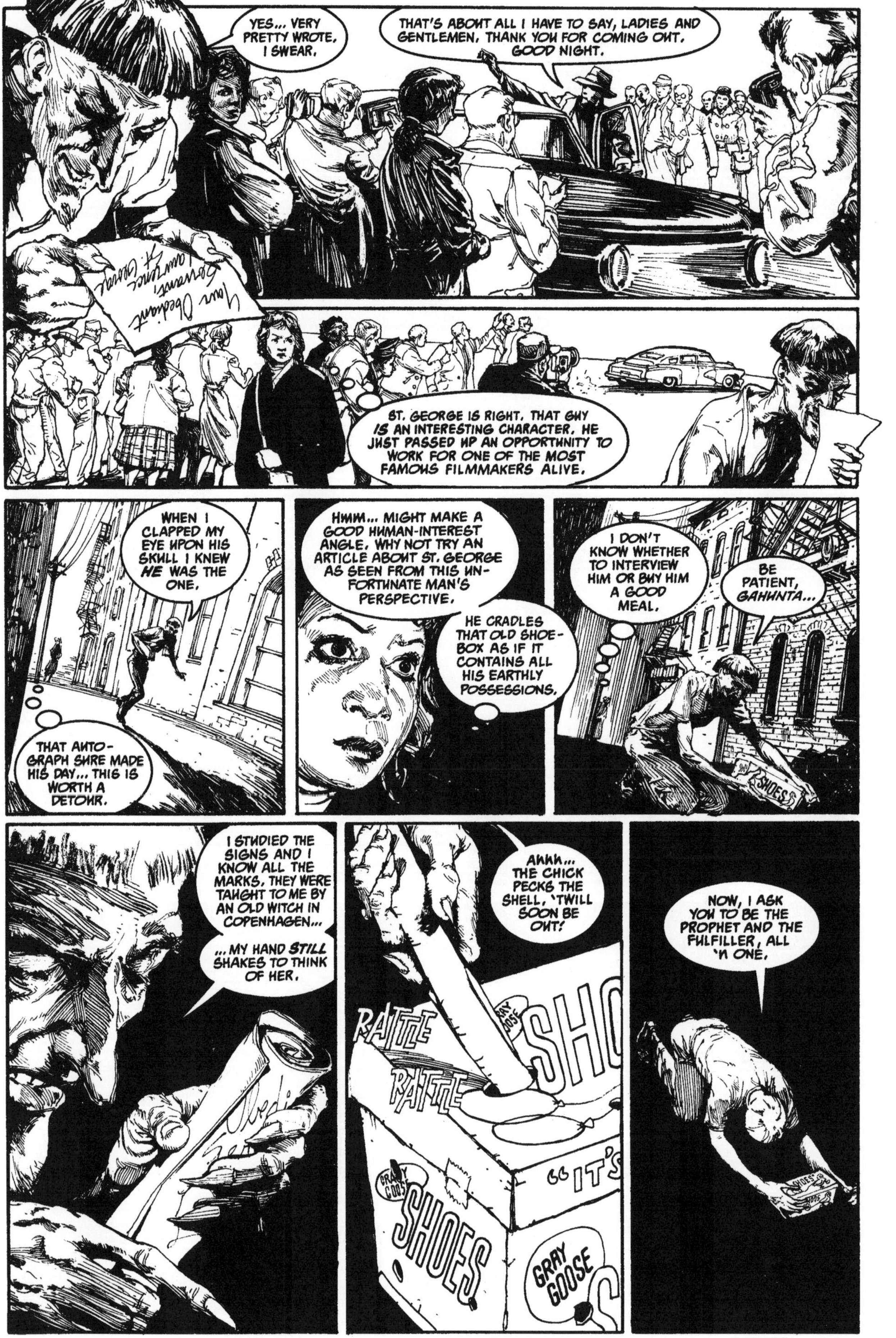
YES... VERY PRETTY WROTE, I SWEAR.
THAT'S ABOUT ALL I HAVE TO SAY, LADIES AND GENTLEMEN, THANK YOU FOR COMING OUT. GOOD NIGHT.
Your Obedient Servant, Lawrence St. George
ST. GEORGE IS RIGHT. THAT GUY IS AN INTERESTING CHARACTER. HE JUST PASSED UP AN OPPORTUNITY TO WORK FOR ONE OF THE MOST FAMOUS FILMMAKERS ALIVE.
WHEN I CLAPPED MY EYE UPON HIS SKULL I KNEW HE WAS THE ONE.
THAT AUTOGRAPH SURE MADE HIS DAY... THIS IS WORTH A DETOUR.
HMM... MIGHT MAKE A GOOD HUMAN-INTEREST ANGLE. WHY NOT TRY AN ARTICLE ABOUT ST. GEORGE AS SEEN FROM THIS UNFORTUNATE MAN'S PERSPECTIVE.
HE CRADLES THAT OLD SHOEBOX AS IF IT CONTAINS ALL HIS EARTHLY POSSESSIONS.
I DON'T KNOW WHETHER TO INTERVIEW HIM OR BUY HIM A GOOD MEAL.
BE PATIENT, GAHUNTA...
SHOES
I STUDIED THE SIGNS AND I KNOW ALL THE MARKS. THEY WERE TAUGHT TO ME BY AN OLD WITCH IN COPENHAGEN...
...MY HAND STILL SHAKES TO THINK OF HER.
AHHH... THE CHICK PECKS THE SHELL, 'TWILL SOON BE OUT!
RATTLE
RATTLE
GRAY GOOSE
SHO
"IT'S
GRAY GOOSE
SHOES
GRAY GOOSE
NOW, I ASK YOU TO BE THE PROPHET AND THE FULFILLER, ALL 'N ONE.

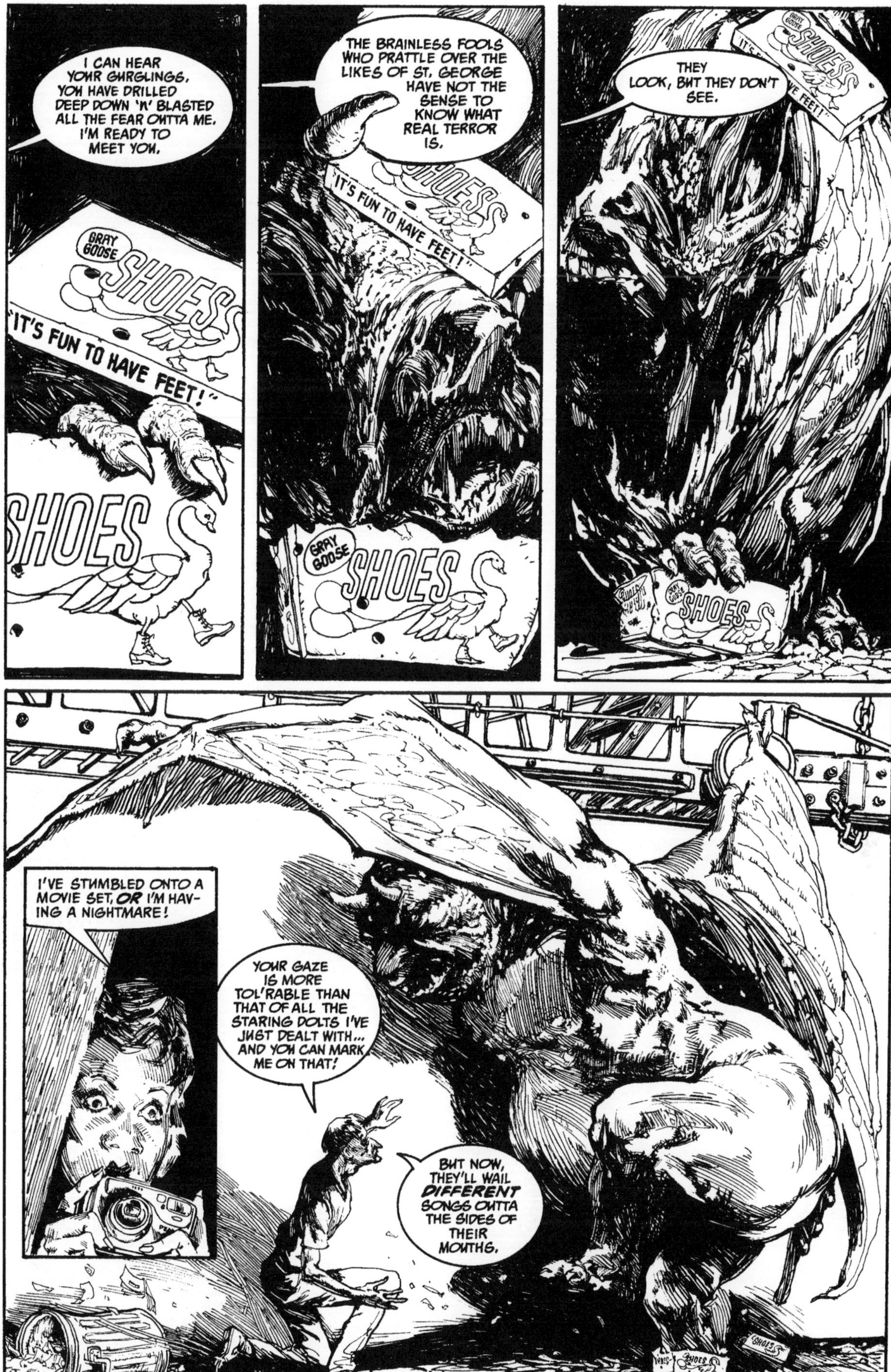
I CAN HEAR YOUR GURGLINGS. YOU HAVE DRILLED DEEP DOWN 'N' BLASTED ALL THE FEAR OUTTA ME. I'M READY TO MEET YOU.
GRAY GOOSE SHOES
"IT'S FUN TO HAVE FEET!"
SHOES
THE BRAINLESS FOOLS WHO PRATTLE OVER THE LIKES OF ST. GEORGE HAVE NOT THE SENSE TO KNOW WHAT REAL TERROR IS.
SHOES
"IT'S FUN TO HAVE FEET!"
GRAY GOOSE SHOES
THEY LOOK, BUT THEY DON'T SEE.
SHOES
"IT'S FUN TO HAVE FEET!"
SHOES
I'VE STUMBLED ONTO A MOVIE SET, OR I'M HAVING A NIGHTMARE!
YOUR GAZE IS MORE TOL'RABLE THAN THAT OF ALL THE STARING DOLTS I'VE JUST DEALT WITH... AND YOU CAN MARK ME ON THAT!
BUT NOW, THEY'LL WAIL DIFFERENT SONGS OUTTA THE SIDES OF THEIR MOUTHS.

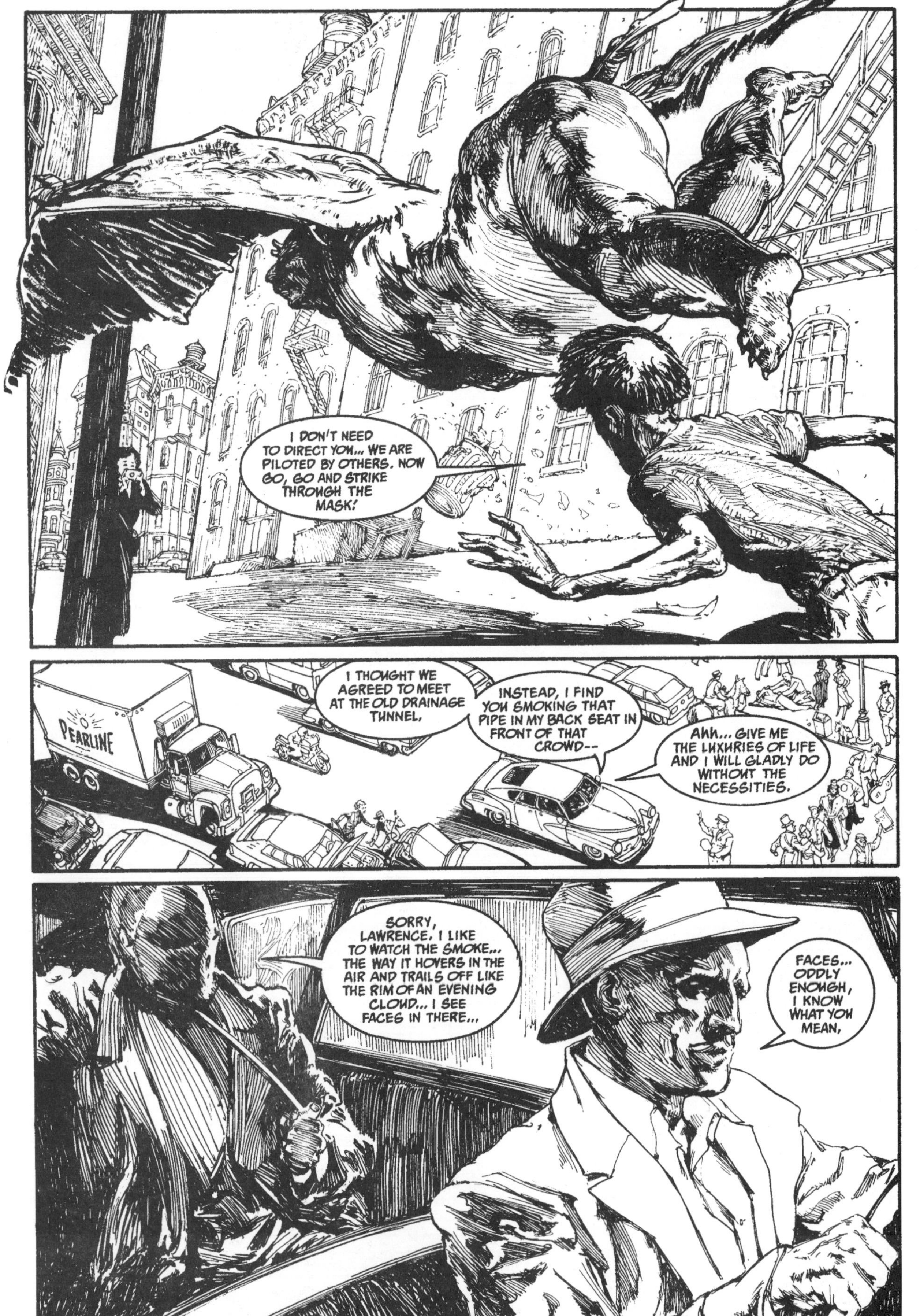
I DON'T NEED TO DIRECT YOU... WE ARE PILOTED BY OTHERS. NOW GO, GO AND STRIKE THROUGH THE MASK!
PEARLINE
I THOUGHT WE AGREED TO MEET AT THE OLD DRAINAGE TUNNEL.
INSTEAD, I FIND YOU SMOKING THAT PIPE IN MY BACK SEAT IN FRONT OF THAT CROWD--
AHH... GIVE ME THE LUXURIES OF LIFE AND I WILL GLADLY DO WITHOUT THE NECESSITIES.
SORRY, LAWRENCE. I LIKE TO WATCH THE SMOKE... THE WAY IT HOVERS IN THE AIR AND TRAILS OFF LIKE THE RIM OF AN EVENING CLOUD... I SEE FACES IN THERE...
FACES... ODDLY ENOUGH, I KNOW WHAT YOU MEAN.

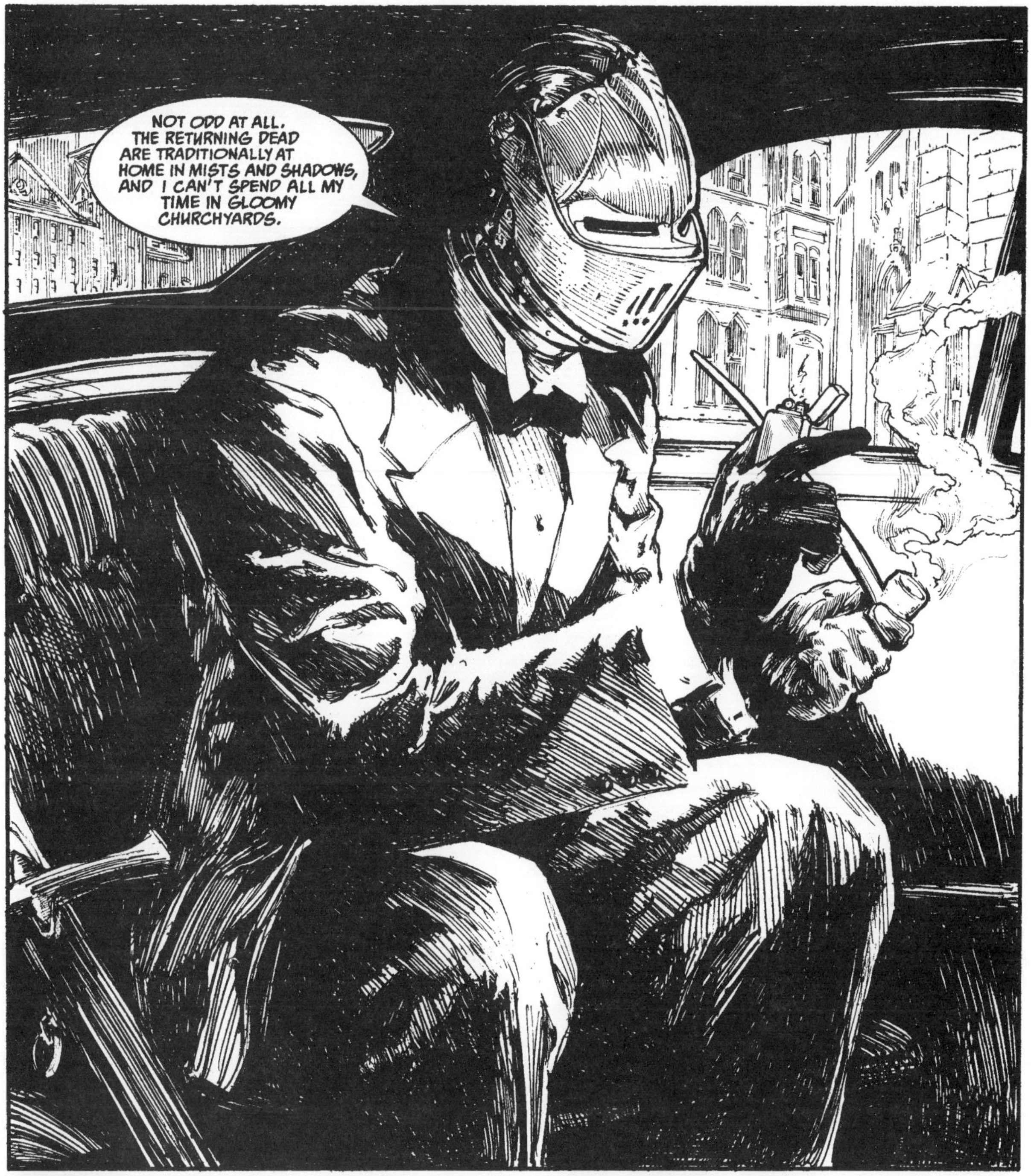
NOT ODD AT ALL. THE RETURNING DEAD ARE TRADITIONALLY AT HOME IN MISTS AND SHADOWS, AND I CAN'T SPEND ALL MY TIME IN GLOOMY CHURCHYARDS.

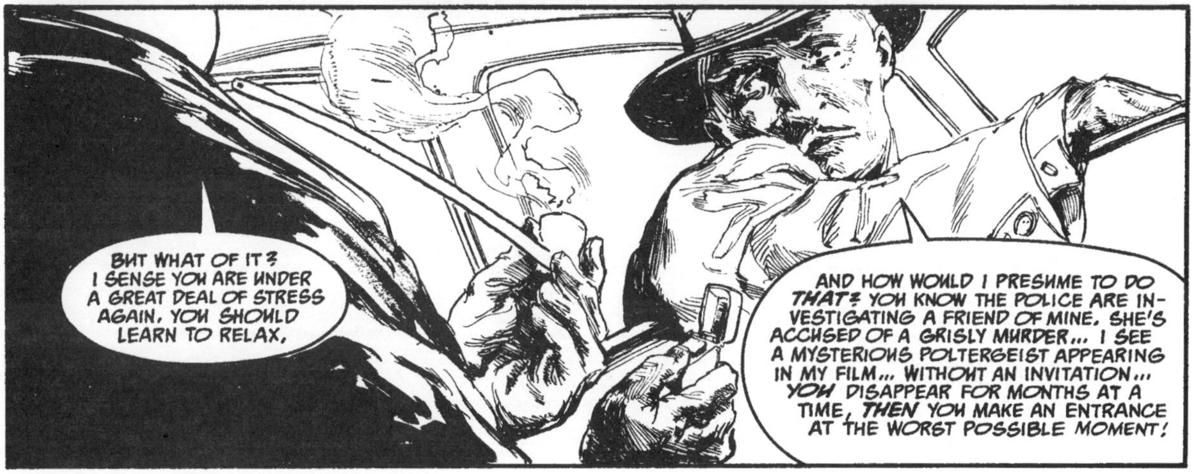
BUT WHAT OF IT? I SENSE YOU ARE UNDER A GREAT DEAL OF STRESS AGAIN. YOU SHOULD LEARN TO RELAX.
AND HOW WOULD I PRESUME TO DO THAT? YOU KNOW THE POLICE ARE INVESTIGATING A FRIEND OF MINE. SHE'S ACCUSED OF A GRISLY MURDER... I SEE A MYSTERIOUS POLTERGEIST APPEARING IN MY FILM... WITHOUT AN INVITATION... YOU DISAPPEAR FOR MONTHS AT A TIME, THEN YOU MAKE AN ENTRANCE AT THE WORST POSSIBLE MOMENT!

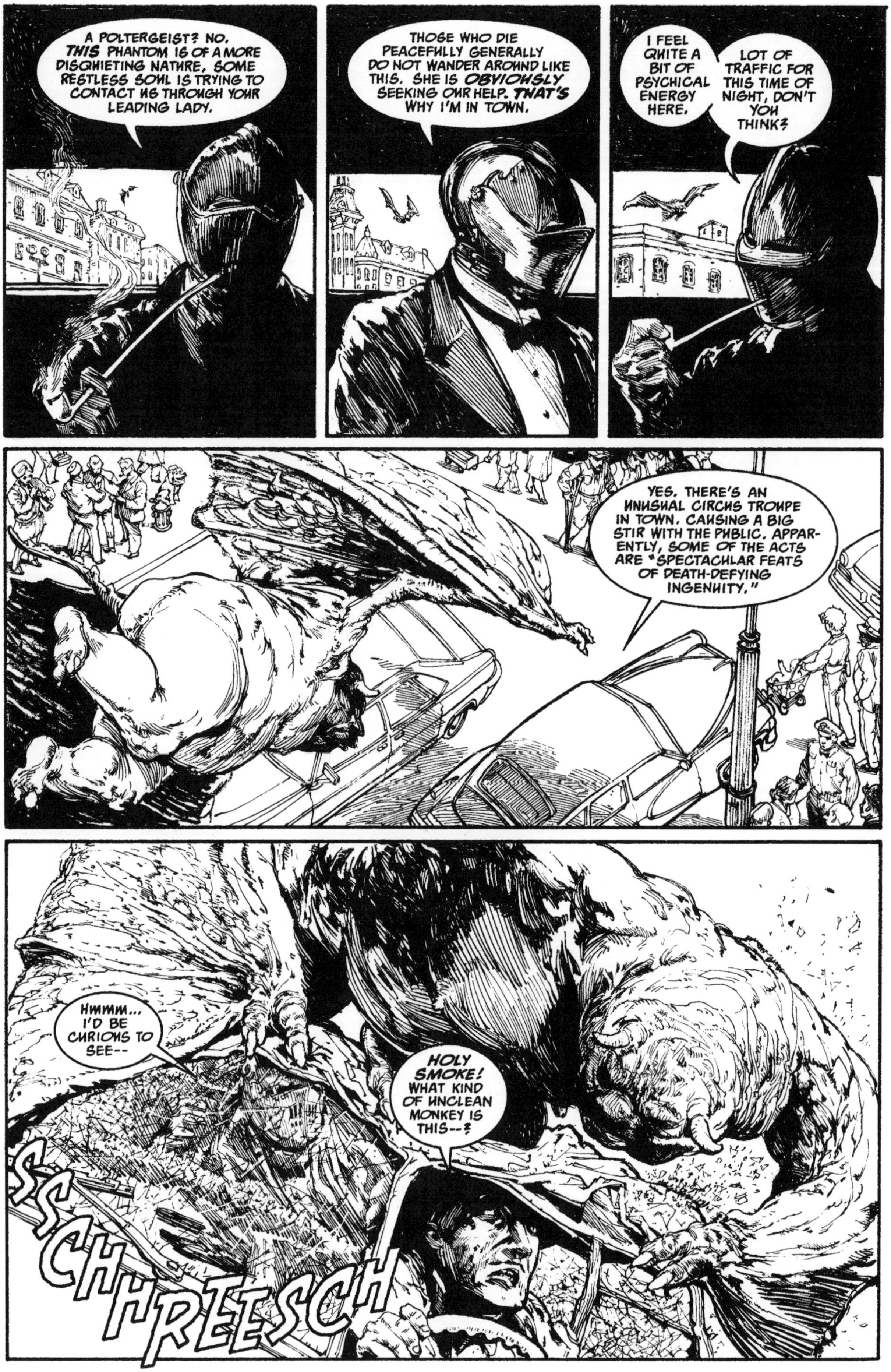
A POLTERGEIST? NO. THIS PHANTOM IS OF A MORE DISQUIETING NATURE. SOME RESTLESS SOUL IS TRYING TO CONTACT US THROUGH YOUR LEADING LADY.
THOSE WHO DIE PEACEFULLY GENERALLY DO NOT WANDER AROUND LIKE THIS. SHE IS OBVIOUSLY SEEKING OUR HELP. THAT'S WHY I'M IN TOWN.
I FEEL QUITE A BIT OF PSYCHICAL ENERGY HERE.
LOT OF TRAFFIC FOR THIS TIME OF NIGHT, DON'T YOU THINK?
YES. THERE'S AN UNUSUAL CIRCUS TROUPE IN TOWN. CAUSING A BIG STIR WITH THE PUBLIC. APPARENTLY, SOME OF THE ACTS ARE "SPECTACULAR FEATS OF DEATH-DEFYING INGENUITY."
HMMMM... I'D BE CURIOUS TO SEE--
HOLY SMOKE! WHAT KIND OF UNCLEAN MONKEY IS THIS--?
SSCHHREESCH

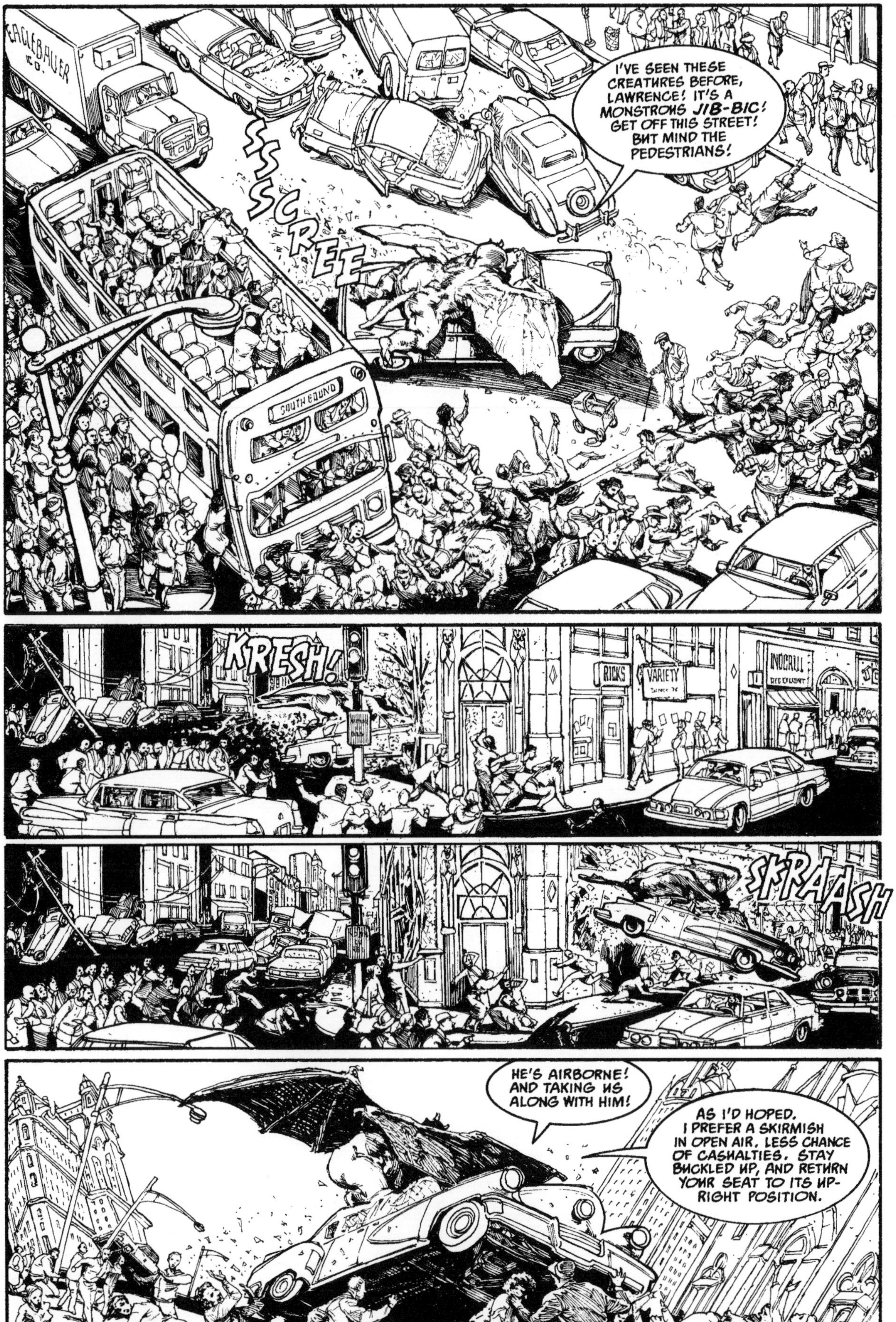
I'VE SEEN THESE CREATURES BEFORE, LAWRENCE! IT'S A MONSTROUS JIB-BIC! GET OFF THIS STREET! BUT MIND THE PEDESTRIANS!
SSSCREEE
SOUTH BOUND
KRESH!
RICKS
VARIETY
SKRAASH
HE'S AIRBORNE! AND TAKING US ALONG WITH HIM!
AS I'D HOPED. I PREFER A SKIRMISH IN OPEN AIR. LESS CHANCE OF CASUALTIES. STAY BUCKLED UP, AND RETURN YOUR SEAT TO ITS UPRIGHT POSITION.

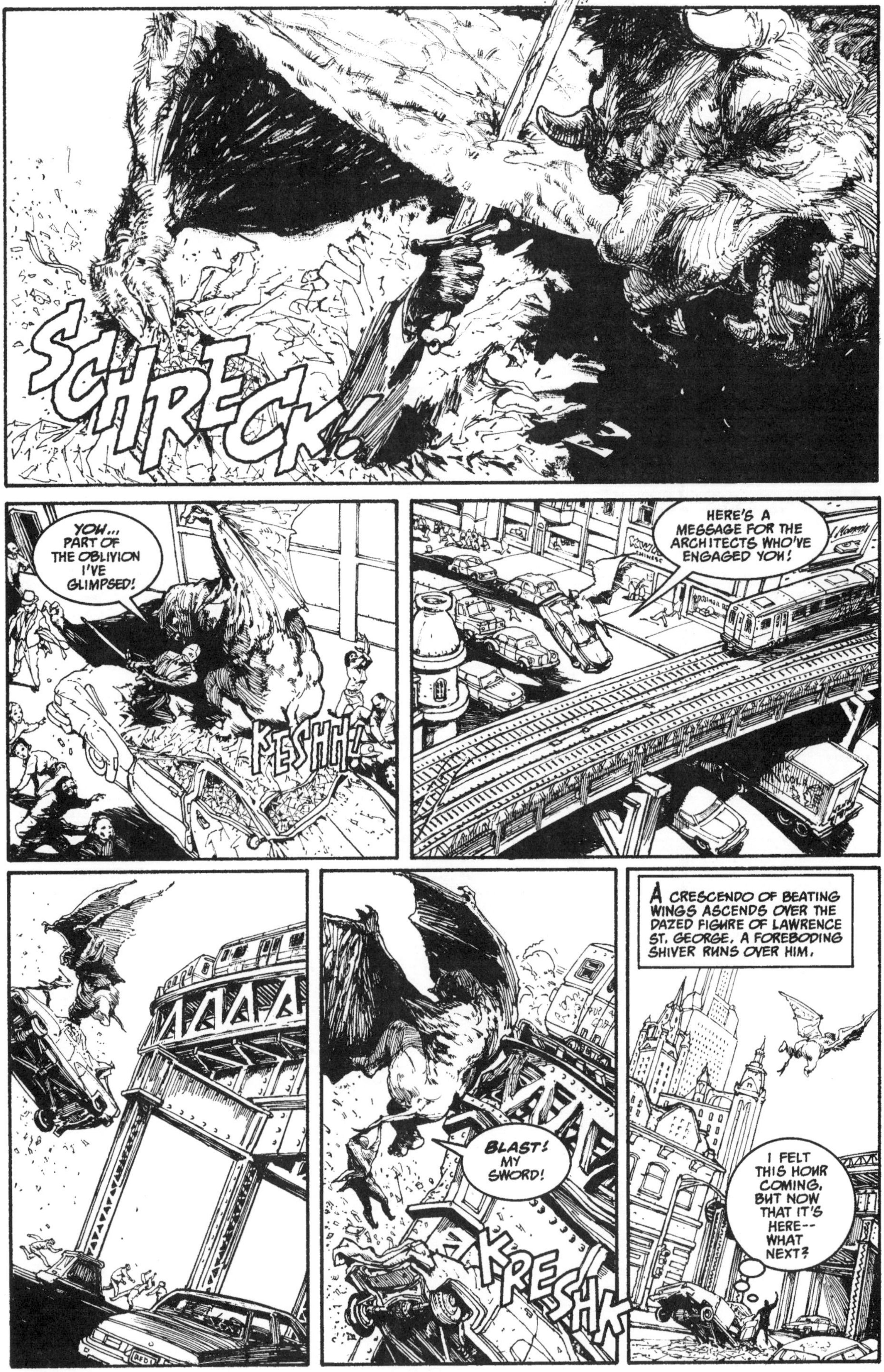
SCHRECK!
YOU... PART OF THE OBLIVION I'VE GLIMPSED!
KESHH!
HERE'S A MESSAGE FOR THE ARCHITECTS WHO'VE ENGAGED YOU!
A CRESCENDO OF BEATING WINGS ASCENDS OVER THE DAZED FIGURE OF LAWRENCE ST. GEORGE. A FOREBODING SHIVER RUNS OVER HIM.
BLAST! MY SWORD!
KRESHK
I FELT THIS HOUR COMING, BUT NOW THAT IT'S HERE-- WHAT NEXT?

THE MONSTERMEN

SILENT AS THE GRAVE

THE WIND IS UP: HARK! HOW IT HOWLS! METHINKS TILL NOW, I NEVER HEARD A SOUND SO DREARY: DOORS CREAK, AND WINDOWS CLAP, AND NIGHT'S FOUL BIRD ROOKED IN THE SPIRE SCREAMS LOUD!

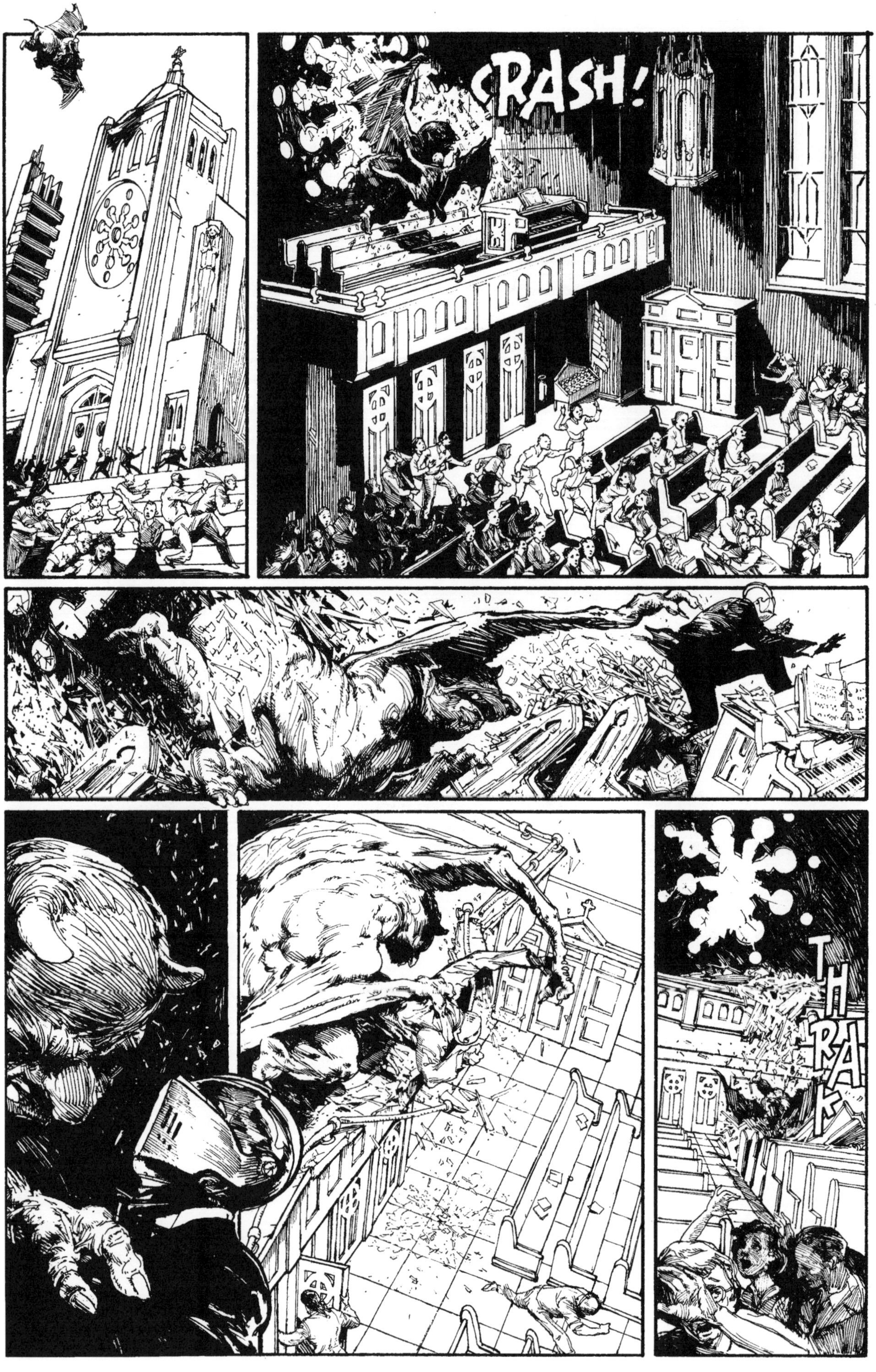
CRASH!
THRAK

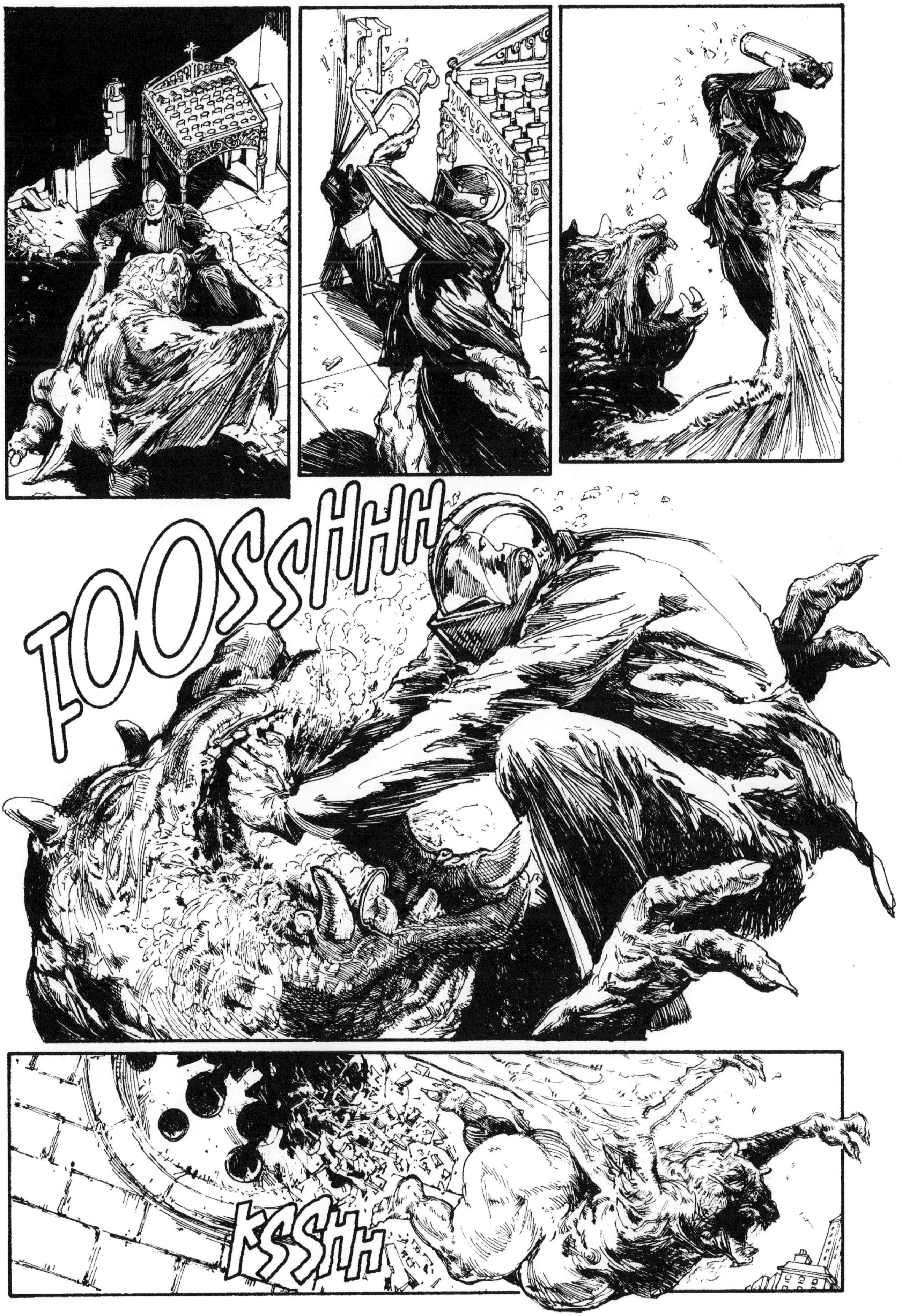

FOOSSHHH
KSSHH

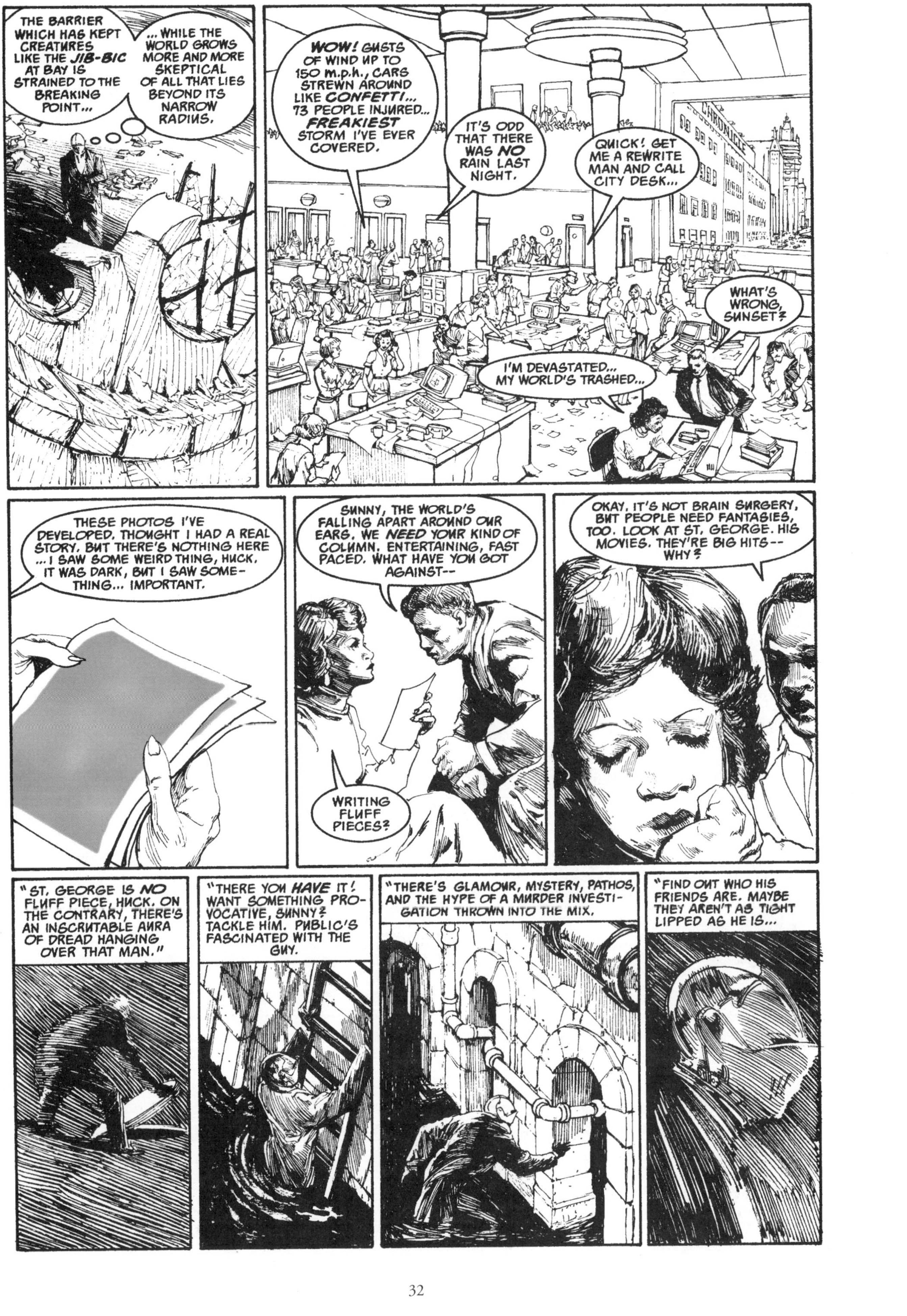
THE BARRIER WHICH HAS KEPT CREATURES LIKE THE JIB-BIC AT BAY IS STRAINED TO THE BREAKING POINT...
...WHILE THE WORLD GROWS MORE AND MORE SKEPTICAL OF ALL THAT LIES BEYOND ITS NARROW RADIUS.
WOW! GUSTS OF WIND UP TO 150 m.p.h., CARS STREWN AROUND LIKE CONFETTI!... 73 PEOPLE INJURED... FREAKIEST STORM I'VE EVER COVERED.
IT'S ODD THAT THERE WAS NO RAIN LAST NIGHT.
QUICK! GET ME A REWRITE MAN AND CALL CITY DESK...
CHRONICLE
WHAT'S WRONG, SUNSET?
I'M DEVASTATED... MY WORLD'S TRASHED...
THESE PHOTOS I'VE DEVELOPED. THOUGHT I HAD A REAL STORY. BUT THERE'S NOTHING HERE ...I SAW SOME WEIRD THING, HUCK. IT WAS DARK, BUT I SAW SOMETHING... IMPORTANT.
SUNNY, THE WORLD'S FALLING APART AROUND OUR EARS. WE NEED YOUR KIND OF COLUMN. ENTERTAINING, FAST PACED. WHAT HAVE YOU GOT AGAINST--
WRITING FLUFF PIECES?
OKAY, IT'S NOT BRAIN SURGERY, BUT PEOPLE NEED FANTASIES, TOO. LOOK AT ST. GEORGE. HIS MOVIES. THEY'RE BIG HITS-- WHY?
"ST. GEORGE IS NO FLUFF PIECE, HUCK. ON THE CONTRARY, THERE'S AN INSCRUTABLE AURA OF DREAD HANGING OVER THAT MAN."
"THERE YOU HAVE IT! WANT SOMETHING PROVOCATIVE, SUNNY? TACKLE HIM. PUBLIC'S FASCINATED WITH THE GUY.
"THERE'S GLAMOUR, MYSTERY, PATHOS, AND THE HYPE OF A MURDER INVESTIGATION THROWN INTO THE MIX.
"FIND OUT WHO HIS FRIENDS ARE. MAYBE THEY AREN'T AS TIGHT LIPPED AS HE IS...

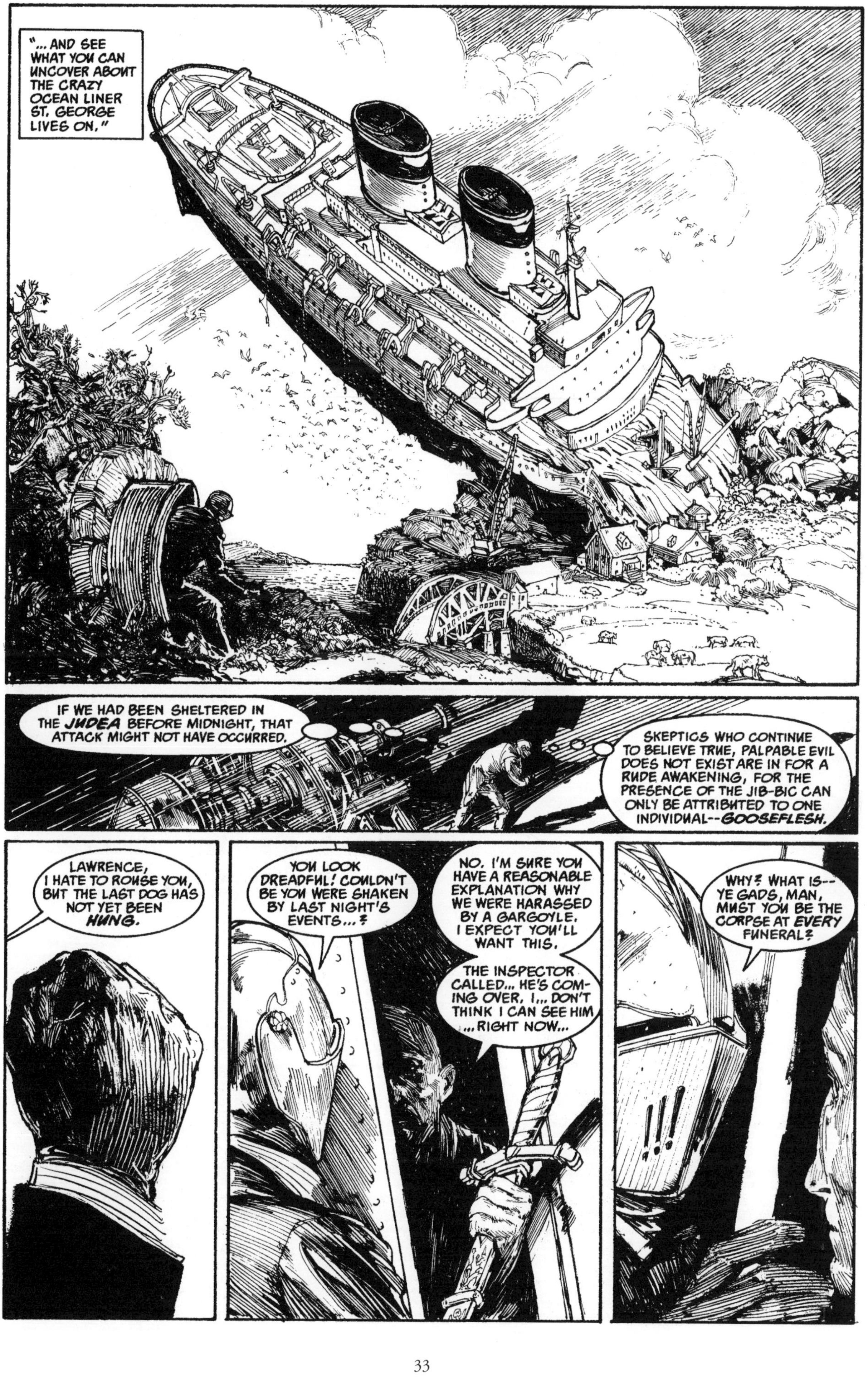
"... AND SEE WHAT YOU CAN UNCOVER ABOUT THE CRAZY OCEAN LINER ST. GEORGE LIVES ON."
IF WE HAD BEEN SHELTERED IN THE JUDEA BEFORE MIDNIGHT, THAT ATTACK MIGHT NOT HAVE OCCURRED.
SKEPTICS WHO CONTINUE TO BELIEVE TRUE, PALPABLE EVIL DOES NOT EXIST ARE IN FOR A RUDE AWAKENING, FOR THE PRESENCE OF THE JIB-BIC CAN ONLY BE ATTRIBUTED TO ONE INDIVIDUAL--GOOSEFLESH.
LAWRENCE, I HATE TO ROUSE YOU, BUT THE LAST DOG HAS NOT YET BEEN HUNG.
YOU LOOK DREADFUL! COULDN'T BE YOU WERE SHAKEN BY LAST NIGHT'S EVENTS...?
NO. I'M SURE YOU HAVE A REASONABLE EXPLANATION WHY WE WERE HARASSED BY A GARGOYLE. I EXPECT YOU'LL WANT THIS.
THE INSPECTOR CALLED... HE'S COMING OVER. I... DON'T THINK I CAN SEE HIM ...RIGHT NOW...
WHY? WHAT IS-- YE GADS, MAN, MUST YOU BE THE CORPSE AT EVERY FUNERAL?
!!!

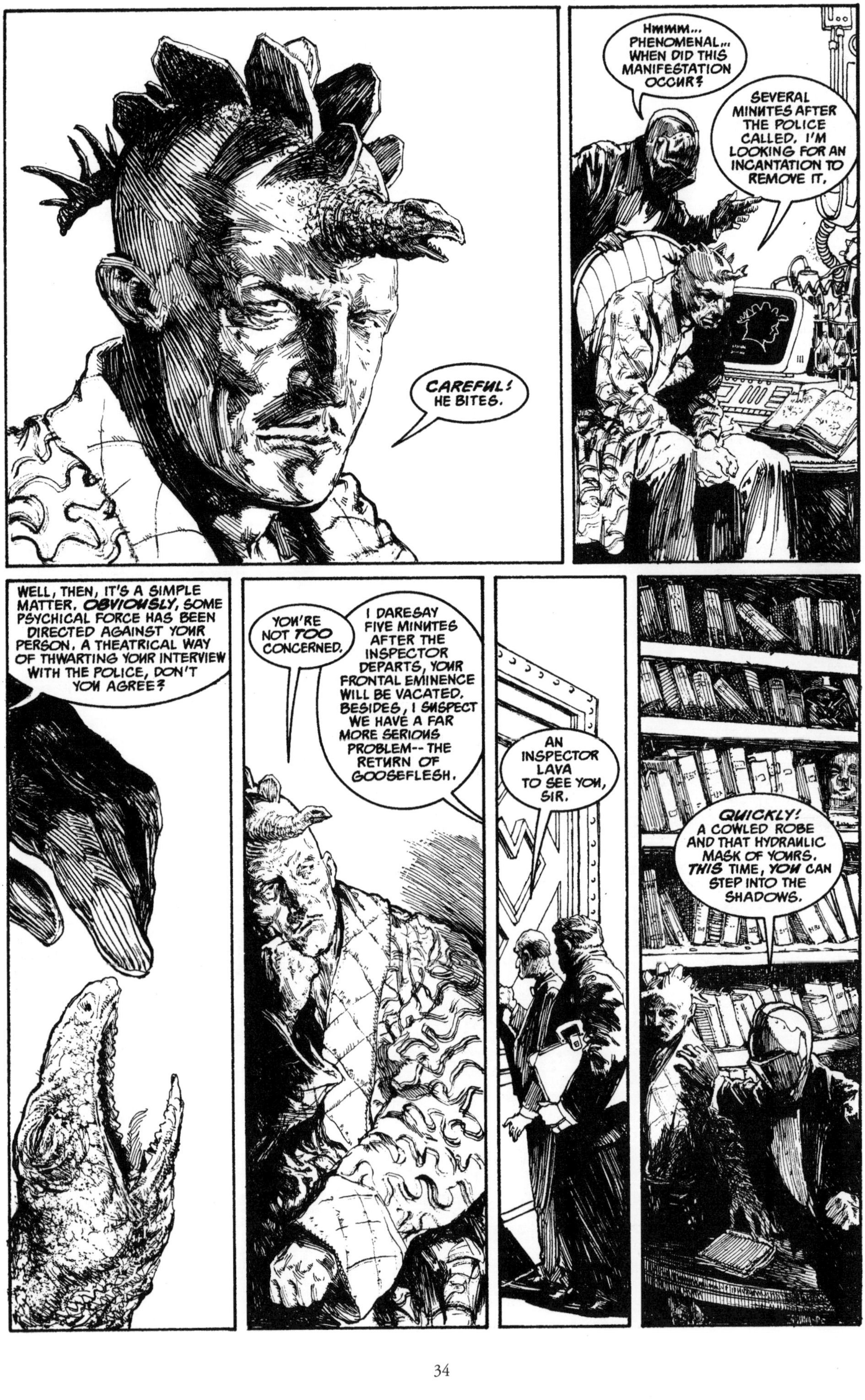
CAREFUL! HE BITES.
HMMMM... PHENOMENAL... WHEN DID THIS MANIFESTATION OCCUR?
SEVERAL MINUTES AFTER THE POLICE CALLED. I'M LOOKING FOR AN INCANTATION TO REMOVE IT.
WELL, THEN, IT'S A SIMPLE MATTER. OBVIOUSLY, SOME PSYCHICAL FORCE HAS BEEN DIRECTED AGAINST YOUR PERSON. A THEATRICAL WAY OF THWARTING YOUR INTERVIEW WITH THE POLICE, DON'T YOU AGREE?
YOU'RE NOT TOO CONCERNED.
I DARESAY FIVE MINUTES AFTER THE INSPECTOR DEPARTS, YOUR FRONTAL EMINENCE WILL BE VACATED. BESIDES, I SUSPECT WE HAVE A FAR MORE SERIOUS PROBLEM-- THE RETURN OF GOOSEFLESH.
AN INSPECTOR LAVA TO SEE YOU, SIR.
QUICKLY! A COWLED ROBE AND THAT HYDRAULIC MASK OF YOURS. THIS TIME, YOU CAN STEP INTO THE SHADOWS.

MORNIN', MR. ST. GEORGE, SOME TUB Y'GOT HERE. NICE OF YOU TO SEE ME THIS EARLY, 'CAUSE I'VE GOT MY HANDS FULL WITH THE STORM AND ALL.

GET TO THE POINT, CAPTAIN.

WE'RE BOOKING JULIA ADLER FOR THE MURDER OF HER BOYFRIEND. SHE'S BEEN MUMBLIN' YOUR NAME, ALSO MENTIONS TWO OTHER GUYS, BENNY AND DICK. EVER HEAR OF 'EM?

NO.

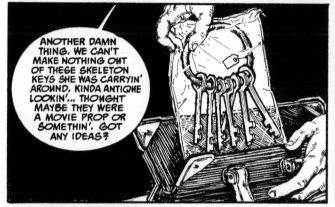

ANOTHER DAMN THING. WE CAN'T MAKE NOTHING OUT OF THESE SKELETON KEYS SHE WAS CARRYIN' AROUND, KINDA ANTIQUE LOOKIN'... THOUGHT MAYBE THEY WERE A MOVIE PROP OR SOMETHIN'. GOT ANY IDEAS?

I UNDERSTAND MISS ADLER'S IN SHOCK. PERHAPS IT'S HER WAY OF RELATING A CLUE.

SHOCK...? SHE'S OUTTA HER MIND!

SHE CUT OFF ALL HER HAIR! WHEN WE FOUND HER SHE WAS CRADLIN' HER LOCKS, AND SHE STILL HASN'T LET GO OF 'EM. CAN'T BLAME HER. SHE'S AS BALD AS A CUE BALL NOW.

THE BODY WE FOUND FLOATIN' IN HER POOL? BURNT TO A CRISP! TRY FIGURIN' THAT OUT.

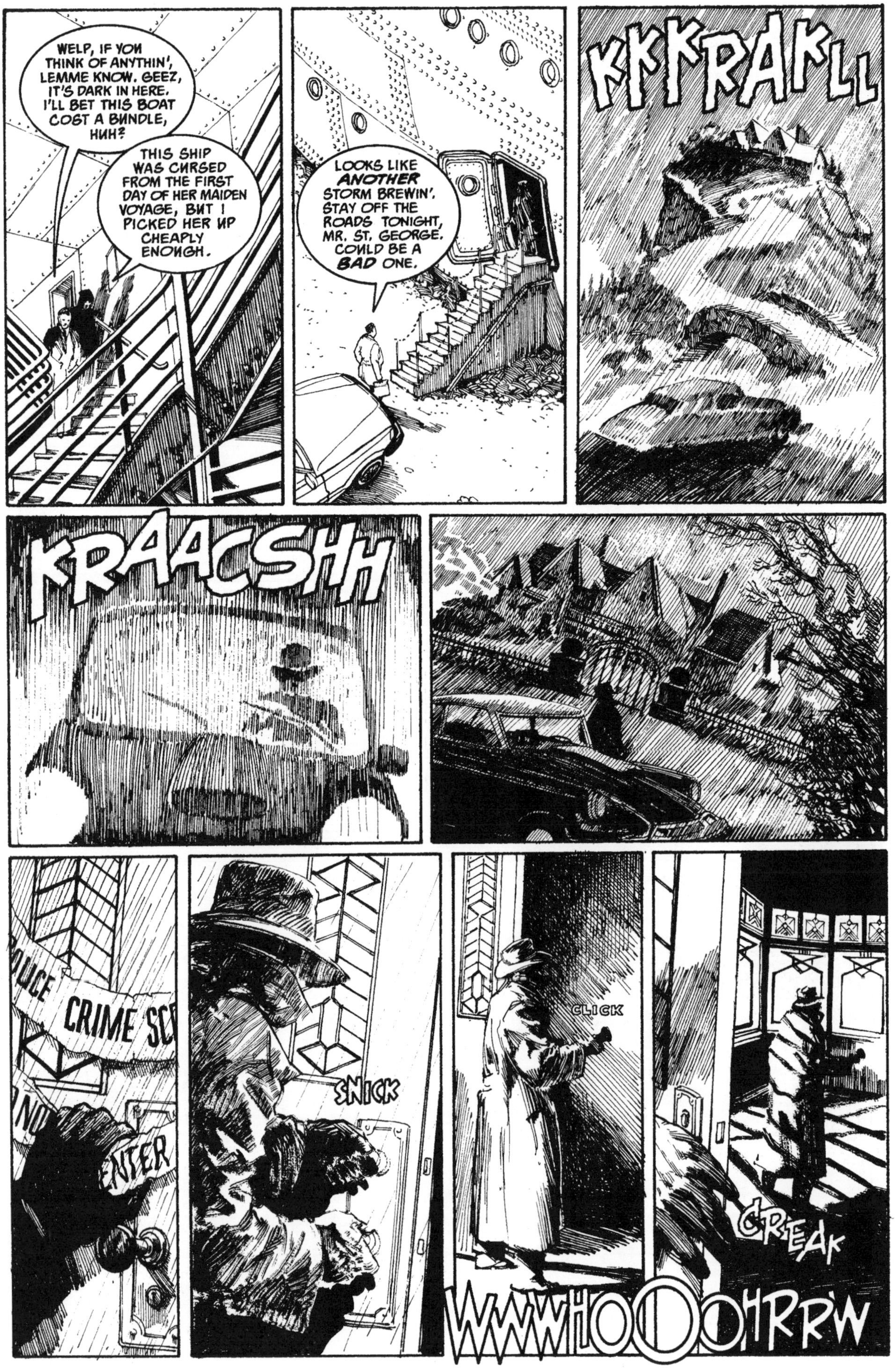
WELP, IF YOU THINK OF ANYTHIN', LEMME KNOW. GEEZ, IT'S DARK IN HERE. I'LL BET THIS BOAT COST A BUNDLE, HUH?
THIS SHIP WAS CURSED FROM THE FIRST DAY OF HER MAIDEN VOYAGE, BUT I PICKED HER UP CHEAPLY ENOUGH.
LOOKS LIKE *ANOTHER* STORM BREWIN'. STAY OFF THE ROADS TONIGHT, MR. ST. GEORGE. COULD BE A *BAD* ONE.
KKKRAKLL
KRAACSHH
POLICE CRIME SC
ENTER
SNICK
CLICK
CREAK
WWWHOOOOHRRW

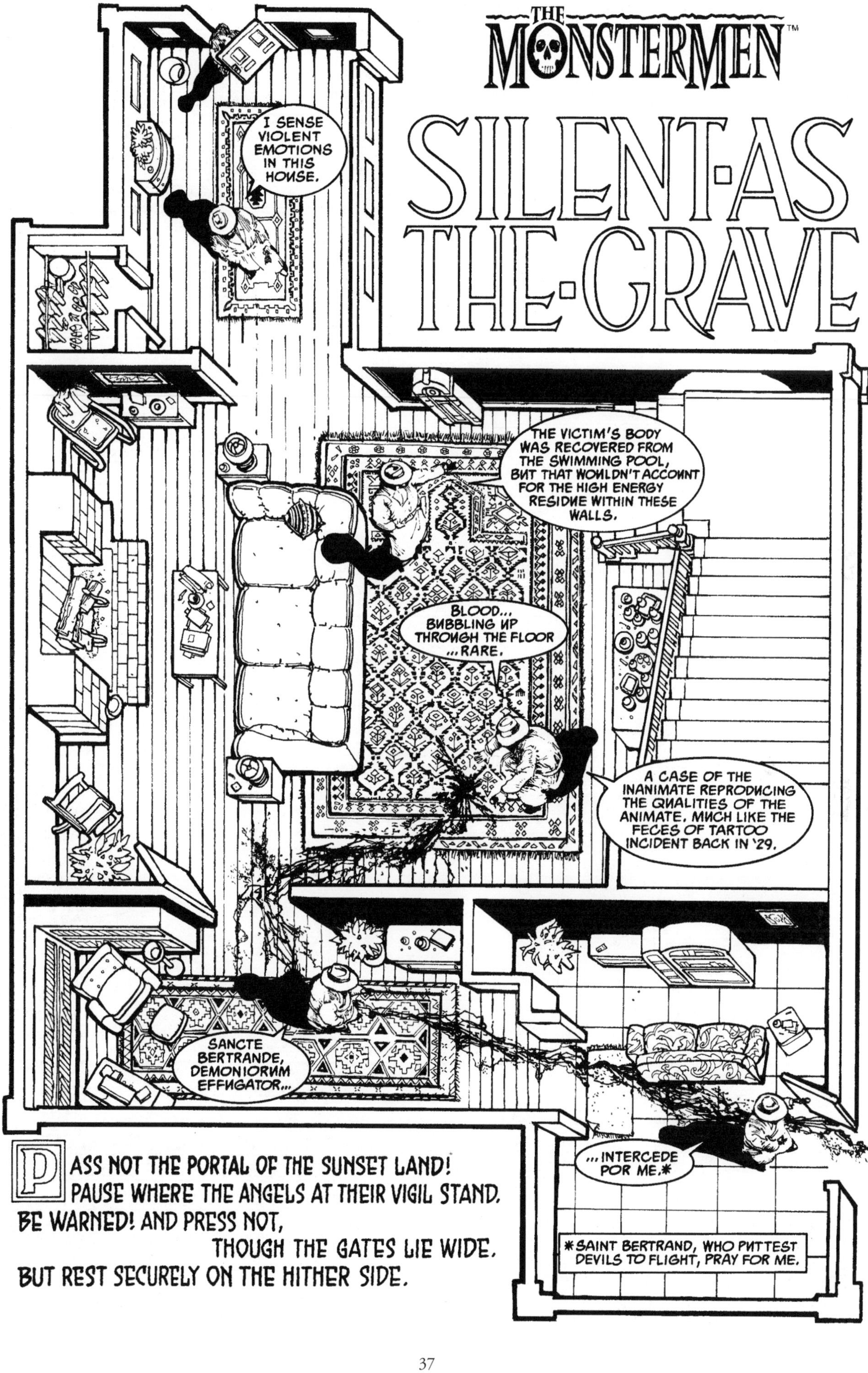
THE MONSTERMEN™
SILENT AS THE GRAVE
I SENSE VIOLENT EMOTIONS IN THIS HOUSE.
THE VICTIM'S BODY WAS RECOVERED FROM THE SWIMMING POOL, BUT THAT WOULDN'T ACCOUNT FOR THE HIGH ENERGY RESIDUE WITHIN THESE WALLS.
BLOOD... BUBBLING UP THROUGH THE FLOOR ...RARE.
A CASE OF THE INANIMATE REPRODUCING THE QUALITIES OF THE ANIMATE. MUCH LIKE THE FECES OF TARTOO INCIDENT BACK IN '29.
SANCTE BERTRANDE, DEMONIORUM EFFUGATOR...
...INTERCEDE PRO ME.*
PASS NOT THE PORTAL OF THE SUNSET LAND!
PAUSE WHERE THE ANGELS AT THEIR VIGIL STAND.
BE WARNED! AND PRESS NOT,
THOUGH THE GATES LIE WIDE.
BUT REST SECURELY ON THE HITHER SIDE.
*SAINT BERTRAND, WHO PUTTEST DEVILS TO FLIGHT, PRAY FOR ME.

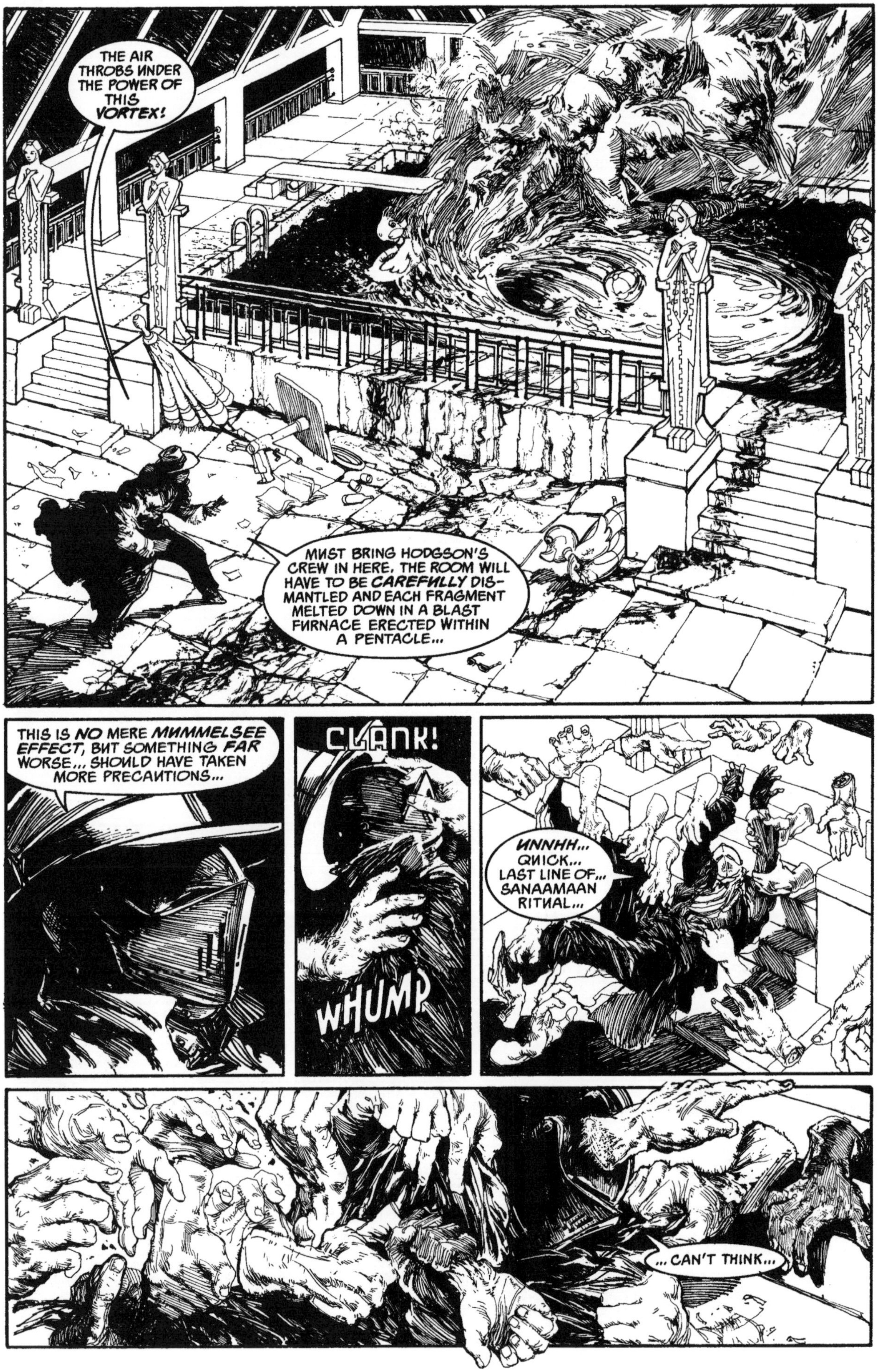
THE AIR THROBS UNDER THE POWER OF THIS VORTEX!
MUST BRING HODGSON'S CREW IN HERE. THE ROOM WILL HAVE TO BE CAREFULLY DISMANTLED AND EACH FRAGMENT MELTED DOWN IN A BLAST FURNACE ERECTED WITHIN A PENTACLE...
THIS IS NO MERE MUMMELSEE EFFECT, BUT SOMETHING FAR WORSE... SHOULD HAVE TAKEN MORE PRECAUTIONS...
CLANK!
WHUMP
UNNHH... QUICK... LAST LINE OF... SANAAMAAN RITUAL...
... CAN'T THINK...

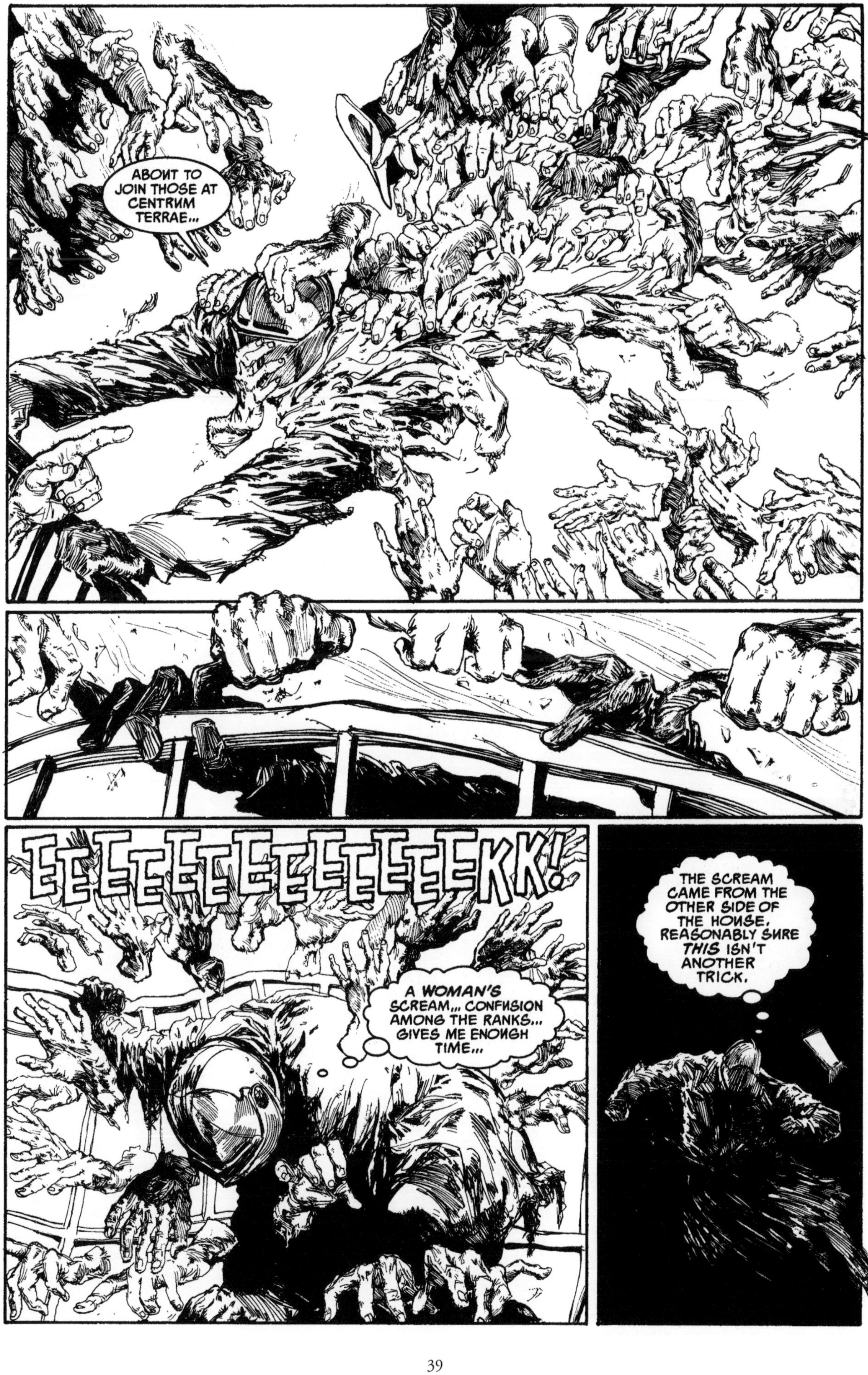
ABOUT TO JOIN THOSE AT CENTRUM TERRAE...
EEEEEEEEEEEEEEKK!
A WOMAN'S SCREAM... CONFUSION AMONG THE RANKS... GIVES ME ENOUGH TIME...
THE SCREAM CAME FROM THE OTHER SIDE OF THE HOUSE. REASONABLY SURE THIS ISN'T ANOTHER TRICK.

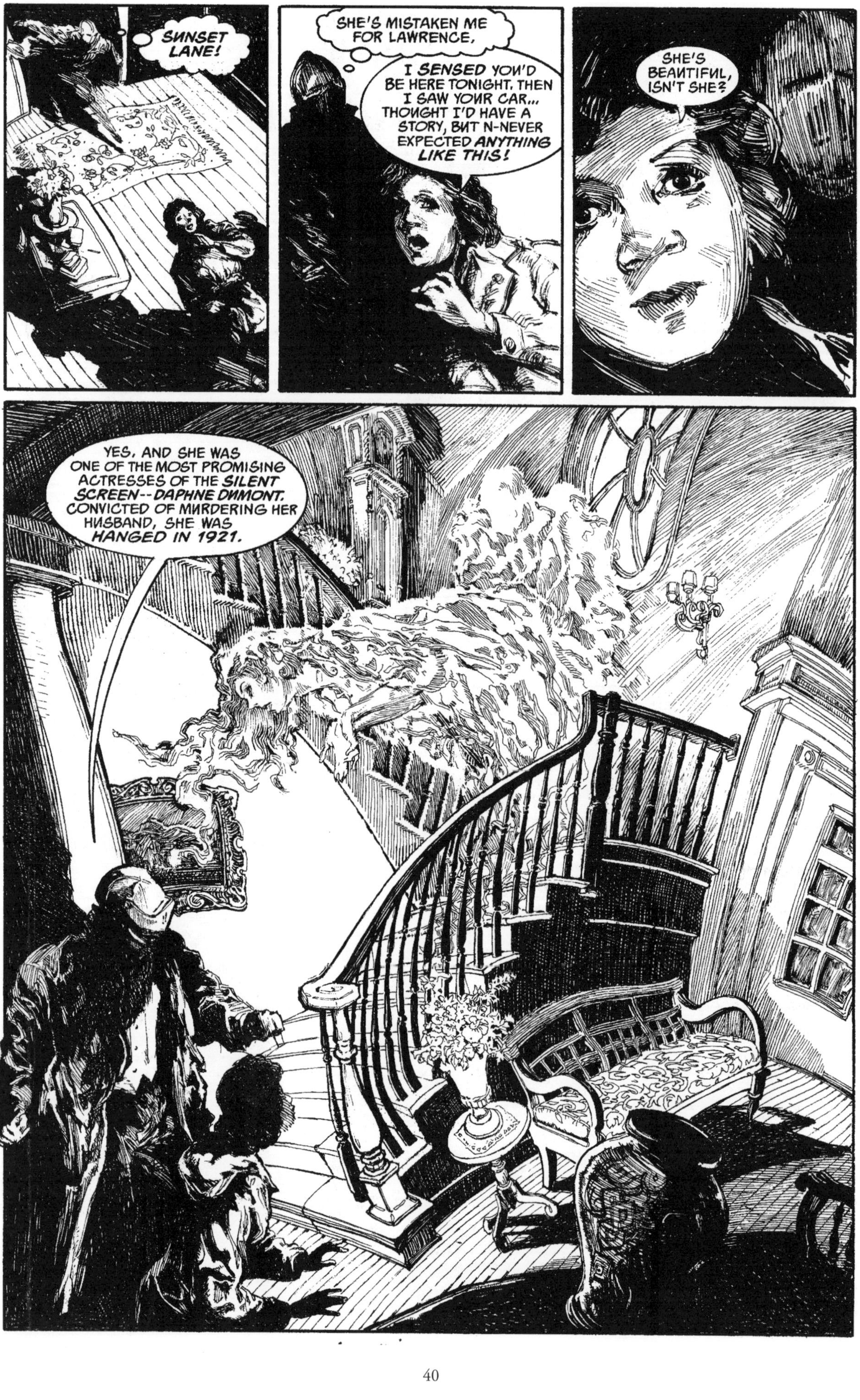
SUNSET LANE!
SHE'S MISTAKEN ME FOR LAWRENCE.
I SENSED YOU'D BE HERE TONIGHT. THEN I SAW YOUR CAR... THOUGHT I'D HAVE A STORY, BUT N-NEVER EXPECTED ANYTHING LIKE THIS!
SHE'S BEAUTIFUL, ISN'T SHE?
YES. AND SHE WAS ONE OF THE MOST PROMISING ACTRESSES OF THE SILENT SCREEN--DAPHNE DUMONT. CONVICTED OF MURDERING HER HUSBAND, SHE WAS HANGED IN 1921.

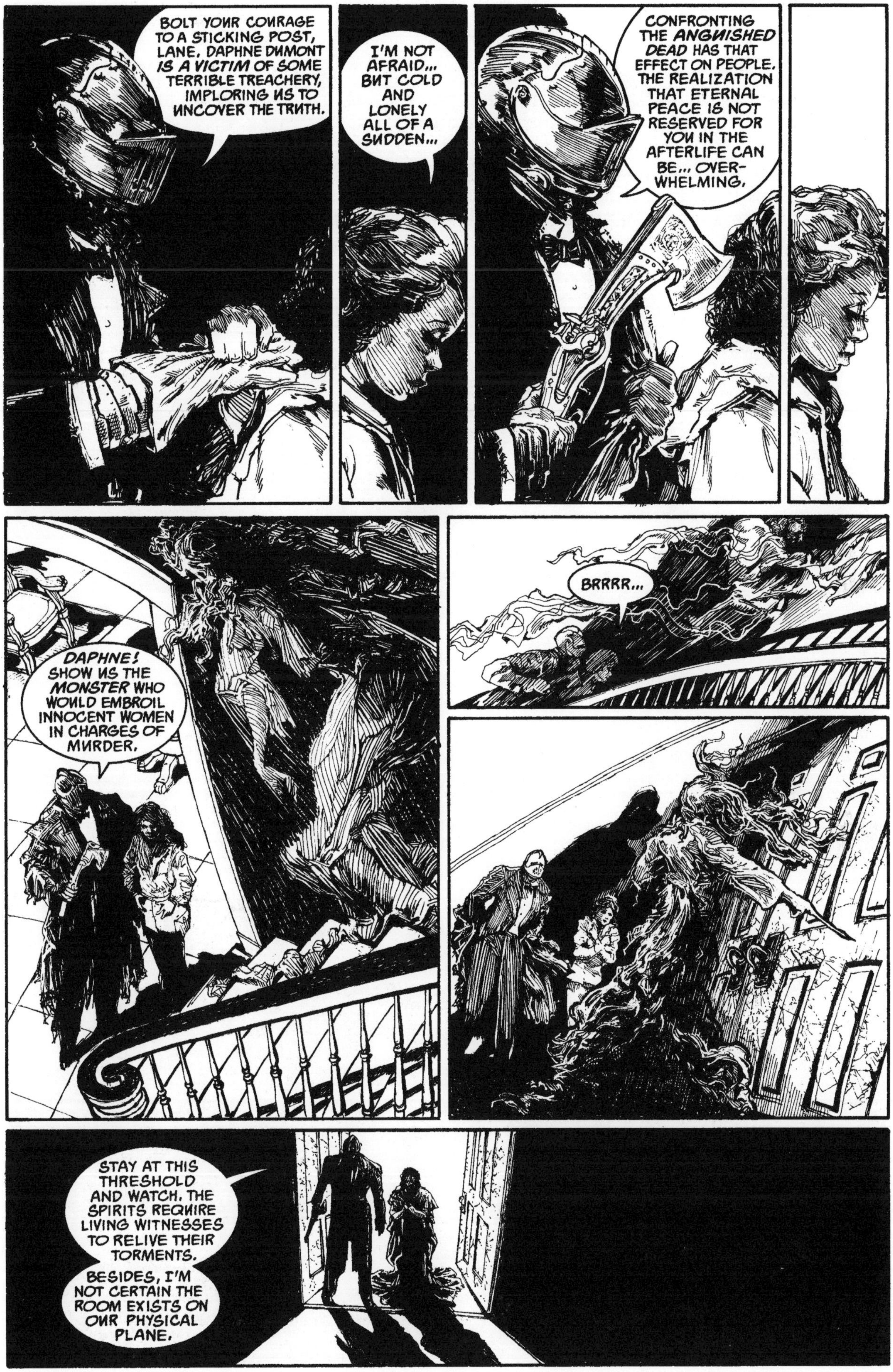
BOLT YOUR COURAGE TO A STICKING POST, LANE. DAPHNE DUMONT IS A VICTIM OF SOME TERRIBLE TREACHERY, IMPLORING US TO UNCOVER THE TRUTH.
I'M NOT AFRAID... BUT COLD AND LONELY ALL OF A SUDDEN...
CONFRONTING THE ANGUISHED DEAD HAS THAT EFFECT ON PEOPLE. THE REALIZATION THAT ETERNAL PEACE IS NOT RESERVED FOR YOU IN THE AFTERLIFE CAN BE... OVER-WHELMING.
DAPHNE! SHOW US THE MONSTER WHO WOULD EMBROIL INNOCENT WOMEN IN CHARGES OF MURDER.
BRRRR...
STAY AT THIS THRESHOLD AND WATCH. THE SPIRITS REQUIRE LIVING WITNESSES TO RELIVE THEIR TORMENTS.
BESIDES, I'M NOT CERTAIN THE ROOM EXISTS ON OUR PHYSICAL PLANE.

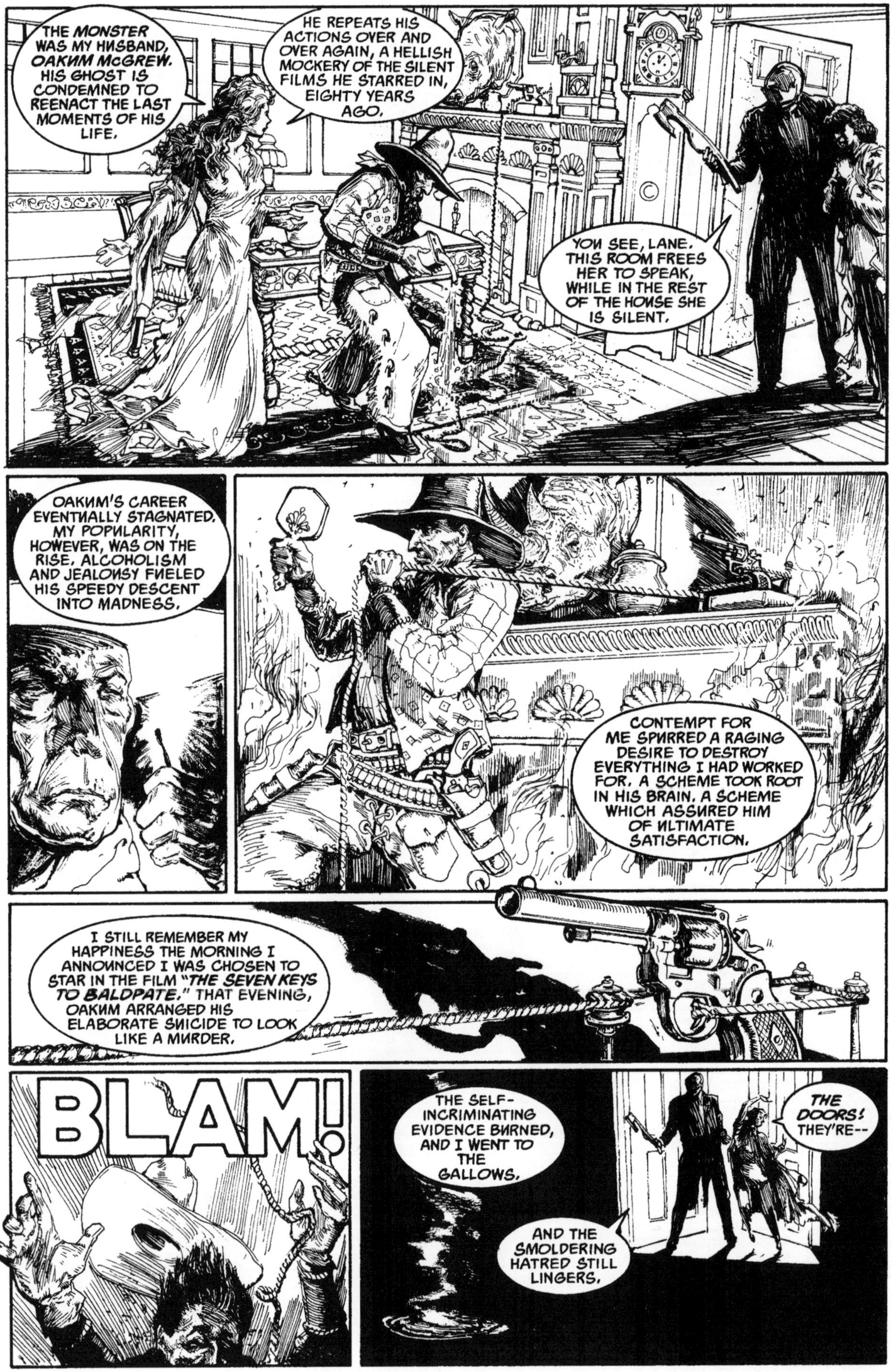
THE MONSTER WAS MY HUSBAND, OAKUM McGREW. HIS GHOST IS CONDEMNED TO REENACT THE LAST MOMENTS OF HIS LIFE.
HE REPEATS HIS ACTIONS OVER AND OVER AGAIN, A HELLISH MOCKERY OF THE SILENT FILMS HE STARRED IN, EIGHTY YEARS AGO.
YOU SEE, LANE. THIS ROOM FREES HER TO SPEAK, WHILE IN THE REST OF THE HOUSE SHE IS SILENT.
OAKUM'S CAREER EVENTUALLY STAGNATED. MY POPULARITY, HOWEVER, WAS ON THE RISE. ALCOHOLISM AND JEALOUSY FUELED HIS SPEEDY DESCENT INTO MADNESS.
CONTEMPT FOR ME SPURRED A RAGING DESIRE TO DESTROY EVERYTHING I HAD WORKED FOR. A SCHEME TOOK ROOT IN HIS BRAIN. A SCHEME WHICH ASSURED HIM OF ULTIMATE SATISFACTION.
I STILL REMEMBER MY HAPPINESS THE MORNING I ANNOUNCED I WAS CHOSEN TO STAR IN THE FILM "THE SEVEN KEYS TO BALDPATE." THAT EVENING, OAKUM ARRANGED HIS ELABORATE SUICIDE TO LOOK LIKE A MURDER.
BLAM!
THE SELF-INCRIMINATING EVIDENCE BURNED, AND I WENT TO THE GALLOWS.
THE DOORS! THEY'RE--
AND THE SMOLDERING HATRED STILL LINGERS.

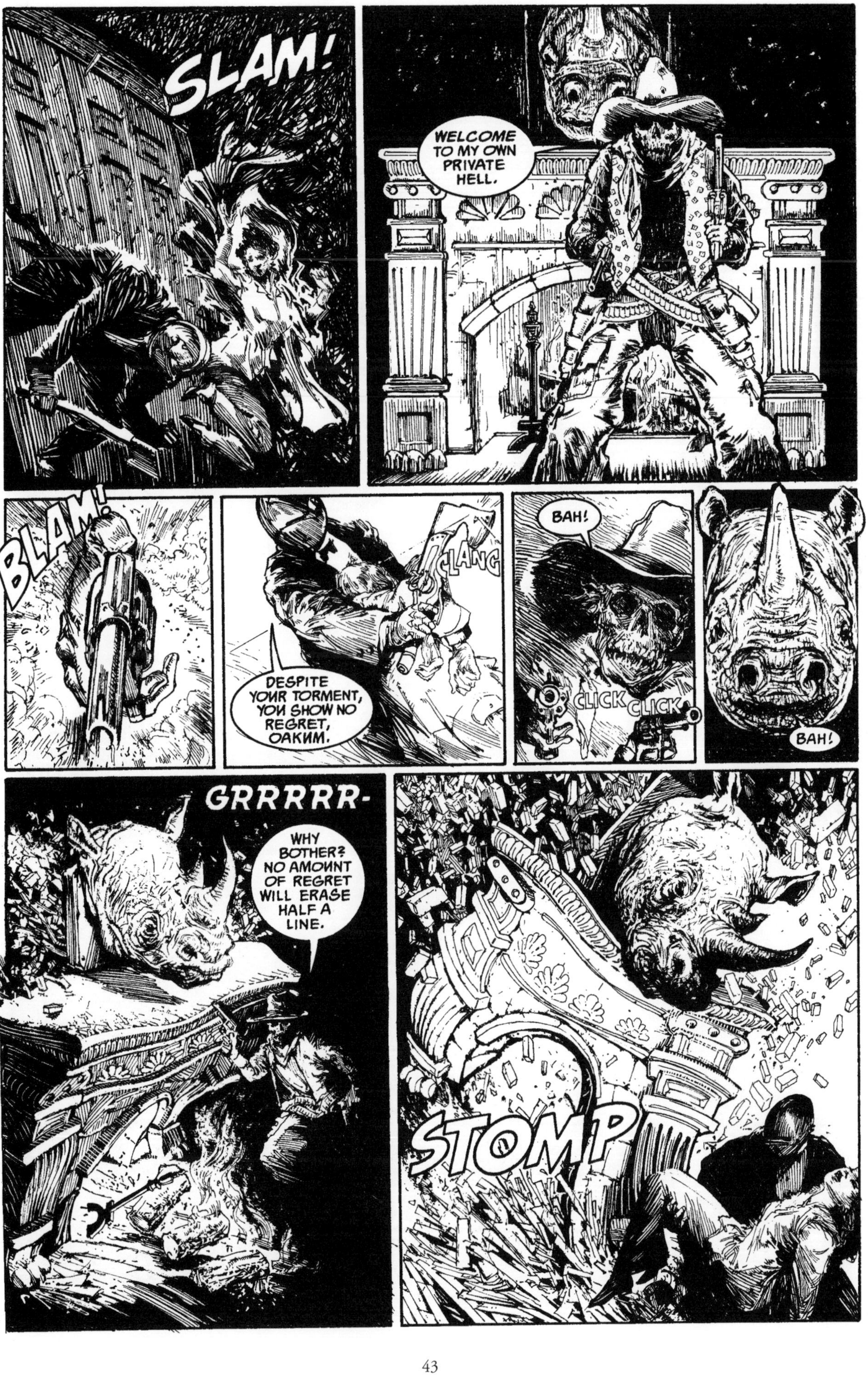
SLAM!
WELCOME TO MY OWN PRIVATE HELL.
BLAM!
CLANG
DESPITE YOUR TORMENT, YOU SHOW NO REGRET, OAKUM.
BAH!
CLICK CLICK
BAH!
GRRRRR-
WHY BOTHER? NO AMOUNT OF REGRET WILL ERASE HALF A LINE.
STOMP

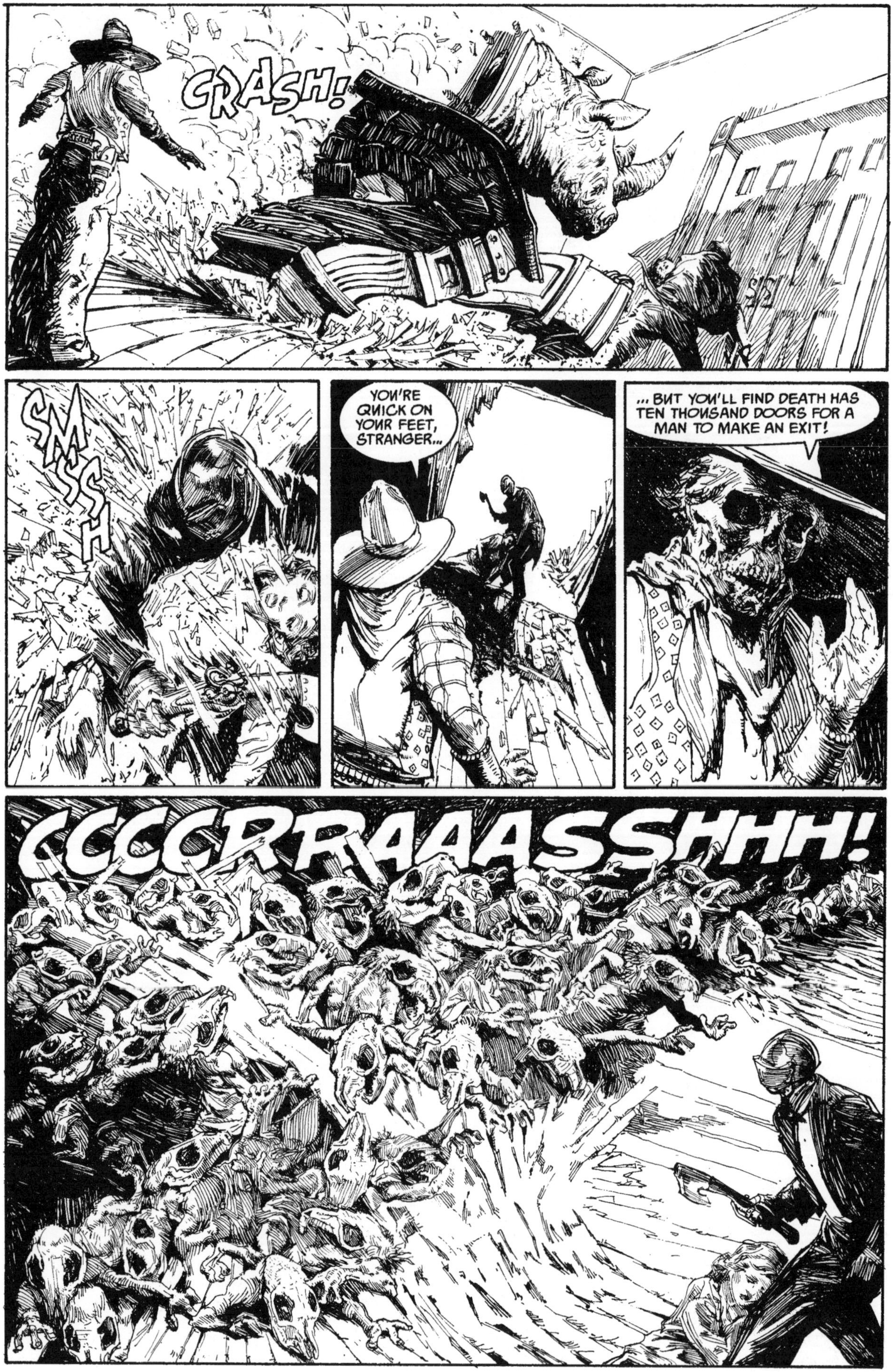
CRASH!
SMASSH
YOU'RE QUICK ON YOUR FEET, STRANGER...
... BUT YOU'LL FIND DEATH HAS TEN THOUSAND DOORS FOR A MAN TO MAKE AN EXIT!
CCCCRRAAASSHHH!

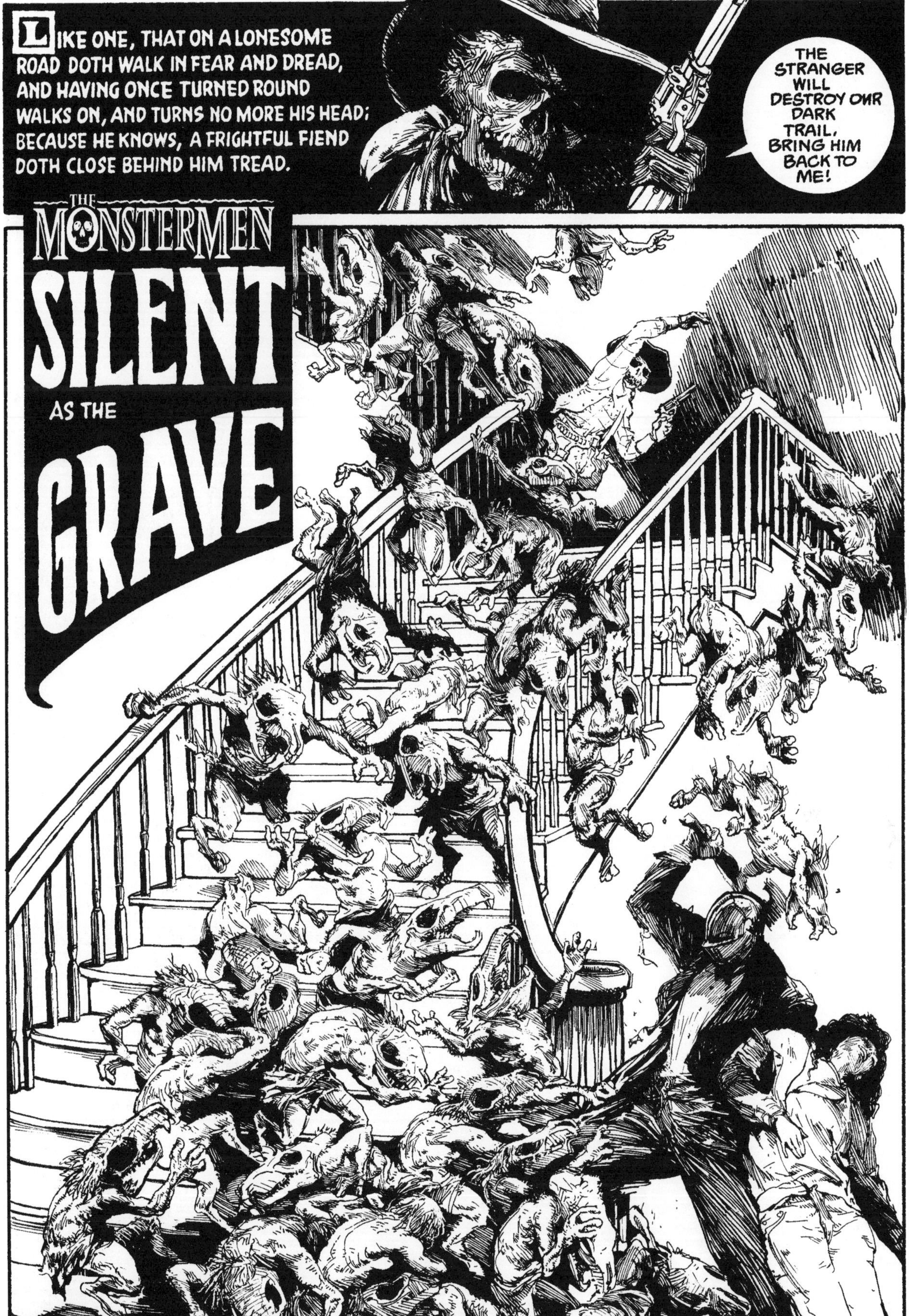
LIKE ONE, THAT ON A LONESOME ROAD DOTH WALK IN FEAR AND DREAD, AND HAVING ONCE TURNED ROUND WALKS ON, AND TURNS NO MORE HIS HEAD; BECAUSE HE KNOWS, A FRIGHTFUL FIEND DOTH CLOSE BEHIND HIM TREAD.
THE STRANGER WILL DESTROY OUR DARK TRAIL, BRING HIM BACK TO ME!
THE MONSTERMEN
SILENT AS THE GRAVE

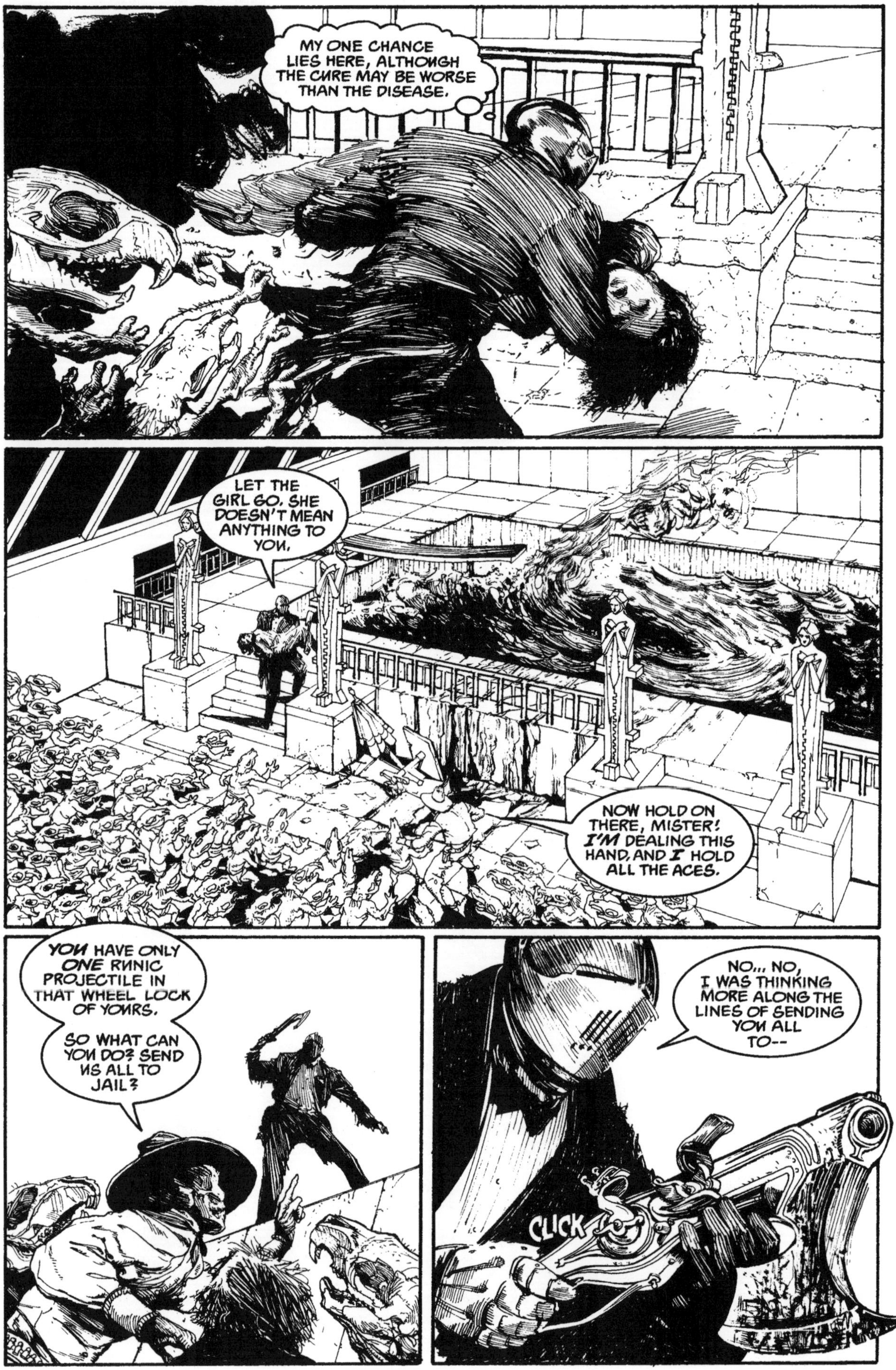
MY ONE CHANCE LIES HERE, ALTHOUGH THE CURE MAY BE WORSE THAN THE DISEASE.
LET THE GIRL GO. SHE DOESN'T MEAN ANYTHING TO YOU.
NOW HOLD ON THERE, MISTER! I'M DEALING THIS HAND, AND I HOLD ALL THE ACES.
YOU HAVE ONLY ONE RUNIC PROJECTILE IN THAT WHEEL LOCK OF YOURS.
SO WHAT CAN YOU DO? SEND US ALL TO JAIL?
NO... NO, I WAS THINKING MORE ALONG THE LINES OF SENDING YOU ALL TO--
CLICK

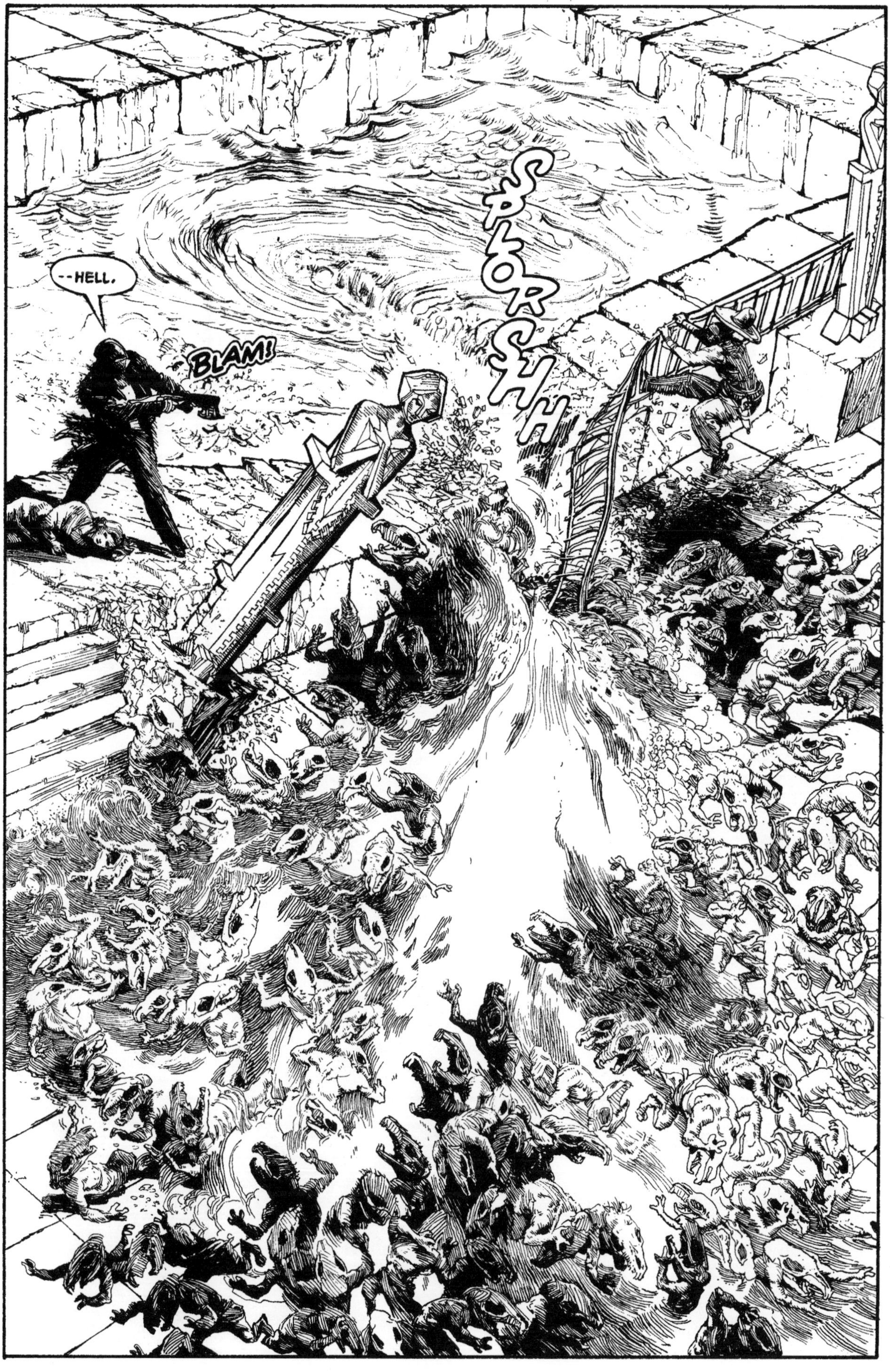
--HELL.
BLAM!
SPLORSHH

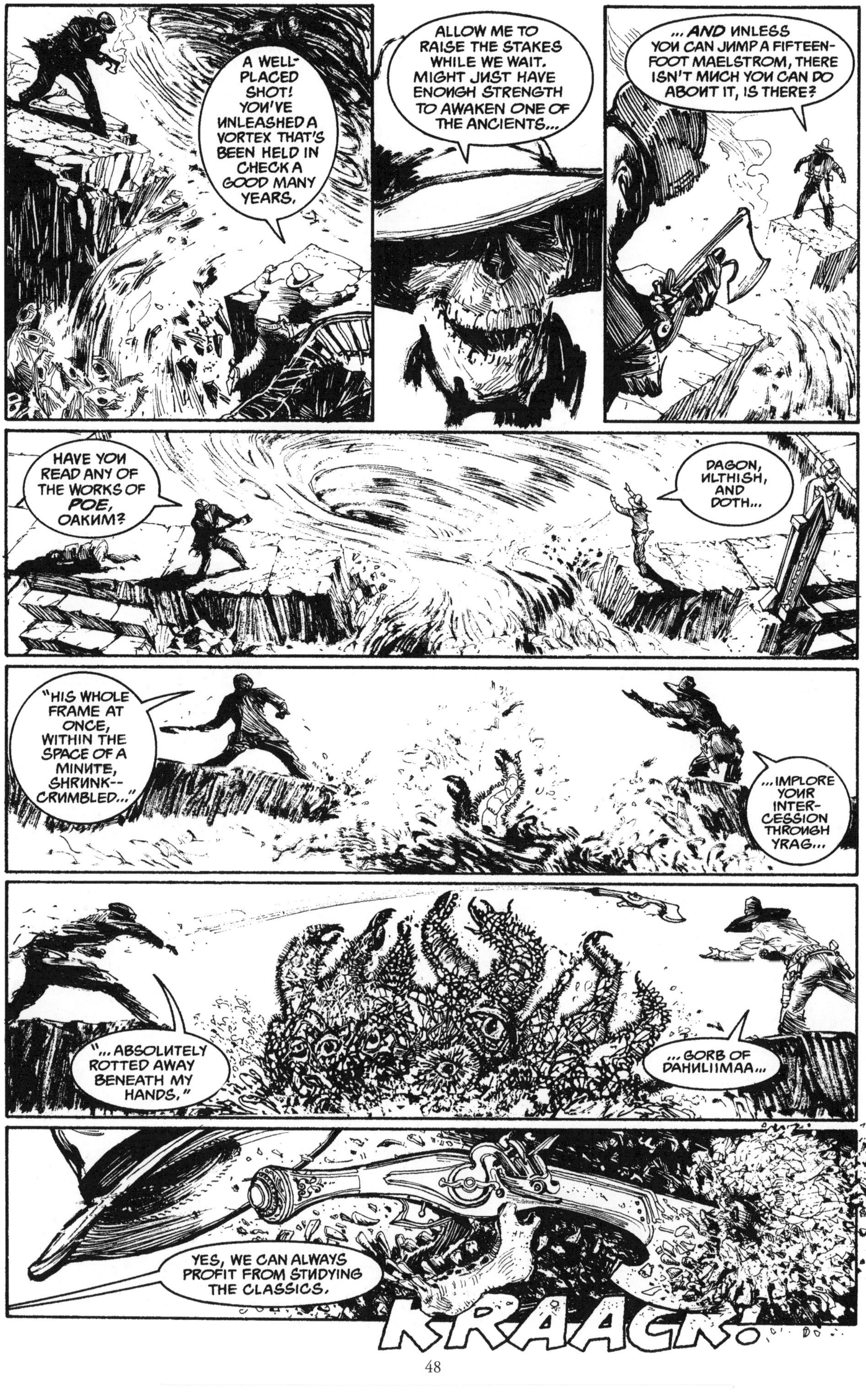
A WELL-PLACED SHOT! YOU'VE UNLEASHED A VORTEX THAT'S BEEN HELD IN CHECK A GOOD MANY YEARS.
ALLOW ME TO RAISE THE STAKES WHILE WE WAIT. MIGHT JUST HAVE ENOUGH STRENGTH TO AWAKEN ONE OF THE ANCIENTS...
...AND UNLESS YOU CAN JUMP A FIFTEEN-FOOT MAELSTROM, THERE ISN'T MUCH YOU CAN DO ABOUT IT, IS THERE?
HAVE YOU READ ANY OF THE WORKS OF POE, OAKUM?
DAGON, ULTHISH, AND DOTH...
"HIS WHOLE FRAME AT ONCE, WITHIN THE SPACE OF A MINUTE, SHRUNK--CRUMBLED..."
...IMPLORE YOUR INTERCESSION THROUGH YRAG...
"...ABSOLUTELY ROTTED AWAY BENEATH MY HANDS."
...GORB OF DAHULIIMAA...
YES, WE CAN ALWAYS PROFIT FROM STUDYING THE CLASSICS.
KRAACK!

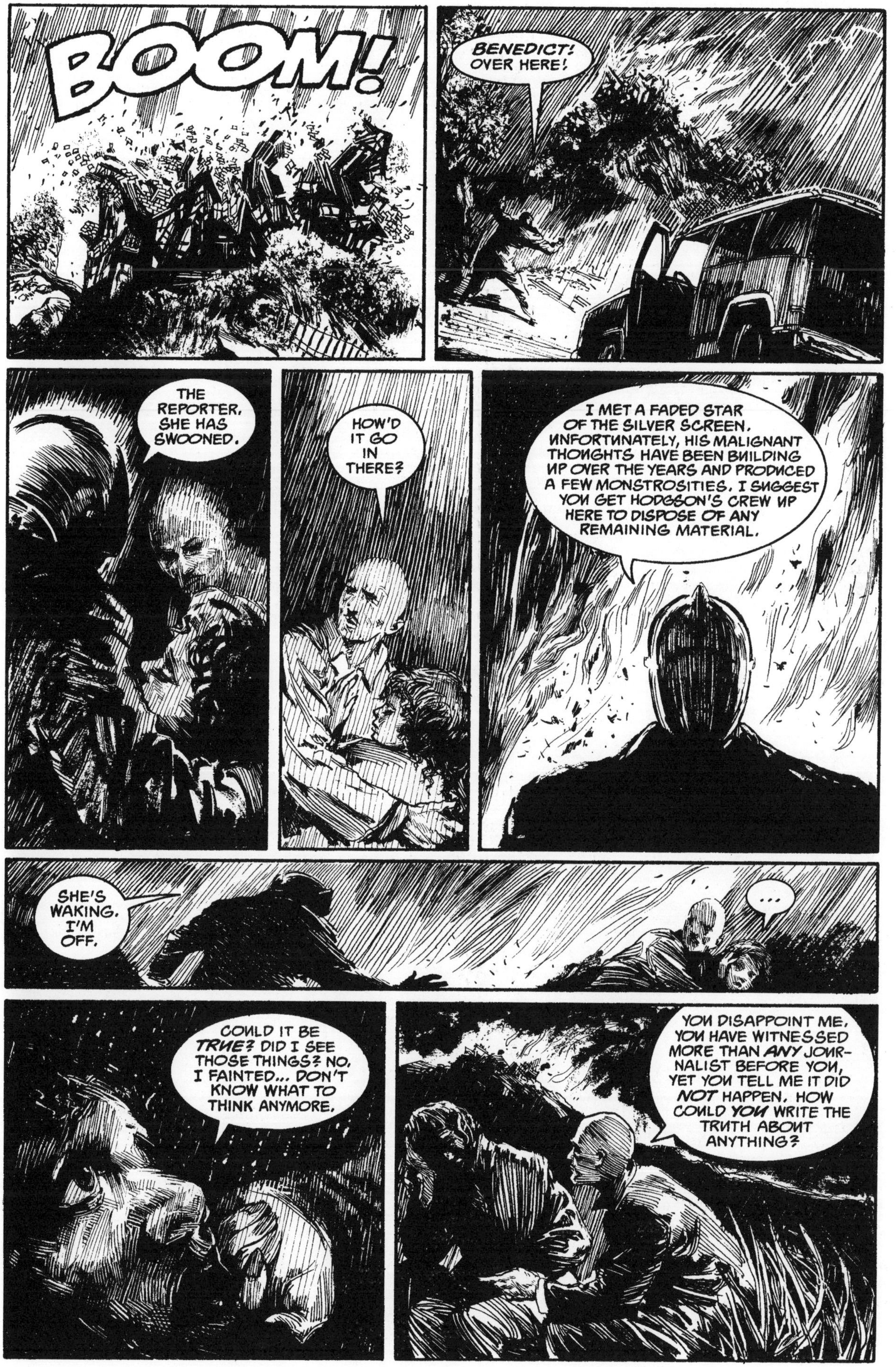
BOOM!
BENEDICT! OVER HERE!
THE REPORTER, SHE HAS SWOONED.
HOW'D IT GO IN THERE?
I MET A FADED STAR OF THE SILVER SCREEN. UNFORTUNATELY, HIS MALIGNANT THOUGHTS HAVE BEEN BUILDING UP OVER THE YEARS AND PRODUCED A FEW MONSTROSITIES. I SUGGEST YOU GET HODGSON'S CREW UP HERE TO DISPOSE OF ANY REMAINING MATERIAL.
SHE'S WAKING. I'M OFF.
...
COULD IT BE TRUE? DID I SEE THOSE THINGS? NO, I FAINTED... DON'T KNOW WHAT TO THINK ANYMORE.
YOU DISAPPOINT ME. YOU HAVE WITNESSED MORE THAN ANY JOURNALIST BEFORE YOU, YET YOU TELL ME IT DID NOT HAPPEN. HOW COULD YOU WRITE THE TRUTH ABOUT ANYTHING?

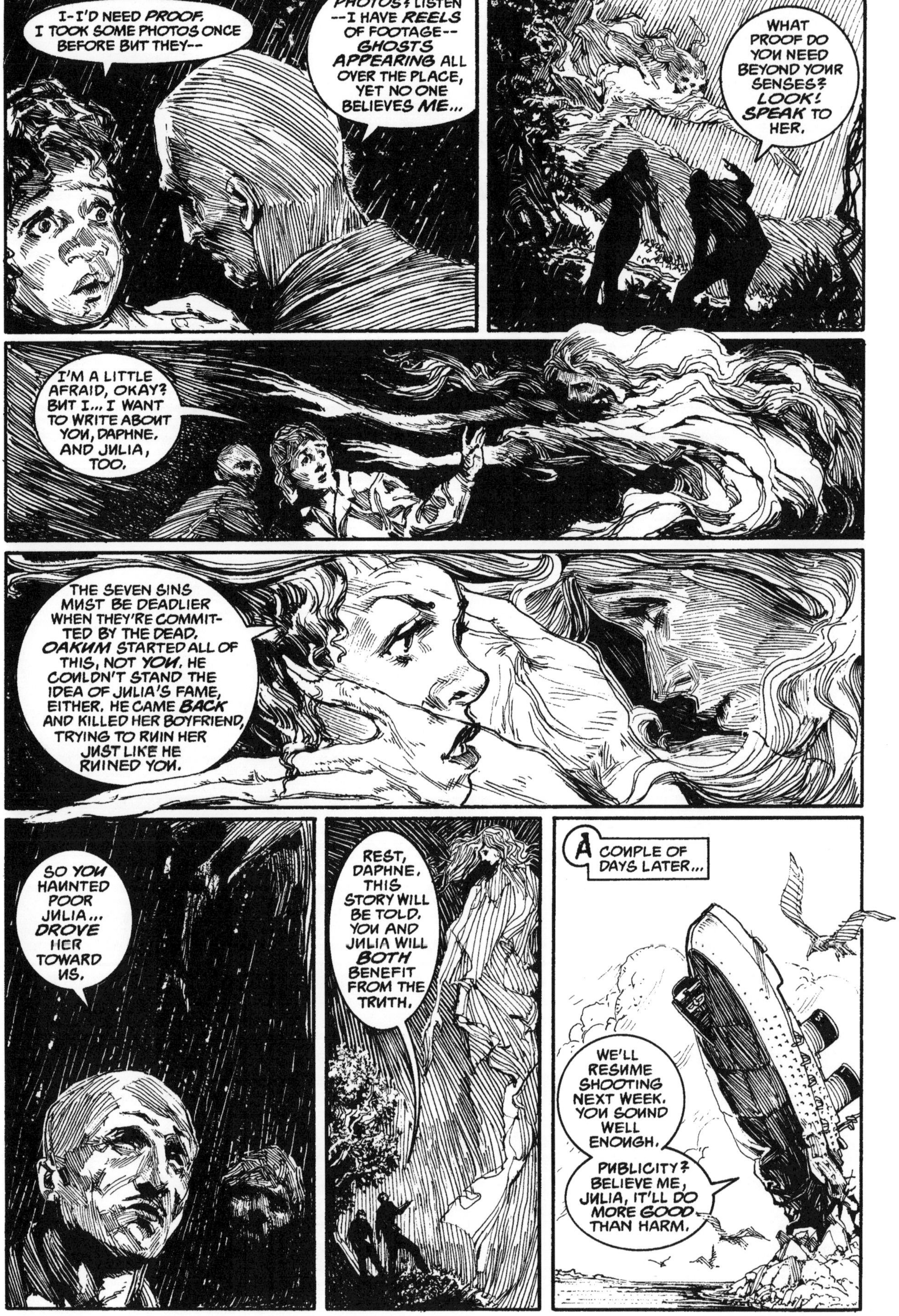
I-I'D NEED PROOF. I TOOK SOME PHOTOS ONCE BEFORE BUT THEY--
PHOTOS? LISTEN --I HAVE REELS OF FOOTAGE-- GHOSTS APPEARING ALL OVER THE PLACE, YET NO ONE BELIEVES ME...
WHAT PROOF DO YOU NEED BEYOND YOUR SENSES? LOOK! SPEAK TO HER.
I'M A LITTLE AFRAID, OKAY? BUT I... I WANT TO WRITE ABOUT YOU, DAPHNE, AND JULIA, TOO.
THE SEVEN SINS MUST BE DEADLIER WHEN THEY'RE COMMITTED BY THE DEAD. OAKUM STARTED ALL OF THIS, NOT YOU. HE COULDN'T STAND THE IDEA OF JULIA'S FAME, EITHER. HE CAME BACK AND KILLED HER BOYFRIEND, TRYING TO RUIN HER JUST LIKE HE RUINED YOU.
SO YOU HAUNTED POOR JULIA... DROVE HER TOWARD US.
REST, DAPHNE. THIS STORY WILL BE TOLD. YOU AND JULIA WILL BOTH BENEFIT FROM THE TRUTH.
A COUPLE OF DAYS LATER...
WE'LL RESUME SHOOTING NEXT WEEK. YOU SOUND WELL ENOUGH.
PUBLICITY? BELIEVE ME, JULIA, IT'LL DO MORE GOOD THAN HARM.

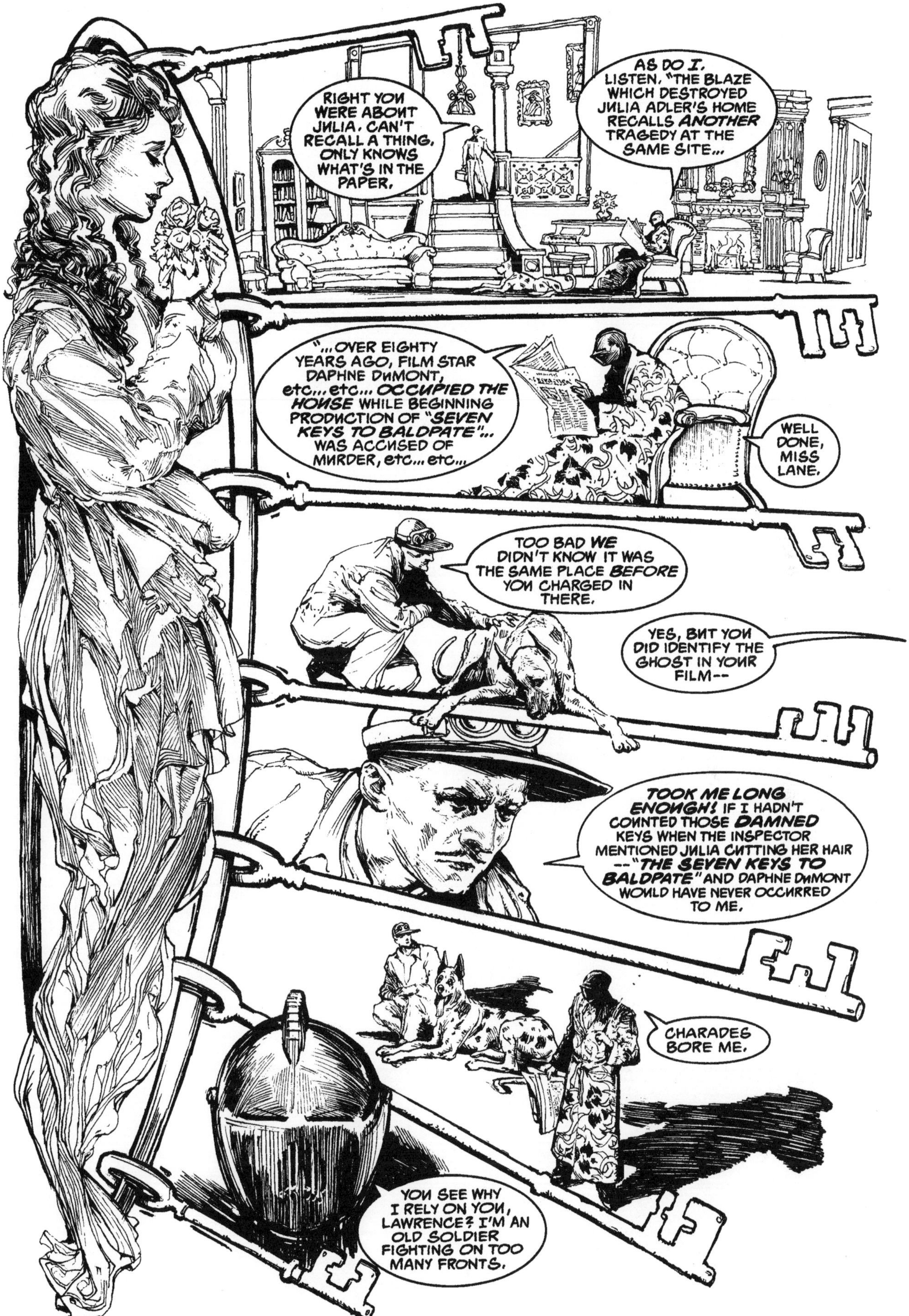
RIGHT YOU WERE ABOUT JULIA. CAN'T RECALL A THING. ONLY KNOWS WHAT'S IN THE PAPER.
AS DO I. LISTEN. "THE BLAZE WHICH DESTROYED JULIA ADLER'S HOME RECALLS ANOTHER TRAGEDY AT THE SAME SITE...
"...OVER EIGHTY YEARS AGO, FILM STAR DAPHNE DUMONT, etc...etc... OCCUPIED THE HOUSE WHILE BEGINNING PRODUCTION OF "SEVEN KEYS TO BALDPATE"... WAS ACCUSED OF MURDER, etc...etc...
WELL DONE, MISS LANE.
TOO BAD WE DIDN'T KNOW IT WAS THE SAME PLACE BEFORE YOU CHARGED IN THERE.
YES, BUT YOU DID IDENTIFY THE GHOST IN YOUR FILM--
TOOK ME LONG ENOUGH! IF I HADN'T COUNTED THOSE DAMNED KEYS WHEN THE INSPECTOR MENTIONED JULIA CUTTING HER HAIR --"THE SEVEN KEYS TO BALDPATE" AND DAPHNE DUMONT WOULD HAVE NEVER OCCURRED TO ME.
CHARADES BORE ME.
YOU SEE WHY I RELY ON YOU, LAWRENCE? I'M AN OLD SOLDIER FIGHTING ON TOO MANY FRONTS.

BUT WHAT CAN *ONE* GUY DO, BENEDICT? IF THE WORLD IS *OVERRUN* BY DEMONS AND MONSTERS...

ENLISTING AID AGAINST THE FORCES OF DARKNESS HAS *ALWAYS* BEEN DIFFICULT. THE IGNORANCE I ENCOUNTER MAKES ME VALUE A MAN OF YOUR KIDNEY.

TAKE HEED, CREATURES LIKE THE JIB-BIC AND GOOSEFLESH LURK BEYOND YOUR VERY DOOR-- AND I WILL NOT ALWAYS BE HERE.

THE FOLLOWING AFTERNOON, AN UNUSUAL CIRCUS TROUPE PROCLAIMING "SPECTACULAR FEATS OF INGENUITY" UNVEILS A NEW ATTRACTION.

STEP THIS WAY, LADIES AND GENTLEMEN!

I TOLD YOU WE'D SEE MONSTERS... HERE'S OUR *LATEST* CURIOSITY. HOW HE GOT THIS WAY, NO ONE WILL EVER KNOW...

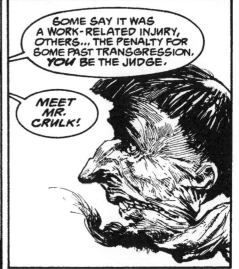

SOME SAY IT WAS A WORK-RELATED INJURY, OTHERS... THE PENALTY FOR SOME PAST TRANSGRESSION. *YOU* BE THE JUDGE.

MEET MR. CRULK!

CRULK, JUST CRULK.

FINI

AUTOPSY IN B-FLAT

THE MONSTERMEN™

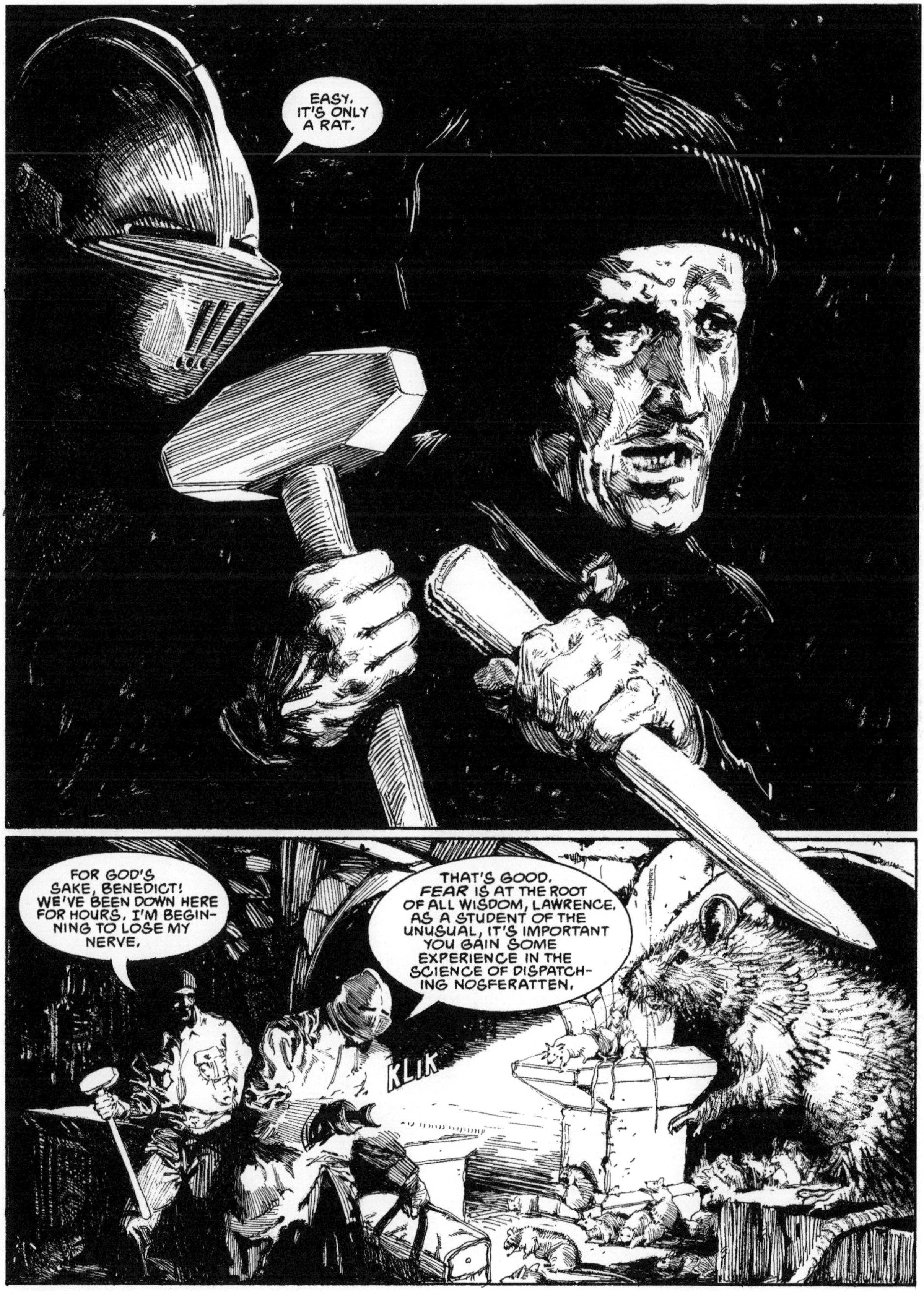
EASY. IT'S ONLY A RAT.
FOR GOD'S SAKE, BENEDICT! WE'VE BEEN DOWN HERE FOR HOURS. I'M BEGINNING TO LOSE MY NERVE.
THAT'S GOOD. FEAR IS AT THE ROOT OF ALL WISDOM, LAWRENCE. AS A STUDENT OF THE UNUSUAL, IT'S IMPORTANT YOU GAIN SOME EXPERIENCE IN THE SCIENCE OF DISPATCHING NOSFERATTEN.
KLIK

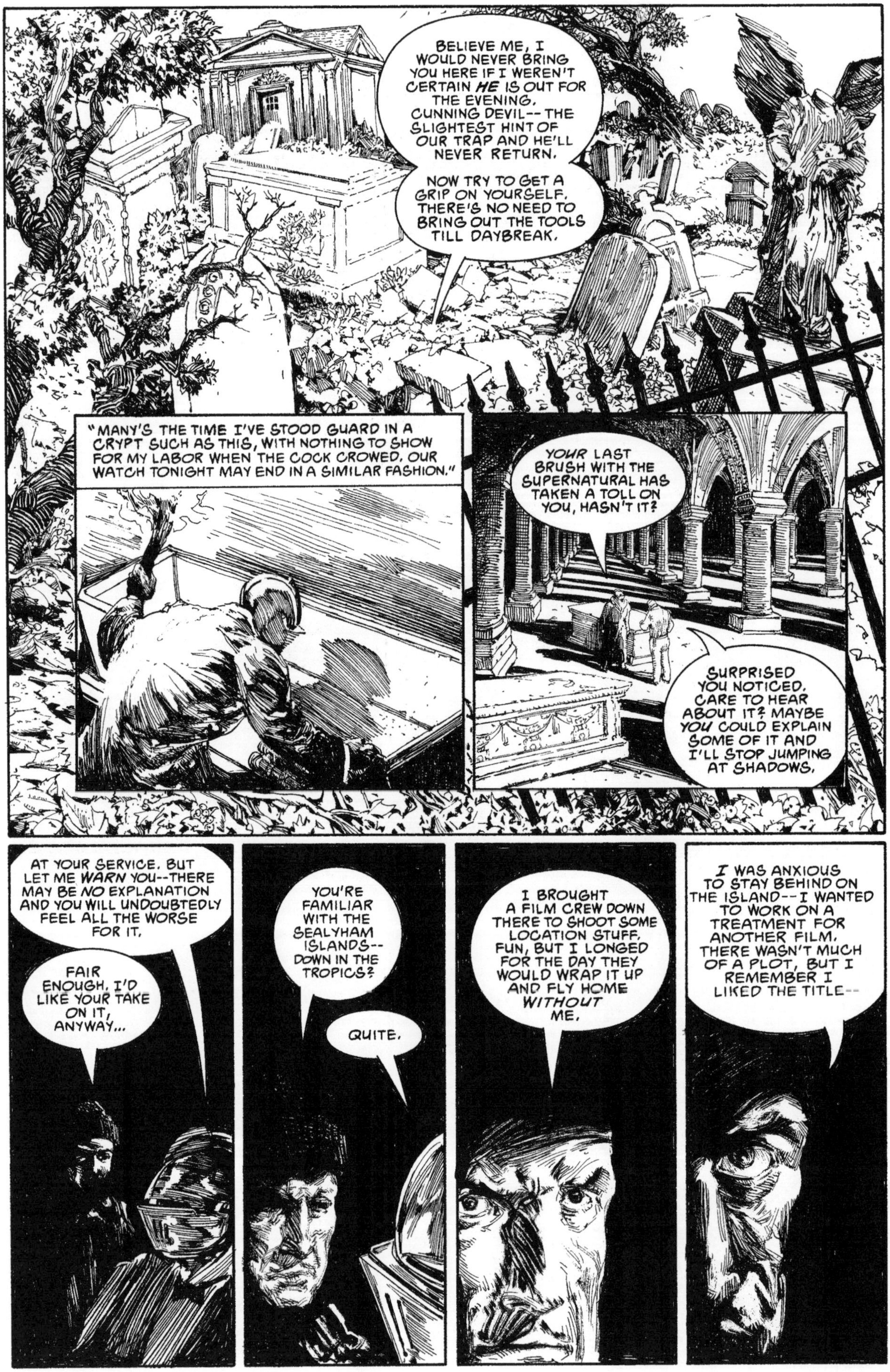
BELIEVE ME, I WOULD NEVER BRING YOU HERE IF I WEREN'T CERTAIN HE IS OUT FOR THE EVENING. CUNNING DEVIL-- THE SLIGHTEST HINT OF OUR TRAP AND HE'LL NEVER RETURN.
NOW TRY TO GET A GRIP ON YOURSELF. THERE'S NO NEED TO BRING OUT THE TOOLS TILL DAYBREAK.
"MANY'S THE TIME I'VE STOOD GUARD IN A CRYPT SUCH AS THIS, WITH NOTHING TO SHOW FOR MY LABOR WHEN THE COCK CROWED. OUR WATCH TONIGHT MAY END IN A SIMILAR FASHION."
YOUR LAST BRUSH WITH THE SUPERNATURAL HAS TAKEN A TOLL ON YOU, HASN'T IT?
SURPRISED YOU NOTICED. CARE TO HEAR ABOUT IT? MAYBE YOU COULD EXPLAIN SOME OF IT AND I'LL STOP JUMPING AT SHADOWS.
AT YOUR SERVICE. BUT LET ME WARN YOU--THERE MAY BE NO EXPLANATION AND YOU WILL UNDOUBTEDLY FEEL ALL THE WORSE FOR IT.
FAIR ENOUGH. I'D LIKE YOUR TAKE ON IT, ANYWAY...
YOU'RE FAMILIAR WITH THE SEALYHAM ISLANDS-- DOWN IN THE TROPICS?
QUITE.
I BROUGHT A FILM CREW DOWN THERE TO SHOOT SOME LOCATION STUFF. FUN, BUT I LONGED FOR THE DAY THEY WOULD WRAP IT UP AND FLY HOME WITHOUT ME.
I WAS ANXIOUS TO STAY BEHIND ON THE ISLAND-- I WANTED TO WORK ON A TREATMENT FOR ANOTHER FILM. THERE WASN'T MUCH OF A PLOT, BUT I REMEMBER I LIKED THE TITLE--

AUTOPSY IN B-FLAT

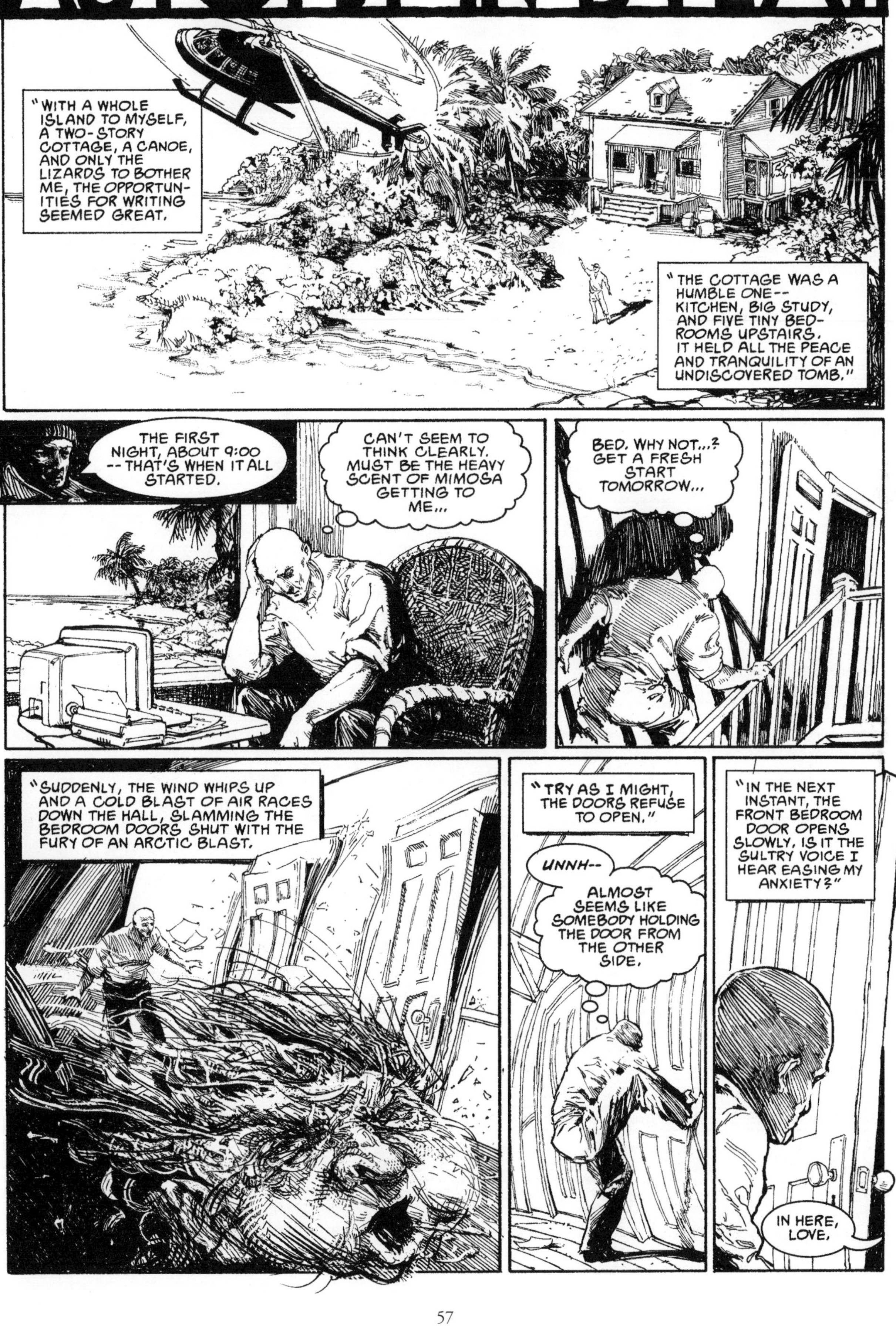

"WITH A WHOLE ISLAND TO MYSELF, A TWO-STORY COTTAGE, A CANOE, AND ONLY THE LIZARDS TO BOTHER ME, THE OPPORTUNITIES FOR WRITING SEEMED GREAT.
"THE COTTAGE WAS A HUMBLE ONE-- KITCHEN, BIG STUDY, AND FIVE TINY BEDROOMS UPSTAIRS. IT HELD ALL THE PEACE AND TRANQUILITY OF AN UNDISCOVERED TOMB."
THE FIRST NIGHT, ABOUT 9:00 -- THAT'S WHEN IT ALL STARTED.
CAN'T SEEM TO THINK CLEARLY. MUST BE THE HEAVY SCENT OF MIMOSA GETTING TO ME...
BED. WHY NOT...? GET A FRESH START TOMORROW...
"SUDDENLY, THE WIND WHIPS UP AND A COLD BLAST OF AIR RACES DOWN THE HALL, SLAMMING THE BEDROOM DOORS SHUT WITH THE FURY OF AN ARCTIC BLAST.
"TRY AS I MIGHT, THE DOORS REFUSE TO OPEN."
UNNH--
ALMOST SEEMS LIKE SOMEBODY HOLDING THE DOOR FROM THE OTHER SIDE.
"IN THE NEXT INSTANT, THE FRONT BEDROOM DOOR OPENS SLOWLY. IS IT THE SULTRY VOICE I HEAR EASING MY ANXIETY?"
IN HERE, LOVE.

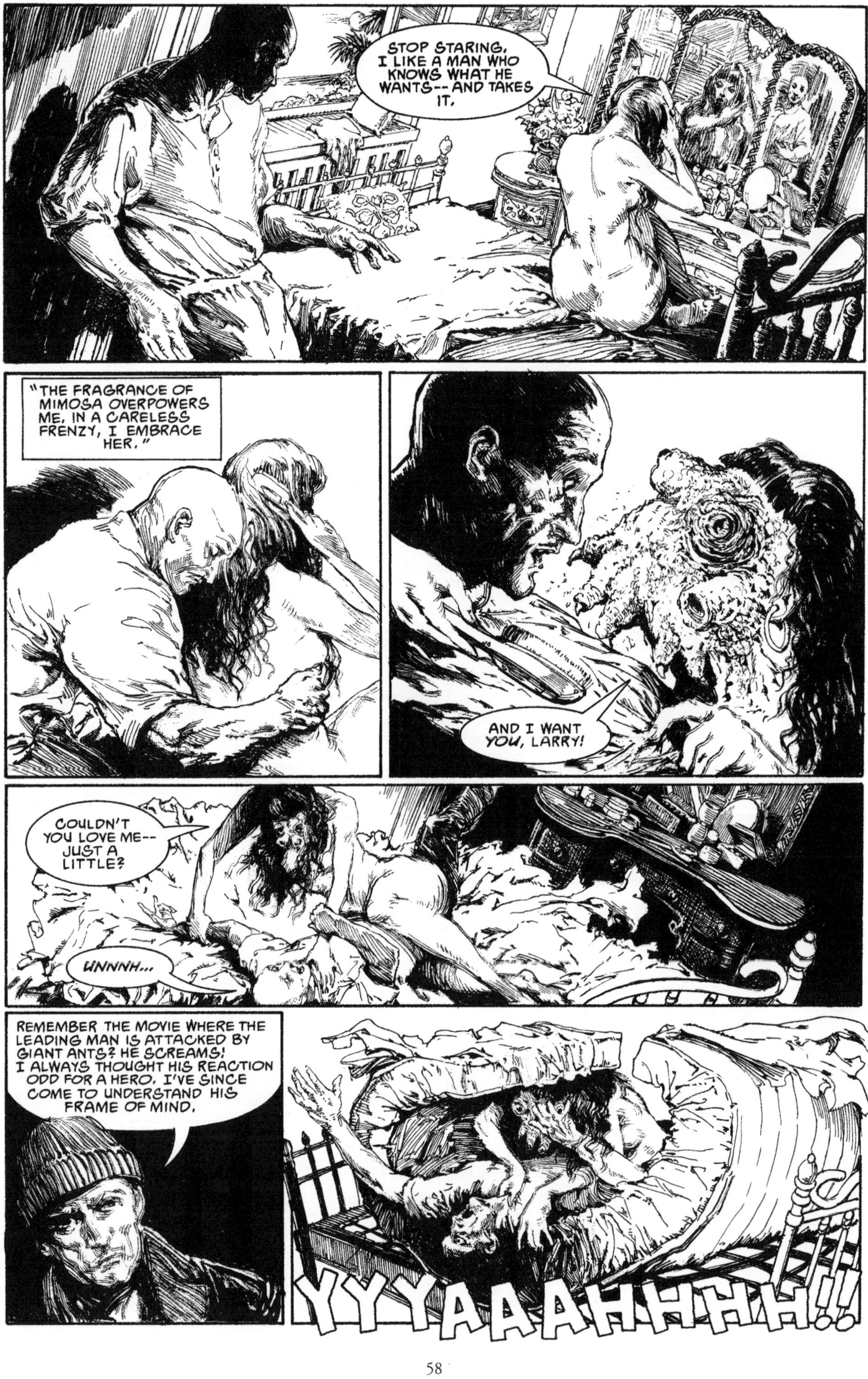
STOP STARING, I LIKE A MAN WHO KNOWS WHAT HE WANTS-- AND TAKES IT.
"THE FRAGRANCE OF MIMOSA OVERPOWERS ME, IN A CARELESS FRENZY, I EMBRACE HER."
AND I WANT YOU, LARRY!
COULDN'T YOU LOVE ME-- JUST A LITTLE?
UNNNH...
REMEMBER THE MOVIE WHERE THE LEADING MAN IS ATTACKED BY GIANT ANTS? HE SCREAMS! I ALWAYS THOUGHT HIS REACTION ODD FOR A HERO. I'VE SINCE COME TO UNDERSTAND HIS FRAME OF MIND.
YYYAAAAHHHHH!!

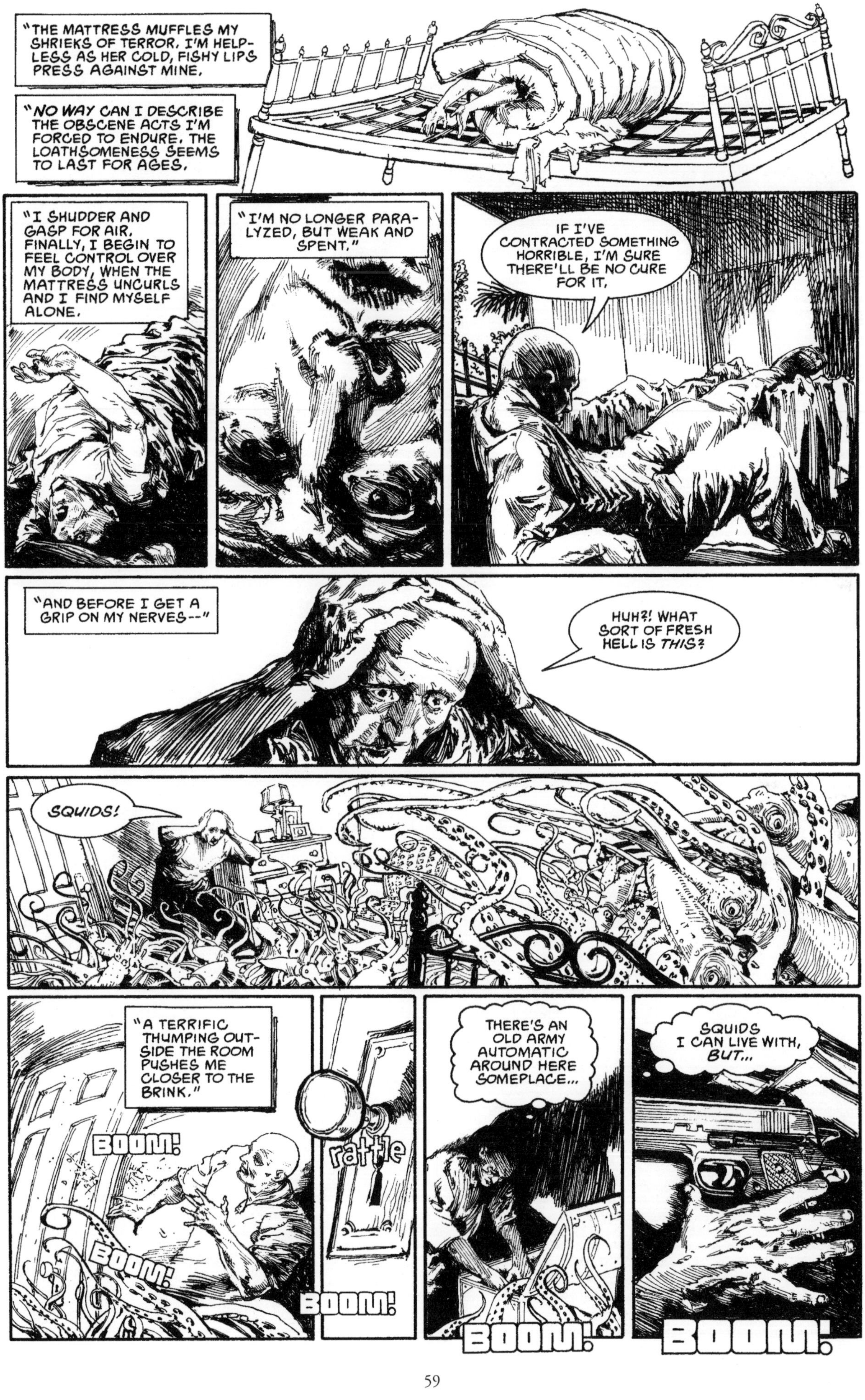
"THE MATTRESS MUFFLES MY SHRIEKS OF TERROR. I'M HELPLESS AS HER COLD, FISHY LIPS PRESS AGAINST MINE.
"NO WAY CAN I DESCRIBE THE OBSCENE ACTS I'M FORCED TO ENDURE. THE LOATHSOMENESS SEEMS TO LAST FOR AGES.
"I SHUDDER AND GASP FOR AIR. FINALLY, I BEGIN TO FEEL CONTROL OVER MY BODY, WHEN THE MATTRESS UNCURLS AND I FIND MYSELF ALONE.
"I'M NO LONGER PARALYZED, BUT WEAK AND SPENT."
IF I'VE CONTRACTED SOMETHING HORRIBLE, I'M SURE THERE'LL BE NO CURE FOR IT.
"AND BEFORE I GET A GRIP ON MY NERVES--"
HUH?! WHAT SORT OF FRESH HELL IS THIS?
SQUIDS!
"A TERRIFIC THUMPING OUTSIDE THE ROOM PUSHES ME CLOSER TO THE BRINK."
BOOM!
BOOM!
BOOM!
rattle
THERE'S AN OLD ARMY AUTOMATIC AROUND HERE SOMEPLACE...
BOOM!
SQUIDS I CAN LIVE WITH, BUT...
BOOM!

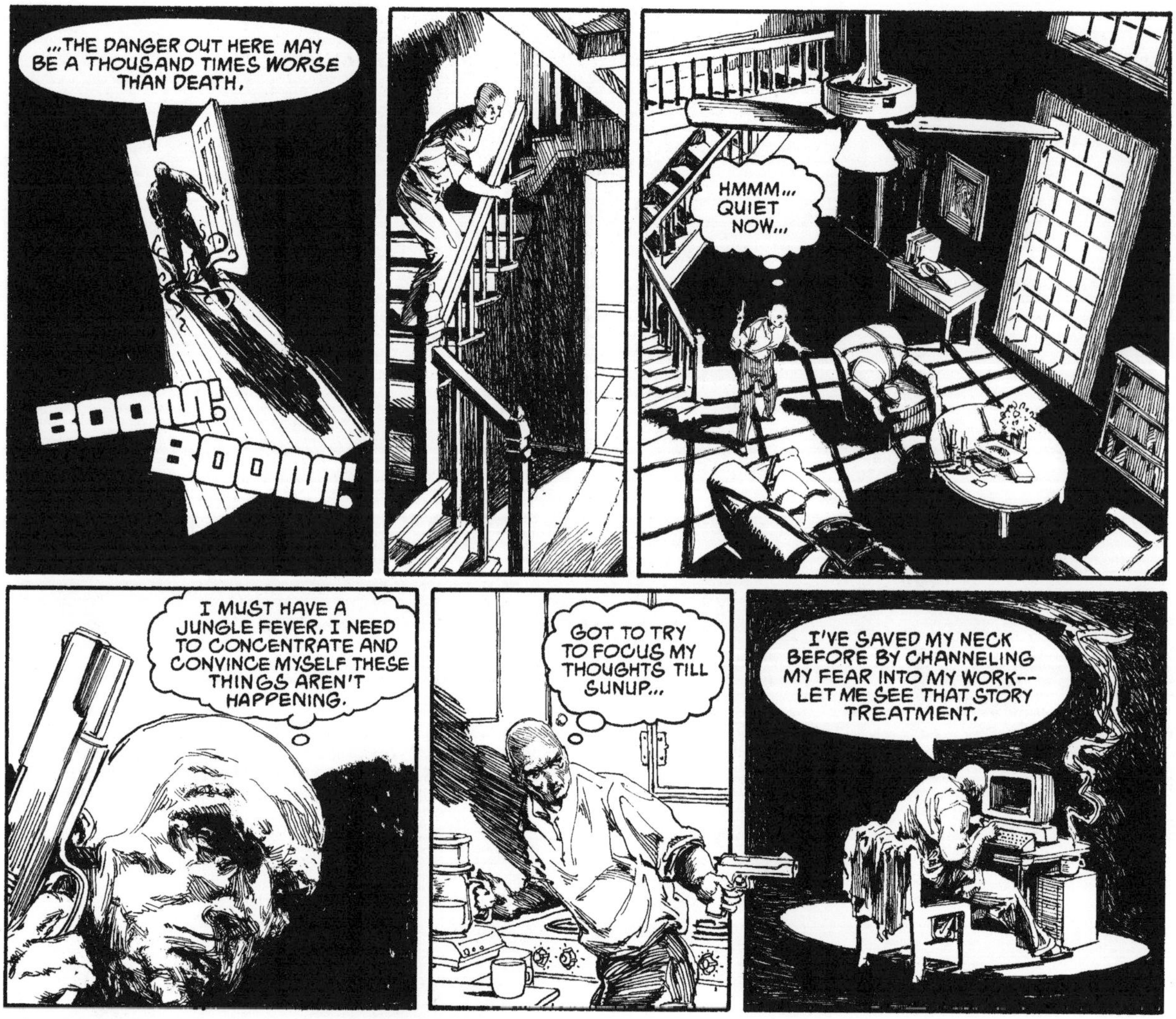
...THE DANGER OUT HERE MAY BE A THOUSAND TIMES WORSE THAN DEATH.
BOOM! BOOM!
HMMM... QUIET NOW...
I MUST HAVE A JUNGLE FEVER. I NEED TO CONCENTRATE AND CONVINCE MYSELF THESE THINGS AREN'T HAPPENING.
GOT TO TRY TO FOCUS MY THOUGHTS TILL SUNUP...
I'VE SAVED MY NECK BEFORE BY CHANNELING MY FEAR INTO MY WORK-- LET ME SEE THAT STORY TREATMENT.

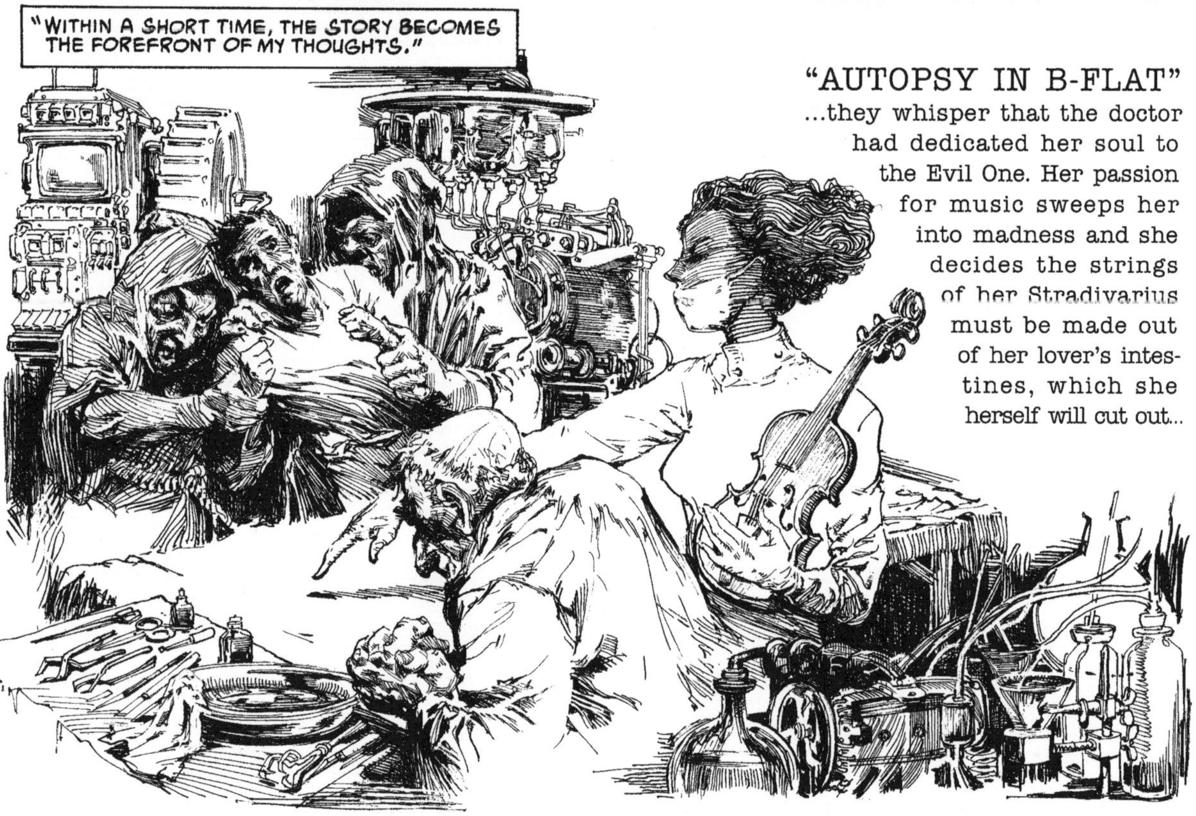
"WITHIN A SHORT TIME, THE STORY BECOMES THE FOREFRONT OF MY THOUGHTS."

"AUTOPSY IN B-FLAT"
...they whisper that the doctor had dedicated her soul to the Evil One. Her passion for music sweeps her into madness and she decides the strings of her Stradivarius must be made out of her lover's intestines, which she herself will cut out...

NOT TOO BAD. UNFORTUNATELY, THE CHOPPER WILL BE BACK IN THE MORNING-- *THAT'LL* PUT AN END TO MY CONCENTRATION.

WONDER WHAT BENEDICT WOULD SAY ABOUT MY NIGHT? GUESS HE'D WANT TO CH--

HEY! WHAT TH-- WHERE'S THAT LIGHT COMING FROM?

A ROWBOAT?! OF *ALL* THINGS! WE'RE A *LONG* WAY FROM WATER TRAFFIC OUT HERE.

APPEARS TO BE COMING ASHORE. MIGHT BE A COUPLE OF LOST BOATERS. THEN AGAIN-- LOTS OF DRUG SMUGGLING IN THESE PARTS.

WELL, WHOEVER THEY ARE, THEY'RE *ONLY* HUMAN, A WELCOME RELIEF FROM WHAT I'M USED TO.

BETTER TAKE TO THE BUSH, THEY'LL HEAD UP THIS WAY BEFORE LONG.

UNLOADING SHOVELS, CRATES --WHAT'S THEIR GAME, ANYWAY?

"THE PARTY HALTS TEN YARDS AWAY. ANY NOTION I HAVE CONCERNING THEIR IDENTITY DOES NOT PRE- PARE ME FOR THEIR ACTUAL APPEARANCE,"

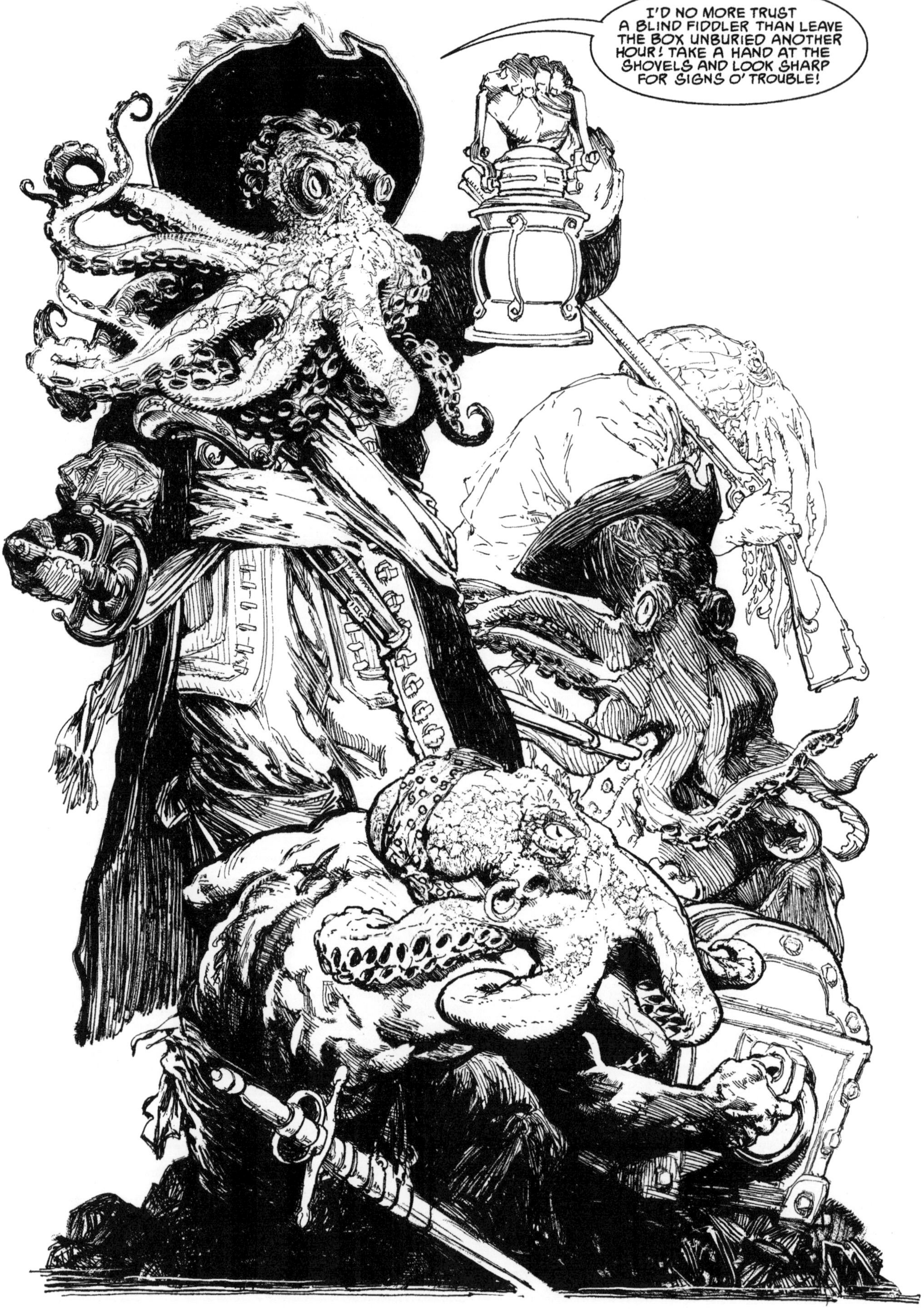
I'D NO MORE TRUST A BLIND FIDDLER THAN LEAVE THE BOX UNBURIED ANOTHER HOUR! TAKE A HAND AT THE SHOVELS AND LOOK SHARP FOR SIGNS O' TROUBLE!

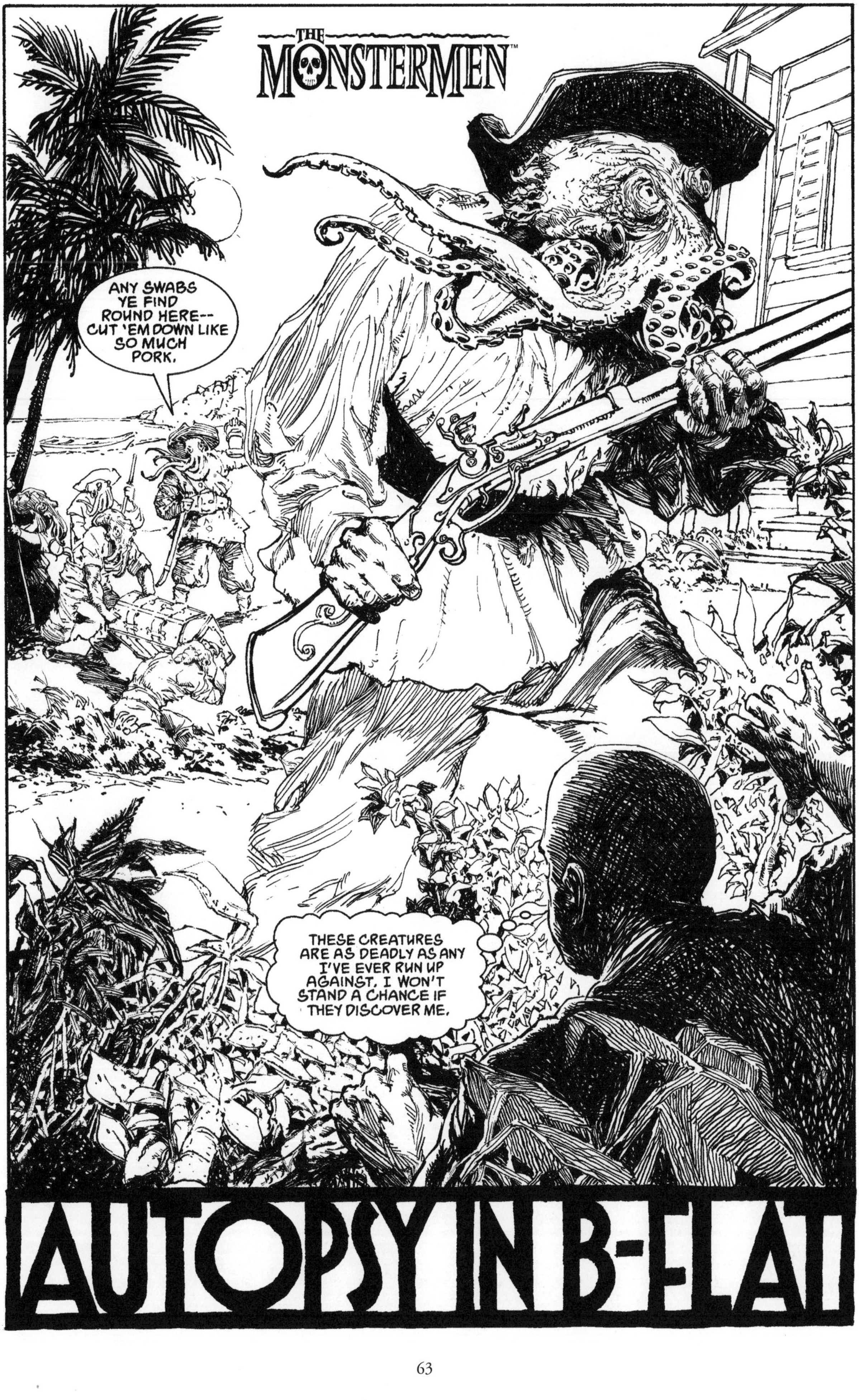
THE MONSTERMEN
ANY SWABS YE FIND ROUND HERE-- CUT 'EM DOWN LIKE SO MUCH PORK.
THESE CREATURES ARE AS DEADLY AS ANY I'VE EVER RUN UP AGAINST. I WON'T STAND A CHANCE IF THEY DISCOVER ME.
AUTOPSY IN B-FLAT

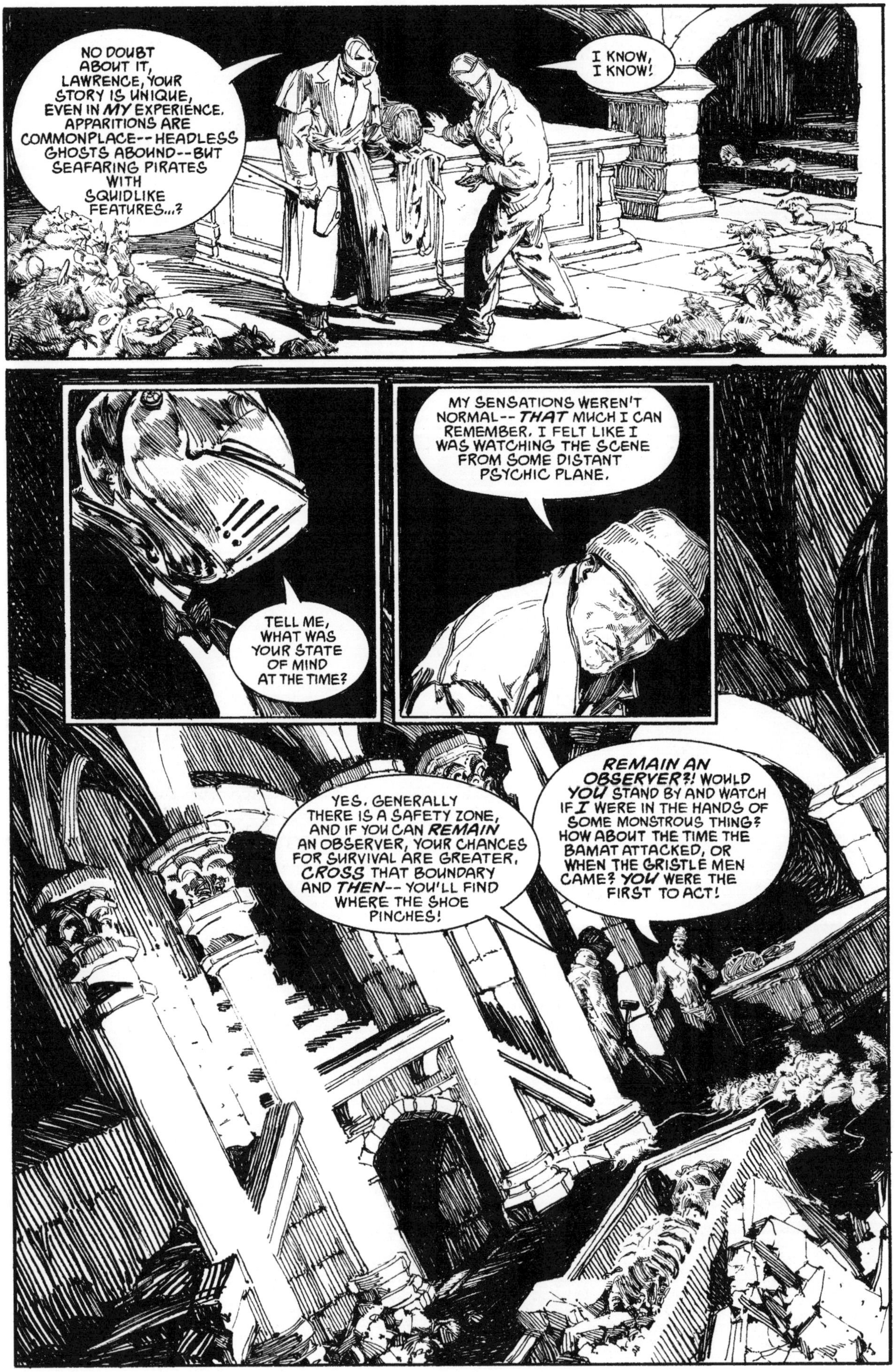
NO DOUBT ABOUT IT, LAWRENCE, YOUR STORY IS UNIQUE, EVEN IN MY EXPERIENCE. APPARITIONS ARE COMMONPLACE--HEADLESS GHOSTS ABOUND--BUT SEAFARING PIRATES WITH SQUIDLIKE FEATURES...?
I KNOW, I KNOW!
TELL ME, WHAT WAS YOUR STATE OF MIND AT THE TIME?
MY SENSATIONS WEREN'T NORMAL--THAT MUCH I CAN REMEMBER. I FELT LIKE I WAS WATCHING THE SCENE FROM SOME DISTANT PSYCHIC PLANE.
YES. GENERALLY THERE IS A SAFETY ZONE, AND IF YOU CAN REMAIN AN OBSERVER, YOUR CHANCES FOR SURVIVAL ARE GREATER. CROSS THAT BOUNDARY AND THEN--YOU'LL FIND WHERE THE SHOE PINCHES!
REMAIN AN OBSERVER?! WOULD YOU STAND BY AND WATCH IF I WERE IN THE HANDS OF SOME MONSTROUS THING? HOW ABOUT THE TIME THE BAMAT ATTACKED, OR WHEN THE GRISTLE MEN CAME? YOU WERE THE FIRST TO ACT!

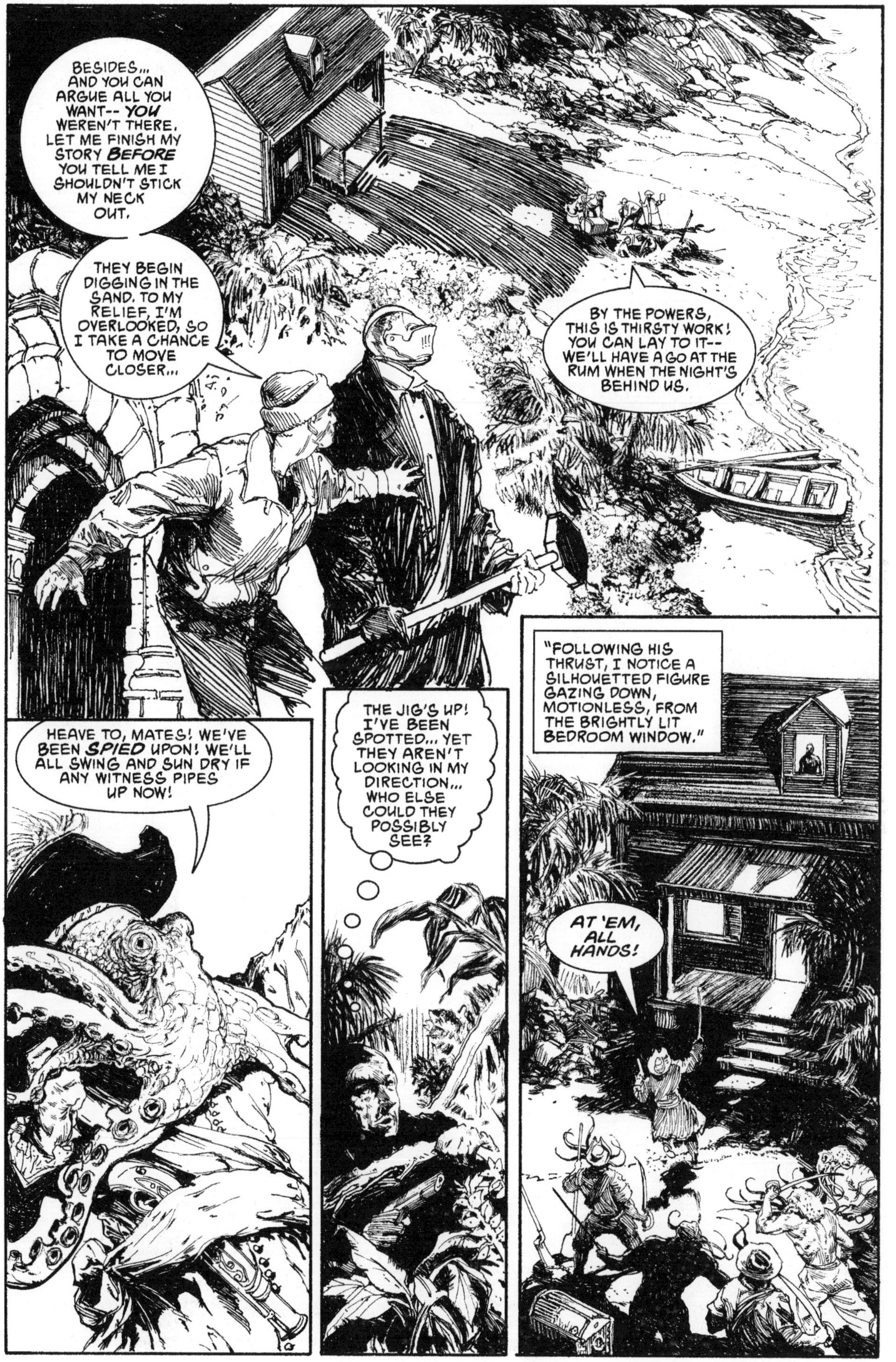
BESIDES... AND YOU CAN ARGUE ALL YOU WANT-- YOU WEREN'T THERE. LET ME FINISH MY STORY BEFORE YOU TELL ME I SHOULDN'T STICK MY NECK OUT.
THEY BEGIN DIGGING IN THE SAND. TO MY RELIEF, I'M OVERLOOKED, SO I TAKE A CHANCE TO MOVE CLOSER...
BY THE POWERS, THIS IS THIRSTY WORK! YOU CAN LAY TO IT-- WE'LL HAVE A GO AT THE RUM WHEN THE NIGHT'S BEHIND US.
HEAVE TO, MATES! WE'VE BEEN SPIED UPON! WE'LL ALL SWING AND SUN DRY IF ANY WITNESS PIPES UP NOW!
THE JIG'S UP! I'VE BEEN SPOTTED... YET THEY AREN'T LOOKING IN MY DIRECTION... WHO ELSE COULD THEY POSSIBLY SEE?
"FOLLOWING HIS THRUST, I NOTICE A SILHOUETTED FIGURE GAZING DOWN, MOTIONLESS, FROM THE BRIGHTLY LIT BEDROOM WINDOW."
AT 'EM, ALL HANDS!

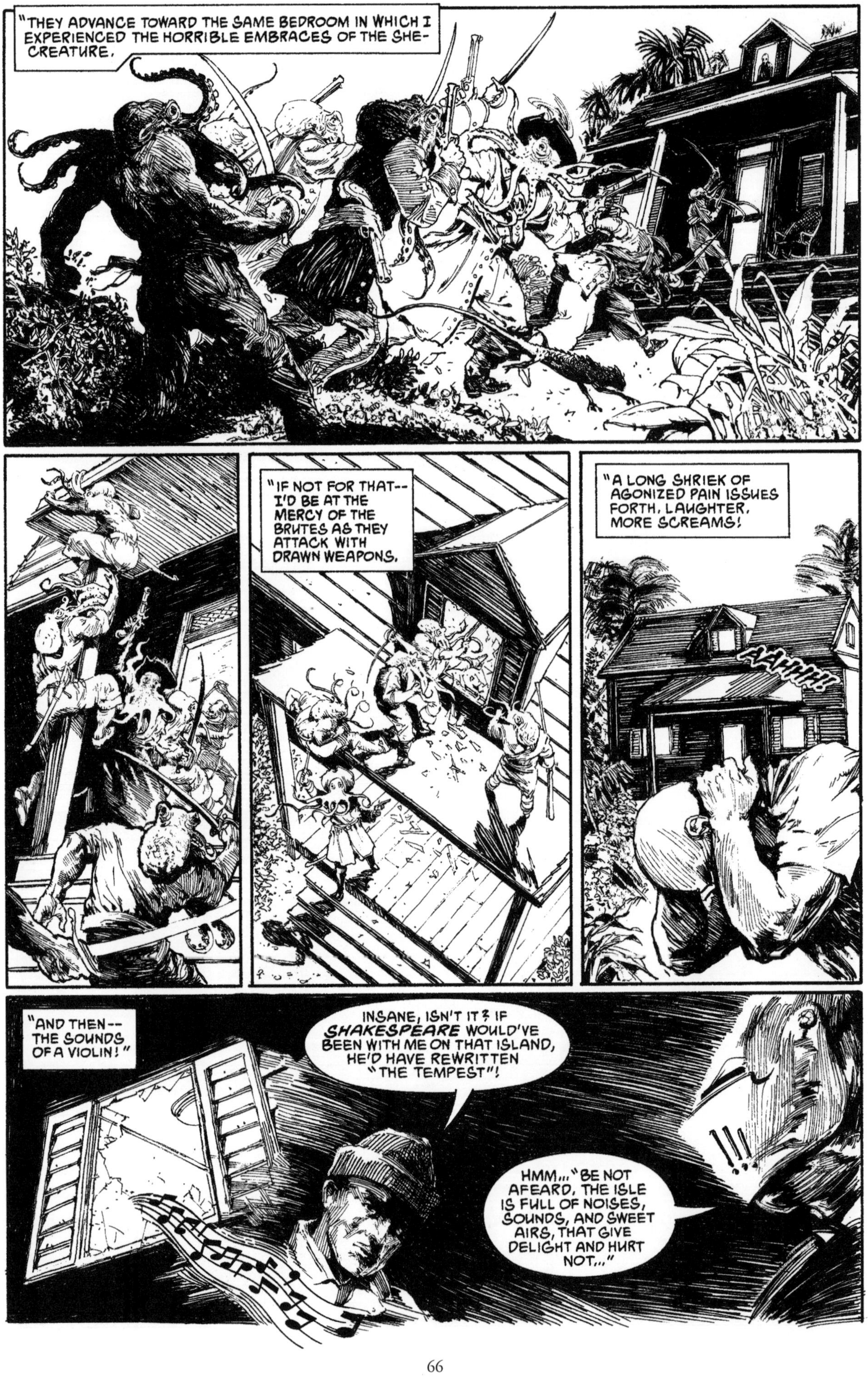
"THEY ADVANCE TOWARD THE SAME BEDROOM IN WHICH I EXPERIENCED THE HORRIBLE EMBRACES OF THE SHE-CREATURE.
"IF NOT FOR THAT-- I'D BE AT THE MERCY OF THE BRUTES AS THEY ATTACK WITH DRAWN WEAPONS.
"A LONG SHRIEK OF AGONIZED PAIN ISSUES FORTH, LAUGHTER, MORE SCREAMS!
AAHHH!
"AND THEN-- THE SOUNDS OF A VIOLIN!"
INSANE, ISN'T IT? IF SHAKESPEARE WOULD'VE BEEN WITH ME ON THAT ISLAND, HE'D HAVE REWRITTEN "THE TEMPEST"!
!!!
HMM... "BE NOT AFEARD, THE ISLE IS FULL OF NOISES, SOUNDS, AND SWEET AIRS, THAT GIVE DELIGHT AND HURT NOT..."

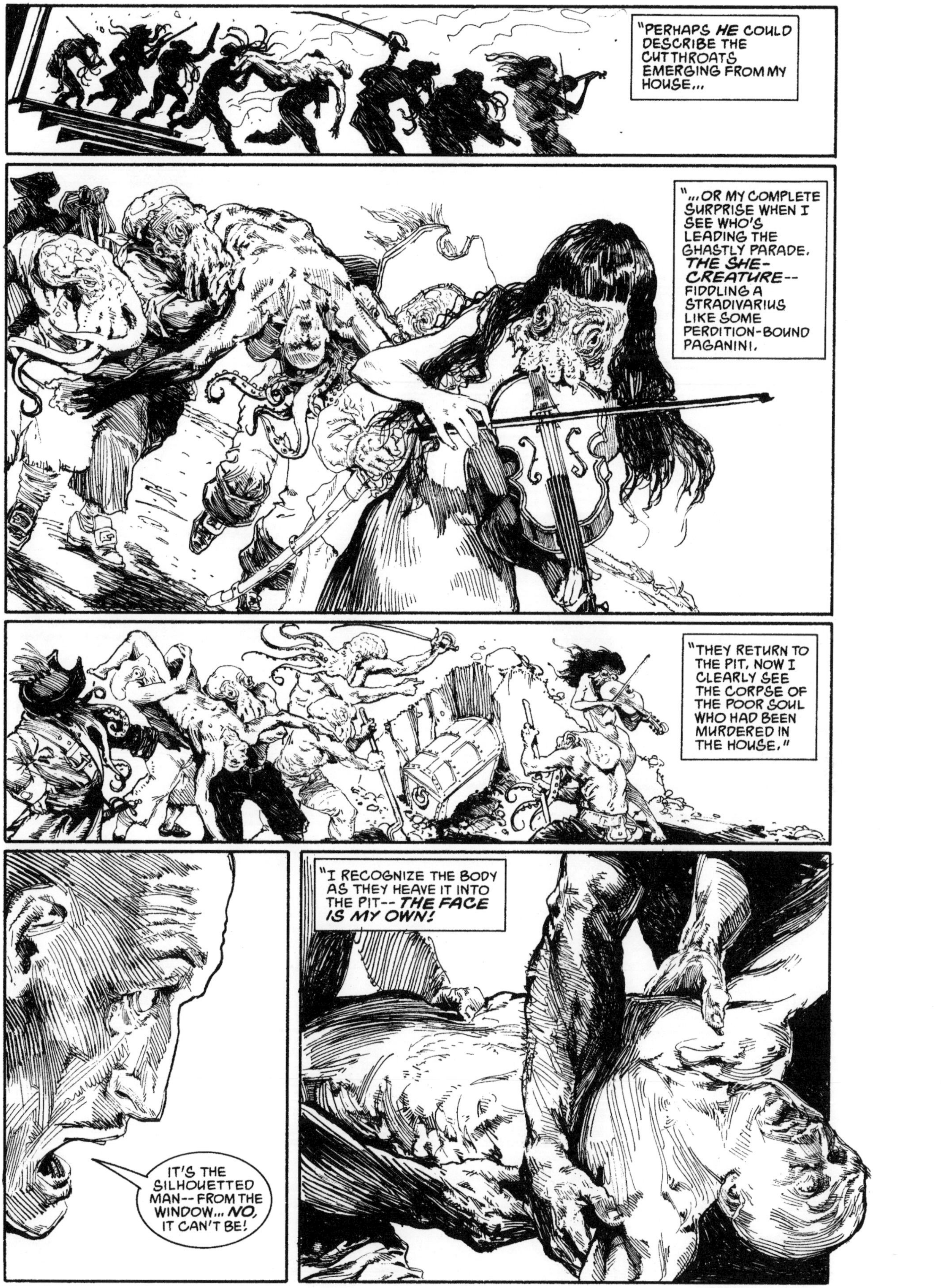
"PERHAPS HE COULD DESCRIBE THE CUTTHROATS EMERGING FROM MY HOUSE...
"...OR MY COMPLETE SURPRISE WHEN I SEE WHO'S LEADING THE GHASTLY PARADE. THE SHE-CREATURE-- FIDDLING A STRADIVARIUS LIKE SOME PERDITION-BOUND PAGANINI.
"THEY RETURN TO THE PIT. NOW I CLEARLY SEE THE CORPSE OF THE POOR SOUL WHO HAD BEEN MURDERED IN THE HOUSE."
IT'S THE SILHOUETTED MAN-- FROM THE WINDOW... NO, IT CAN'T BE!
"I RECOGNIZE THE BODY AS THEY HEAVE IT INTO THE PIT-- THE FACE IS MY OWN!

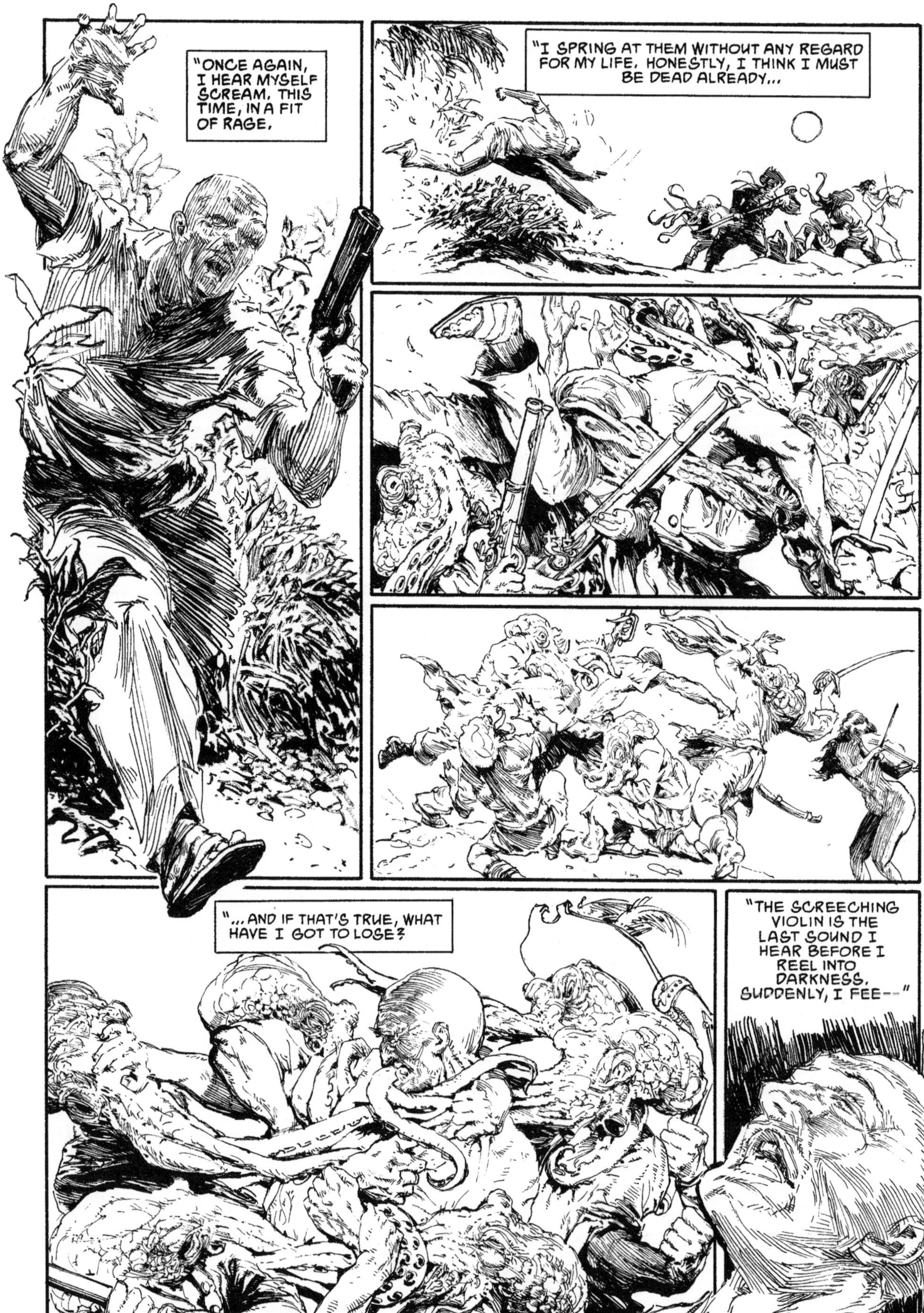
"ONCE AGAIN, I HEAR MYSELF SCREAM. THIS TIME, IN A FIT OF RAGE.
"I SPRING AT THEM WITHOUT ANY REGARD FOR MY LIFE. HONESTLY, I THINK I MUST BE DEAD ALREADY...
"...AND IF THAT'S TRUE, WHAT HAVE I GOT TO LOSE?
"THE SCREECHING VIOLIN IS THE LAST SOUND I HEAR BEFORE I REEL INTO DARKNESS. SUDDENLY, I FEE--"

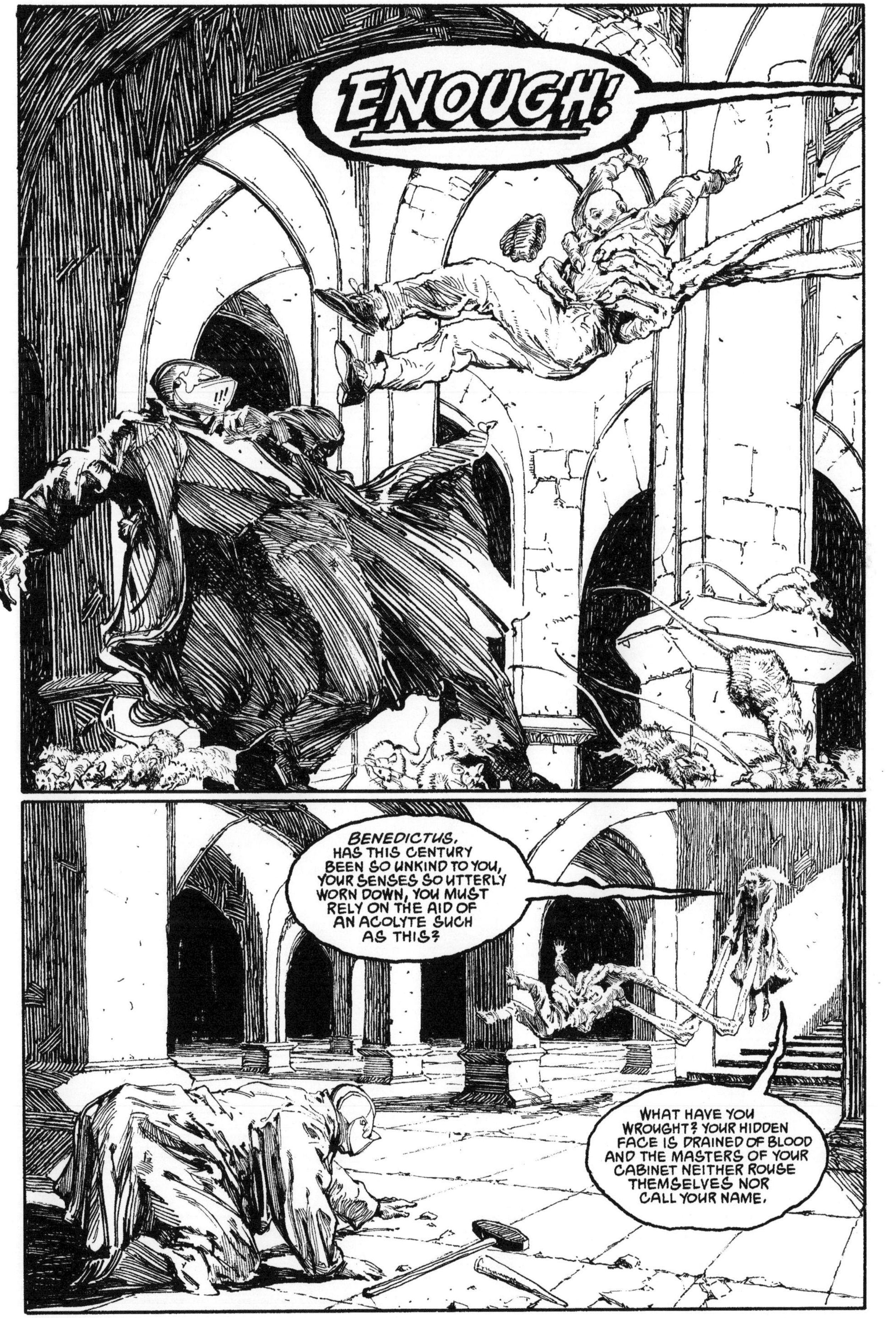
ENOUGH!
BENEDICTUS, HAS THIS CENTURY BEEN SO UNKIND TO YOU, YOUR SENSES SO UTTERLY WORN DOWN, YOU MUST RELY ON THE AID OF AN ACOLYTE SUCH AS THIS?
WHAT HAVE YOU WROUGHT? YOUR HIDDEN FACE IS DRAINED OF BLOOD AND THE MASTERS OF YOUR CABINET NEITHER ROUSE THEMSELVES NOR CALL YOUR NAME.

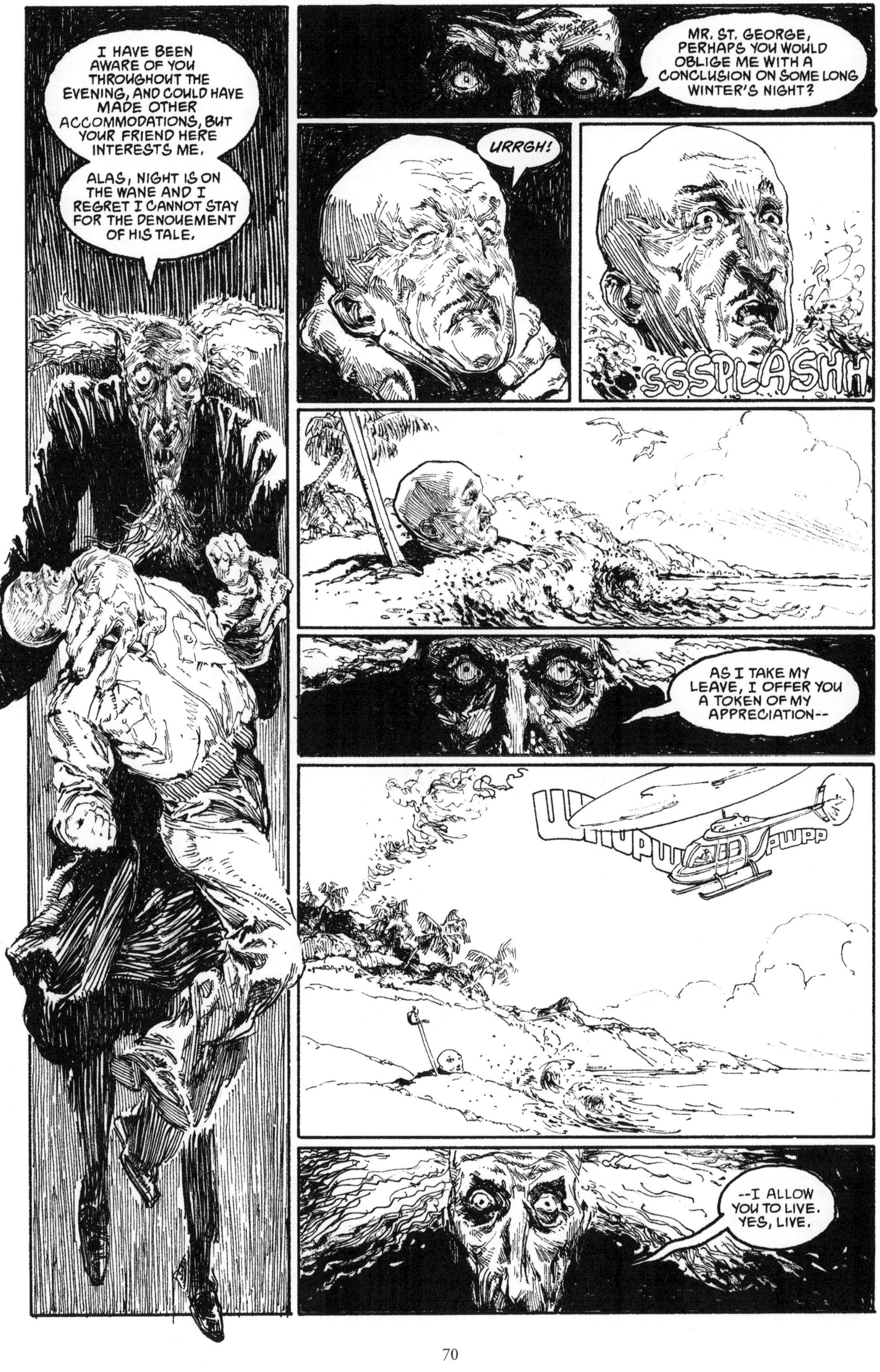
I HAVE BEEN AWARE OF YOU THROUGHOUT THE EVENING, AND COULD HAVE MADE OTHER ACCOMMODATIONS, BUT YOUR FRIEND HERE INTERESTS ME.
ALAS, NIGHT IS ON THE WANE AND I REGRET I CANNOT STAY FOR THE DENOUEMENT OF HIS TALE.
MR. ST. GEORGE, PERHAPS YOU WOULD OBLIGE ME WITH A CONCLUSION ON SOME LONG WINTER'S NIGHT?
URRGH!
SSSPLASHH
AS I TAKE MY LEAVE, I OFFER YOU A TOKEN OF MY APPRECIATION--
PWPP
--I ALLOW YOU TO LIVE. YES, LIVE.

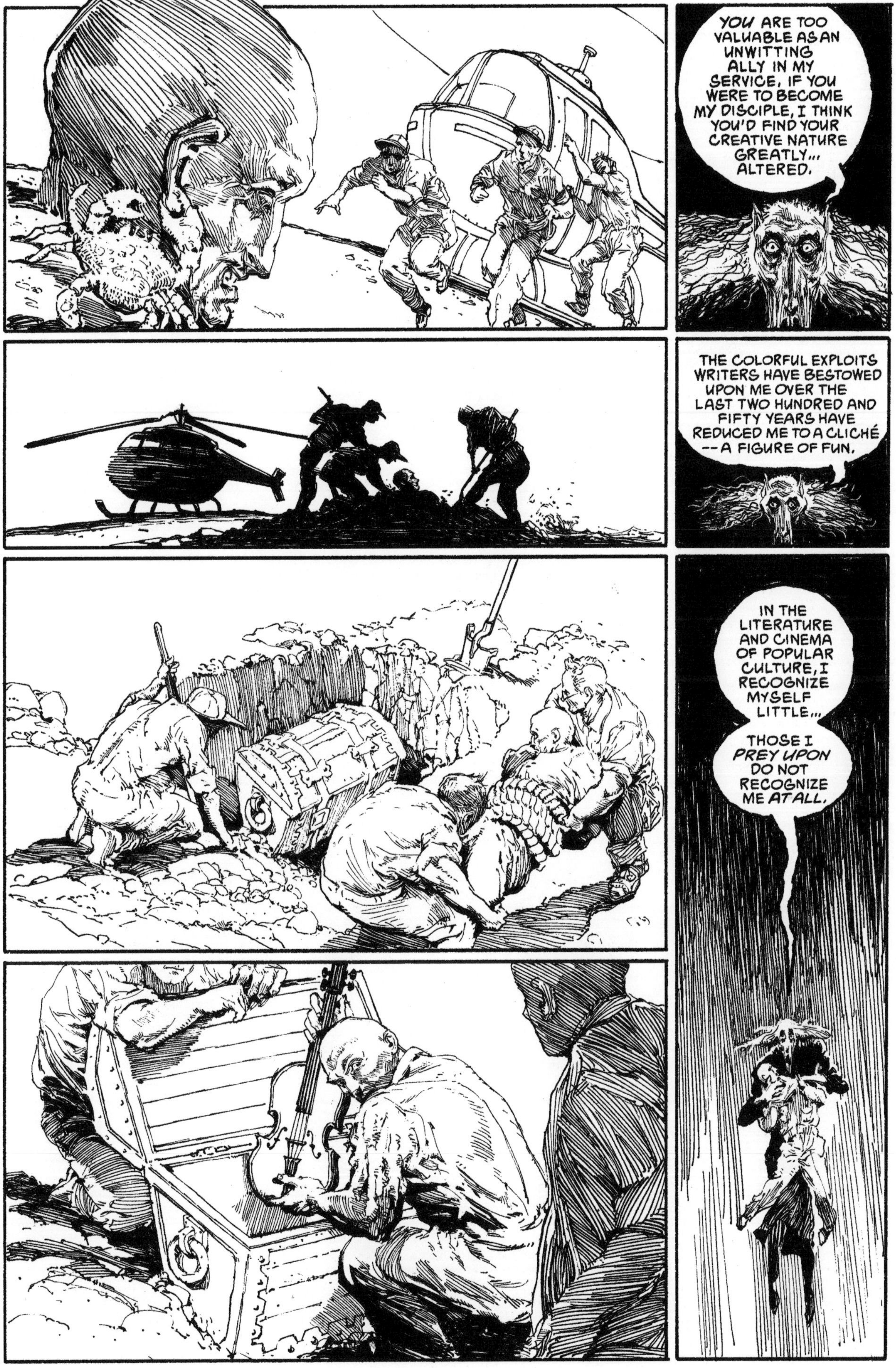
YOU ARE TOO VALUABLE AS AN UNWITTING ALLY IN MY SERVICE. IF YOU WERE TO BECOME MY DISCIPLE, I THINK YOU'D FIND YOUR CREATIVE NATURE GREATLY... ALTERED.
THE COLORFUL EXPLOITS WRITERS HAVE BESTOWED UPON ME OVER THE LAST TWO HUNDRED AND FIFTY YEARS HAVE REDUCED ME TO A CLICHÉ --A FIGURE OF FUN.
IN THE LITERATURE AND CINEMA OF POPULAR CULTURE, I RECOGNIZE MYSELF LITTLE...
THOSE I PREY UPON DO NOT RECOGNIZE ME AT ALL.

YES, MR. ST. GEORGE. *YOU* HAVE HELPED FOSTER THIS CULTURE OF DISBELIEF, AND I USE THAT TO MY GREAT ADVANTAGE.

YOU HAVE MY UNDYING GRATITUDE.

BENEDICTUS, I LEAVE OUR FRIEND UNDER THE YEW TREE-- UNHARMED. FAREWELL.

YOUR SEARCH FOR ALLIES AMONG THE DISBELIEVERS CONTINUES TO BE THE *MOST* PROFOUND FORM OF ENTERTAINMENT.

NO. IT IS NOT THAT MEN DISBELIEVE...

IT'S MUCH WORSE.

CLATER

IT'S MORE THEY DO NOT CARE.

THE END

A GIFT FOR THE WICKED

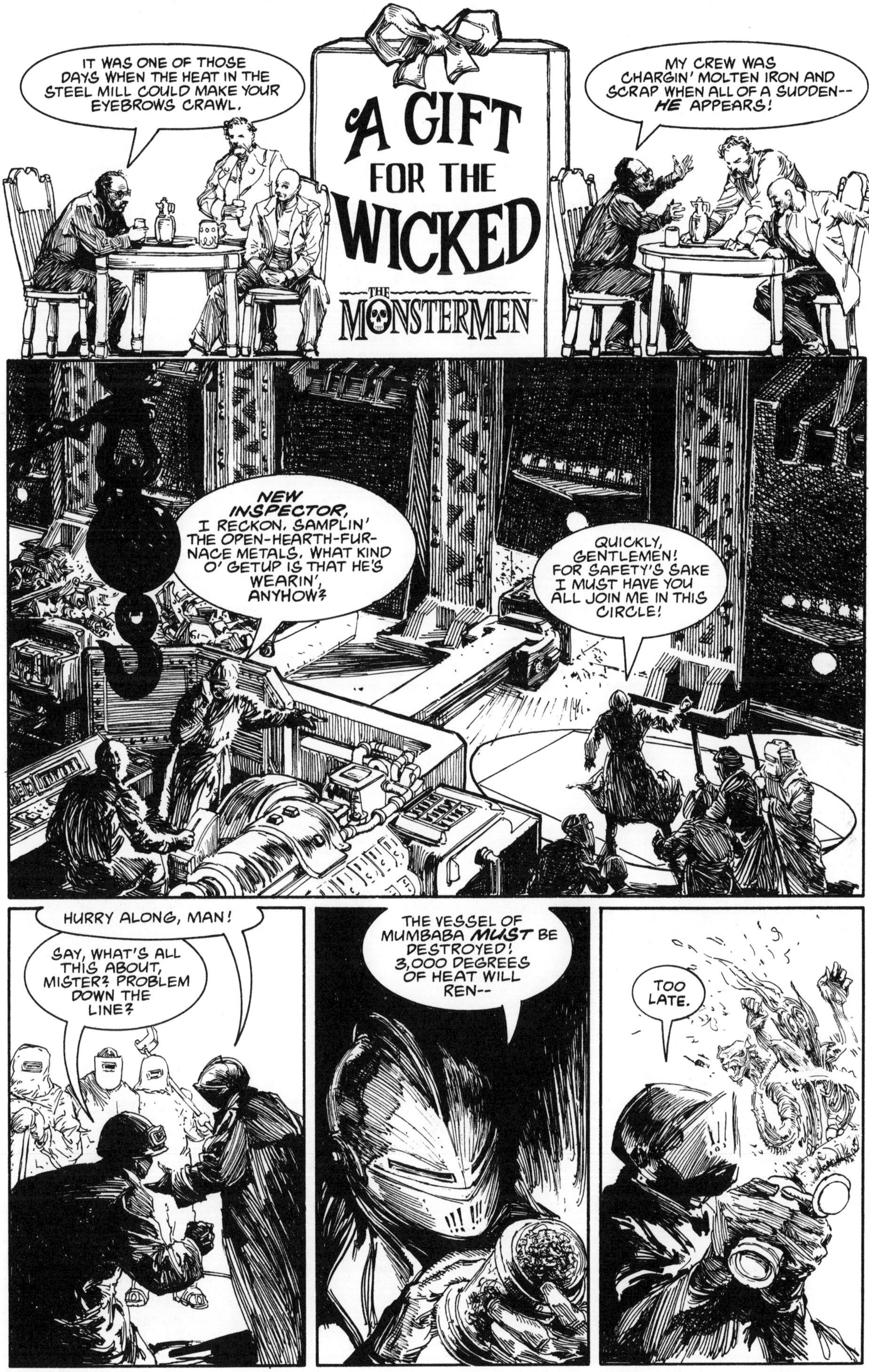
IT WAS ONE OF THOSE DAYS WHEN THE HEAT IN THE STEEL MILL COULD MAKE YOUR EYEBROWS CRAWL.
A GIFT FOR THE WICKED
THE MONSTERMEN™
MY CREW WAS CHARGIN' MOLTEN IRON AND SCRAP WHEN ALL OF A SUDDEN-- HE APPEARS!
NEW INSPECTOR, I RECKON. SAMPLIN' THE OPEN-HEARTH-FURNACE METALS. WHAT KIND O' GETUP IS THAT HE'S WEARIN', ANYHOW?
QUICKLY, GENTLEMEN! FOR SAFETY'S SAKE I MUST HAVE YOU ALL JOIN ME IN THIS CIRCLE!
HURRY ALONG, MAN!
SAY, WHAT'S ALL THIS ABOUT, MISTER? PROBLEM DOWN THE LINE?
THE VESSEL OF MUMBABA MUST BE DESTROYED! 3,000 DEGREES OF HEAT WILL REN--
TOO LATE.

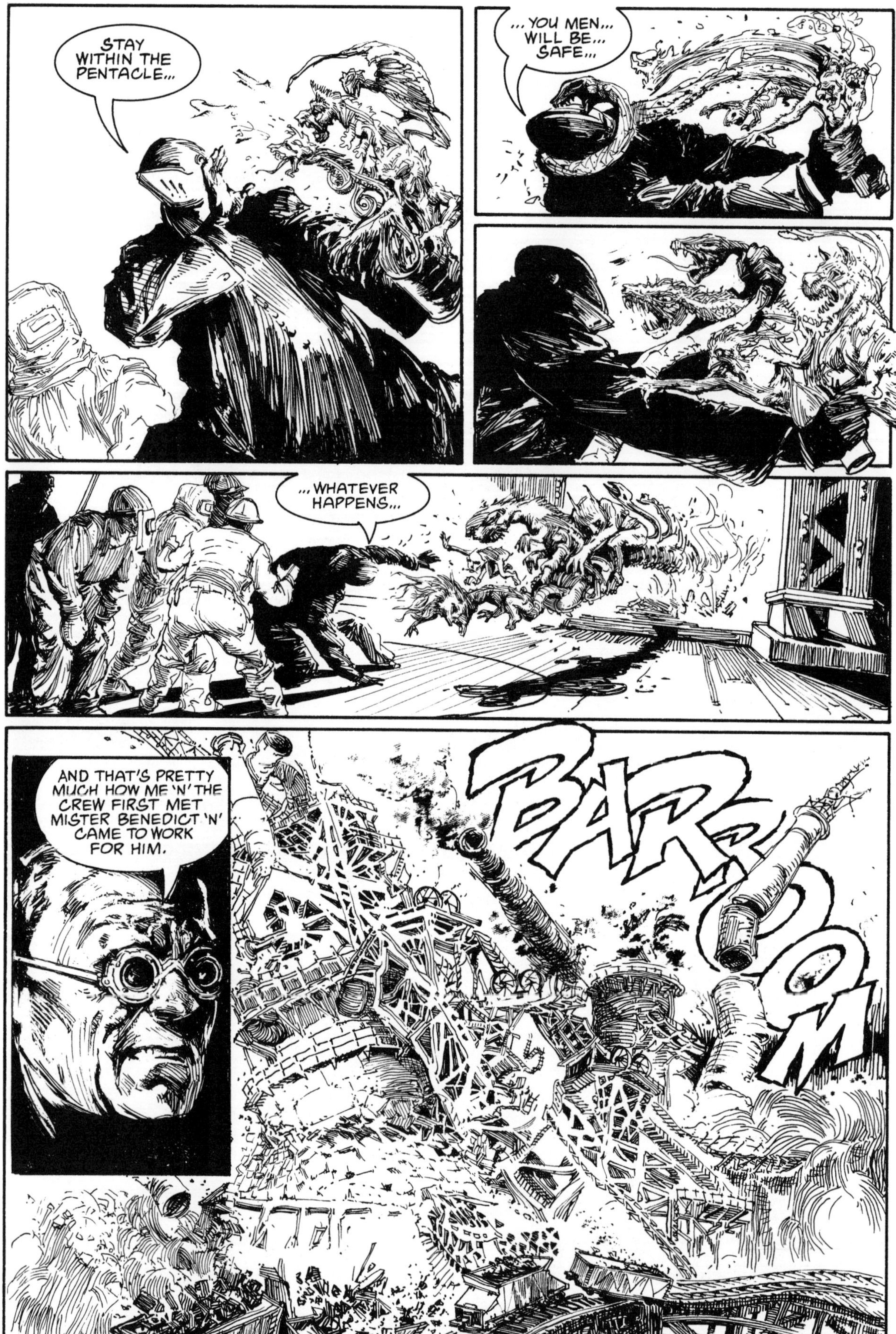
STAY WITHIN THE PENTACLE...
...YOU MEN... WILL BE... SAFE...
...WHATEVER HAPPENS...
AND THAT'S PRETTY MUCH HOW ME 'N' THE CREW FIRST MET MISTER BENEDICT 'N' CAME TO WORK FOR HIM.
BARROOM

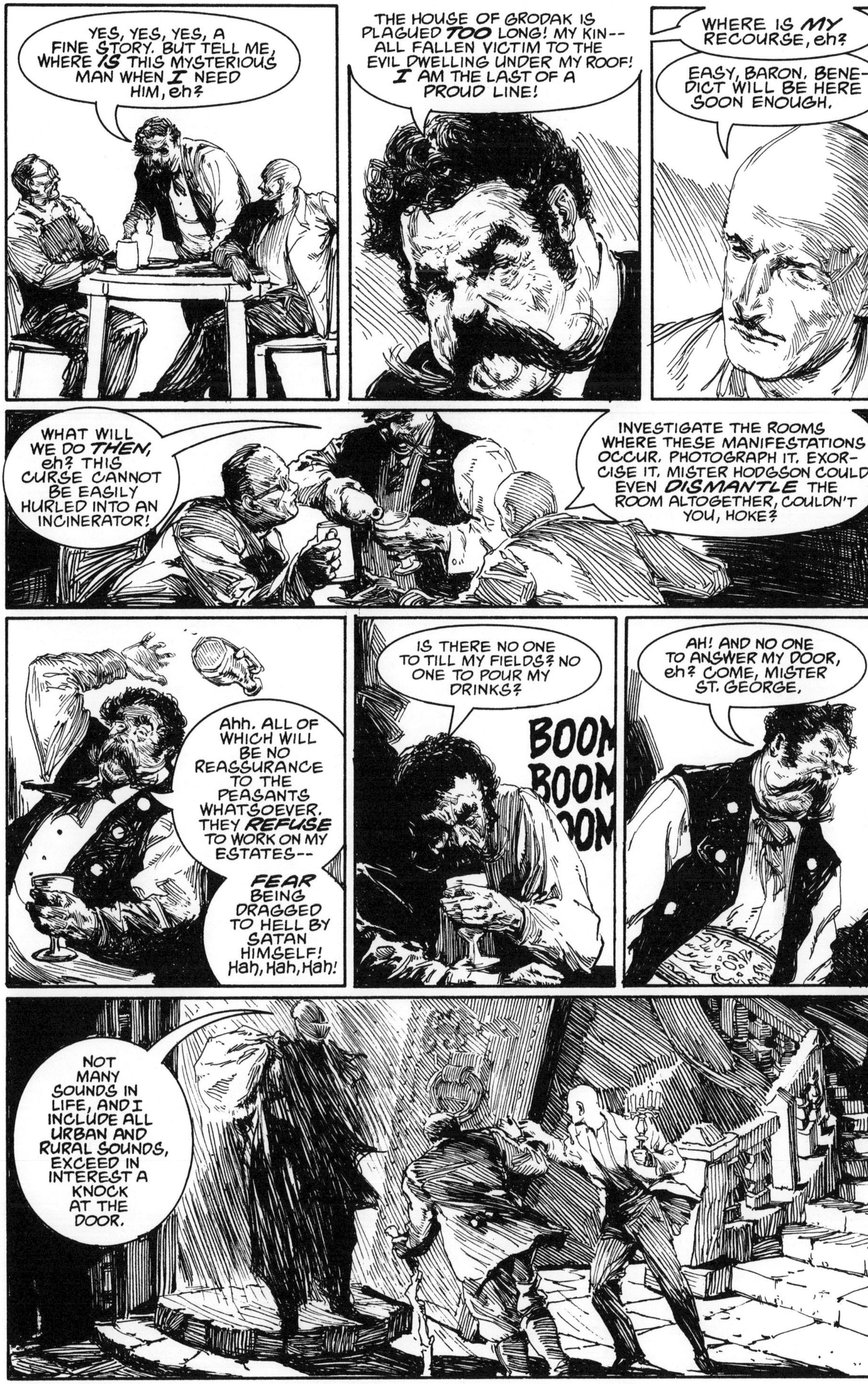
YES, YES, YES, A FINE STORY. BUT TELL ME, WHERE IS THIS MYSTERIOUS MAN WHEN I NEED HIM, eh?
THE HOUSE OF GRODAK IS PLAGUED TOO LONG! MY KIN-- ALL FALLEN VICTIM TO THE EVIL DWELLING UNDER MY ROOF! I AM THE LAST OF A PROUD LINE!
WHERE IS MY RECOURSE, eh?
EASY, BARON. BENEDICT WILL BE HERE SOON ENOUGH.
WHAT WILL WE DO THEN, eh? THIS CURSE CANNOT BE EASILY HURLED INTO AN INCINERATOR!
INVESTIGATE THE ROOMS WHERE THESE MANIFESTATIONS OCCUR. PHOTOGRAPH IT. EXORCISE IT. MISTER HODGSON COULD EVEN DISMANTLE THE ROOM ALTOGETHER, COULDN'T YOU, HOKE?
Ahh. ALL OF WHICH WILL BE NO REASSURANCE TO THE PEASANTS WHATSOEVER. THEY REFUSE TO WORK ON MY ESTATES--
FEAR BEING DRAGGED TO HELL BY SATAN HIMSELF! Hah, Hah, Hah!
IS THERE NO ONE TO TILL MY FIELDS? NO ONE TO POUR MY DRINKS?
BOOM
BOOM
BOOM
AH! AND NO ONE TO ANSWER MY DOOR, eh? COME, MISTER ST. GEORGE.
NOT MANY SOUNDS IN LIFE, AND I INCLUDE ALL URBAN AND RURAL SOUNDS, EXCEED IN INTEREST A KNOCK AT THE DOOR.

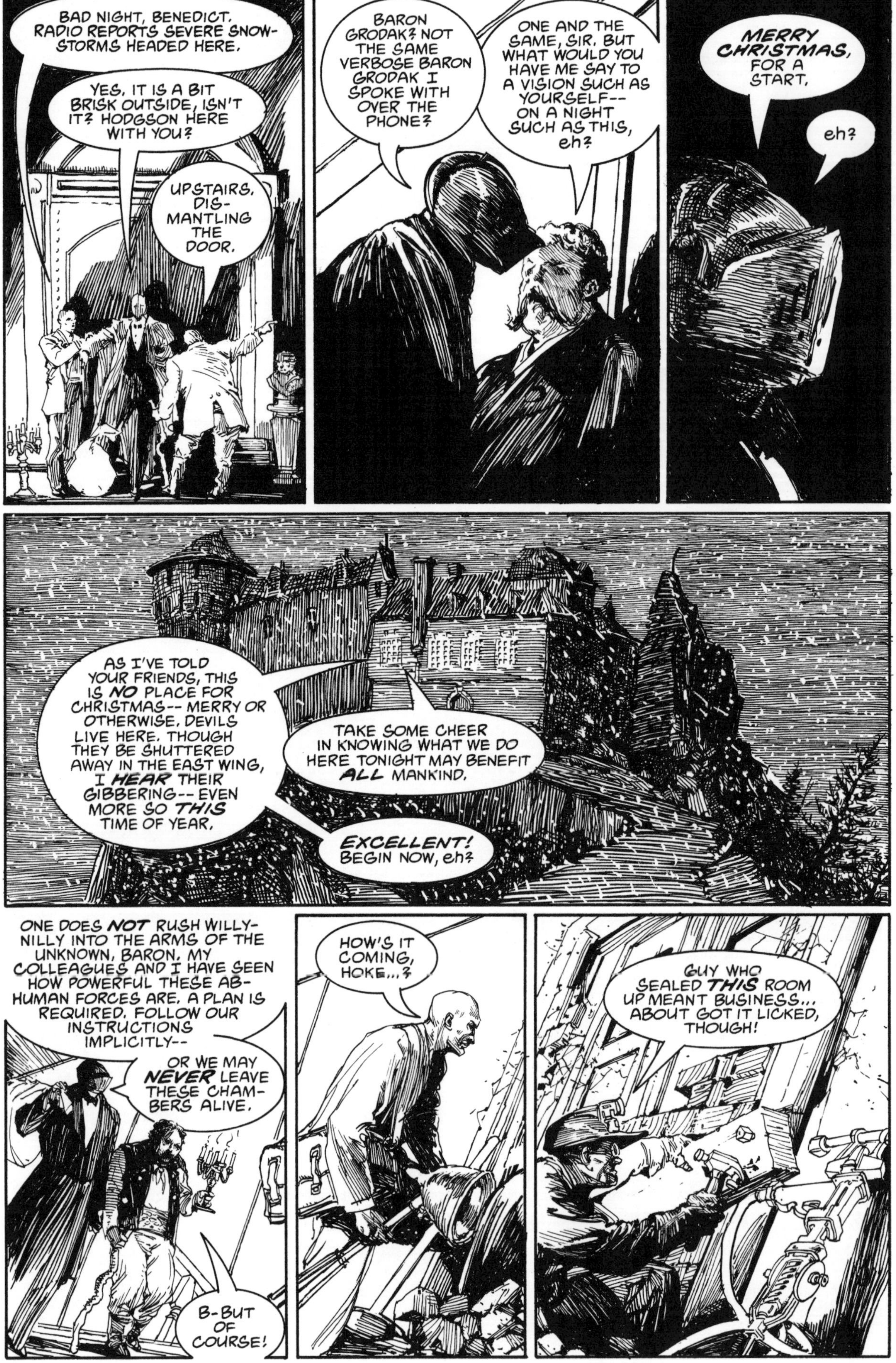
BAD NIGHT, BENEDICT. RADIO REPORTS SEVERE SNOWSTORMS HEADED HERE.
YES, IT IS A BIT BRISK OUTSIDE, ISN'T IT? HODGSON HERE WITH YOU?
UPSTAIRS, DISMANTLING THE DOOR.
BARON GRODAK? NOT THE SAME VERBOSE BARON GRODAK I SPOKE WITH OVER THE PHONE?
ONE AND THE SAME, SIR. BUT WHAT WOULD YOU HAVE ME SAY TO A VISION SUCH AS YOURSELF-- ON A NIGHT SUCH AS THIS, eh?
MERRY CHRISTMAS, FOR A START.
eh?
AS I'VE TOLD YOUR FRIENDS, THIS IS NO PLACE FOR CHRISTMAS-- MERRY OR OTHERWISE. DEVILS LIVE HERE. THOUGH THEY BE SHUTTERED AWAY IN THE EAST WING, I HEAR THEIR GIBBERING-- EVEN MORE SO THIS TIME OF YEAR.
TAKE SOME CHEER IN KNOWING WHAT WE DO HERE TONIGHT MAY BENEFIT ALL MANKIND.
EXCELLENT! BEGIN NOW, eh?
ONE DOES NOT RUSH WILLY-NILLY INTO THE ARMS OF THE UNKNOWN, BARON. MY COLLEAGUES AND I HAVE SEEN HOW POWERFUL THESE AB-HUMAN FORCES ARE. A PLAN IS REQUIRED. FOLLOW OUR INSTRUCTIONS IMPLICITLY--
OR WE MAY NEVER LEAVE THESE CHAMBERS ALIVE.
B-BUT OF COURSE!
HOW'S IT COMING, HOKE...?
GUY WHO SEALED THIS ROOM UP MEANT BUSINESS... ABOUT GOT IT LICKED, THOUGH!

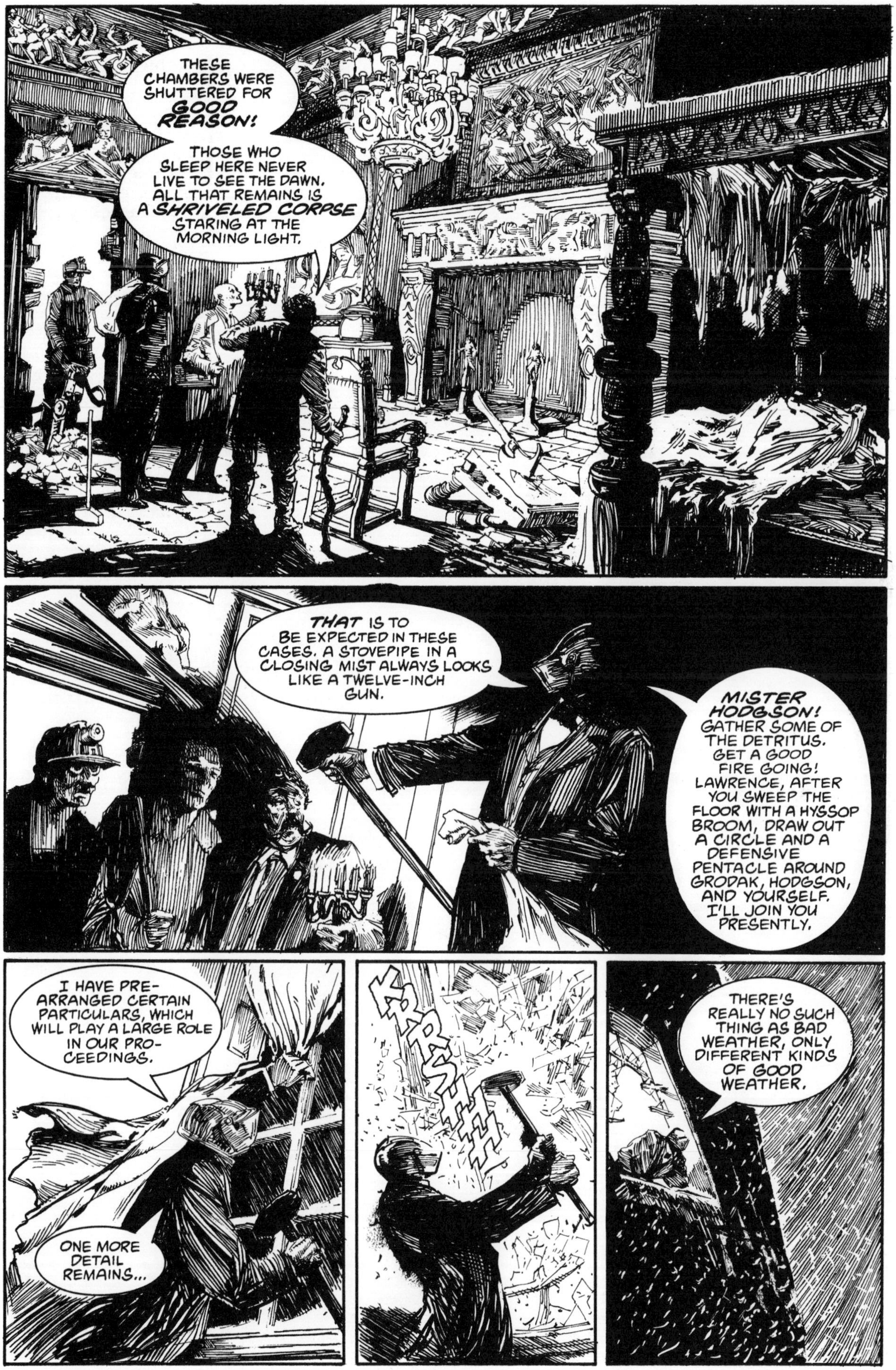
THESE CHAMBERS WERE SHUTTERED FOR GOOD REASON!
THOSE WHO SLEEP HERE NEVER LIVE TO SEE THE DAWN. ALL THAT REMAINS IS A SHRIVELED CORPSE STARING AT THE MORNING LIGHT.
THAT IS TO BE EXPECTED IN THESE CASES. A STOVEPIPE IN A CLOSING MIST ALWAYS LOOKS LIKE A TWELVE-INCH GUN.
MISTER HODGSON! GATHER SOME OF THE DETRITUS. GET A GOOD FIRE GOING! LAWRENCE, AFTER YOU SWEEP THE FLOOR WITH A HYSSOP BROOM, DRAW OUT A CIRCLE AND A DEFENSIVE PENTACLE AROUND GRODAK, HODGSON, AND YOURSELF. I'LL JOIN YOU PRESENTLY.
I HAVE PRE-ARRANGED CERTAIN PARTICULARS, WHICH WILL PLAY A LARGE ROLE IN OUR PRO-CEEDINGS.
ONE MORE DETAIL REMAINS...
KRASHHH
THERE'S REALLY NO SUCH THING AS BAD WEATHER, ONLY DIFFERENT KINDS OF GOOD WEATHER.

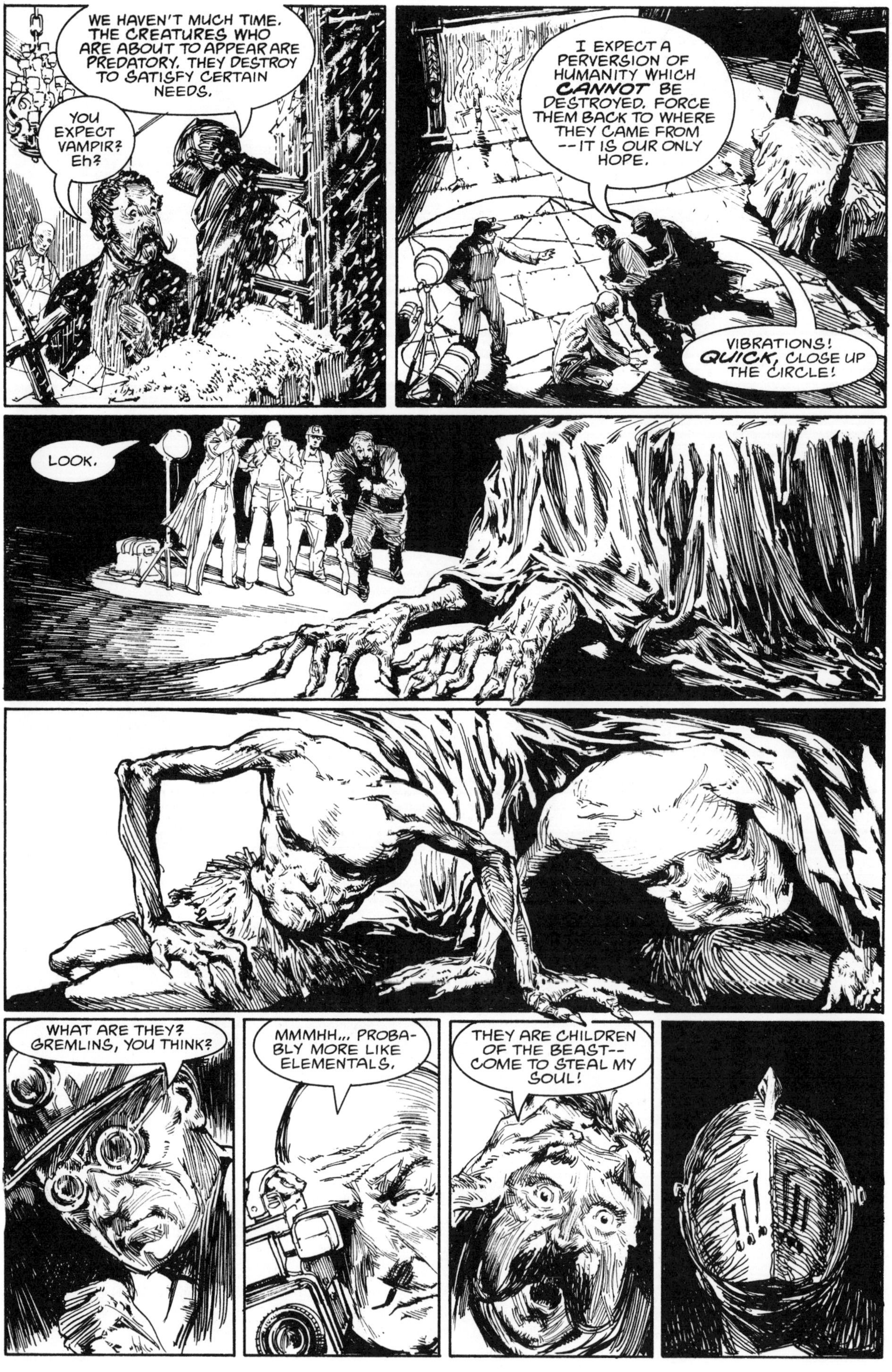
WE HAVEN'T MUCH TIME. THE CREATURES WHO ARE ABOUT TO APPEAR ARE PREDATORY. THEY DESTROY TO SATISFY CERTAIN NEEDS.
YOU EXPECT VAMPIR? Eh?
I EXPECT A PERVERSION OF HUMANITY WHICH CANNOT BE DESTROYED. FORCE THEM BACK TO WHERE THEY CAME FROM --IT IS OUR ONLY HOPE.
VIBRATIONS! QUICK, CLOSE UP THE CIRCLE!
LOOK.
WHAT ARE THEY? GREMLINS, YOU THINK?
MMMHH... PROBA-BLY MORE LIKE ELEMENTALS.
THEY ARE CHILDREN OF THE BEAST-- COME TO STEAL MY SOUL!

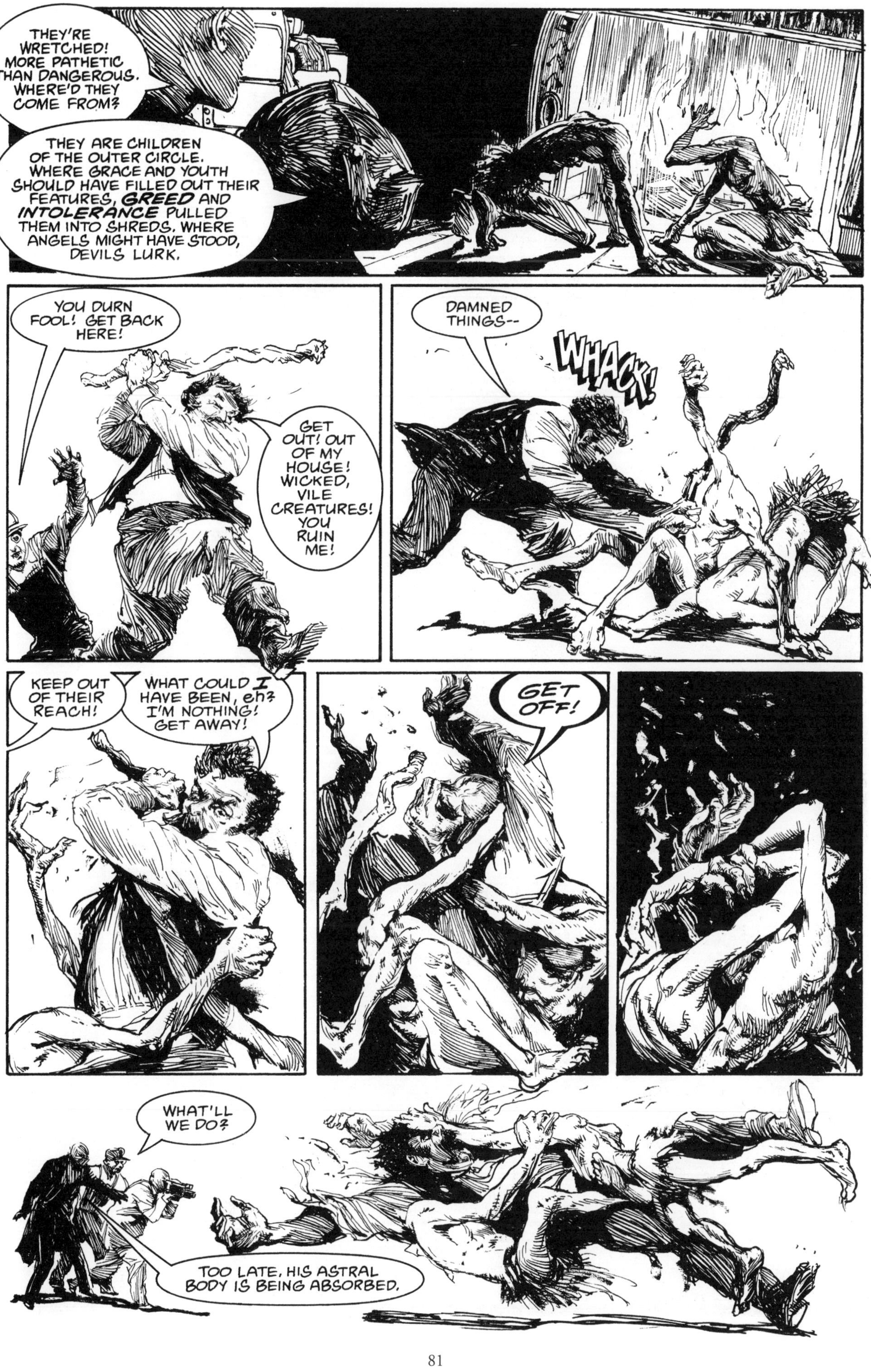
THEY'RE WRETCHED! MORE PATHETIC THAN DANGEROUS. WHERE'D THEY COME FROM?
THEY ARE CHILDREN OF THE OUTER CIRCLE. WHERE GRACE AND YOUTH SHOULD HAVE FILLED OUT THEIR FEATURES, GREED AND INTOLERANCE PULLED THEM INTO SHREDS. WHERE ANGELS MIGHT HAVE STOOD, DEVILS LURK.
YOU DURN FOOL! GET BACK HERE!
GET OUT! OUT OF MY HOUSE! WICKED, VILE CREATURES! YOU RUIN ME!
DAMNED THINGS--
WHACK!
KEEP OUT OF THEIR REACH!
WHAT COULD I HAVE BEEN, eh? I'M NOTHING! GET AWAY!
GET OFF!
WHAT'LL WE DO?
TOO LATE. HIS ASTRAL BODY IS BEING ABSORBED.

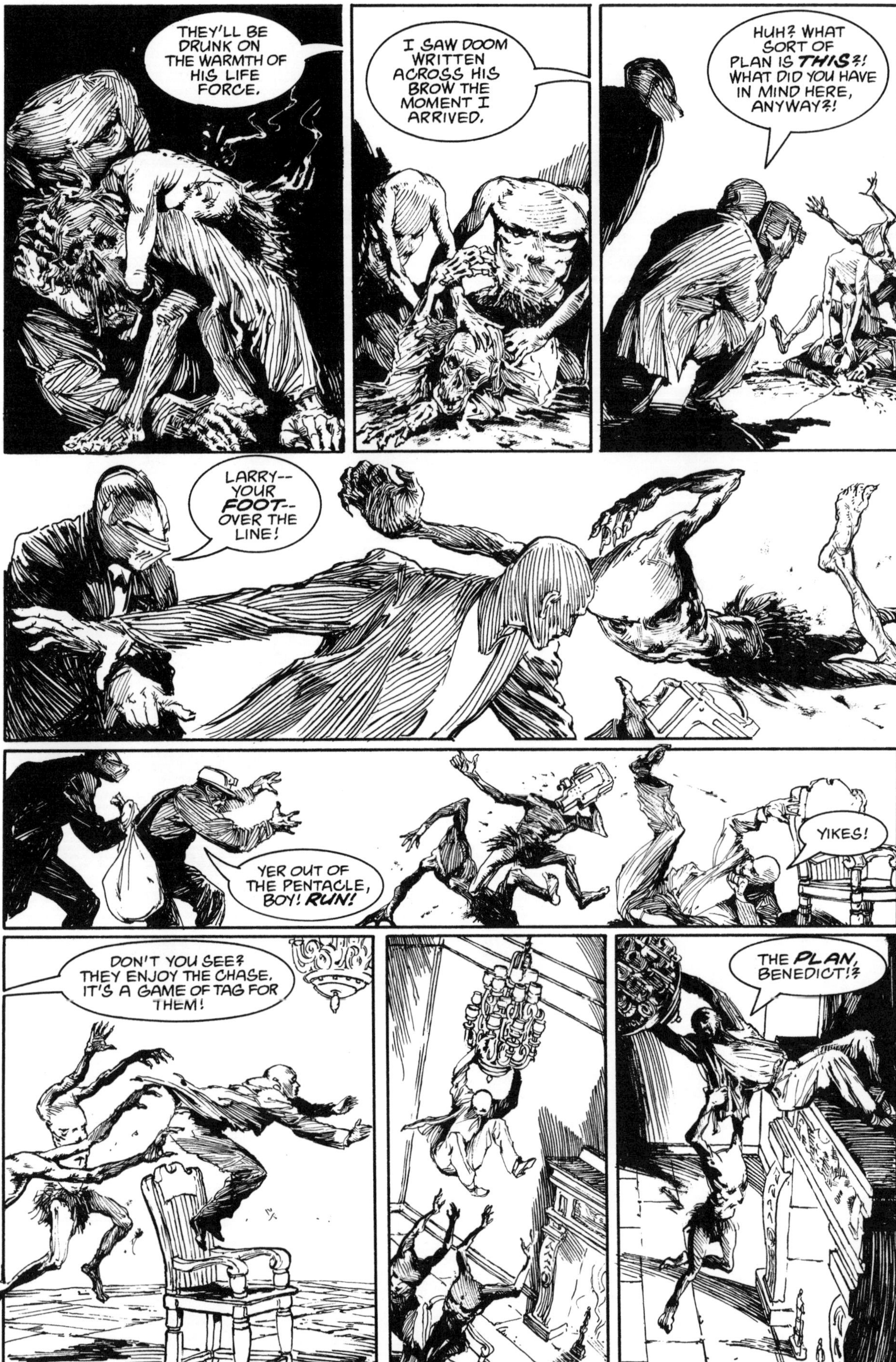
THEY'LL BE DRUNK ON THE WARMTH OF HIS LIFE FORCE.
I SAW DOOM WRITTEN ACROSS HIS BROW THE MOMENT I ARRIVED.
HUH? WHAT SORT OF PLAN IS THIS?! WHAT DID YOU HAVE IN MIND HERE, ANYWAY?!
LARRY-- YOUR FOOT-- OVER THE LINE!
YER OUT OF THE PENTACLE, BOY! RUN!
YIKES!
DON'T YOU SEE? THEY ENJOY THE CHASE. IT'S A GAME OF TAG FOR THEM!
THE PLAN, BENEDICT!?

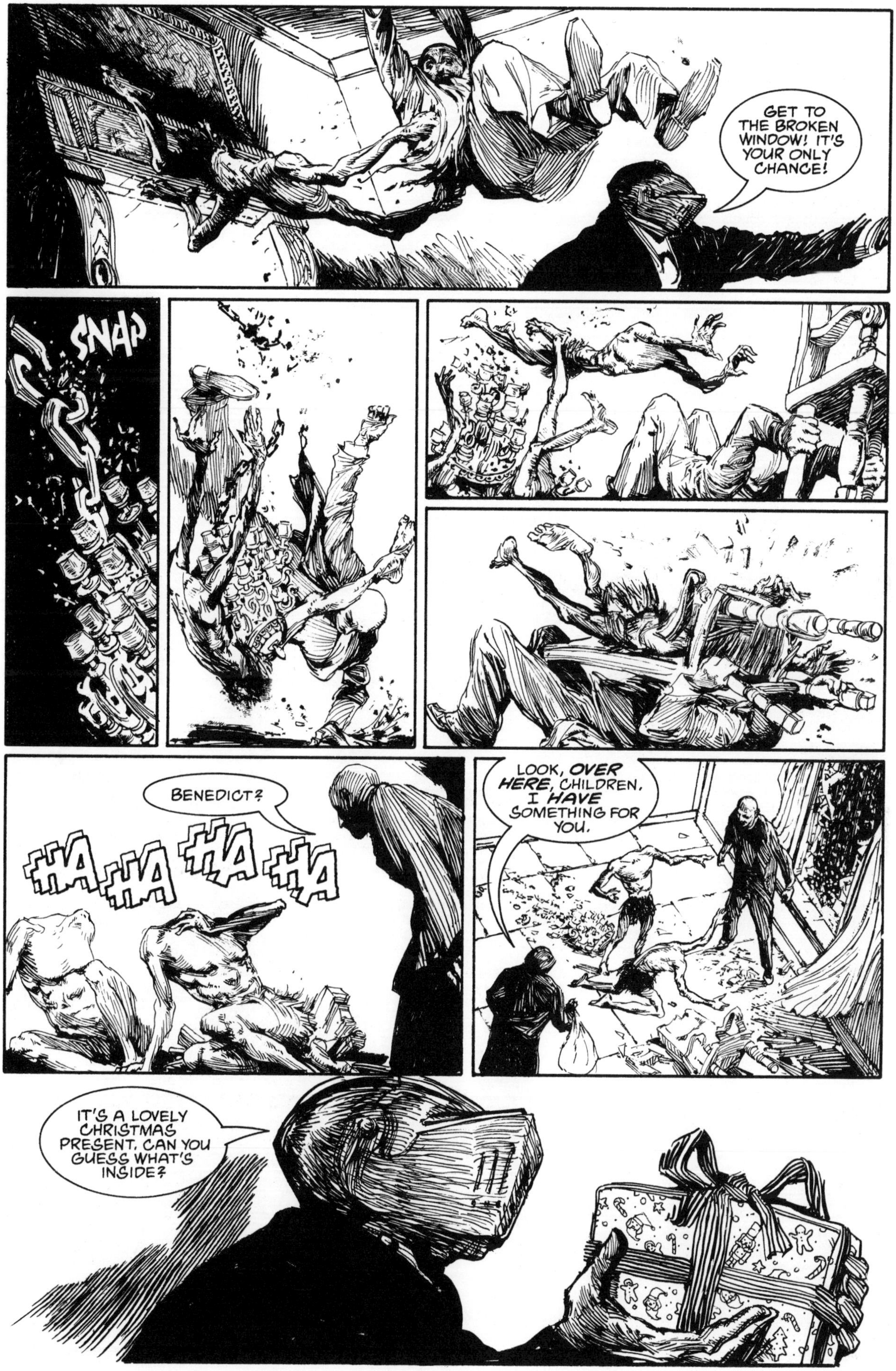
GET TO THE BROKEN WINDOW! IT'S YOUR ONLY CHANCE!
SNAP
BENEDICT?
HA HA HA HA
LOOK, OVER HERE, CHILDREN. I HAVE SOMETHING FOR YOU.
IT'S A LOVELY CHRISTMAS PRESENT. CAN YOU GUESS WHAT'S INSIDE?

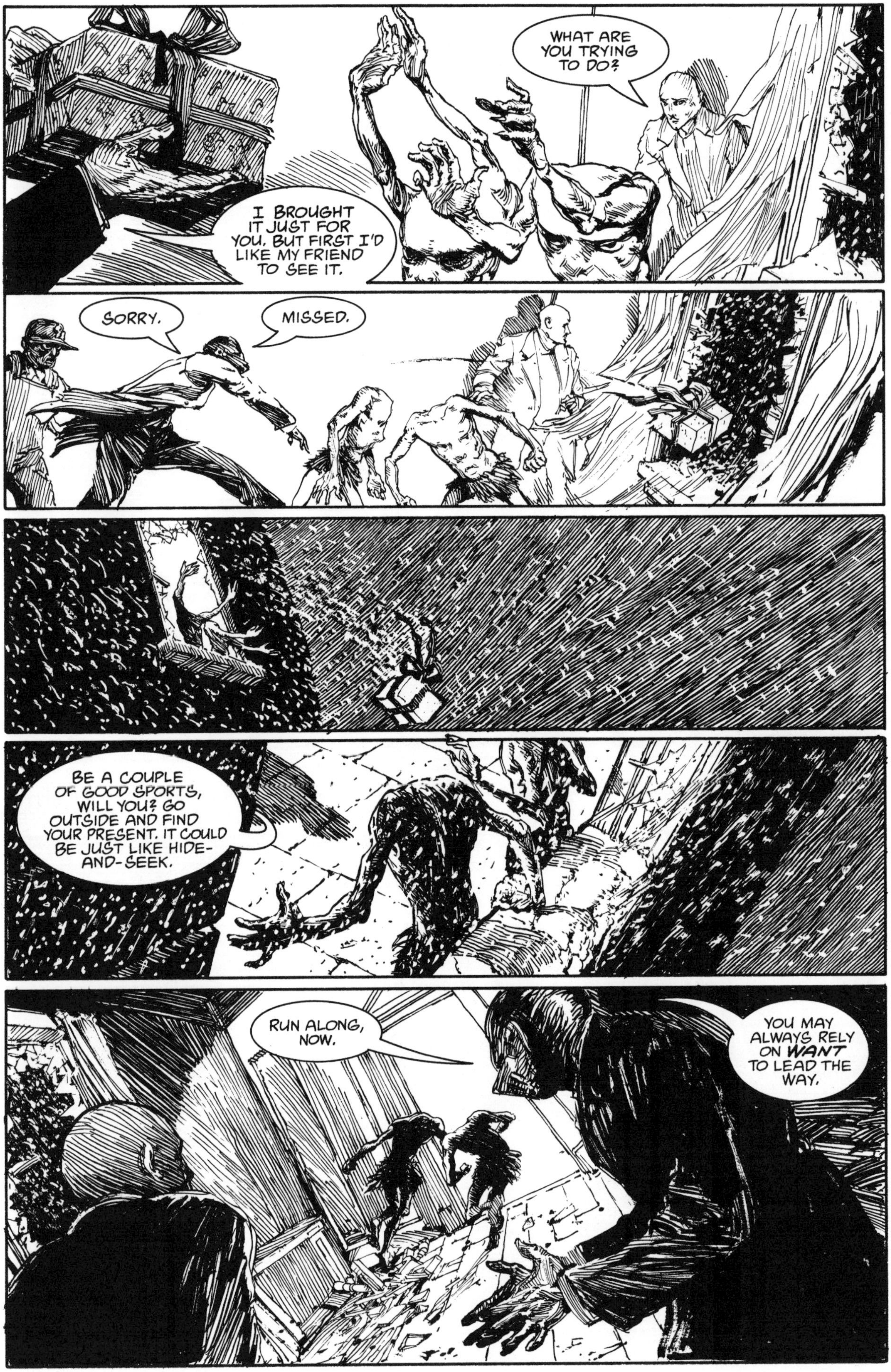
WHAT ARE YOU TRYING TO DO?
I BROUGHT IT JUST FOR YOU. BUT FIRST I'D LIKE MY FRIEND TO SEE IT.
SORRY.
MISSED.
BE A COUPLE OF GOOD SPORTS, WILL YOU? GO OUTSIDE AND FIND YOUR PRESENT. IT COULD BE JUST LIKE HIDE-AND-SEEK.
RUN ALONG, NOW.
YOU MAY ALWAYS RELY ON *WANT* TO LEAD THE WAY.

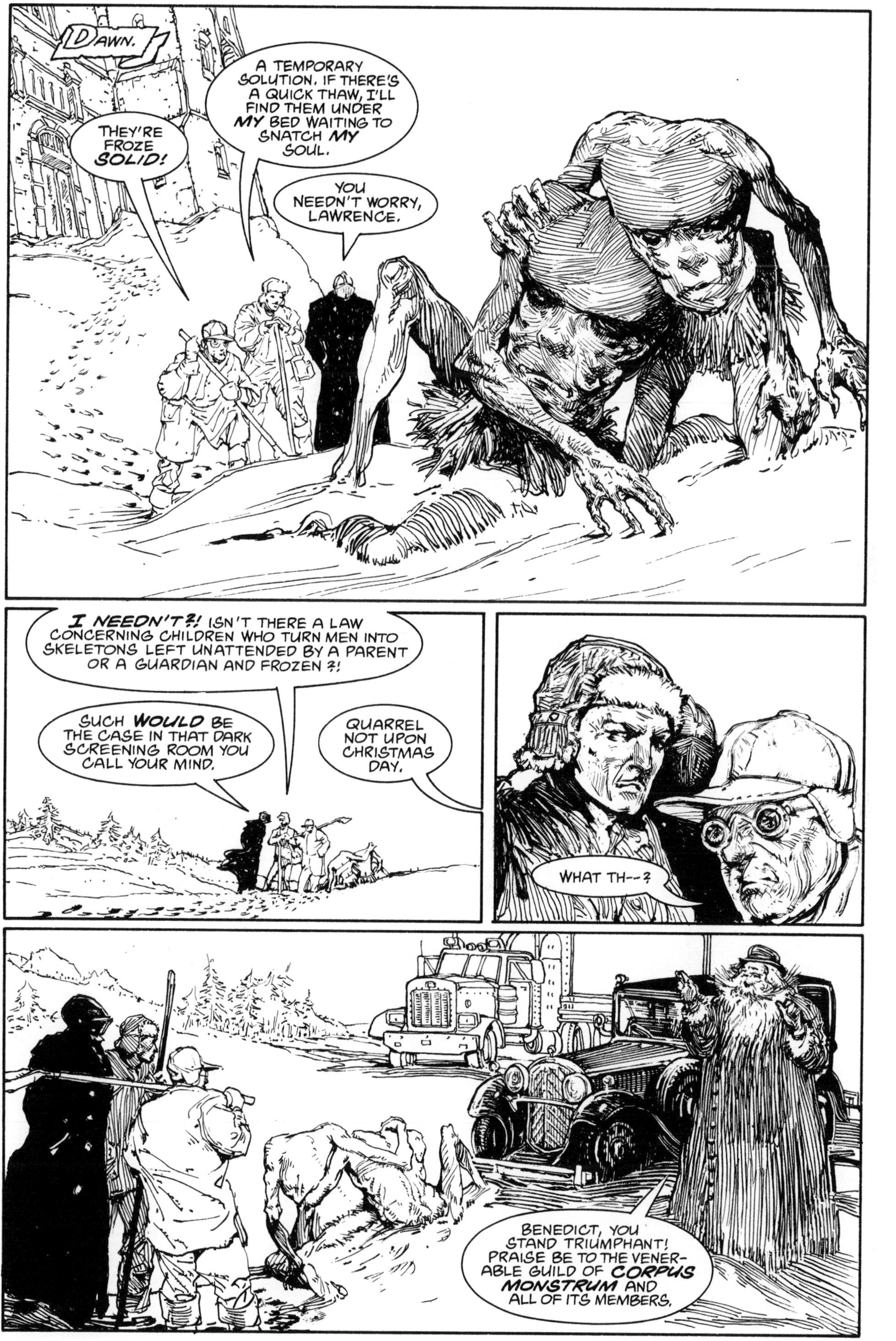

DAWN.
THEY'RE FROZE SOLID!
A TEMPORARY SOLUTION. IF THERE'S A QUICK THAW, I'LL FIND THEM UNDER MY BED WAITING TO SNATCH MY SOUL.
YOU NEEDN'T WORRY, LAWRENCE.
I NEEDN'T?! ISN'T THERE A LAW CONCERNING CHILDREN WHO TURN MEN INTO SKELETONS LEFT UNATTENDED BY A PARENT OR A GUARDIAN AND FROZEN?!
SUCH WOULD BE THE CASE IN THAT DARK SCREENING ROOM YOU CALL YOUR MIND.
QUARREL NOT UPON CHRISTMAS DAY.
WHAT TH--?
BENEDICT, YOU STAND TRIUMPHANT! PRAISE BE TO THE VENERABLE GUILD OF CORPUS MONSTRUM AND ALL OF ITS MEMBERS.

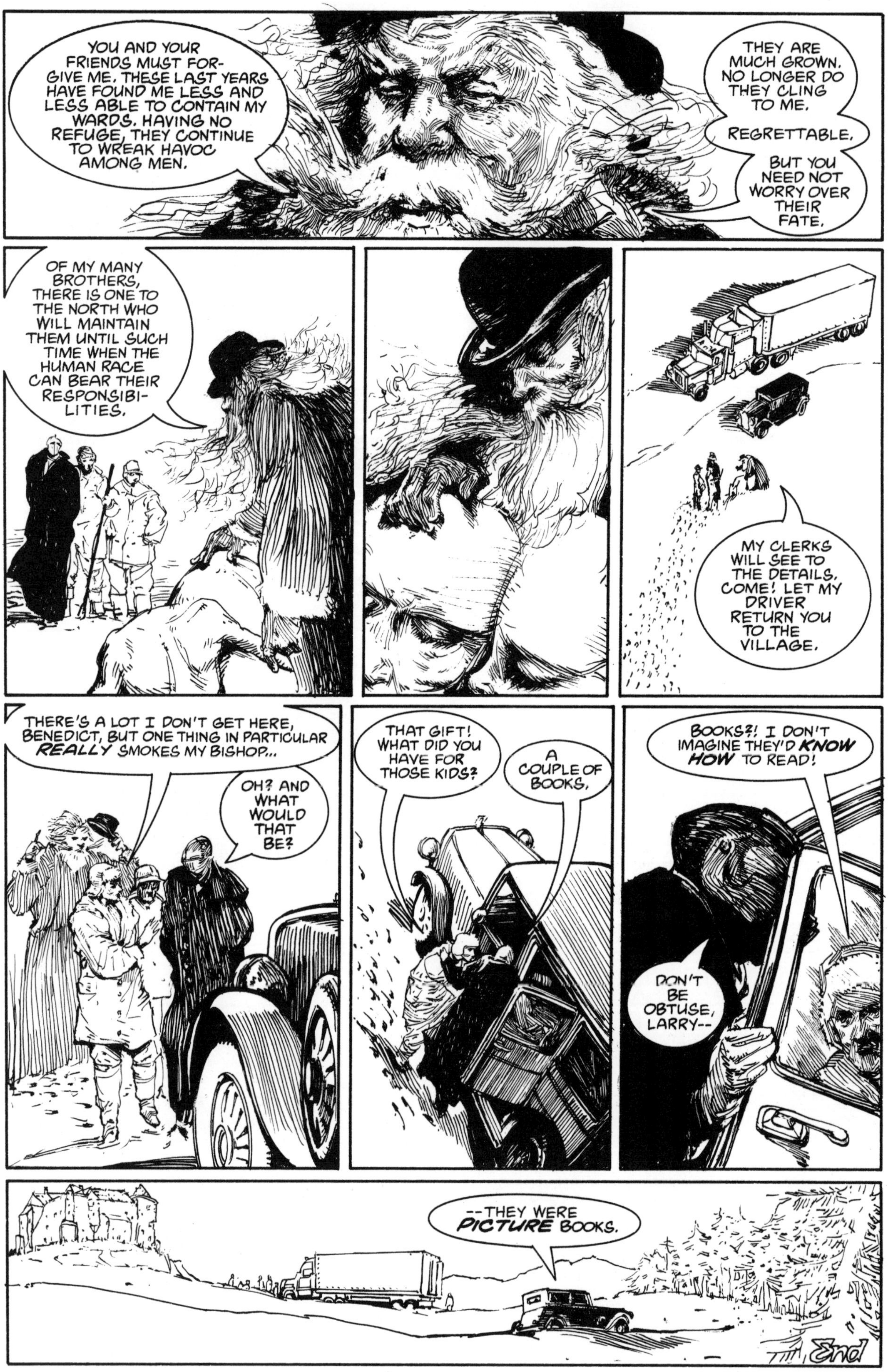
YOU AND YOUR FRIENDS MUST FORGIVE ME. THESE LAST YEARS HAVE FOUND ME LESS AND LESS ABLE TO CONTAIN MY WARDS. HAVING NO REFUGE, THEY CONTINUE TO WREAK HAVOC AMONG MEN.
THEY ARE MUCH GROWN. NO LONGER DO THEY CLING TO ME.
REGRETTABLE.
BUT YOU NEED NOT WORRY OVER THEIR FATE.
OF MY MANY BROTHERS, THERE IS ONE TO THE NORTH WHO WILL MAINTAIN THEM UNTIL SUCH TIME WHEN THE HUMAN RACE CAN BEAR THEIR RESPONSIBILITIES.
MY CLERKS WILL SEE TO THE DETAILS. COME! LET MY DRIVER RETURN YOU TO THE VILLAGE.
THERE'S A LOT I DON'T GET HERE, BENEDICT, BUT ONE THING IN PARTICULAR REALLY SMOKES MY BISHOP...
OH? AND WHAT WOULD THAT BE?
THAT GIFT! WHAT DID YOU HAVE FOR THOSE KIDS?
A COUPLE OF BOOKS.
BOOKS?! I DON'T IMAGINE THEY'D KNOW HOW TO READ!
DON'T BE OBTUSE, LARRY--
--THEY WERE PICTURE BOOKS.
End

THE SKULL AND THE SNOWMAN

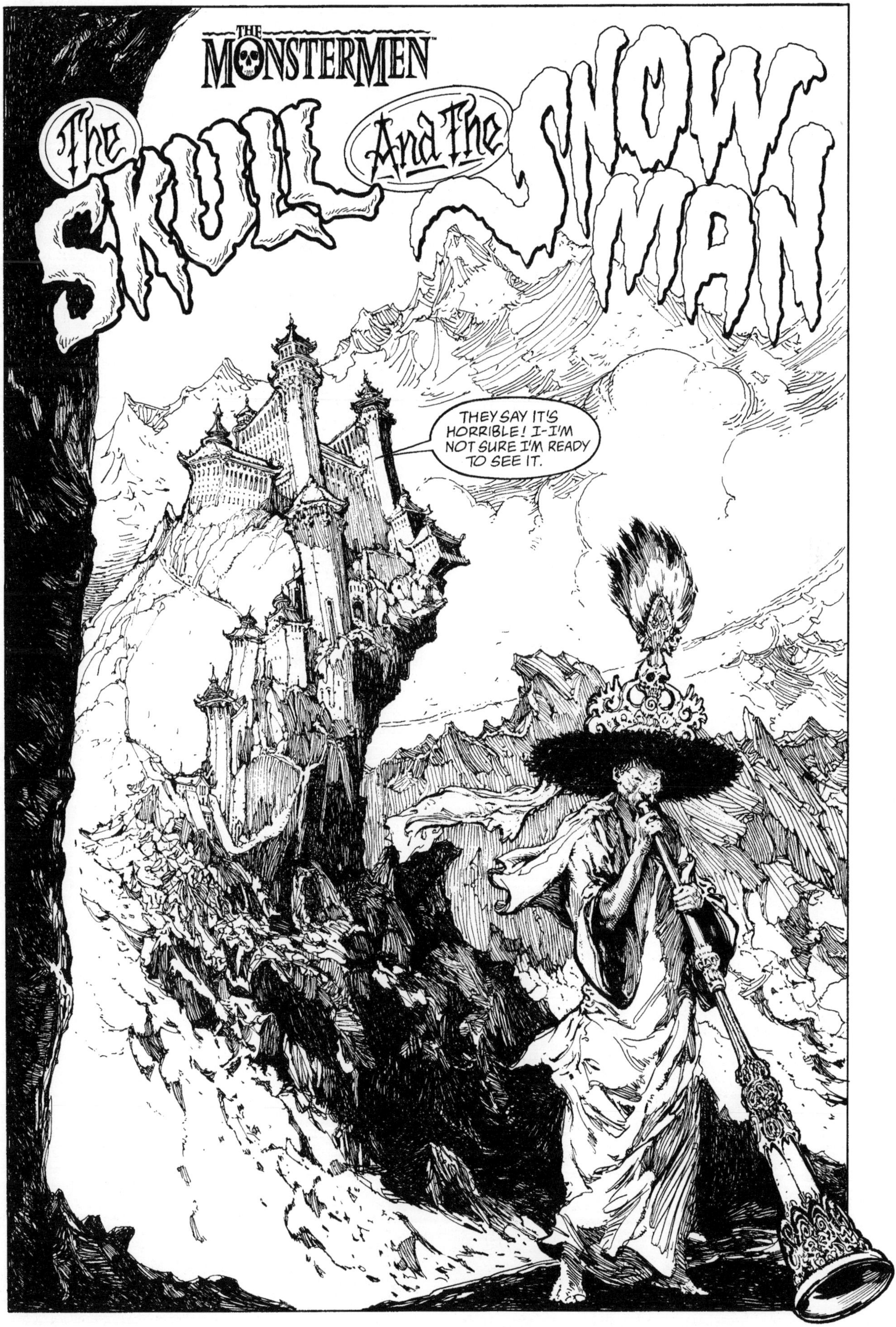
THE MONSTERMEN
The SKULL And The SNOW MAN
THEY SAY IT'S HORRIBLE! I-I'M NOT SURE I'M READY TO SEE IT.

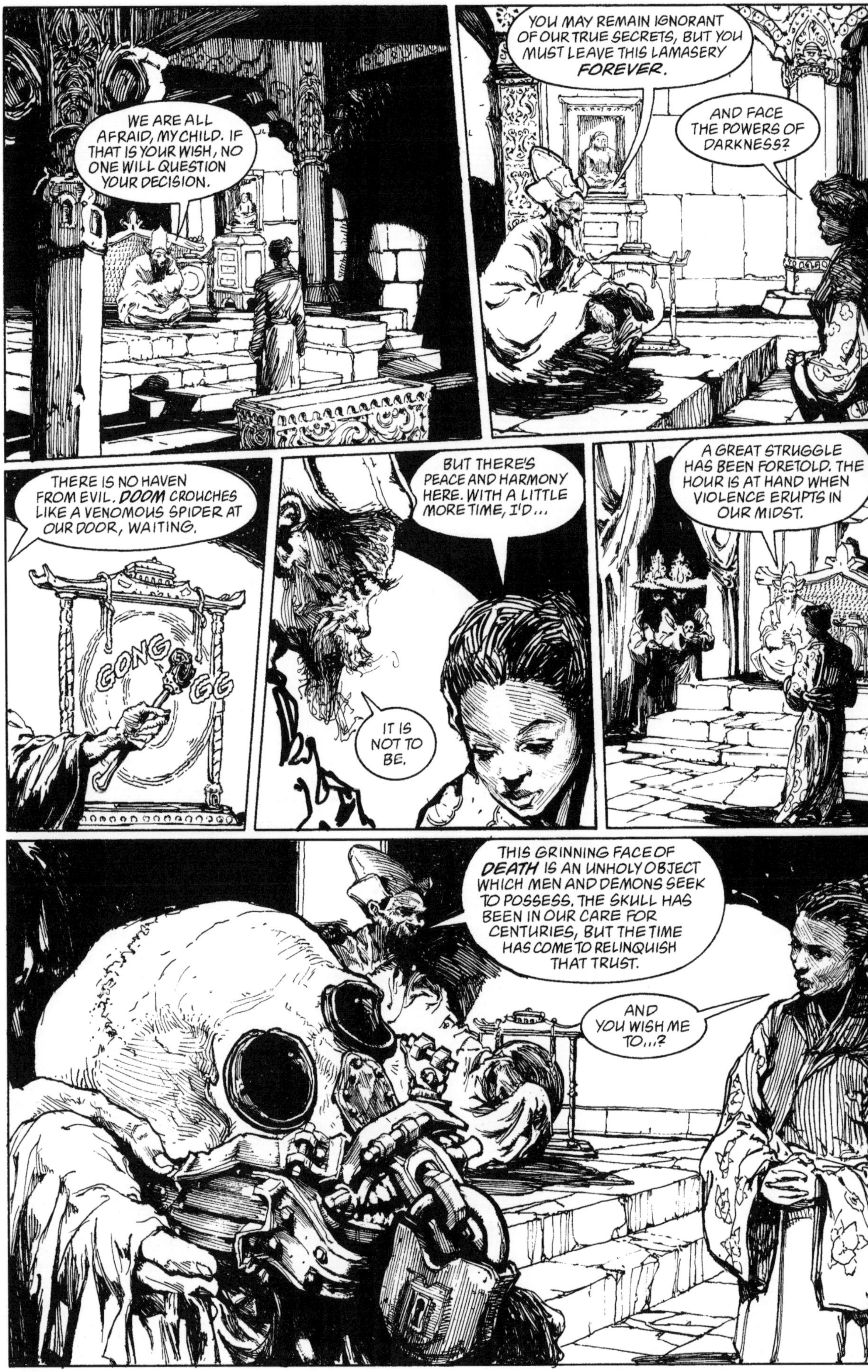
WE ARE ALL AFRAID, MY CHILD. IF THAT IS YOUR WISH, NO ONE WILL QUESTION YOUR DECISION.
YOU MAY REMAIN IGNORANT OF OUR TRUE SECRETS, BUT YOU MUST LEAVE THIS LAMASERY FOREVER.
AND FACE THE POWERS OF DARKNESS?
THERE IS NO HAVEN FROM EVIL. DOOM CROUCHES LIKE A VENOMOUS SPIDER AT OUR DOOR, WAITING.
GONG
GG
BUT THERE'S PEACE AND HARMONY HERE. WITH A LITTLE MORE TIME, I'D...
IT IS NOT TO BE.
A GREAT STRUGGLE HAS BEEN FORETOLD. THE HOUR IS AT HAND WHEN VIOLENCE ERUPTS IN OUR MIDST.
THIS GRINNING FACE OF DEATH IS AN UNHOLY OBJECT WHICH MEN AND DEMONS SEEK TO POSSESS. THE SKULL HAS BEEN IN OUR CARE FOR CENTURIES, BUT THE TIME HAS COME TO RELINQUISH THAT TRUST.
AND YOU WISH ME TO...?

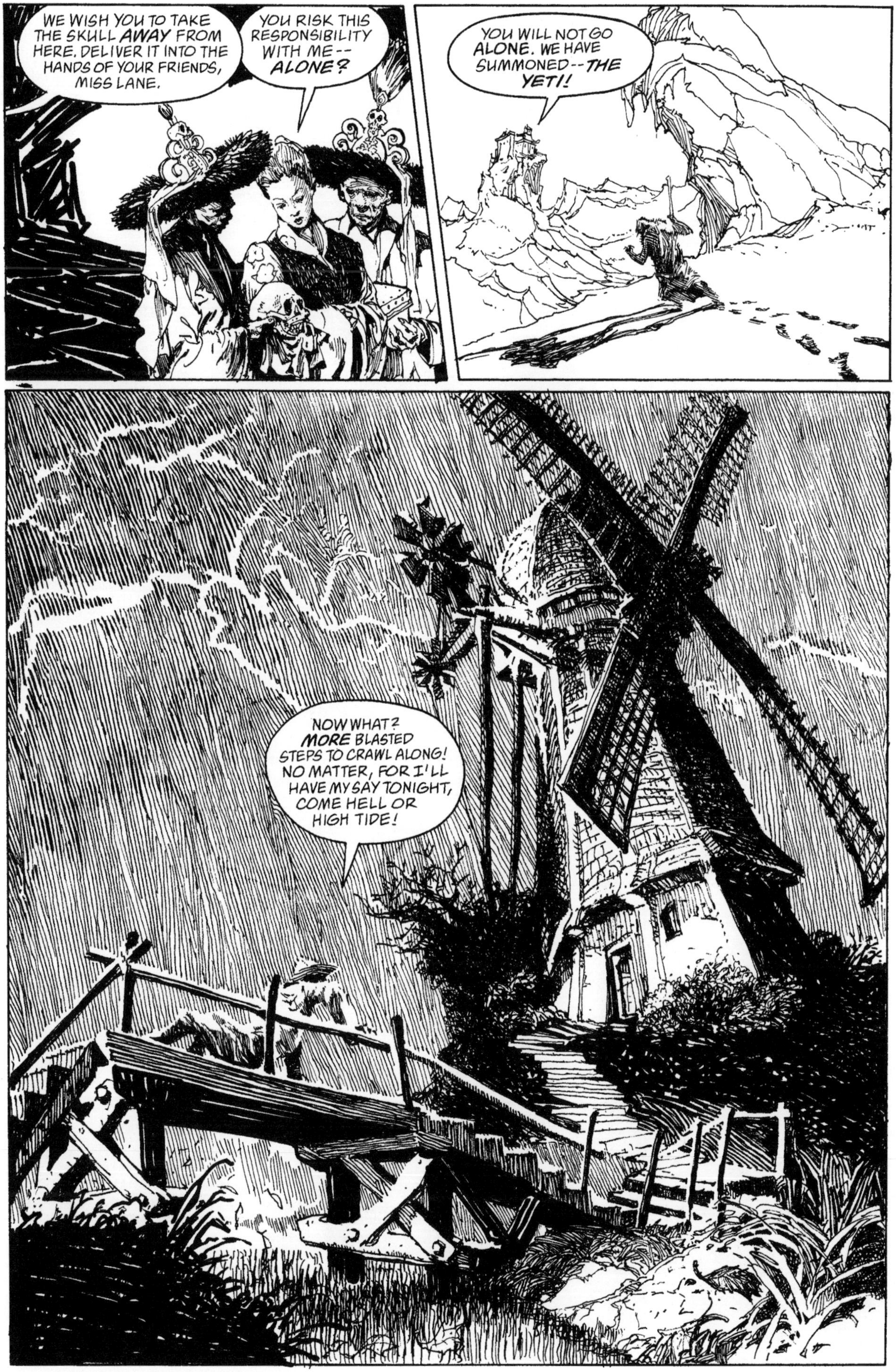
WE WISH YOU TO TAKE THE SKULL AWAY FROM HERE. DELIVER IT INTO THE HANDS OF YOUR FRIENDS, MISS LANE.
YOU RISK THIS RESPONSIBILITY WITH ME-- ALONE?
YOU WILL NOT GO ALONE. WE HAVE SUMMONED--THE YETI!
NOW WHAT? MORE BLASTED STEPS TO CRAWL ALONG! NO MATTER, FOR I'LL HAVE MY SAY TONIGHT, COME HELL OR HIGH TIDE!

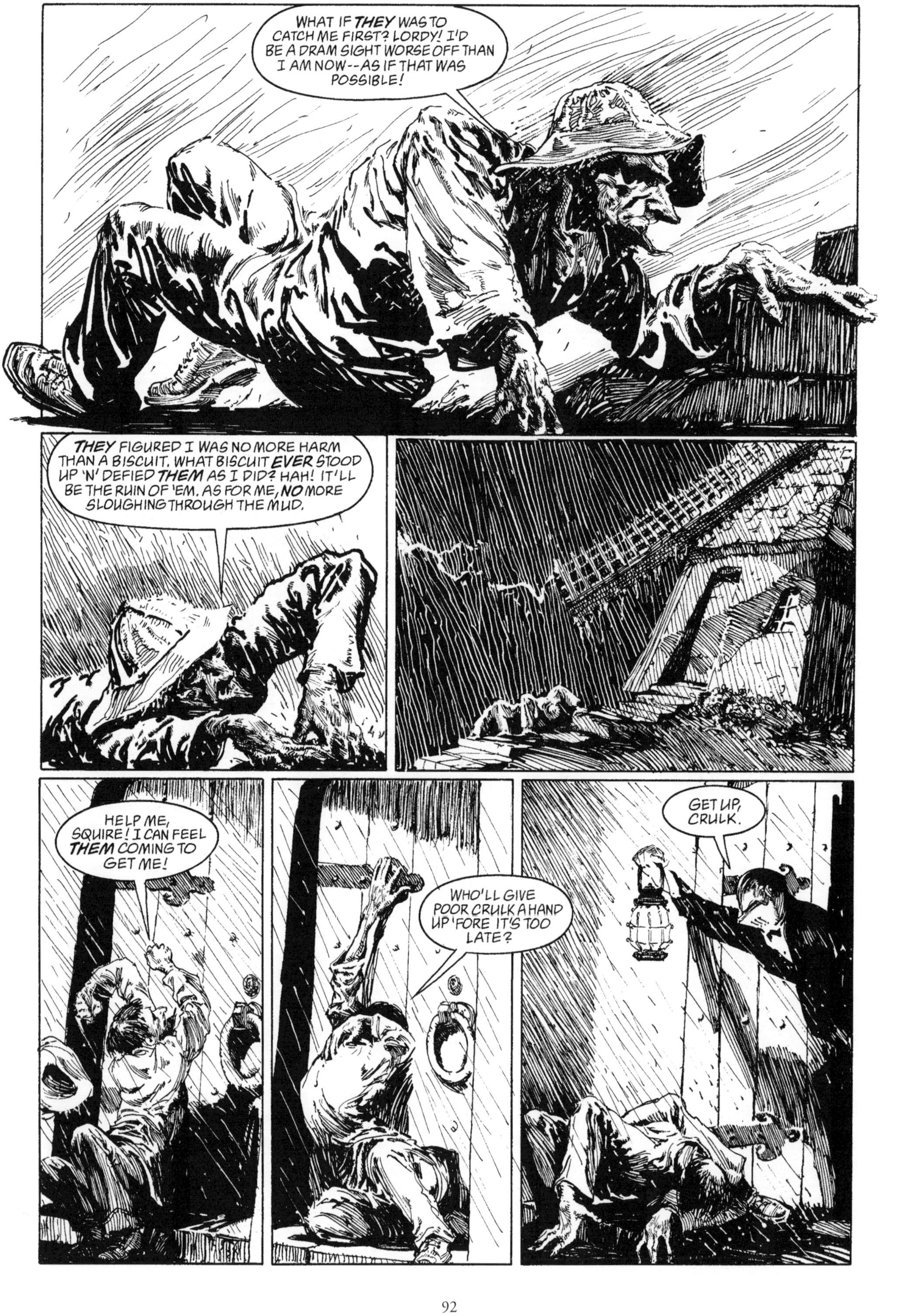
WHAT IF THEY WAS TO CATCH ME FIRST? LORDY! I'D BE A DRAM SIGHT WORSE OFF THAN I AM NOW--AS IF THAT WAS POSSIBLE!
THEY FIGURED I WAS NO MORE HARM THAN A BISCUIT. WHAT BISCUIT EVER STOOD UP 'N' DEFIED THEM AS I DID? HAH! IT'LL BE THE RUIN OF 'EM. AS FOR ME, NO MORE SLOUGHING THROUGH THE MUD.
HELP ME, SQUIRE! I CAN FEEL THEM COMING TO GET ME!
WHO'LL GIVE POOR CRULK A HAND UP 'FORE IT'S TOO LATE?
GET UP, CRULK.

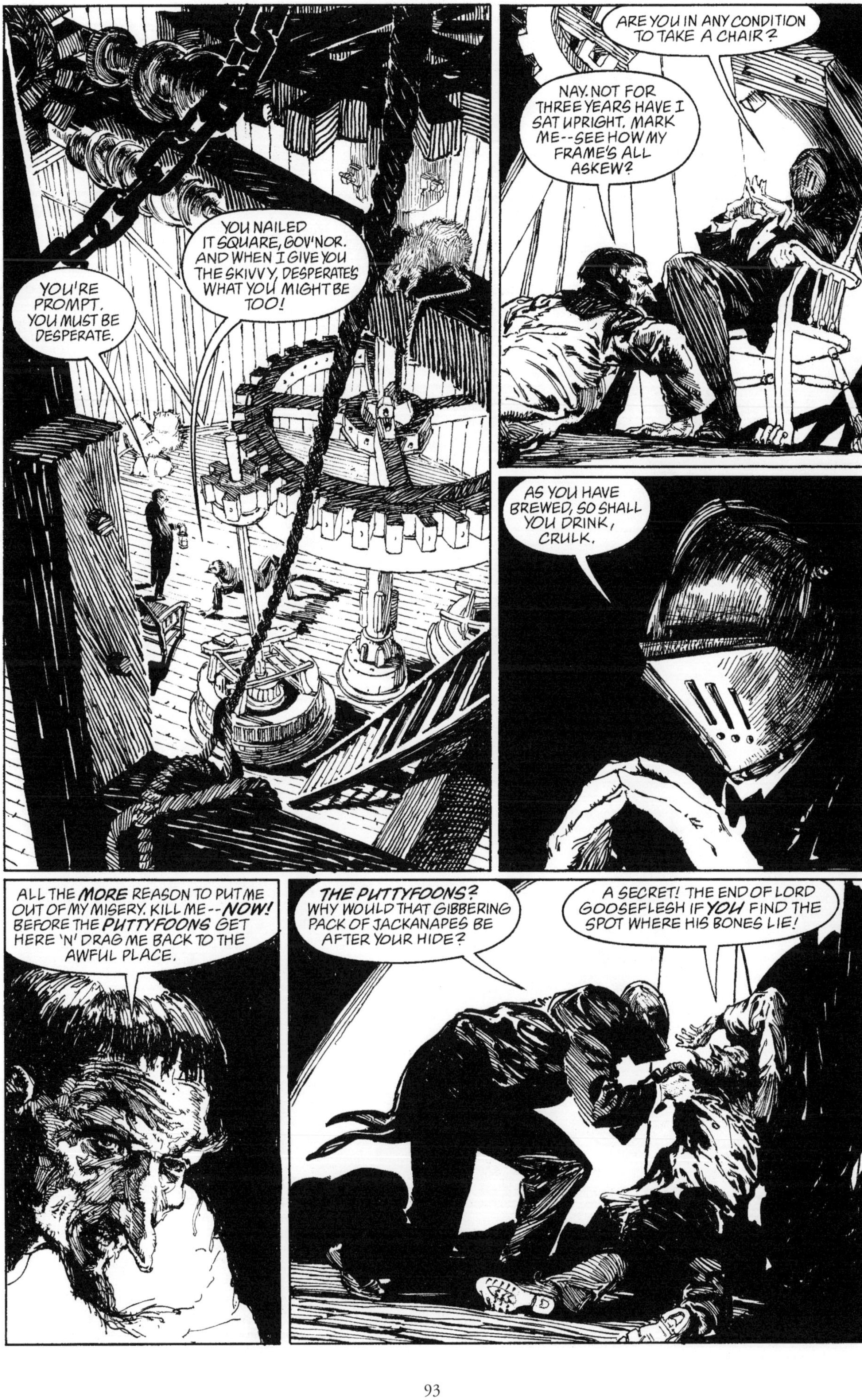

YOU'RE PROMPT. YOU MUST BE DESPERATE.
YOU NAILED IT SQUARE, GOV'NOR. AND WHEN I GIVE YOU THE SKIVVY, DESPERATE'S WHAT YOU MIGHT BE TOO!
ARE YOU IN ANY CONDITION TO TAKE A CHAIR?
NAY. NOT FOR THREE YEARS HAVE I SAT UPRIGHT. MARK ME--SEE HOW MY FRAME'S ALL ASKEW?
AS YOU HAVE BREWED, SO SHALL YOU DRINK, CRULK.
ALL THE MORE REASON TO PUT ME OUT OF MY MISERY. KILL ME--NOW! BEFORE THE PUTTYFOONS GET HERE 'N' DRAG ME BACK TO THE AWFUL PLACE.
THE PUTTYFOONS? WHY WOULD THAT GIBBERING PACK OF JACKANAPES BE AFTER YOUR HIDE?
A SECRET! THE END OF LORD GOOSEFLESH IF YOU FIND THE SPOT WHERE HIS BONES LIE!

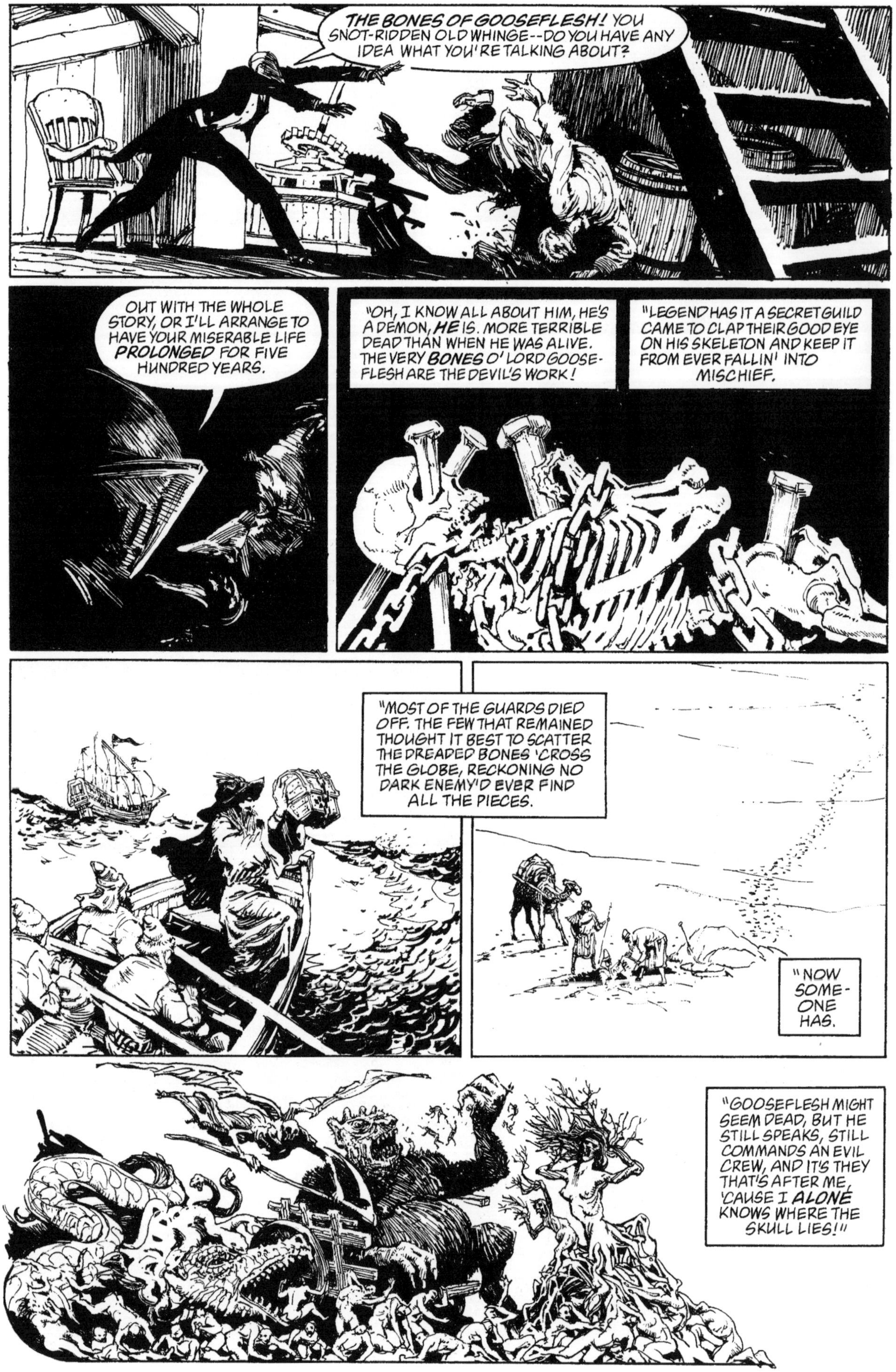
THE BONES OF GOOSEFLESH! YOU SNOT-RIDDEN OLD WHINGE--DO YOU HAVE ANY IDEA WHAT YOU'RE TALKING ABOUT?
OUT WITH THE WHOLE STORY, OR I'LL ARRANGE TO HAVE YOUR MISERABLE LIFE PROLONGED FOR FIVE HUNDRED YEARS.
"OH, I KNOW ALL ABOUT HIM, HE'S A DEMON, HE IS. MORE TERRIBLE DEAD THAN WHEN HE WAS ALIVE. THE VERY BONES O' LORD GOOSE-FLESH ARE THE DEVIL'S WORK!
"LEGEND HAS IT A SECRET GUILD CAME TO CLAP THEIR GOOD EYE ON HIS SKELETON AND KEEP IT FROM EVER FALLIN' INTO MISCHIEF.
"MOST OF THE GUARDS DIED OFF. THE FEW THAT REMAINED THOUGHT IT BEST TO SCATTER THE DREADED BONES 'CROSS THE GLOBE, RECKONING NO DARK ENEMY'D EVER FIND ALL THE PIECES.
"NOW SOME-ONE HAS.
"GOOSEFLESH MIGHT SEEM DEAD, BUT HE STILL SPEAKS, STILL COMMANDS AN EVIL CREW, AND IT'S THEY THAT'S AFTER ME, 'CAUSE I ALONE KNOWS WHERE THE SKULL LIES!"

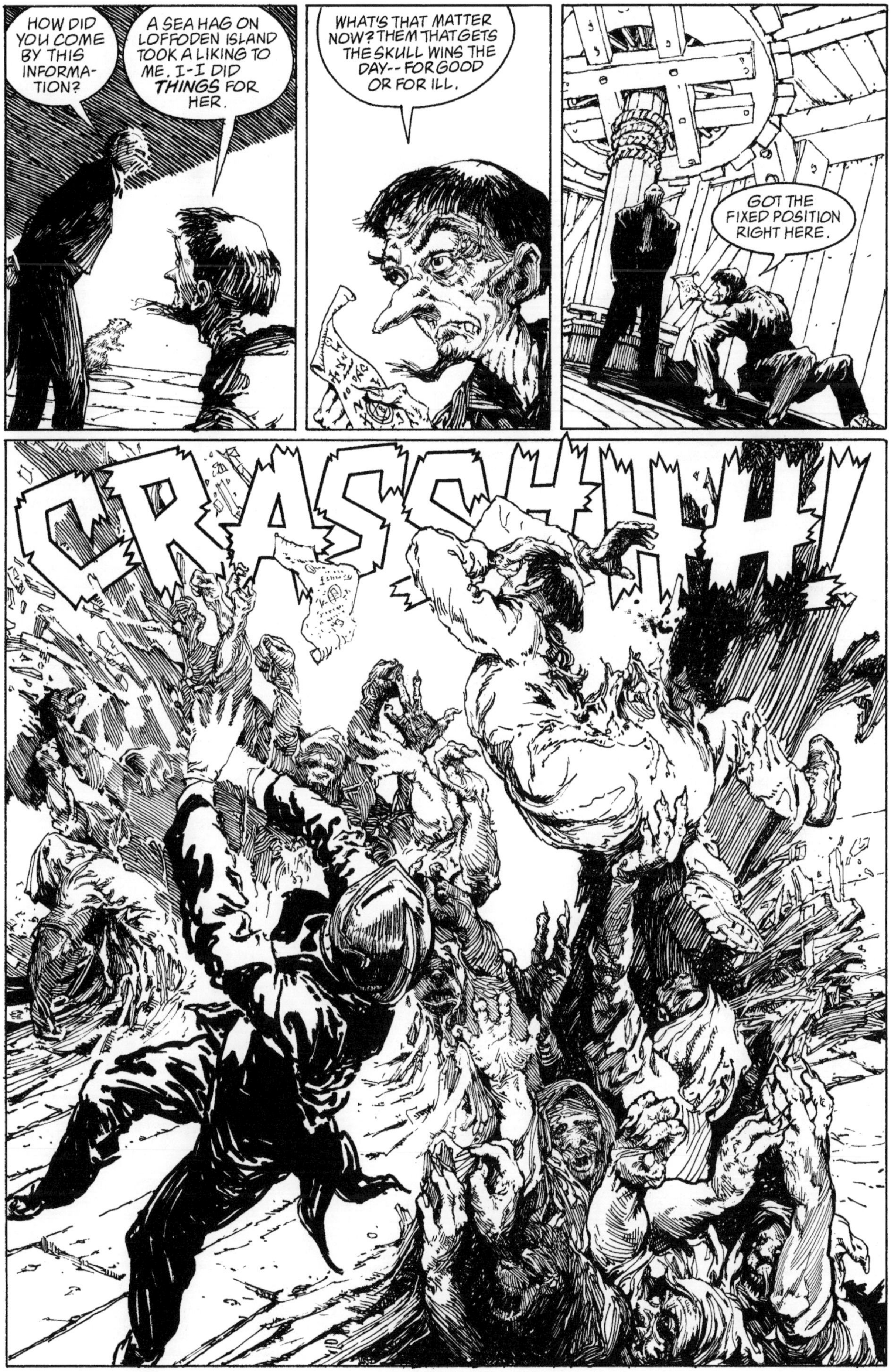
HOW DID YOU COME BY THIS INFORMATION?
A SEA HAG ON LOFFODEN ISLAND TOOK A LIKING TO ME. I-I DID *THINGS* FOR HER.
WHAT'S THAT MATTER NOW? THEM THAT GETS THE SKULL WINS THE DAY--FOR GOOD OR FOR ILL.
GOT THE FIXED POSITION RIGHT HERE.
CRASSHH!

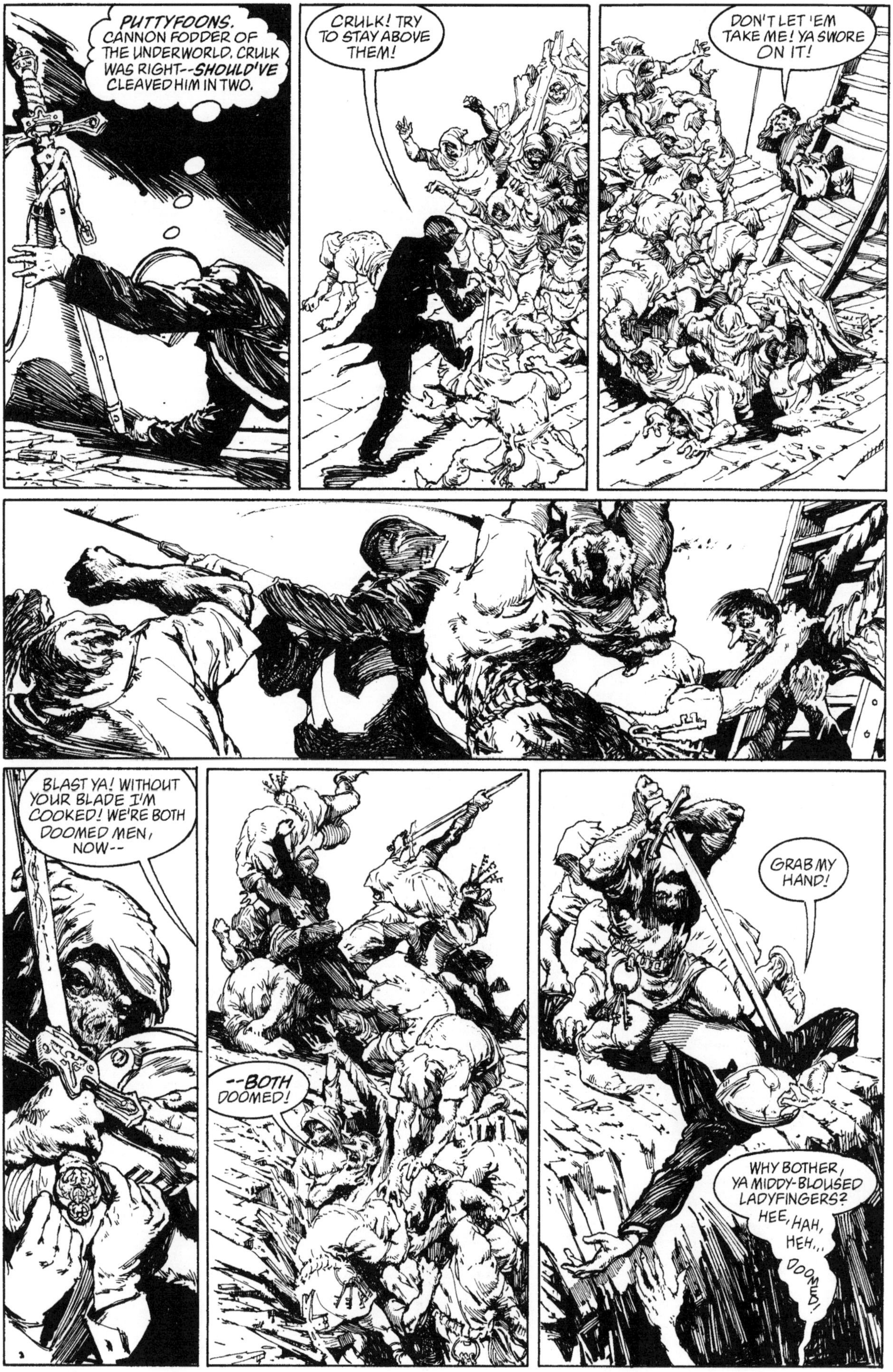
PUTTYFOONS. CANNON FODDER OF THE UNDERWORLD. CRULK WAS RIGHT--SHOULD'VE CLEAVED HIM IN TWO.
CRULK! TRY TO STAY ABOVE THEM!
DON'T LET 'EM TAKE ME! YA SWORE ON IT!
BLAST YA! WITHOUT YOUR BLADE I'M COOKED! WE'RE BOTH DOOMED MEN, NOW--
--BOTH DOOMED!
GRAB MY HAND!
WHY BOTHER, YA MIDDY-BLOUSED LADYFINGERS? HEE, HAH, HEH... DOOMED!

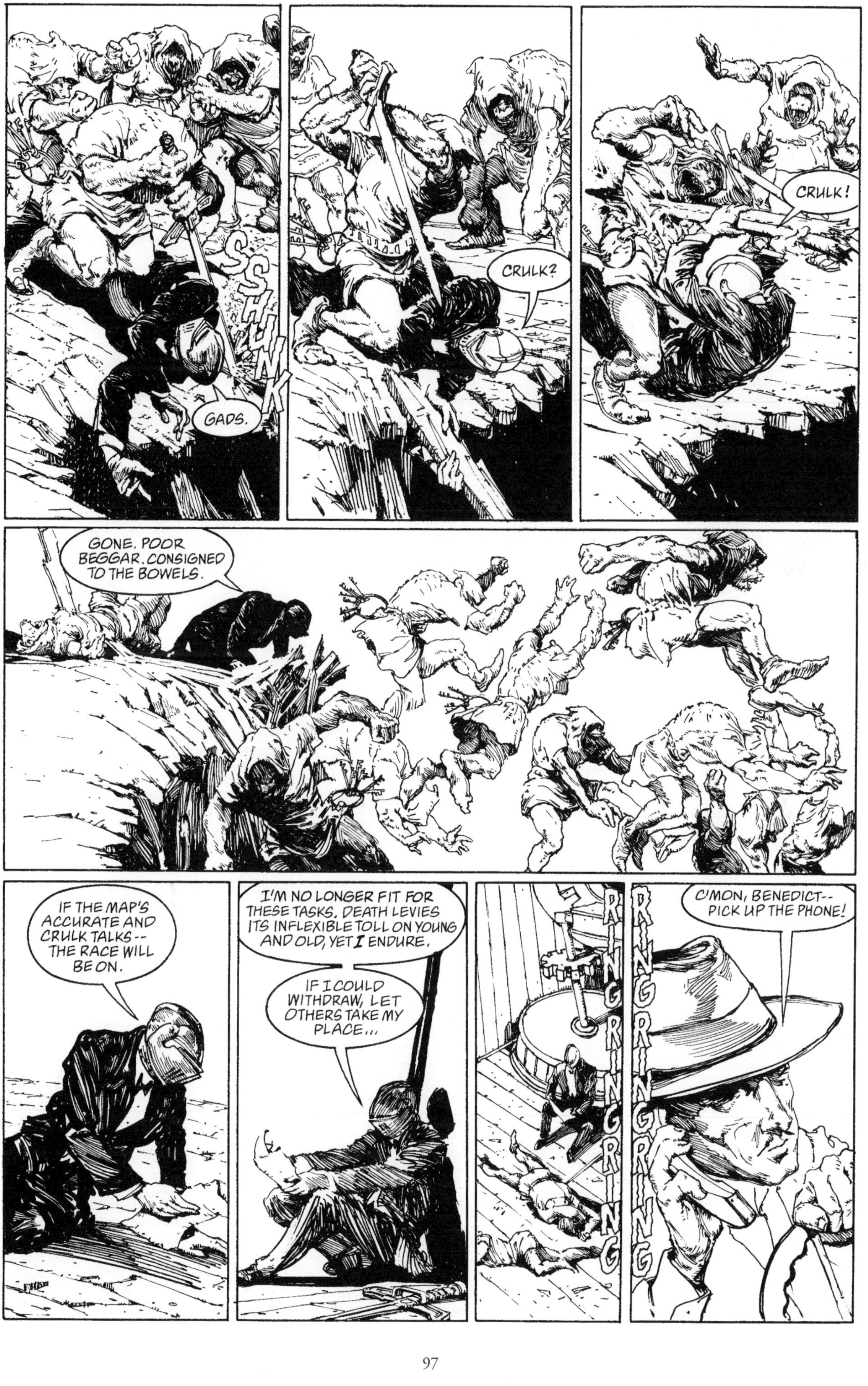
SSHUNK
GADS.
CRULK?
CRULK!
GONE. POOR BEGGAR. CONSIGNED TO THE BOWELS.
IF THE MAP'S ACCURATE AND CRULK TALKS -- THE RACE WILL BE ON.
I'M NO LONGER FIT FOR THESE TASKS. DEATH LEVIES ITS INFLEXIBLE TOLL ON YOUNG AND OLD, YET I ENDURE.
IF I COULD WITHDRAW, LET OTHERS TAKE MY PLACE...
RINGRING
RINGRINGRING
C'MON, BENEDICT-- PICK UP THE PHONE!

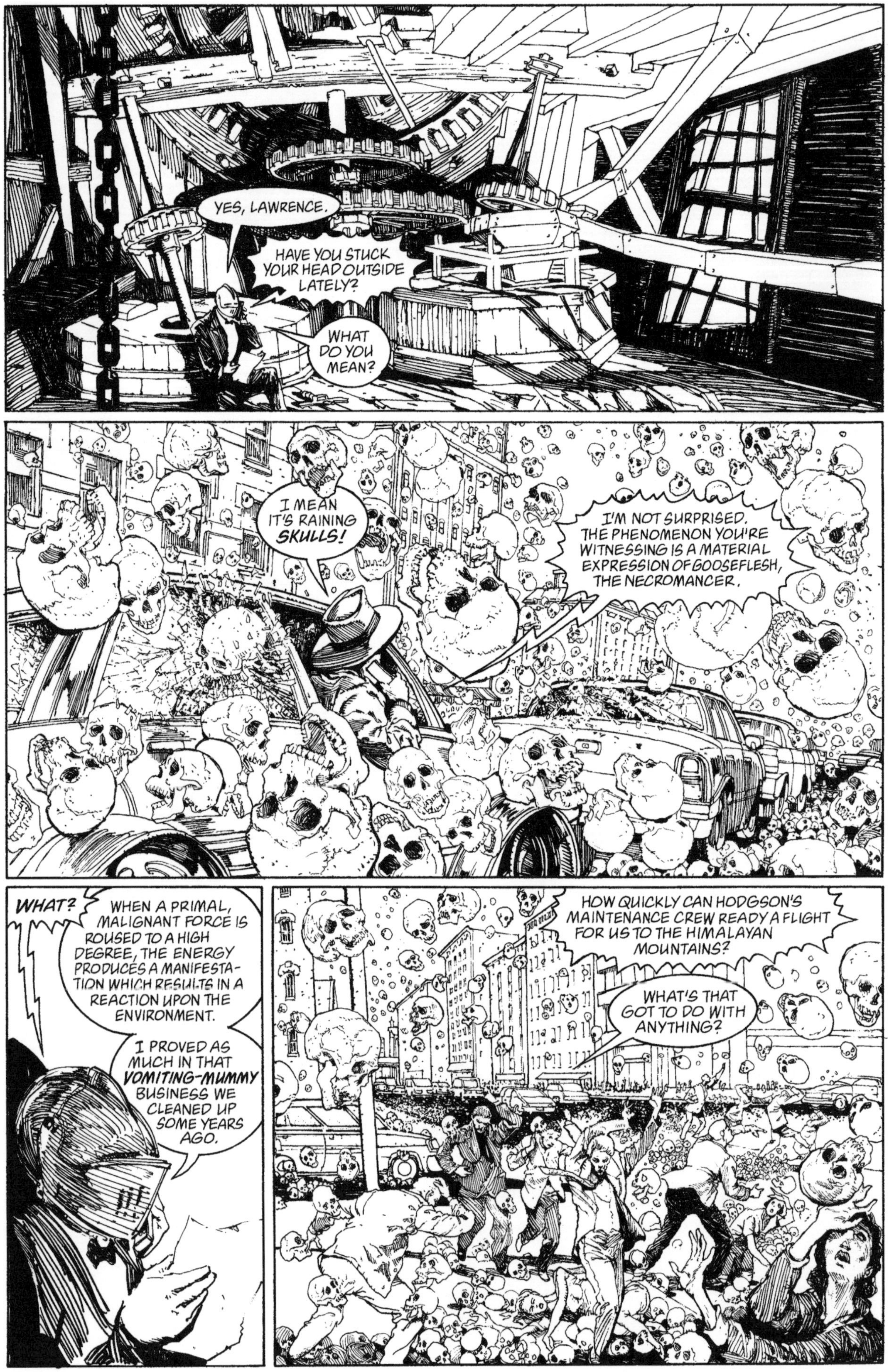
YES, LAWRENCE.
HAVE YOU STUCK YOUR HEAD OUTSIDE LATELY?
WHAT DO YOU MEAN?
I MEAN IT'S RAINING SKULLS!
I'M NOT SURPRISED. THE PHENOMENON YOU'RE WITNESSING IS A MATERIAL EXPRESSION OF GOOSEFLESH, THE NECROMANCER.
WHAT?
WHEN A PRIMAL, MALIGNANT FORCE IS ROUSED TO A HIGH DEGREE, THE ENERGY PRODUCES A MANIFESTATION WHICH RESULTS IN A REACTION UPON THE ENVIRONMENT.
I PROVED AS MUCH IN THAT VOMITING-MUMMY BUSINESS WE CLEANED UP SOME YEARS AGO.
HOW QUICKLY CAN HODGSON'S MAINTENANCE CREW READY A FLIGHT FOR US TO THE HIMALAYAN MOUNTAINS?
WHAT'S THAT GOT TO DO WITH ANYTHING?

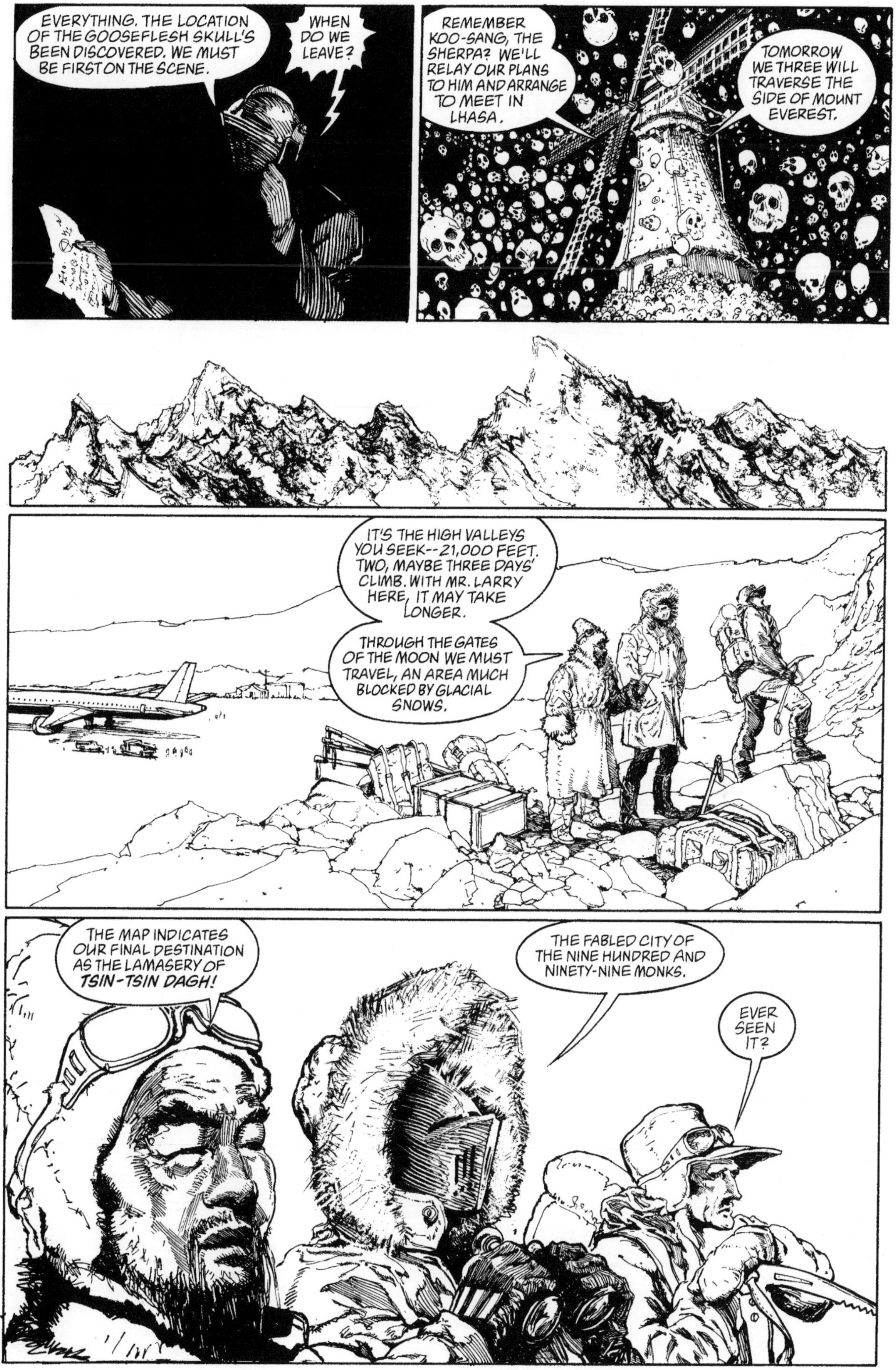
EVERYTHING. THE LOCATION OF THE GOOSEFLESH SKULL'S BEEN DISCOVERED. WE MUST BE FIRST ON THE SCENE.
WHEN DO WE LEAVE?
REMEMBER KOO-SANG, THE SHERPA? WE'LL RELAY OUR PLANS TO HIM AND ARRANGE TO MEET IN LHASA.
TOMORROW WE THREE WILL TRAVERSE THE SIDE OF MOUNT EVEREST.
IT'S THE HIGH VALLEYS YOU SEEK--21,000 FEET. TWO, MAYBE THREE DAYS' CLIMB. WITH MR. LARRY HERE, IT MAY TAKE LONGER.
THROUGH THE GATES OF THE MOON WE MUST TRAVEL, AN AREA MUCH BLOCKED BY GLACIAL SNOWS.
THE MAP INDICATES OUR FINAL DESTINATION AS THE LAMASERY OF TSIN-TSIN DAGH!
THE FABLED CITY OF THE NINE HUNDRED AND NINETY-NINE MONKS.
EVER SEEN IT?

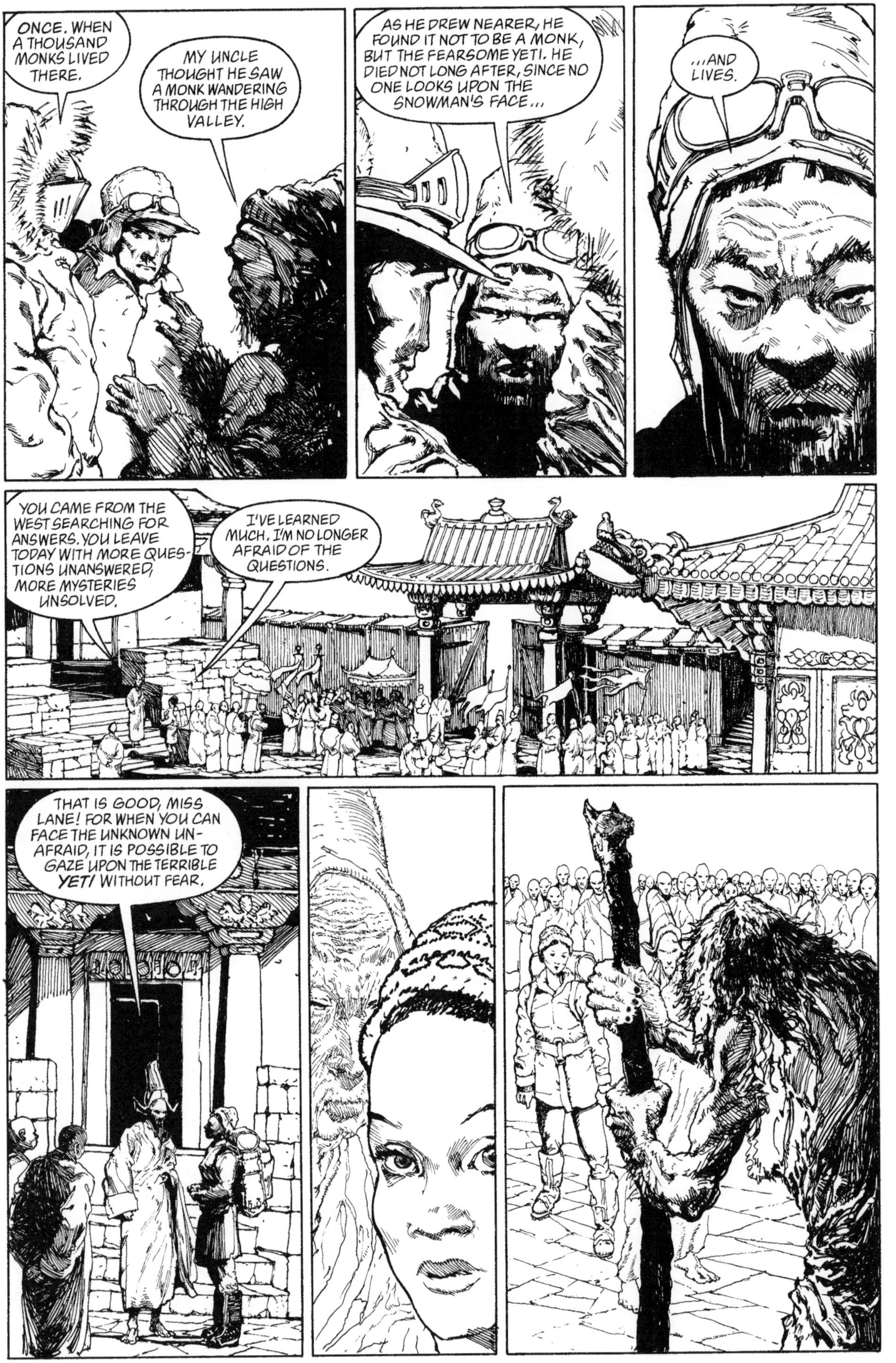
ONCE. WHEN A THOUSAND MONKS LIVED THERE.
MY UNCLE THOUGHT HE SAW A MONK WANDERING THROUGH THE HIGH VALLEY.
AS HE DREW NEARER, HE FOUND IT NOT TO BE A MONK, BUT THE FEARSOME YETI. HE DIED NOT LONG AFTER, SINCE NO ONE LOOKS UPON THE SNOWMAN'S FACE...
...AND LIVES.
YOU CAME FROM THE WEST SEARCHING FOR ANSWERS. YOU LEAVE TODAY WITH MORE QUESTIONS UNANSWERED, MORE MYSTERIES UNSOLVED.
I'VE LEARNED MUCH. I'M NO LONGER AFRAID OF THE QUESTIONS.
THAT IS GOOD, MISS LANE! FOR WHEN YOU CAN FACE THE UNKNOWN UNAFRAID, IT IS POSSIBLE TO GAZE UPON THE TERRIBLE YETI WITHOUT FEAR.

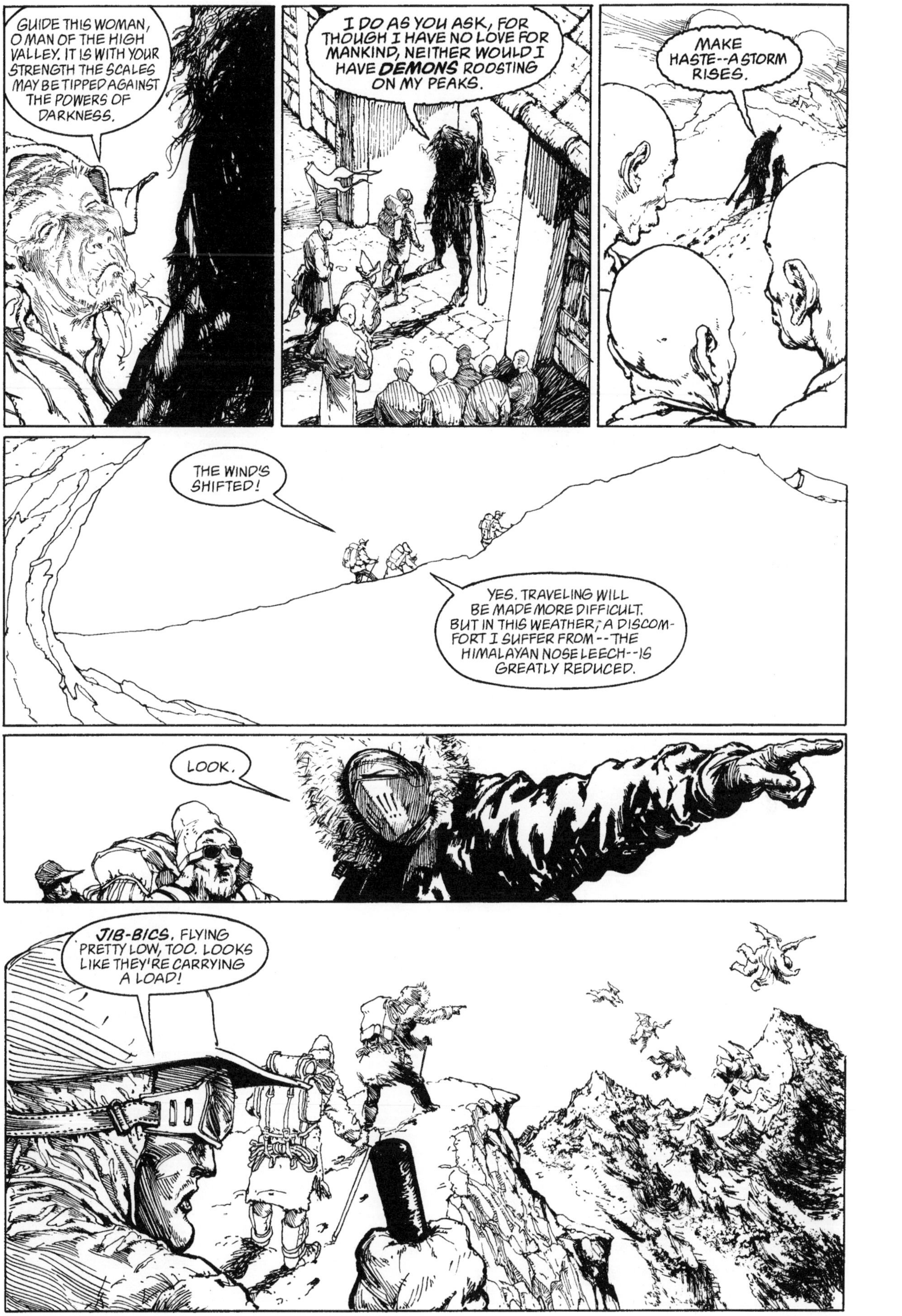
GUIDE THIS WOMAN, O MAN OF THE HIGH VALLEY. IT IS WITH YOUR STRENGTH THE SCALES MAY BE TIPPED AGAINST THE POWERS OF DARKNESS.
I DO AS YOU ASK, FOR THOUGH I HAVE NO LOVE FOR MANKIND, NEITHER WOULD I HAVE **DEMONS** ROOSTING ON MY PEAKS.
MAKE HASTE--A STORM RISES.
THE WIND'S SHIFTED!
YES. TRAVELING WILL BE MADE MORE DIFFICULT. BUT IN THIS WEATHER, A DISCOMFORT I SUFFER FROM--THE HIMALAYAN NOSE LEECH--IS GREATLY REDUCED.
LOOK.
JIB-BICS. FLYING PRETTY LOW, TOO. LOOKS LIKE THEY'RE CARRYING A LOAD!

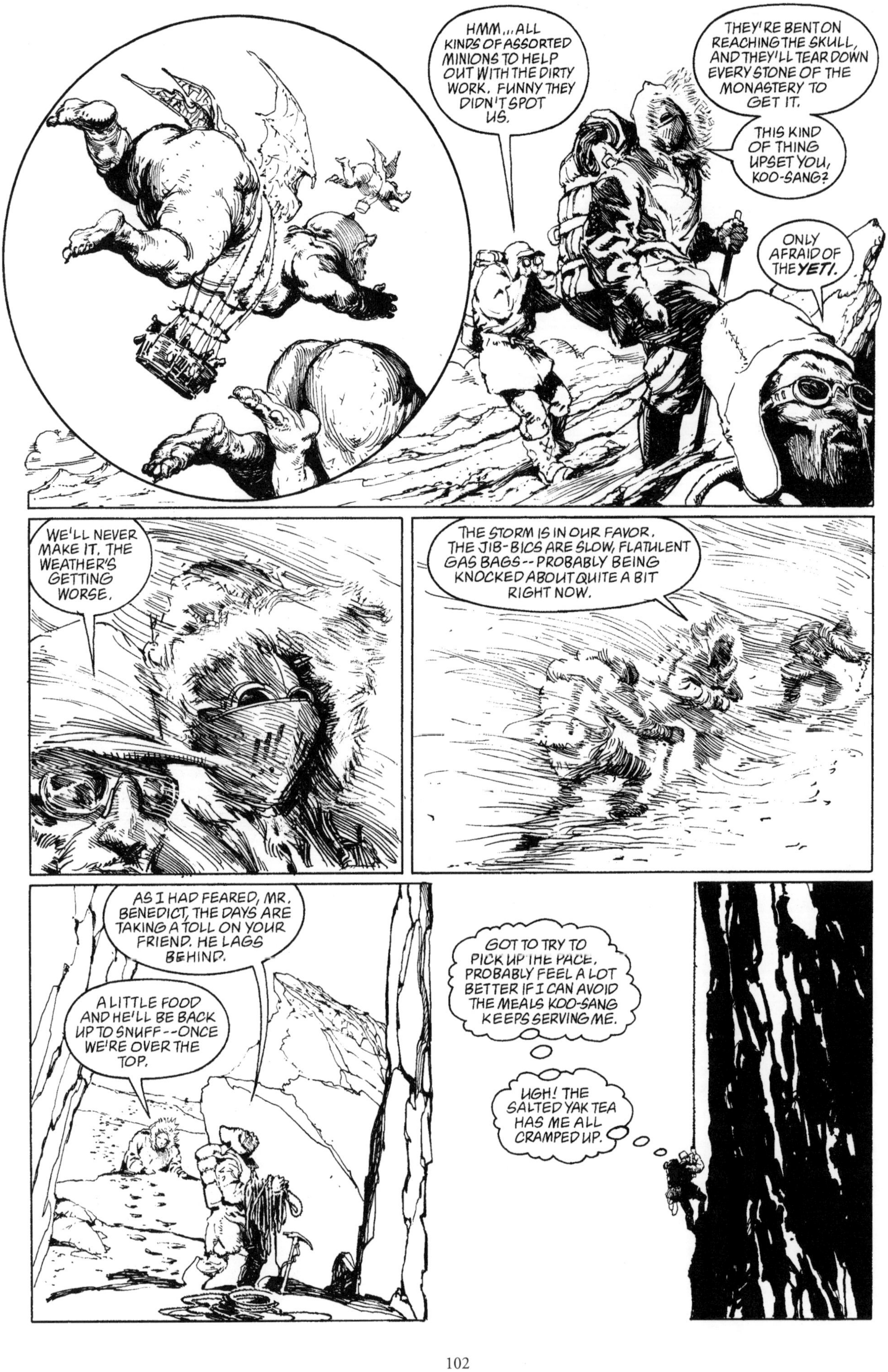

HMM... ALL KINDS OF ASSORTED MINIONS TO HELP OUT WITH THE DIRTY WORK. FUNNY THEY DIDN'T SPOT US.
THEY'RE BENT ON REACHING THE SKULL, AND THEY'LL TEAR DOWN EVERY STONE OF THE MONASTERY TO GET IT.
THIS KIND OF THING UPSET YOU, KOO-SANG?
ONLY AFRAID OF THE *YETI.*
WE'LL NEVER MAKE IT. THE WEATHER'S GETTING WORSE.
THE STORM IS IN OUR FAVOR. THE JIB-BICS ARE SLOW, FLATULENT GAS BAGS--PROBABLY BEING KNOCKED ABOUT QUITE A BIT RIGHT NOW.
AS I HAD FEARED, MR. BENEDICT, THE DAYS ARE TAKING A TOLL ON YOUR FRIEND. HE LAGS BEHIND.
A LITTLE FOOD AND HE'LL BE BACK UP TO SNUFF--ONCE WE'RE OVER THE TOP.
GOT TO TRY TO PICK UP THE PACE. PROBABLY FEEL A LOT BETTER IF I CAN AVOID THE MEALS KOO-SANG KEEPS SERVING ME.
UGH! THE SALTED YAK TEA HAS ME ALL CRAMPED UP.

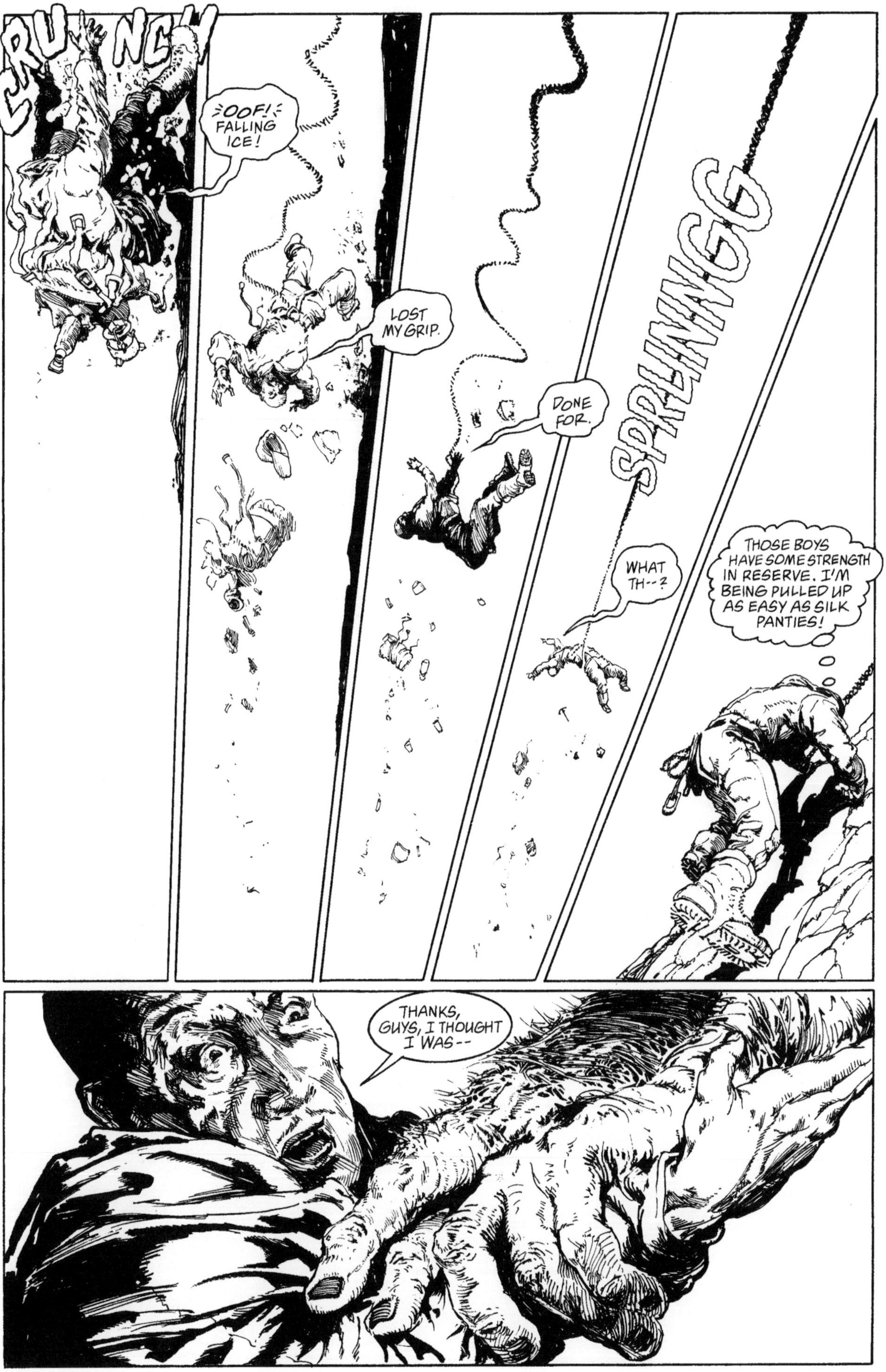
CRUNCH
OOF! FALLING ICE!
LOST MY GRIP.
DONE FOR.
SPRUNNGG
WHAT TH--?
THOSE BOYS HAVE SOME STRENGTH IN RESERVE. I'M BEING PULLED UP AS EASY AS SILK PANTIES!
THANKS, GUYS, I THOUGHT I WAS--

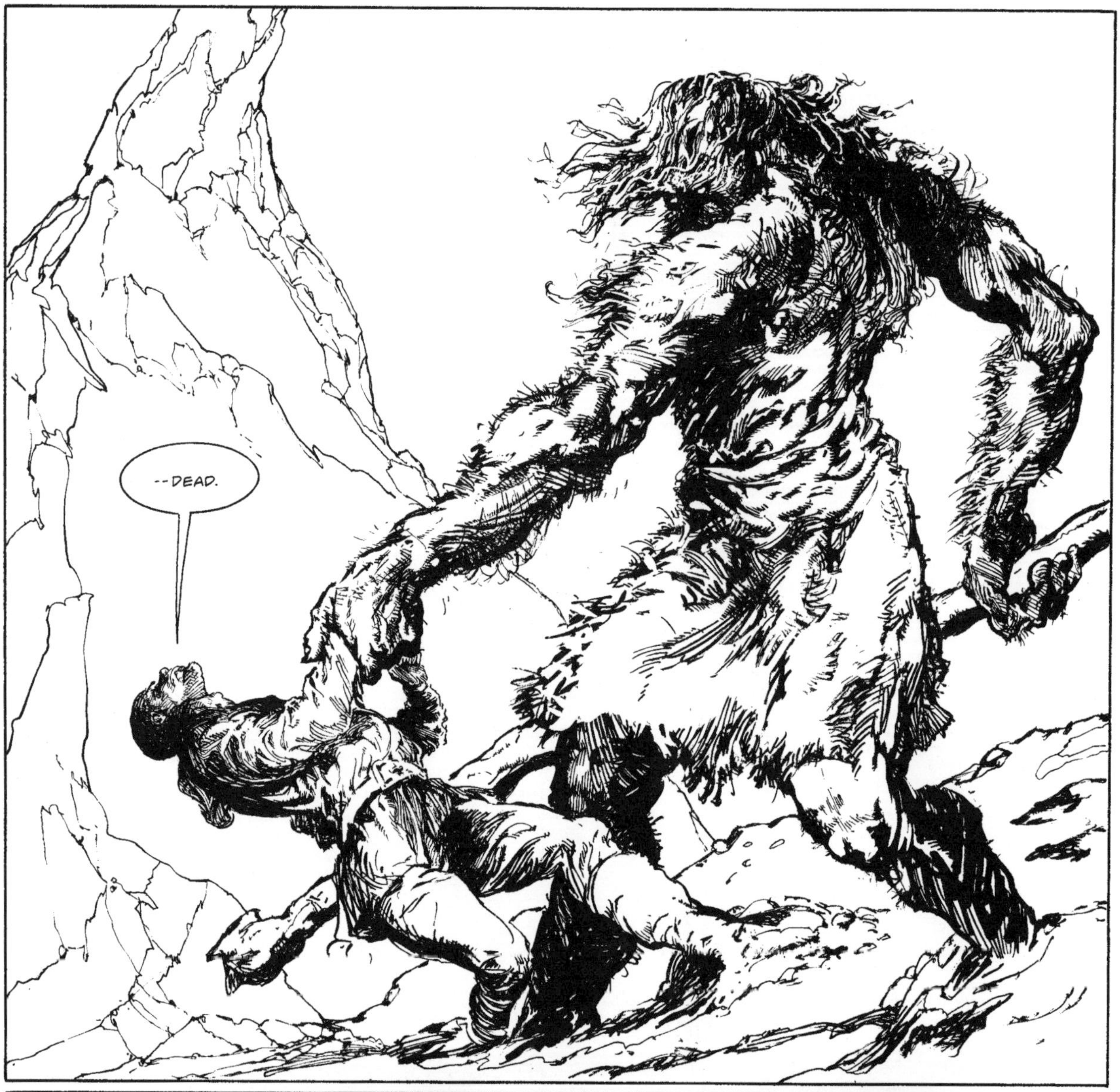
--DEAD.

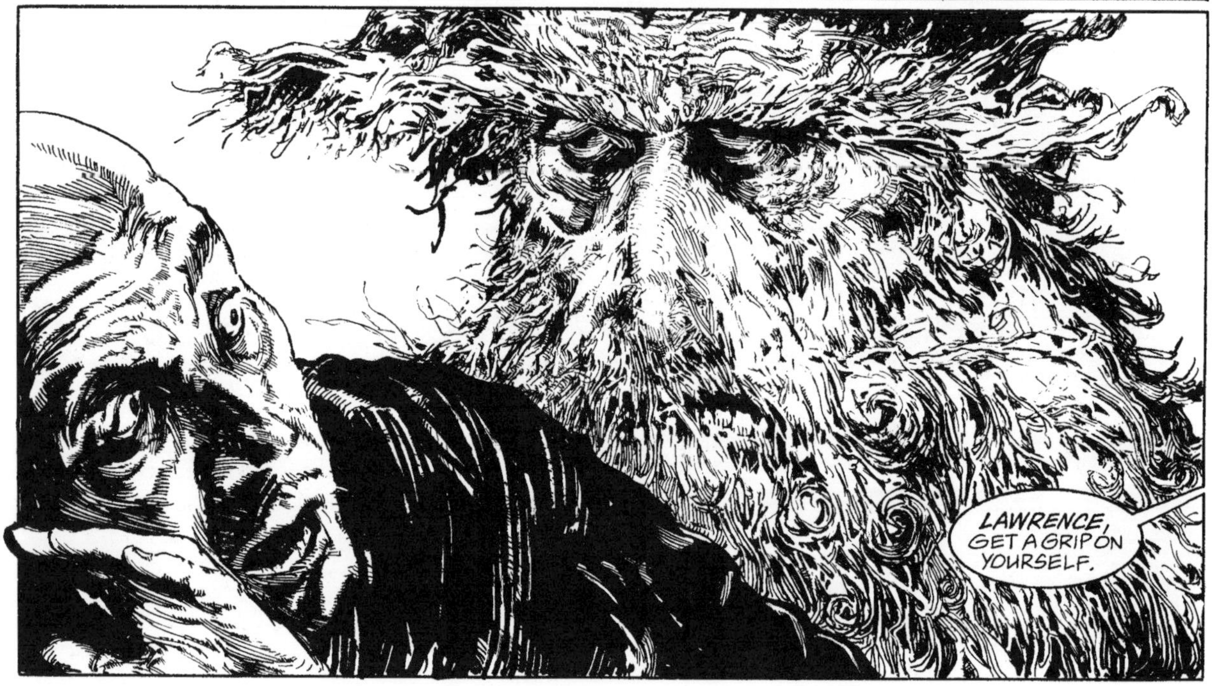
LAWRENCE, GET A GRIP ON YOURSELF.

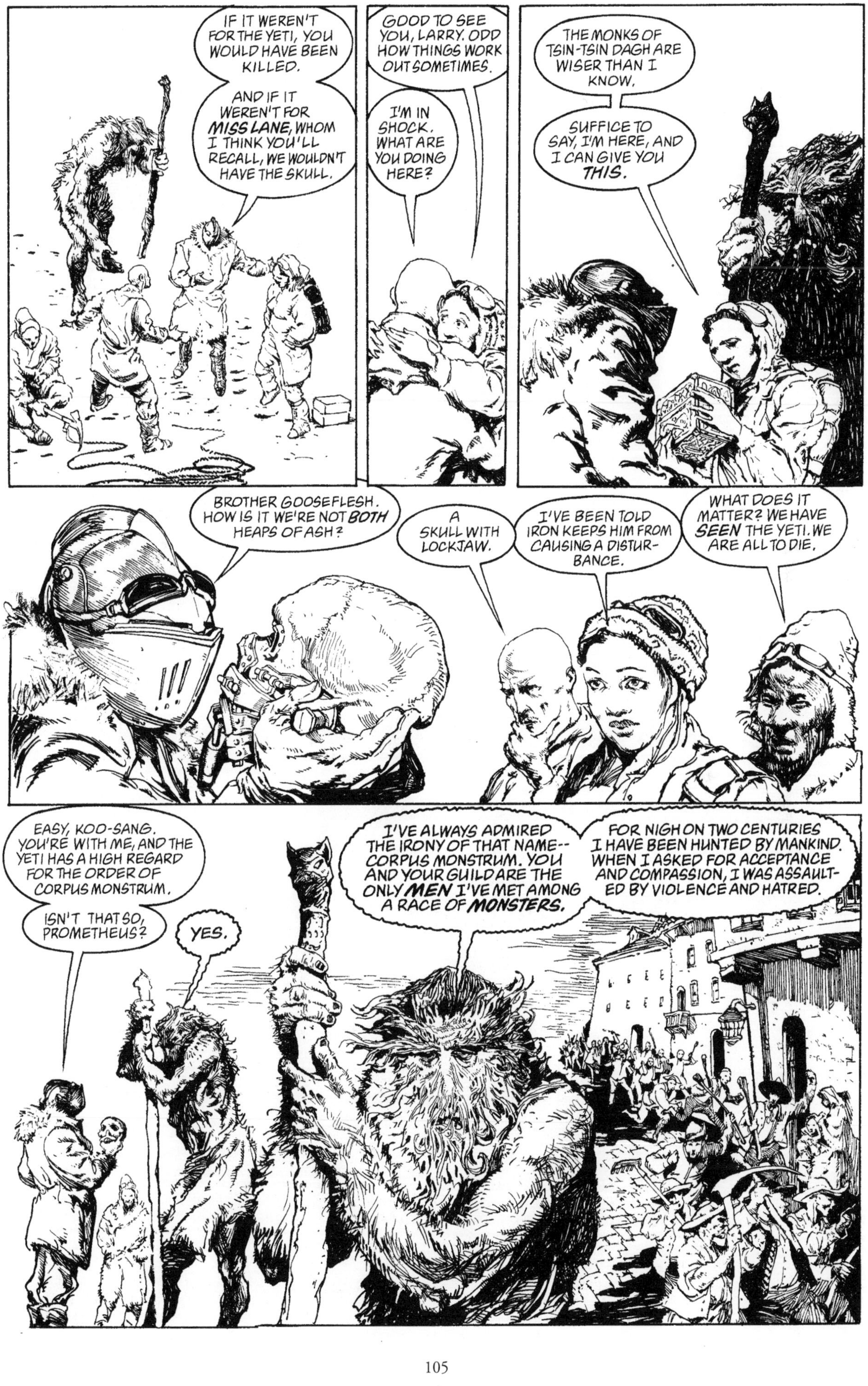
IF IT WEREN'T FOR THE YETI, YOU WOULD HAVE BEEN KILLED.
AND IF IT WEREN'T FOR MISS LANE, WHOM I THINK YOU'LL RECALL, WE WOULDN'T HAVE THE SKULL.
GOOD TO SEE YOU, LARRY. ODD HOW THINGS WORK OUT SOMETIMES.
I'M IN SHOCK. WHAT ARE YOU DOING HERE?
THE MONKS OF TSIN-TSIN DAGH ARE WISER THAN I KNOW.
SUFFICE TO SAY, I'M HERE, AND I CAN GIVE YOU THIS.
BROTHER GOOSEFLESH. HOW IS IT WE'RE NOT BOTH HEAPS OF ASH?
A SKULL WITH LOCKJAW.
I'VE BEEN TOLD IRON KEEPS HIM FROM CAUSING A DISTURBANCE.
WHAT DOES IT MATTER? WE HAVE SEEN THE YETI. WE ARE ALL TO DIE.
EASY, KOO-SANG. YOU'RE WITH ME, AND THE YETI HAS A HIGH REGARD FOR THE ORDER OF CORPUS MONSTRUM.
ISN'T THAT SO, PROMETHEUS?
YES.
I'VE ALWAYS ADMIRED THE IRONY OF THAT NAME--CORPUS MONSTRUM. YOU AND YOUR GUILD ARE THE ONLY MEN I'VE MET AMONG A RACE OF MONSTERS.
FOR NIGH ON TWO CENTURIES I HAVE BEEN HUNTED BY MANKIND. WHEN I ASKED FOR ACCEPTANCE AND COMPASSION, I WAS ASSAULTED BY VIOLENCE AND HATRED.

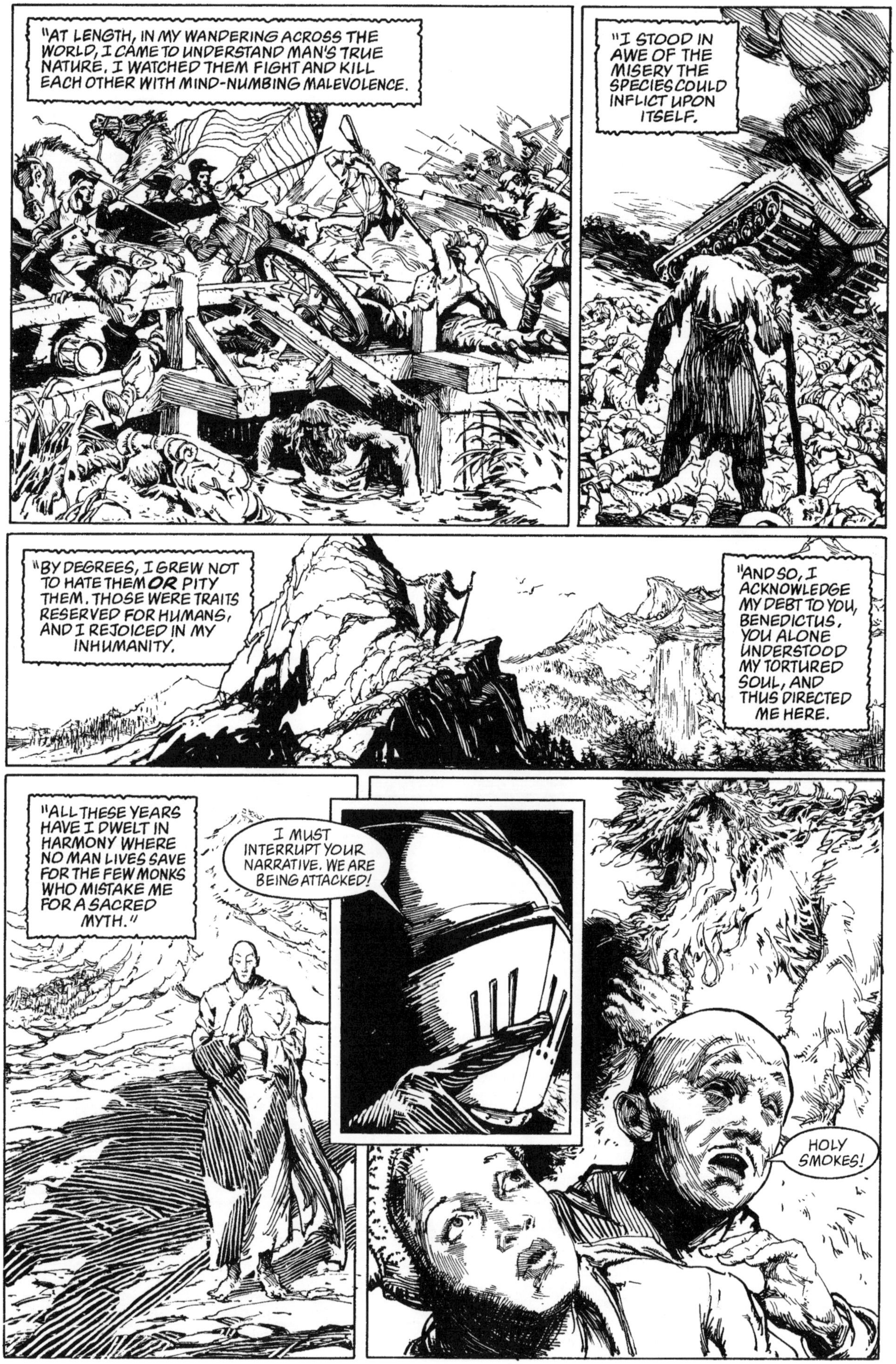
"AT LENGTH, IN MY WANDERING ACROSS THE WORLD, I CAME TO UNDERSTAND MAN'S TRUE NATURE. I WATCHED THEM FIGHT AND KILL EACH OTHER WITH MIND-NUMBING MALEVOLENCE.
"I STOOD IN AWE OF THE MISERY THE SPECIES COULD INFLICT UPON ITSELF.
"BY DEGREES, I GREW NOT TO HATE THEM OR PITY THEM. THOSE WERE TRAITS RESERVED FOR HUMANS, AND I REJOICED IN MY INHUMANITY.
"AND SO, I ACKNOWLEDGE MY DEBT TO YOU, BENEDICTUS. YOU ALONE UNDERSTOOD MY TORTURED SOUL, AND THUS DIRECTED ME HERE.
"ALL THESE YEARS HAVE I DWELT IN HARMONY WHERE NO MAN LIVES SAVE FOR THE FEW MONKS WHO MISTAKE ME FOR A SACRED MYTH."
I MUST INTERRUPT YOUR NARRATIVE. WE ARE BEING ATTACKED!
HOLY SMOKES!

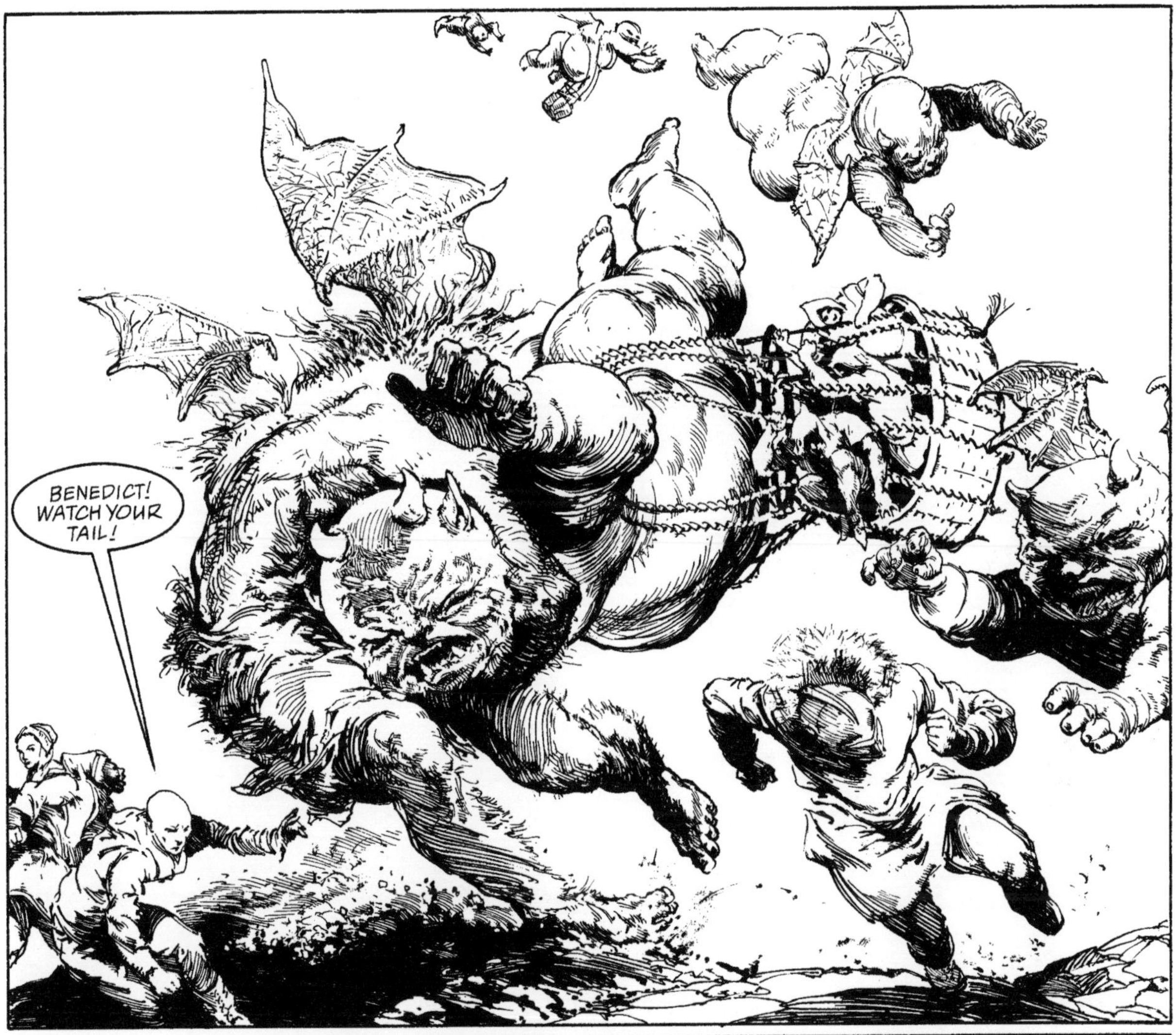
BENEDICT! WATCH YOUR TAIL!

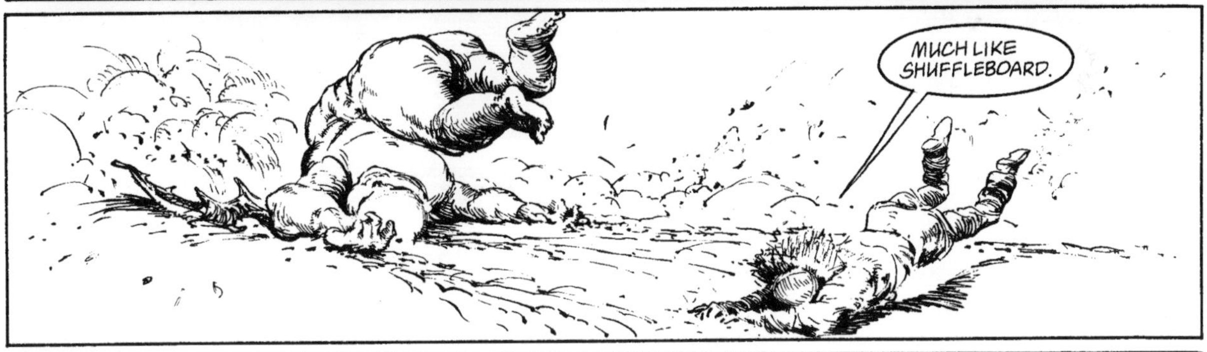
MUCH LIKE SHUFFLEBOARD.

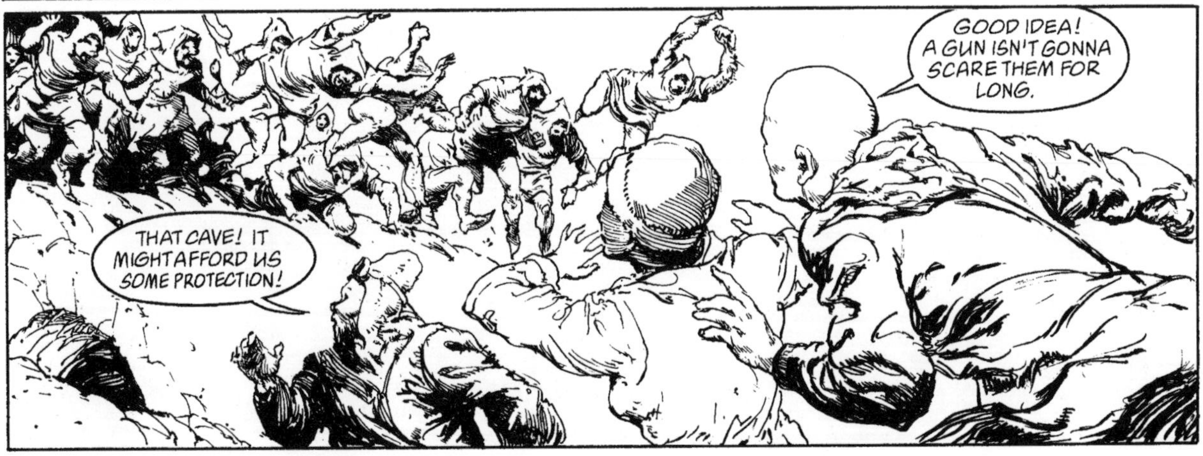
GOOD IDEA! A GUN ISN'T GONNA SCARE THEM FOR LONG.
THAT CAVE! IT MIGHT AFFORD US SOME PROTECTION!

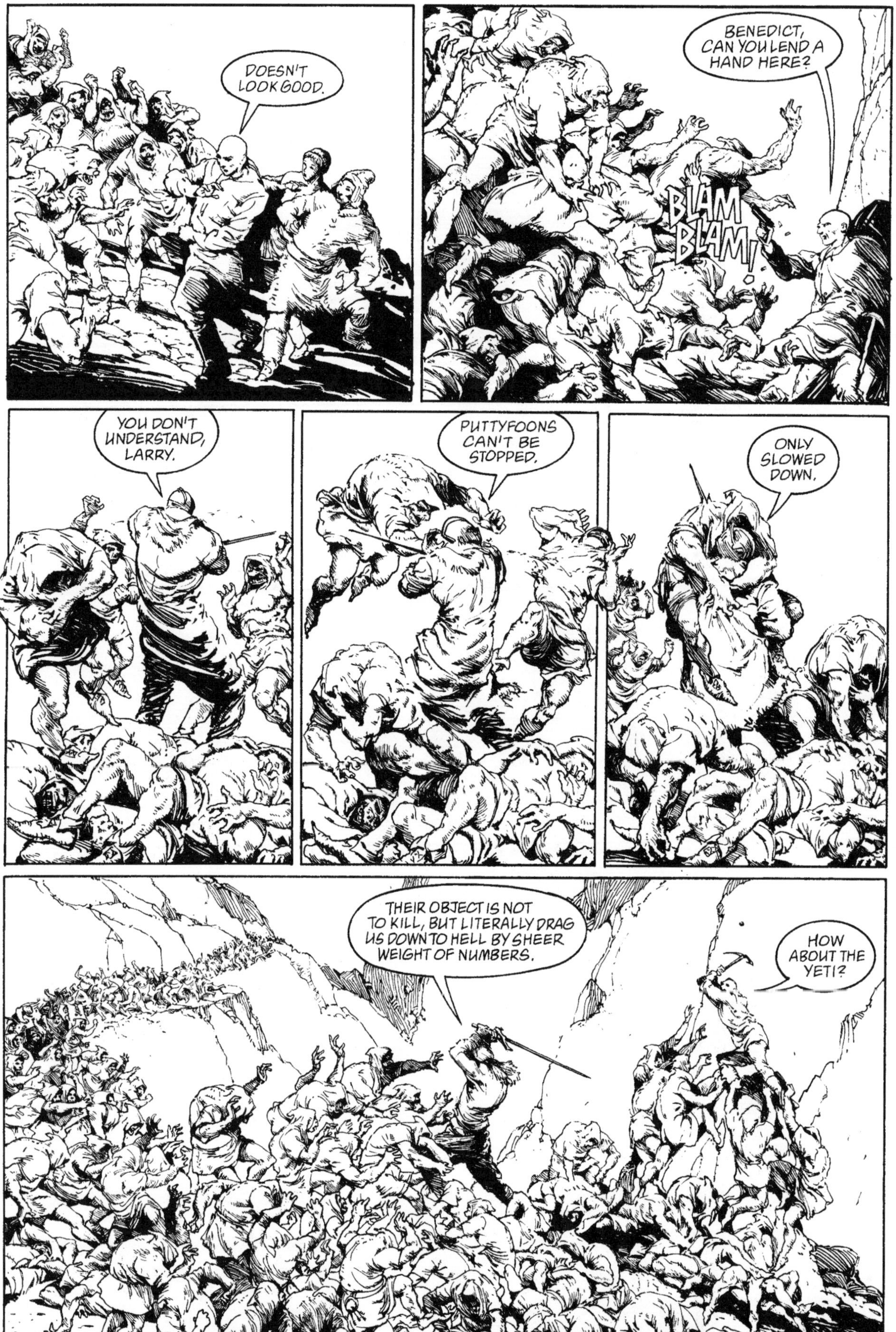
DOESN'T LOOK GOOD.
BENEDICT, CAN YOU LEND A HAND HERE?
BLAM BLAM!
YOU DON'T UNDERSTAND, LARRY.
PUTTYFOONS CAN'T BE STOPPED.
ONLY SLOWED DOWN.
THEIR OBJECT IS NOT TO KILL, BUT LITERALLY DRAG US DOWN TO HELL BY SHEER WEIGHT OF NUMBERS.
HOW ABOUT THE YETI?

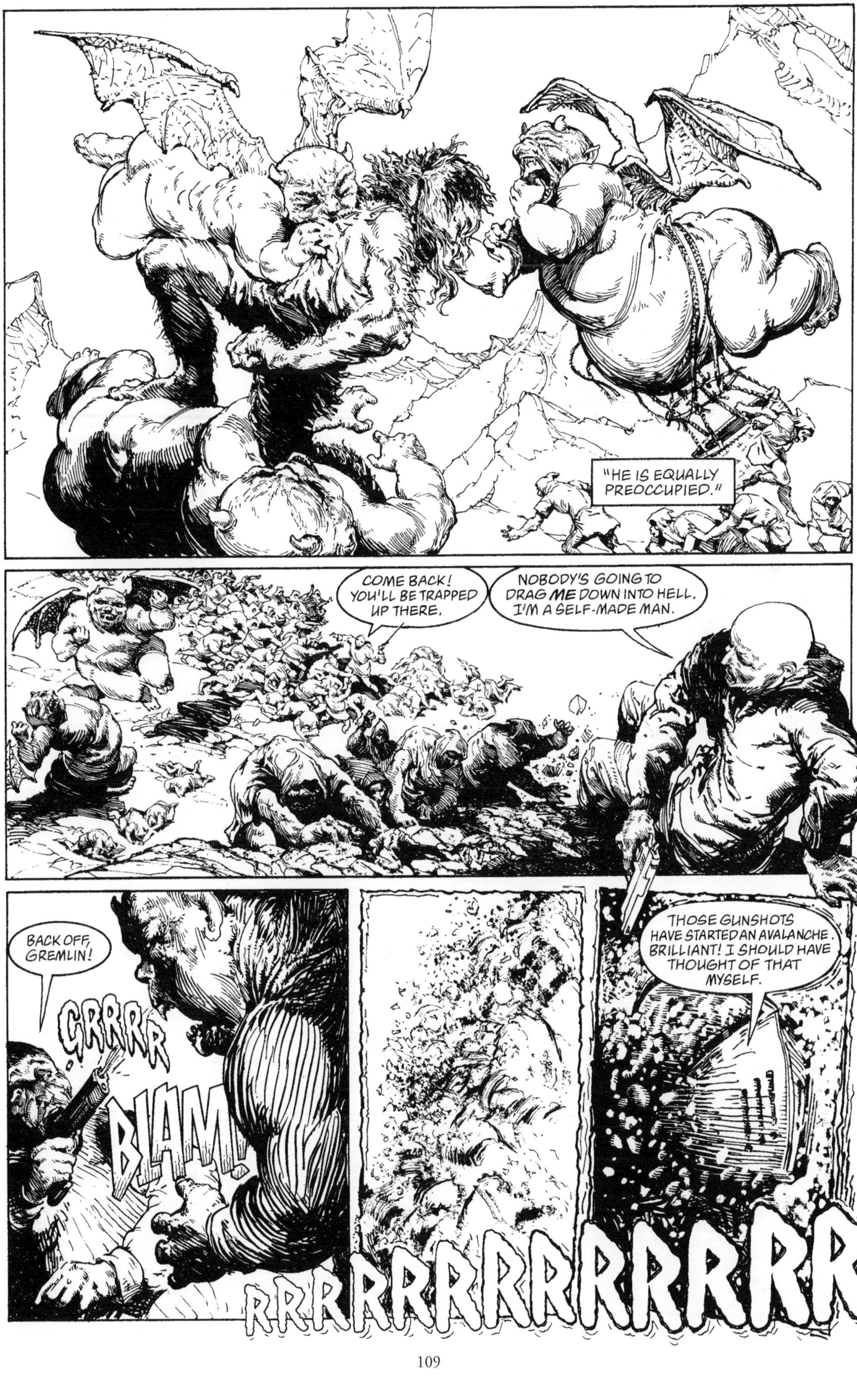
"HE IS EQUALLY PREOCCUPIED."
COME BACK! YOU'LL BE TRAPPED UP THERE.
NOBODY'S GOING TO DRAG ME DOWN INTO HELL. I'M A SELF-MADE MAN.
BACK OFF, GREMLIN!
GRRRR
BLAM!
THOSE GUNSHOTS HAVE STARTED AN AVALANCHE. BRILLIANT! I SHOULD HAVE THOUGHT OF THAT MYSELF.
RRRRRRRRRRRRRR

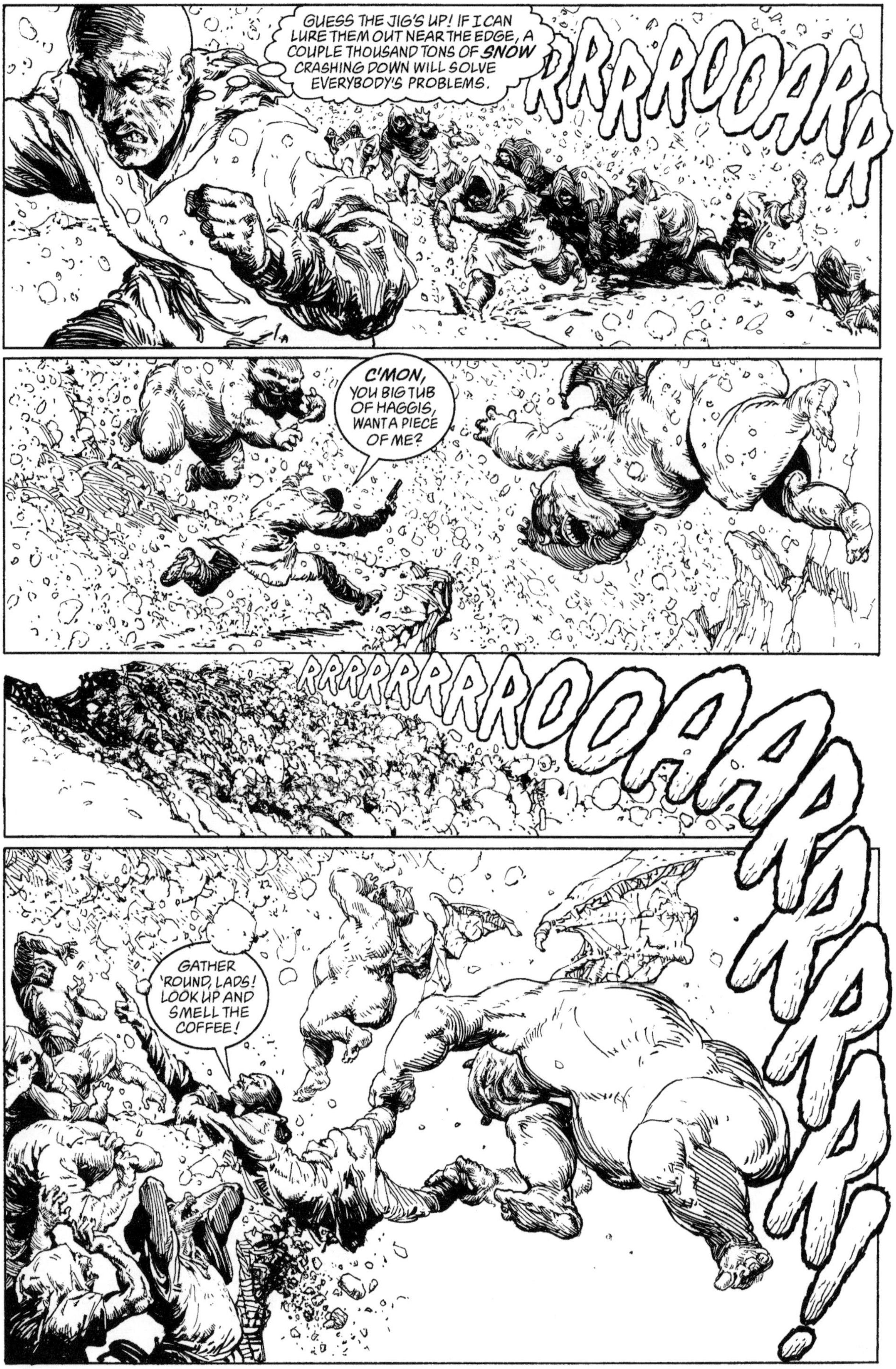
GUESS THE JIG'S UP! IF I CAN LURE THEM OUT NEAR THE EDGE, A COUPLE THOUSAND TONS OF SNOW CRASHING DOWN WILL SOLVE EVERYBODY'S PROBLEMS.
RRRROOARR
C'MON, YOU BIG TUB OF HAGGIS, WANTA PIECE OF ME?
RRRRRRRRROOAARRRRRR!
GATHER 'ROUND, LADS! LOOK UP AND SMELL THE COFFEE!

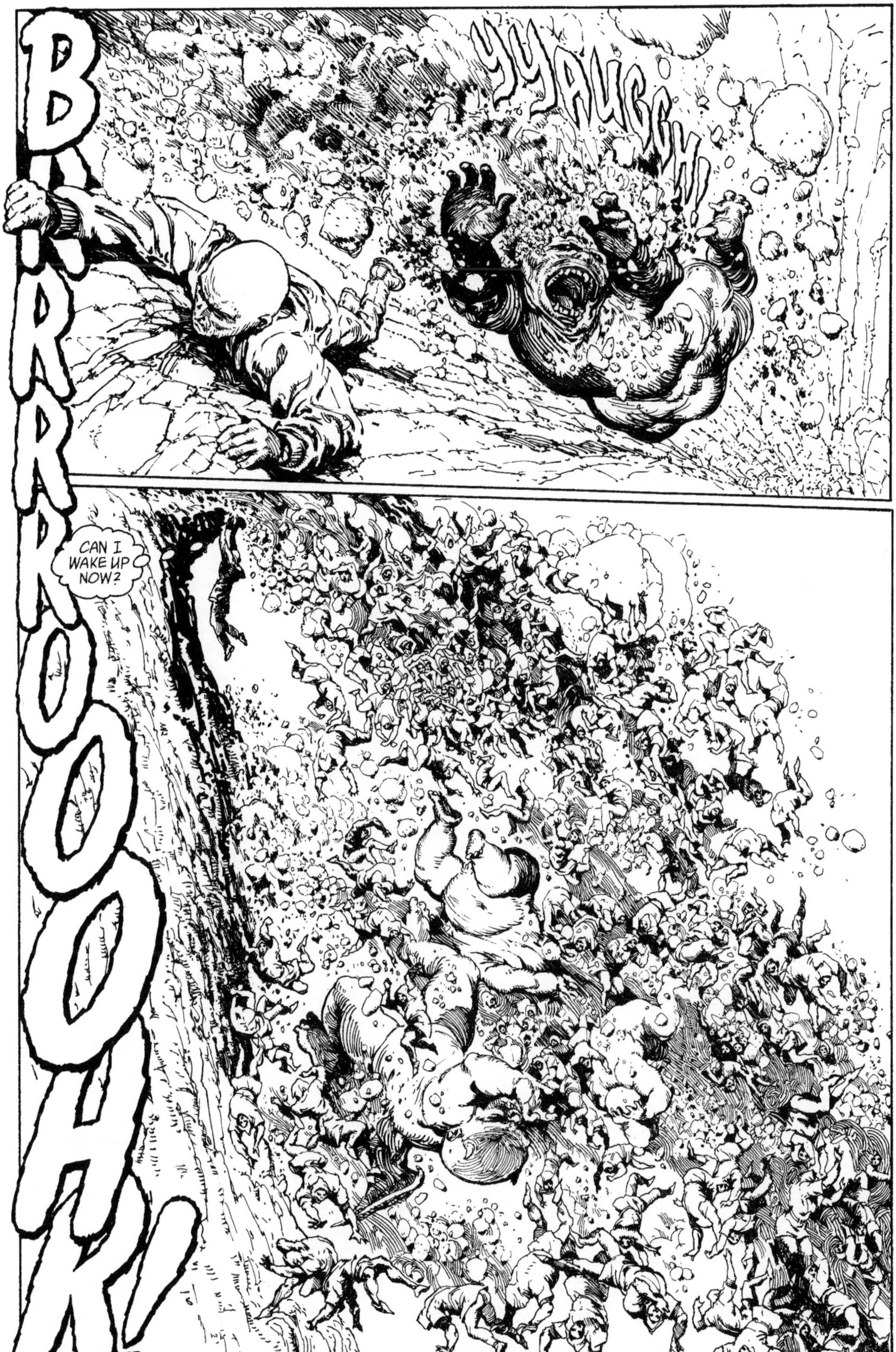
YYAUGGH!
CAN I WAKE UP NOW?

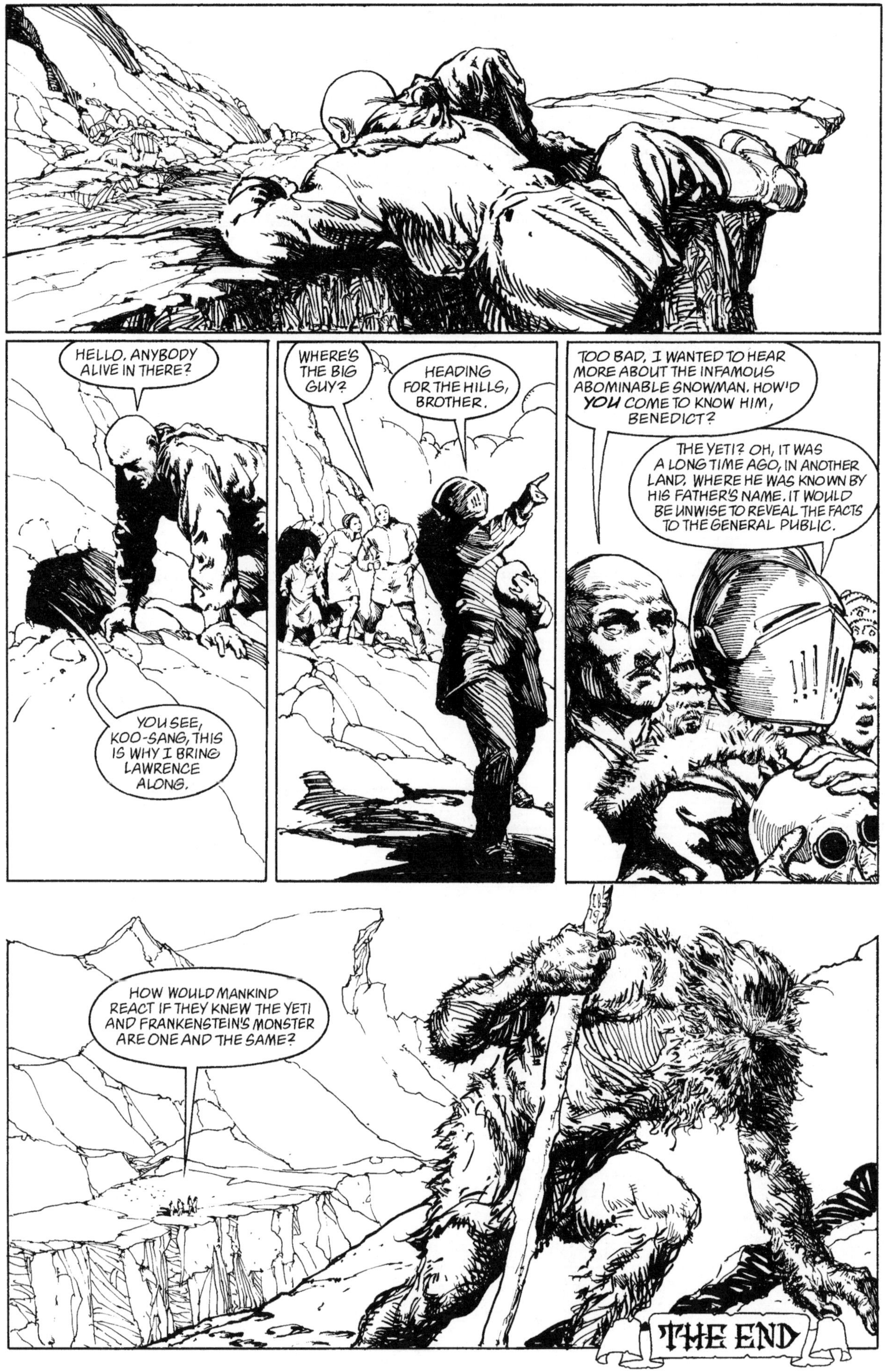
HELLO. ANYBODY ALIVE IN THERE?
YOU SEE, KOO-SANG, THIS IS WHY I BRING LAWRENCE ALONG.
WHERE'S THE BIG GUY?
HEADING FOR THE HILLS, BROTHER.
TOO BAD, I WANTED TO HEAR MORE ABOUT THE INFAMOUS ABOMINABLE SNOWMAN. HOW'D YOU COME TO KNOW HIM, BENEDICT?
THE YETI? OH, IT WAS A LONG TIME AGO, IN ANOTHER LAND, WHERE HE WAS KNOWN BY HIS FATHER'S NAME. IT WOULD BE UNWISE TO REVEAL THE FACTS TO THE GENERAL PUBLIC.
HOW WOULD MANKIND REACT IF THEY KNEW THE YETI AND FRANKENSTEIN'S MONSTER ARE ONE AND THE SAME?
THE END

O SINNER BENEATH US

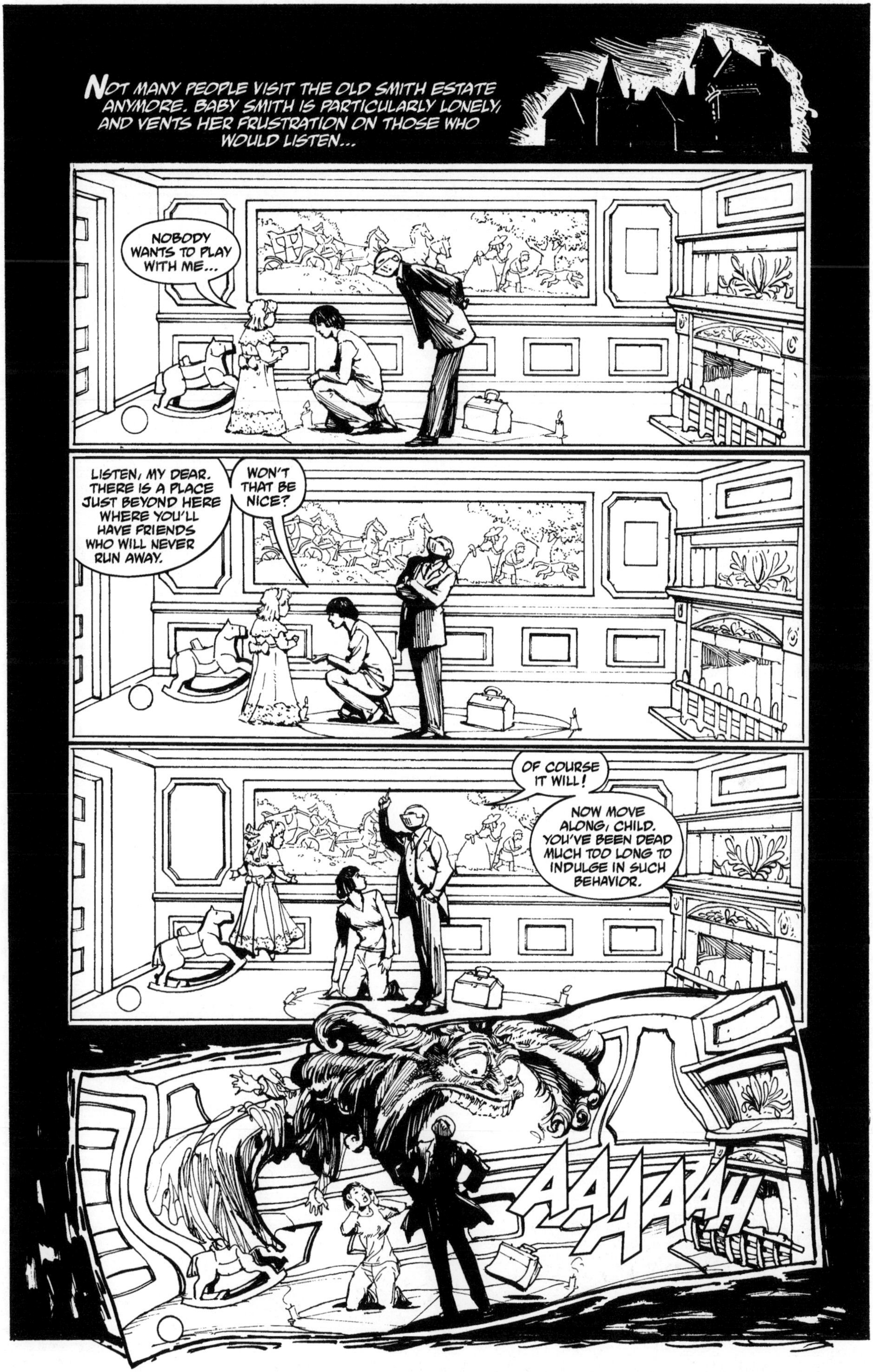
NOT MANY PEOPLE VISIT THE OLD SMITH ESTATE ANYMORE. BABY SMITH IS PARTICULARLY LONELY, AND VENTS HER FRUSTRATION ON THOSE WHO WOULD LISTEN...
NOBODY WANTS TO PLAY WITH ME...
LISTEN, MY DEAR. THERE IS A PLACE JUST BEYOND HERE WHERE YOU'LL HAVE FRIENDS WHO WILL NEVER RUN AWAY.
WON'T THAT BE NICE?
OF COURSE IT WILL!
NOW MOVE ALONG, CHILD. YOU'VE BEEN DEAD MUCH TOO LONG TO INDULGE IN SUCH BEHAVIOR.
AAAAAAH

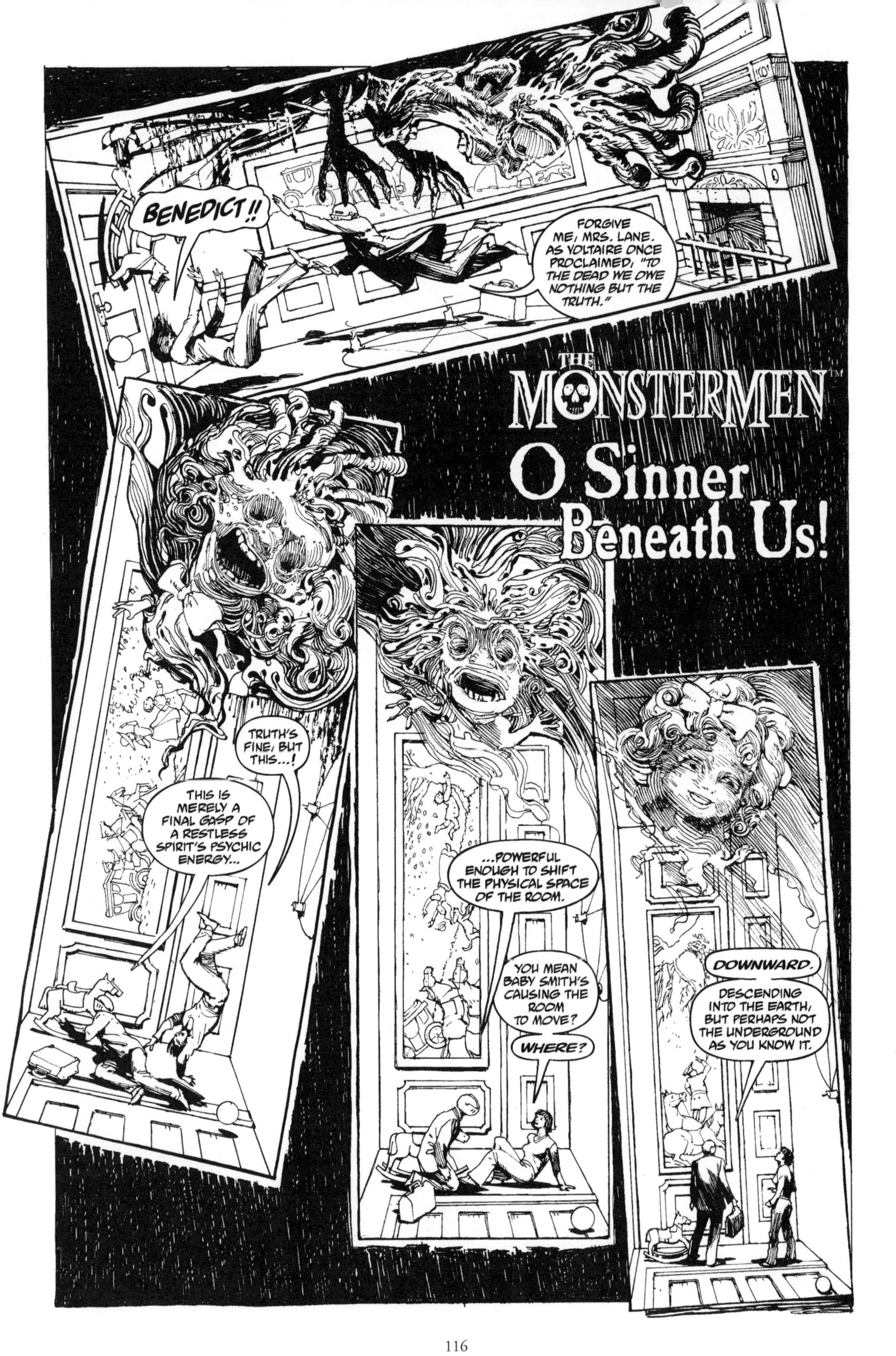

BENEDICT!!
FORGIVE ME, MRS. LANE. AS VOLTAIRE ONCE PROCLAIMED, "TO THE DEAD WE OWE NOTHING BUT THE TRUTH."
THE MONSTERMEN™
O Sinner Beneath Us!
TRUTH'S FINE, BUT THIS...!
THIS IS MERELY A FINAL GASP OF A RESTLESS SPIRIT'S PSYCHIC ENERGY...
...POWERFUL ENOUGH TO SHIFT THE PHYSICAL SPACE OF THE ROOM.
YOU MEAN BABY SMITH'S CAUSING THE ROOM TO MOVE?
WHERE?
DOWNWARD.
DESCENDING INTO THE EARTH, BUT PERHAPS NOT THE UNDERGROUND AS YOU KNOW IT.

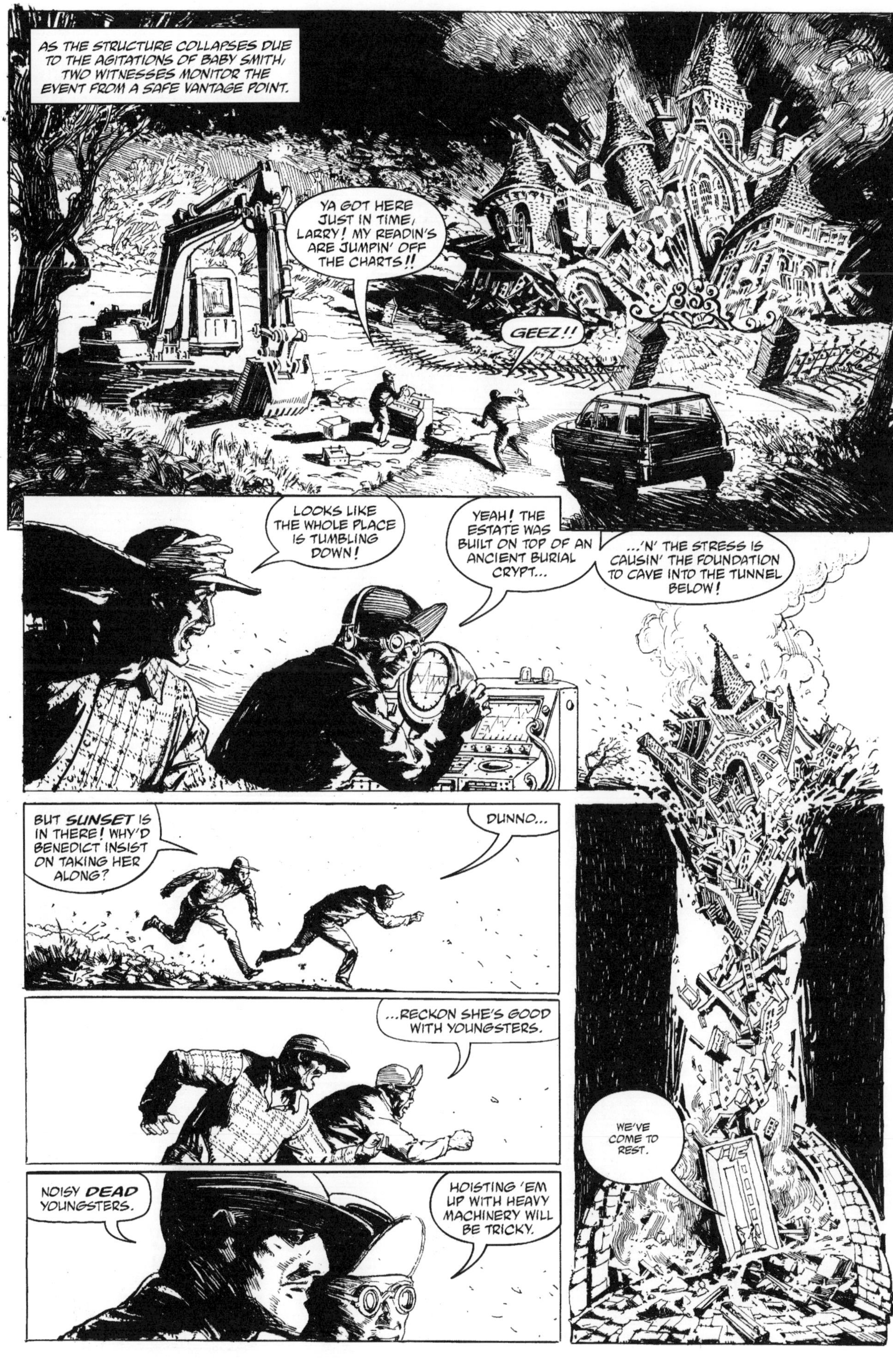
AS THE STRUCTURE COLLAPSES DUE TO THE AGITATIONS OF BABY SMITH, TWO WITNESSES MONITOR THE EVENT FROM A SAFE VANTAGE POINT.
YA GOT HERE JUST IN TIME, LARRY! MY READIN'S ARE JUMPIN' OFF THE CHARTS!!
GEEZ!!
LOOKS LIKE THE WHOLE PLACE IS TUMBLING DOWN!
YEAH! THE ESTATE WAS BUILT ON TOP OF AN ANCIENT BURIAL CRYPT...
...'N' THE STRESS IS CAUSIN' THE FOUNDATION TO CAVE INTO THE TUNNEL BELOW!
BUT SUNSET IS IN THERE! WHY'D BENEDICT INSIST ON TAKING HER ALONG?
DUNNO...
...RECKON SHE'S GOOD WITH YOUNGSTERS.
NOISY DEAD YOUNGSTERS.
HOISTING 'EM UP WITH HEAVY MACHINERY WILL BE TRICKY.
WE'VE COME TO REST.

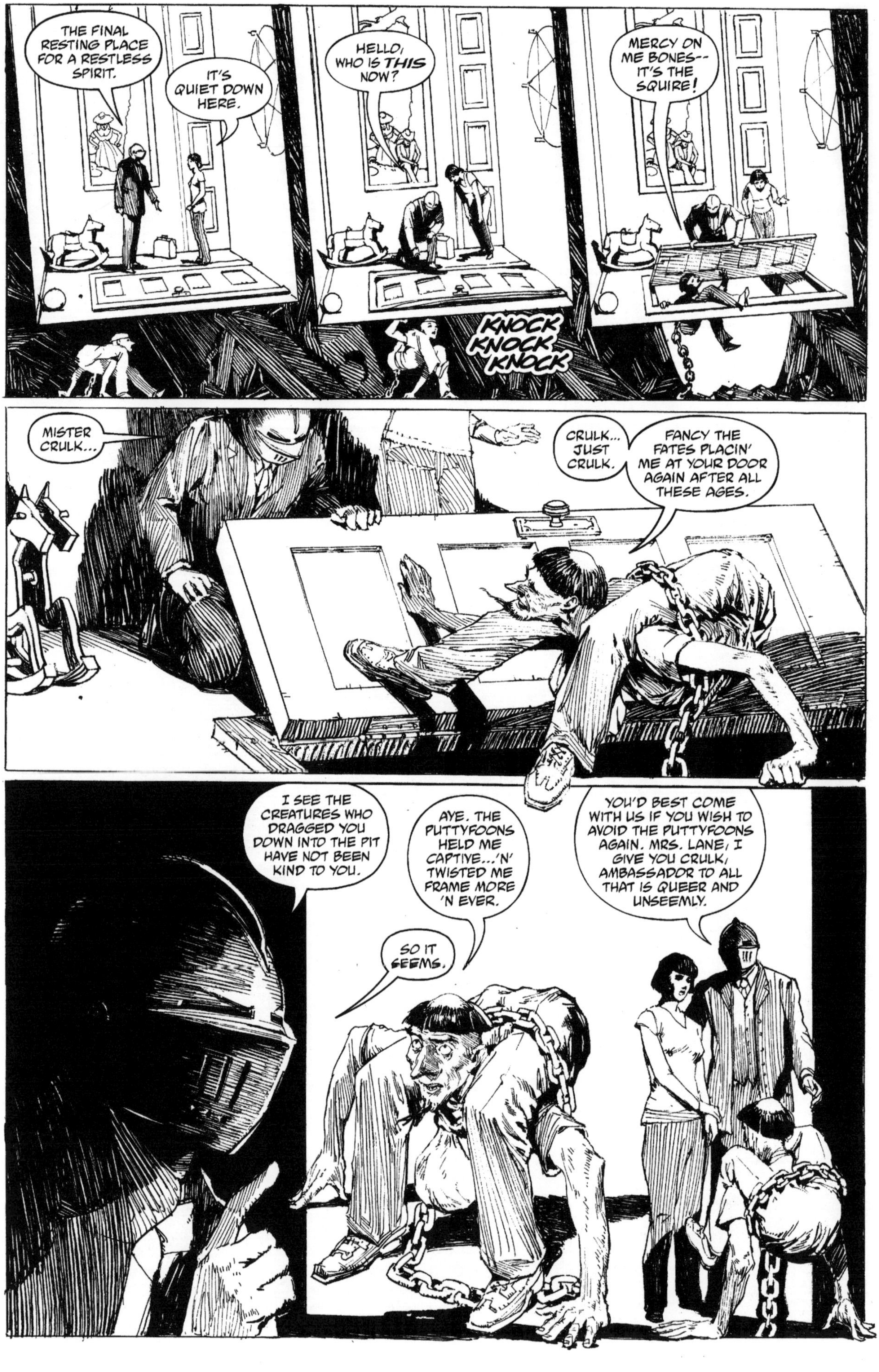
THE FINAL RESTING PLACE FOR A RESTLESS SPIRIT.
IT'S QUIET DOWN HERE.
HELLO, WHO IS THIS NOW?
MERCY ON ME BONES-- IT'S THE SQUIRE!
KNOCK KNOCK KNOCK
MISTER CRULK...
CRULK... JUST CRULK.
FANCY THE FATES PLACIN' ME AT YOUR DOOR AGAIN AFTER ALL THESE AGES.
I SEE THE CREATURES WHO DRAGGED YOU DOWN INTO THE PIT HAVE NOT BEEN KIND TO YOU.
AYE. THE PUTTYFOONS HELD ME CAPTIVE...'N' TWISTED ME FRAME MORE 'N EVER.
SO IT SEEMS.
YOU'D BEST COME WITH US IF YOU WISH TO AVOID THE PUTTYFOONS AGAIN. MRS. LANE, I GIVE YOU CRULK, AMBASSADOR TO ALL THAT IS QUEER AND UNSEEMLY.

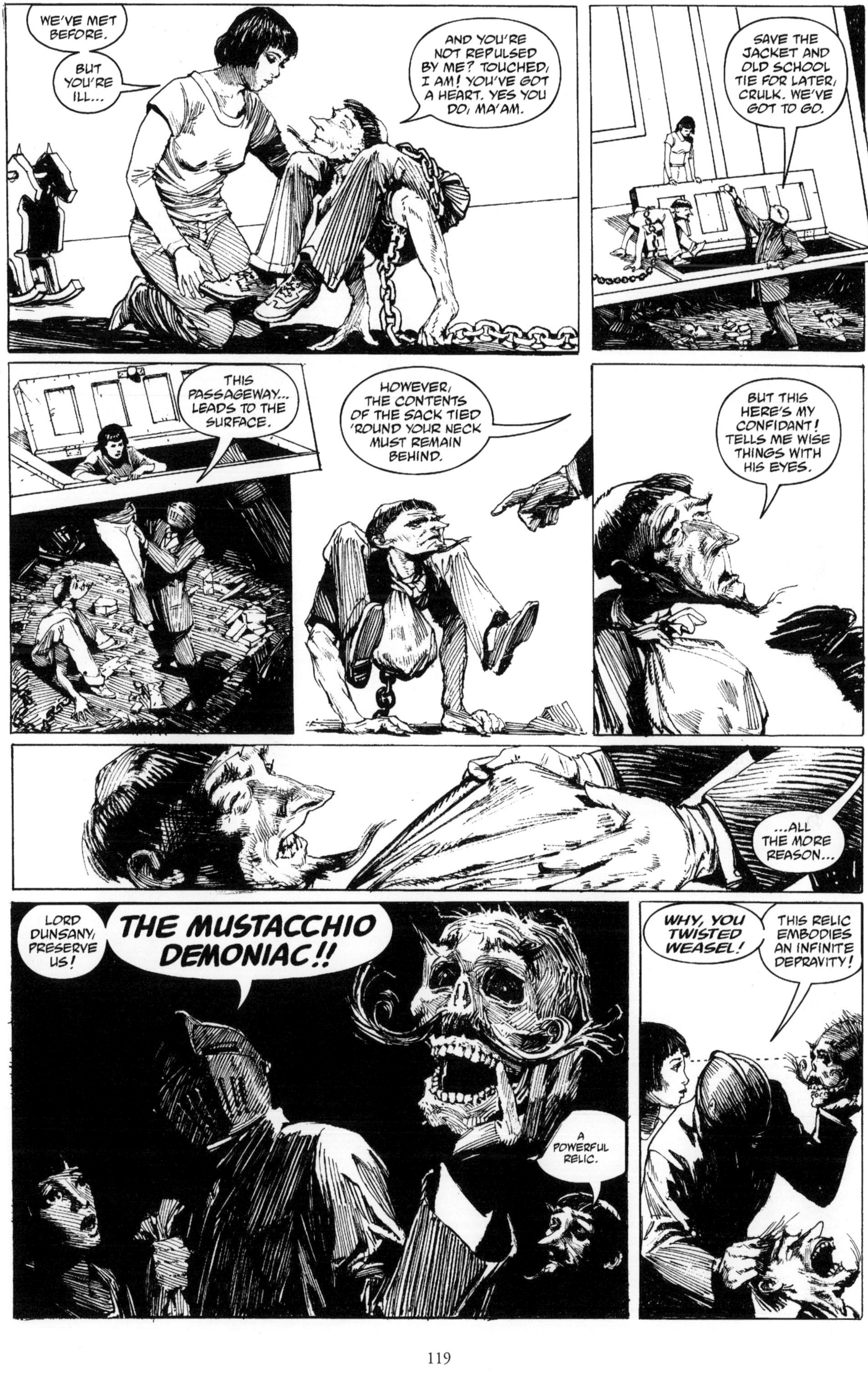
WE'VE MET BEFORE.
BUT YOU'RE ILL...
AND YOU'RE NOT REPULSED BY ME? TOUCHED, I AM! YOU'VE GOT A HEART. YES YOU DO, MA'AM.
SAVE THE JACKET AND OLD SCHOOL TIE FOR LATER, CRULK. WE'VE GOT TO GO.
THIS PASSAGEWAY... LEADS TO THE SURFACE.
HOWEVER, THE CONTENTS OF THE SACK TIED 'ROUND YOUR NECK MUST REMAIN BEHIND.
BUT THIS HERE'S MY CONFIDANT! TELLS ME WISE THINGS WITH HIS EYES.
...ALL THE MORE REASON...
LORD DUNSANY, PRESERVE US!
THE MUSTACCHIO DEMONIAC!!
A POWERFUL RELIC.
WHY, YOU TWISTED WEASEL!
THIS RELIC EMBODIES AN INFINITE DEPRAVITY!

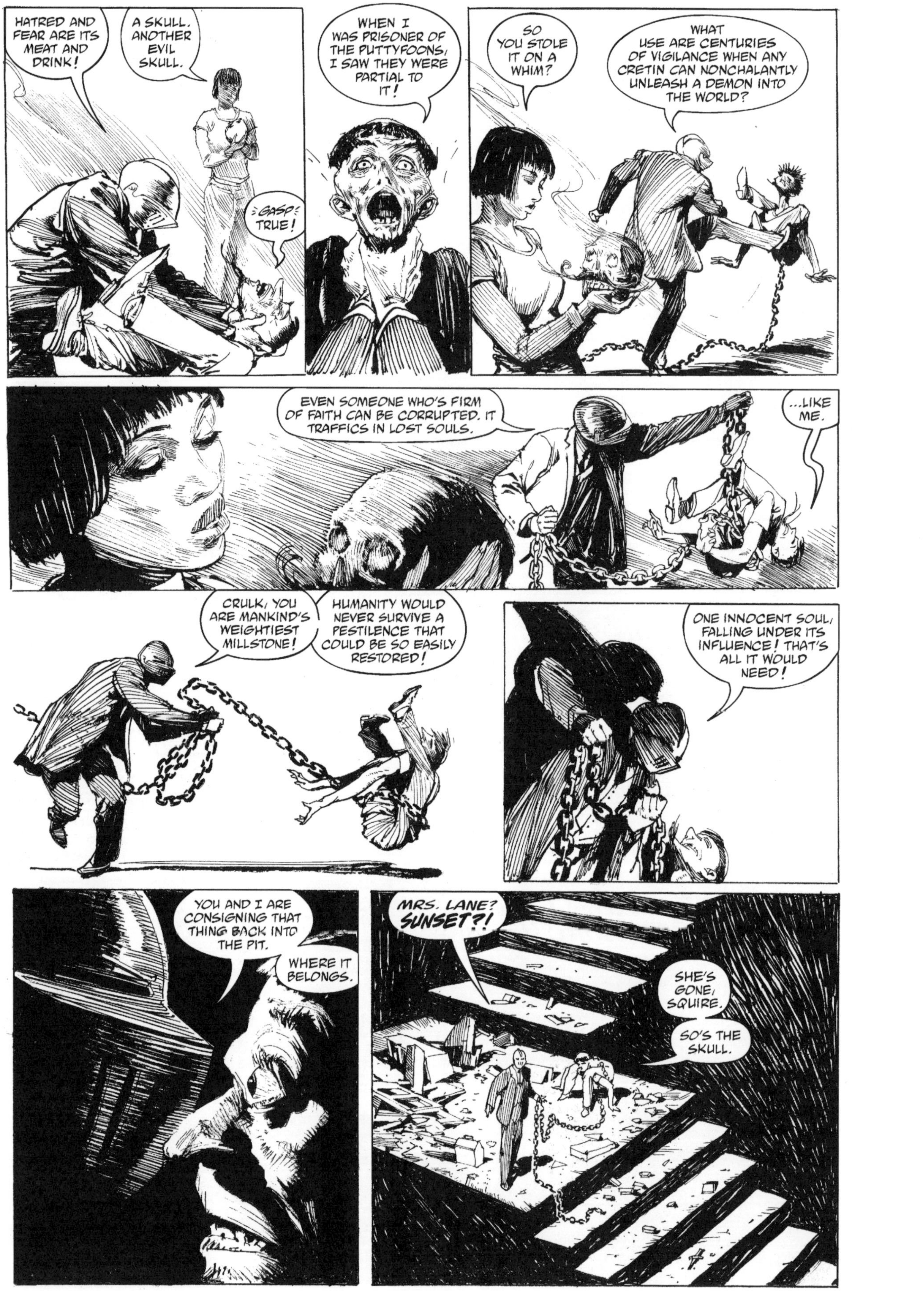
HATRED AND FEAR ARE ITS MEAT AND DRINK!
A SKULL. ANOTHER EVIL SKULL.
GASP TRUE!
WHEN I WAS PRISONER OF THE PUTTYFOONS, I SAW THEY WERE PARTIAL TO IT!
SO YOU STOLE IT ON A WHIM?
WHAT USE ARE CENTURIES OF VIGILANCE WHEN ANY CRETIN CAN NONCHALANTLY UNLEASH A DEMON INTO THE WORLD?
EVEN SOMEONE WHO'S FIRM OF FAITH CAN BE CORRUPTED. IT TRAFFICS IN LOST SOULS.
...LIKE ME.
CRULK, YOU ARE MANKIND'S WEIGHTIEST MILLSTONE!
HUMANITY WOULD NEVER SURVIVE A PESTILENCE THAT COULD BE SO EASILY RESTORED!
ONE INNOCENT SOUL, FALLING UNDER ITS INFLUENCE! THAT'S ALL IT WOULD NEED!
YOU AND I ARE CONSIGNING THAT THING BACK INTO THE PIT.
WHERE IT BELONGS.
MRS. LANE? SUNSET?!
SHE'S GONE, SQUIRE.
SO'S THE SKULL.

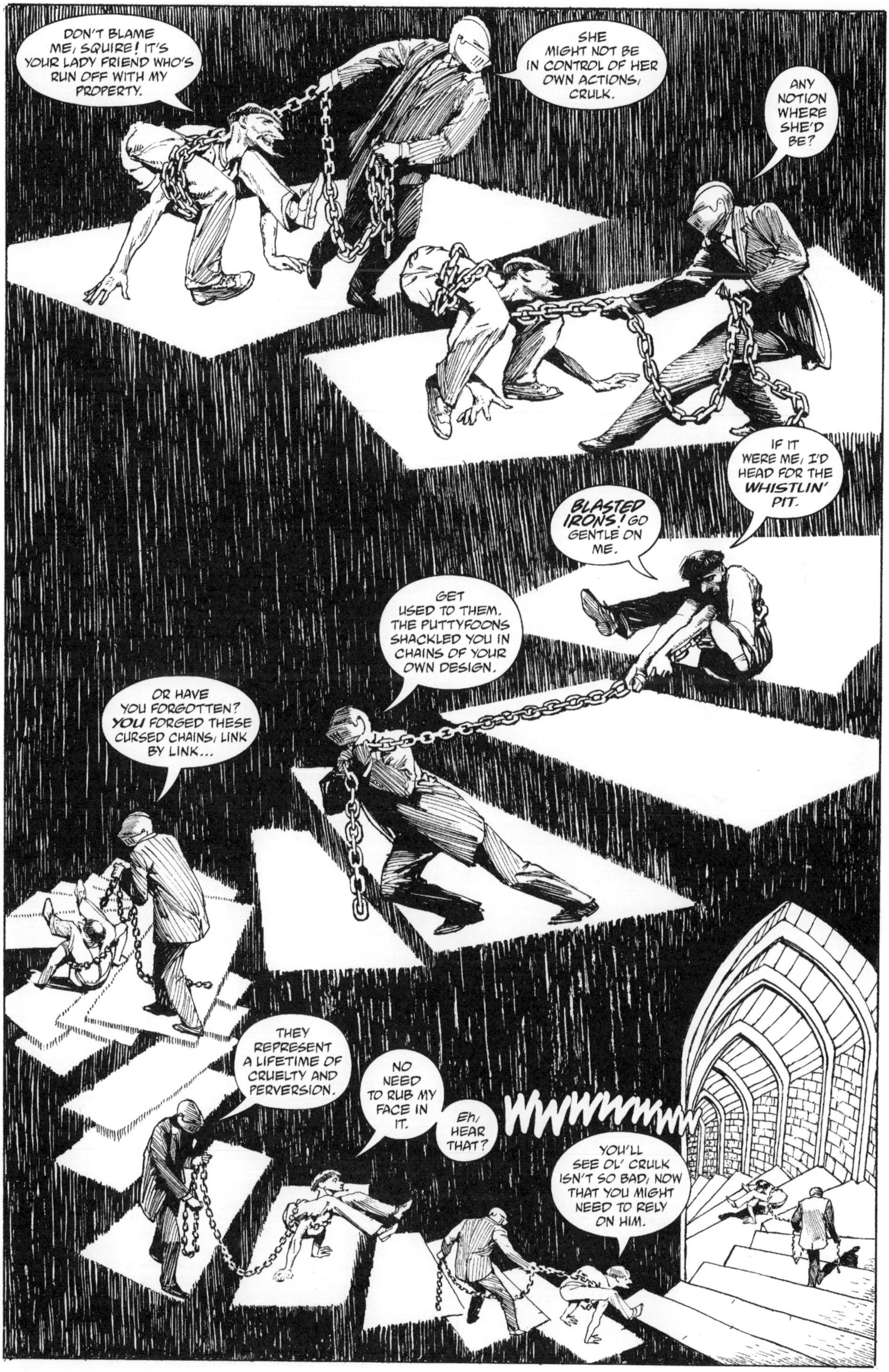
DON'T BLAME ME, SQUIRE! IT'S YOUR LADY FRIEND WHO'S RUN OFF WITH MY PROPERTY.
SHE MIGHT NOT BE IN CONTROL OF HER OWN ACTIONS, CRULK.
ANY NOTION WHERE SHE'D BE?
IF IT WERE ME, I'D HEAD FOR THE WHISTLIN' PIT.
BLASTED IRONS! GO GENTLE ON ME.
GET USED TO THEM. THE PUTTYFOONS SHACKLED YOU IN CHAINS OF YOUR OWN DESIGN.
OR HAVE YOU FORGOTTEN? YOU FORGED THESE CURSED CHAINS, LINK BY LINK...
THEY REPRESENT A LIFETIME OF CRUELTY AND PERVERSION.
NO NEED TO RUB MY FACE IN IT.
Eh, HEAR THAT?
WWWWWWWW
YOU'LL SEE OL' CRULK ISN'T SO BAD, NOW THAT YOU MIGHT NEED TO RELY ON HIM.

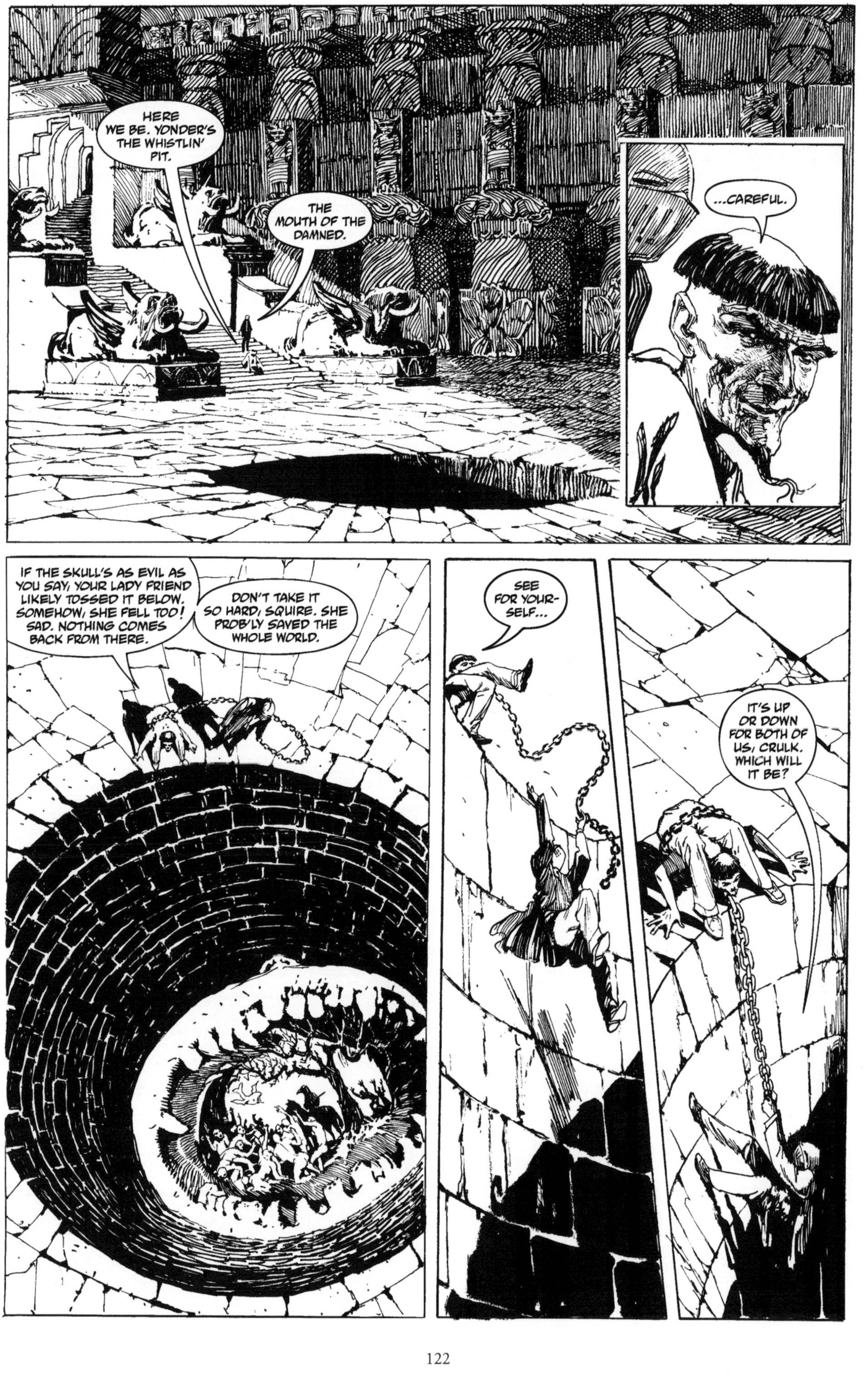
HERE WE BE. YONDER'S THE WHISTLIN' PIT.
THE MOUTH OF THE DAMNED.
...CAREFUL.
IF THE SKULL'S AS EVIL AS YOU SAY, YOUR LADY FRIEND LIKELY TOSSED IT BELOW. SOMEHOW, SHE FELL TOO! SAD. NOTHING COMES BACK FROM THERE.
DON'T TAKE IT SO HARD, SQUIRE. SHE PROB'LY SAVED THE WHOLE WORLD.
SEE FOR YOURSELF...
IT'S UP OR DOWN FOR BOTH OF US, CRULK. WHICH WILL IT BE?

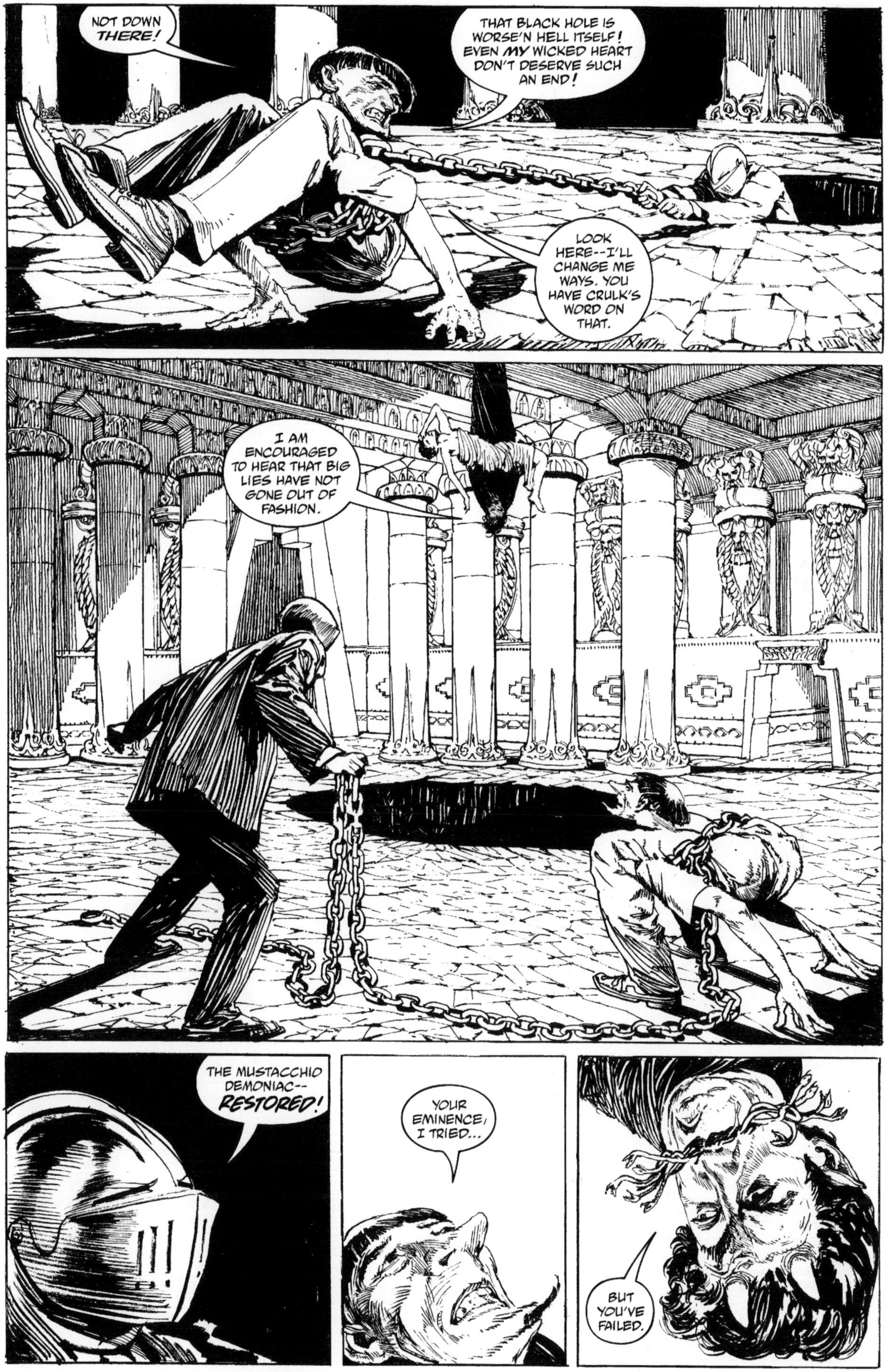
NOT DOWN THERE!
THAT BLACK HOLE IS WORSE'N HELL ITSELF! EVEN MY WICKED HEART DON'T DESERVE SUCH AN END!
LOOK HERE--I'LL CHANGE ME WAYS. YOU HAVE CRULK'S WORD ON THAT.
I AM ENCOURAGED TO HEAR THAT BIG LIES HAVE NOT GONE OUT OF FASHION.
THE MUSTACCHIO DEMONIAC-- RESTORED!
YOUR EMINENCE, I TRIED...
BUT YOU'VE FAILED.

YOU FAILED TO DESTROY AN ENEMY.

WHUMP

HOWEVER, IT WAS THROUGH YOUR DECEIT THAT AN INNOCENT BECAME THE MEANS OF MY REJUVENATION.

COME! YOU MAY PROVE SOME WORTH AS I GO ABROAD TO GATHER MY FLOCK.

IT WILL MAKE MY NEXT TERRITORIAL CLAIM THAT MUCH EASIER.

NOT SO FAST, CRULK. YOU HEARD THE MAESTRO...

YOU'RE FINALLY CALLED UPON...

...FOR A USEFUL...

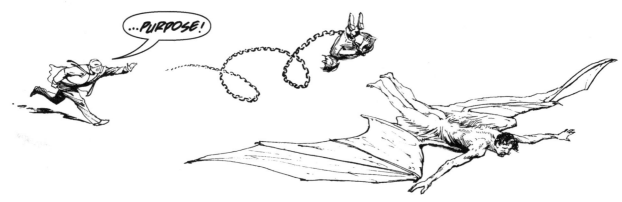

...PURPOSE!

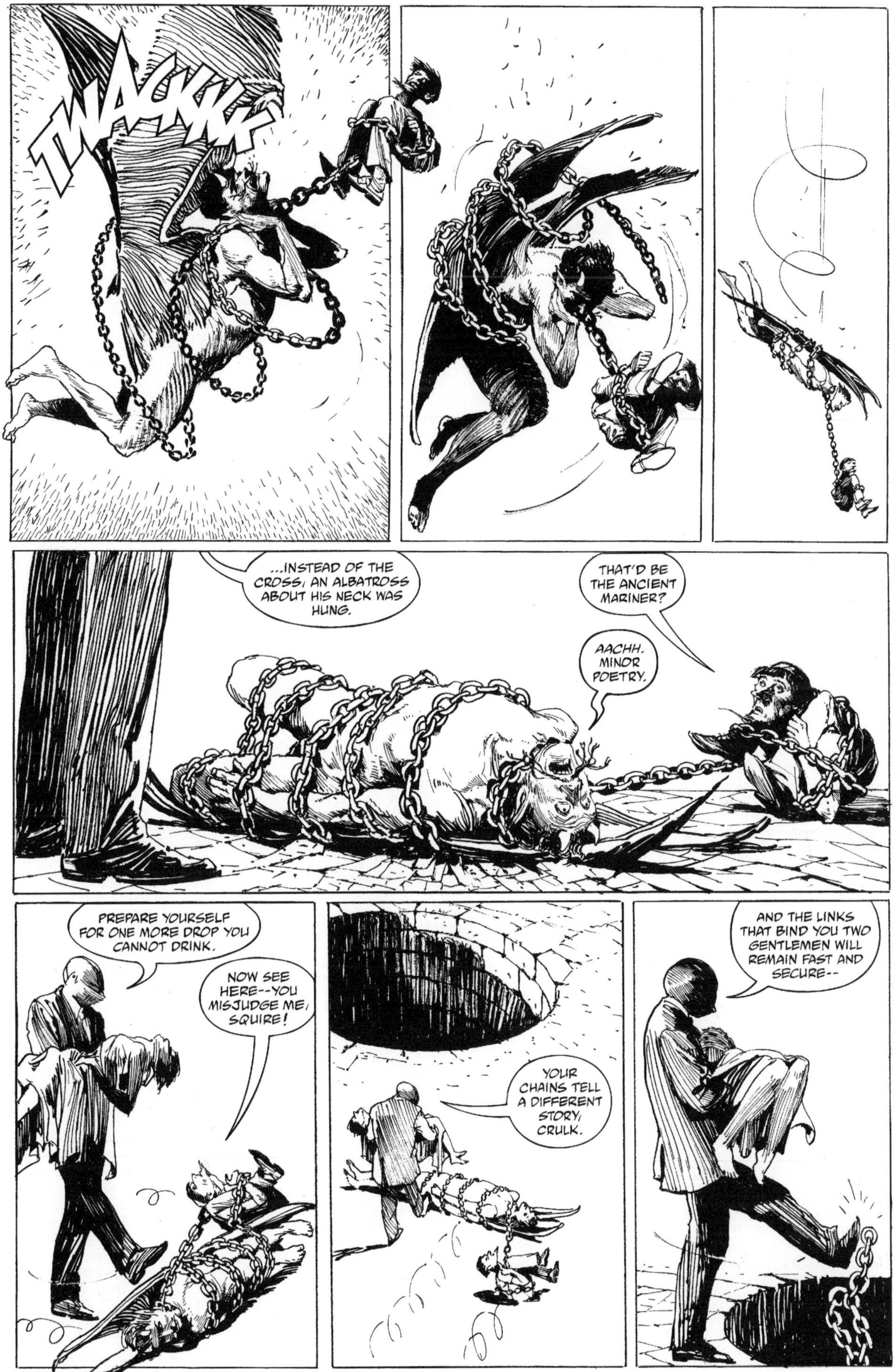
TWACKK
...INSTEAD OF THE CROSS, AN ALBATROSS ABOUT HIS NECK WAS HUNG.
THAT'D BE THE ANCIENT MARINER?
AACHH. MINOR POETRY.
PREPARE YOURSELF FOR ONE MORE DROP YOU CANNOT DRINK.
NOW SEE HERE--YOU MISJUDGE ME, SQUIRE!
YOUR CHAINS TELL A DIFFERENT STORY, CRULK.
AND THE LINKS THAT BIND YOU TWO GENTLEMEN WILL REMAIN FAST AND SECURE--

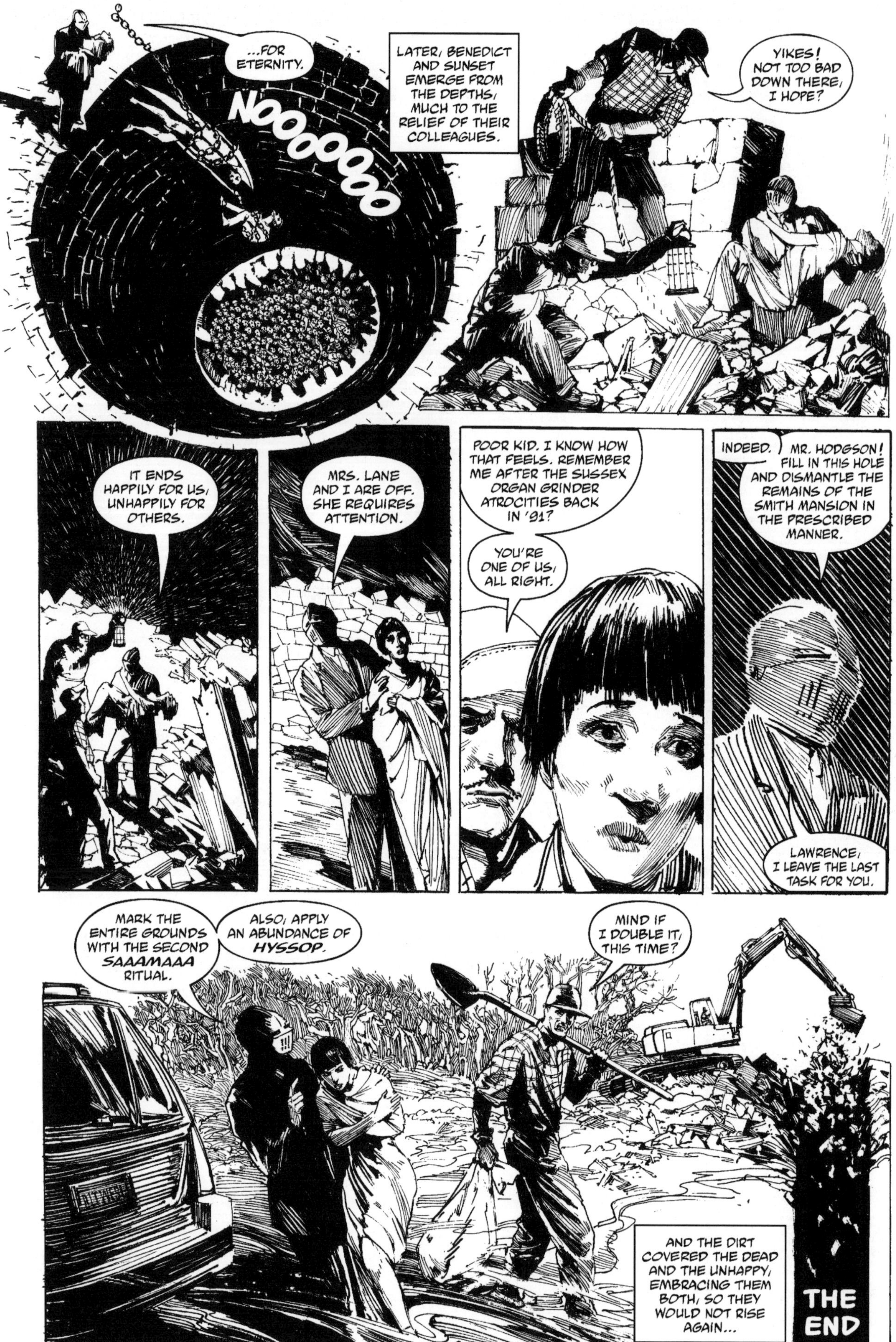

...FOR ETERNITY.
NOOOOOOOO
LATER, BENEDICT AND SUNSET EMERGE FROM THE DEPTHS, MUCH TO THE RELIEF OF THEIR COLLEAGUES.
YIKES! NOT TOO BAD DOWN THERE, I HOPE?
IT ENDS HAPPILY FOR US, UNHAPPILY FOR OTHERS.
MRS. LANE AND I ARE OFF. SHE REQUIRES ATTENTION.
POOR KID. I KNOW HOW THAT FEELS. REMEMBER ME AFTER THE SUSSEX ORGAN GRINDER ATROCITIES BACK IN '91?
YOU'RE ONE OF US, ALL RIGHT.
INDEED.
MR. HODGSON! FILL IN THIS HOLE AND DISMANTLE THE REMAINS OF THE SMITH MANSION IN THE PRESCRIBED MANNER.
LAWRENCE, I LEAVE THE LAST TASK FOR YOU.
MARK THE ENTIRE GROUNDS WITH THE SECOND SAAAMAAA RITUAL.
ALSO, APPLY AN ABUNDANCE OF HYSSOP.
MIND IF I DOUBLE IT, THIS TIME?
AND THE DIRT COVERED THE DEAD AND THE UNHAPPY, EMBRACING THEM BOTH, SO THEY WOULD NOT RISE AGAIN...
THE END

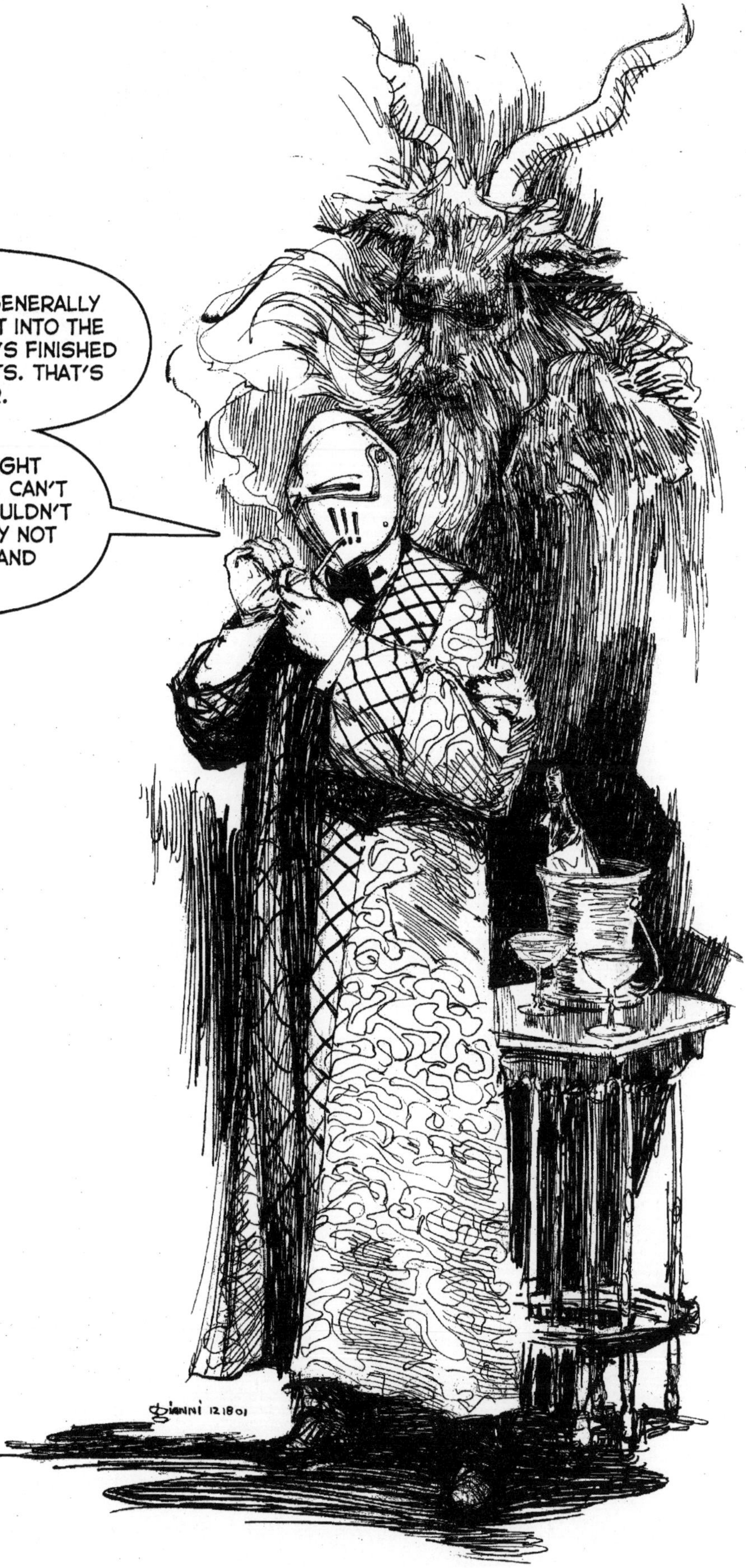
AN OCCULT DETECTIVE GENERALLY BOOTS HIS AUDIENCE OUT INTO THE COLD NIGHT AIR AFTER HE'S FINISHED RECOUNTING HIS EXPLOITS. THAT'S WHERE I DIFFER.
THERE'S SOMETHING DOWNRIGHT TERRIFYING IN THE AIR TONIGHT. CAN'T YOU FEEL IT? PERHAPS YOU SHOULDN'T VENTURE OUT IN THE DARK. WHY NOT TAKE A SEAT NEAR THE FIRE AND THUMB THROUGH SOME...

OTHER SCARY STORIES

Carnacki, the Ghost-Finder

in William Hope Hodgson's

THE GATEWAY OF THE MONSTER

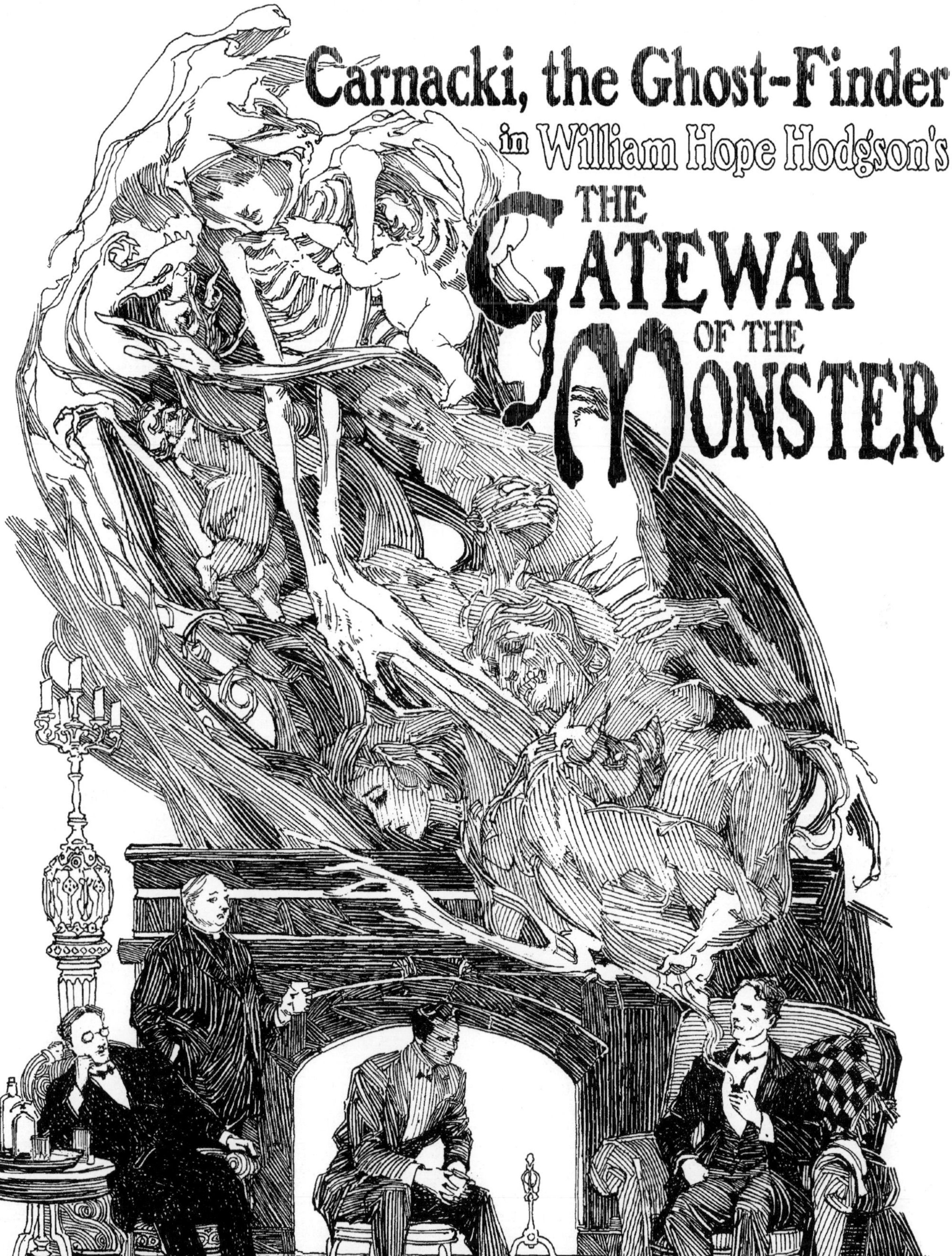

gianni

(Thomas Carnacki, the famous investigator of "real" ghost stories, tells here his incredibly weird experience in the Electric Pentacle.)

From *The Idler*, January 1910

I N RESPONSE TO CARNACKI'S USUAL card of invitation to have dinner and listen to a story, I arrived promptly at No. 427, Cheyne Walk, to find the three others who were always invited to these happy little times, there before me. Five minutes later, Carnacki, Arkright, Jessop, Taylor and I were all engaged in the "pleasant occupation" of dining.

"You've not been long away, this time," I remarked, as I finished my soup; forgetting momentarily, Carnacki's dislike of being asked even to skirt the borders of his story until such time as he was ready. Then he would not stint words.

"That's all," he replied, with brevity; and I changed the subject, remarking that I had been buying a new gun, to which piece of news he gave an intelligent nod, and a smile which I think showed a genuinely good-humoured appreciation of my intentional changing of the conversation.

Later, when dinner was finished, Carnacki snugged himself comfortably down in his big chair, along with his pipe, and began his story, with very little circumlocution:—

"As Dodgson was remarking just now, I've only been away a short time, and for a very good reason too—I've only been away a short distance. The exact locality I am afraid I must not tell you; but it is less than twenty miles from here; though, except for changing a name, that won't spoil the story. And it *is* a story too! One of the most extraordinary things ever I have run against.

"I received a letter a fortnight ago from a man I must call Anderson, asking for an appointment. I arranged a time, and when he came, I found that he wished me to investigate, and see whether I could not clear up a long-standing and well—too well—authenticated case of what he termed 'haunting.' He gave me very full particulars, and, finally, as the thing seemed to present something unique, I decided to take it up.

"Two days later, I drove to the house, late in the afternoon. I found it a very old place, standing quite alone in its own grounds.

Anderson had left a letter with the butler, I found, pleading excuses for his absence, and leaving the whole house at my disposal for my investigations. The butler evidently knew the object of my visit, and I questioned him pretty thoroughly during dinner, which I had in rather lonely state. He is an old and privileged servant, and had the history of the Grey Room exact in detail. From him I learned more particulars regarding two things that Anderson had mentioned in but a casual manner. The first was that the door of the Grey Room would be heard in the dead of night to open, and slam heavily, and this even though the butler knew it was locked, and the key on the bunch in his pantry. The second was that the bedclothes would always be found torn off the bed, and hurled in a heap into a corner.

"But it was the door slamming that chiefly bothered the old butler. Many and many a time, he told me, had he lain awake and just got shivering with fright, listening; for sometimes the door would be slammed time after time—thud! thud! thud!—so that sleep was impossible.

"From Anderson, I knew already that the room had a history extending back over a hundred and fifty years. Three people had been strangled in it—an ancestor of his and his wife and child. This is authentic, as I had taken very great pains to discover; so that you can imagine it was with a feeling I had a striking case to investigate, that I went upstairs after dinner to have a look at the Grey Room.

"Peter, the old butler, was in rather a state about my going, and assured me with much solemnity that in all the twenty years of his service, no one had ever entered that room after nightfall. He begged me, in quite a fatherly way, to wait till the morning, when there would be no danger, and then he could accompany me himself.

"Of course, I smiled a little at him, and told him not to bother. I explained that I should do no more than look round a bit, and, perhaps, affix a few seals. He need not fear; I was used to that sort of thing. But he shook his head, when I said that.

" 'There isn't many ghosts like ours, sir,' he assured me, with mournful pride. And, by Jove! he was right, as you will see.

"I took a couple of candles, and Peter followed, with his bunch of keys. He unlocked the door; but would not come inside with me. He was evidently in a fright, and he renewed his request, that I would put off my examination, until daylight. Of course, I laughed at him again, and told him he could stand sentry at the door, and catch anything that came out.

" 'It never comes outside, sir,' he said, in his funny, old, solemn manner. Somehow, he managed to make me feel as if I were going to have the 'creeps' right away. Anyway, it was one to him, you know.

"I left him there, and examined the room. It is a big apartment, and well furnished in the grand style, with a huge four-poster, which stands with its head to the end wall. There were two candles on the mantelpiece, and two on each of the three tables that were in the room. I lit the lot, and after that, the room felt a little less inhumanly dreary; though, mind you, it was quite fresh, and well kept in every way.

"After I had taken a good look round, I sealed lengths of *bebe* ribbon across the windows, along the walls, over the pictures, and over the fireplace and the wall-closets. All the time, as I worked, the butler stood just without the door, and I could not persuade him to enter; though I jested him a little, as I stretched the ribbons, and went here and there about my work. Every now and again, he would say:—'You'll excuse me, I'm sure, sir; but I do wish you would come out, sir. I'm fair in a quake for you.'

"I told him he need not wait; but he was loyal enough in his way to what he considered his duty. He said he could not go away and leave me all alone there. He apologised; but made it very clear that I did not realise the danger of the room; and I could see, generally, that he was in a pretty frightened state. All the same, I had to make the room so that I should know if anything material entered it; so I asked him not to bother me, unless he really heard or saw something. He was beginning to get on my nerves, and the 'feel' of the room was bad enough, without making it any nastier.

"For a time further, I worked, stretching ribbons across the floor, and sealing them, so that the merest touch would have broken them, were anyone to venture into the room in the dark with the intention of playing the fool. All this had taken me far longer than I had anticipated; and, suddenly, I heard a clock strike eleven. I had taken off my coat soon after commencing work; now, however, as I had practically made an end of all that I intended to do, I walked across to the settee, and picked it up. I was in the act of getting into it, when the old butler's voice (he had not said a word for the last hour) came sharp and frightened:—'Come out, sir, quick! There's something going to happen!' Jove! but I jumped, and then, in the same moment, one of the candles on the table to the left went out. Now whether it was the wind, or what, I do not know; but, just for a moment, I was enough startled to make a run for the door; though I am glad to say that I pulled up, before I reached it. I simply could not bunk out, with the butler standing there, after having, as it were, read him a sort of lesson on 'bein' brave, y'know.' So I just turned right round, picked up the two candles off the mantelpiece, and

walked across to the table near the bed. Well, I saw nothing. I blew out the candle that was still alight; then I went to those on the two tables, and blew them out. Then, outside of the door, the old man called again:—'Oh! sir, do be told! Do be told!'

" 'All right, Peter,' I said, and by Jove, my voice was not as steady as I should have liked! I made for the door, and had a bit of work, not to start running. I took some thundering long strides, as you can imagine. Near the door, I had a sudden feeling that there was a cold wind in the room. It was almost as if the window had been suddenly opened a little. I got to the door, and the old butler gave back a step, in a sort of instinctive way. 'Collar the candles, Peter!' I said, pretty sharply, and shoved them into his hands. I turned, and caught the handle, and slammed the door shut with a crash. Somehow, do you know, as I did so, I thought I felt something pull back on it; but it must have been only fancy. I turned the key in the lock, and then again, double-locking the door. I felt easier

then, and set-to and sealed the door. In addition, I put my card over the keyhole, and sealed it there; after which I pocketed the key, and went downstairs—with Peter; who was nervous and silent, leading the way. Poor old beggar! It had not struck me until that moment that he had been enduring a considerable strain during the last two or three hours.

"About midnight, I went to bed. My room lay at the end of the corridor upon which opens the door of the Grey Room. I counted the doors between it and mine, and found that five rooms lay between. And I am sure you can understand that I was not sorry. Then, just as I was beginning to undress, an idea came to me, and I took my candle and sealing wax, and sealed the doors of all five rooms. If any door slammed in the night, I should know just which one.

"I returned to my room, locked the door, and went to bed. I was waked suddenly from a deep sleep by a loud crash somewhere

glad as any lost child to have a live human being close to me. 'Where are you off to with the refreshments?'

"The old man gave a start, and slopped some of the coffee. He stared up at me, and I could see that he looked white and done-up. He came on up the stairs, and held out the little tray to me. 'I'm very thankful indeed, sir, to see you safe and well,' he said. 'I feared, one time, you might risk going into the Grey Room, sir. I've lain awake all night, with the sound of the Door. And when it came light, I thought I'd make you a cup of coffee. I knew you would want to look at the seals, and somehow it seems safer if there's two, sir.'

" 'Peter,' I said, 'you're a brick. This is very thoughtful of you.' And I drank the coffee. 'Come along,' I told him, and handed him back the tray. 'I'm going to have a look at what the Brutes have been up to. I simply hadn't the pluck to in the night.'

" 'I'm very thankful, sir,' he replied. 'Flesh and blood can do nothing, sir, against devils; and that's what's in the Grey Room after dark.'

"I examined the seals on all the doors, as I went along, and found them right; but when I got to the Grey Room, the seal was broken; though the card, over the keyhole, was untouched. I ripped it off, and unlocked the door, and went in, rather cautiously, as you can imagine; but the whole room was empty of anything to frighten one, and there was heaps of light. I examined all my seals, and not a single one was disturbed. The old butler had followed me in, and, suddenly, he called out:—'The bedclothes, sir!'

"I ran up to the bed, and looked over; and, surely, they were lying in the corner to the left of the bed. Jove! you can imagine how queer I felt. Something *had* been in the room. I stared for a while, from the bed, to the clothes on the floor. I had a feeling that I did not want to touch either. Old Peter, though, did not seem to be affected that way. He went over to the bed-coverings, and was going to pick them up, as, doubtless, he had done every day these twenty years back; but I stopped him. I wanted nothing

out in the passage. I sat up in bed, and listened, but heard nothing. Then I lit my candle. I was in the very act of lighting it when there came the bang of a door being violently slammed, along the corridor. I jumped out of bed and got my revolver. I unlocked the door, and went out into the passage, holding my candle high, and keeping the pistol ready. Then a queer thing happened. I could not go a step towards the Grey Room. You all know I am not really a cowardly chap. I've gone into too many cases connected with ghostly things, to be accused of that; but I tell you I funked it; simply funked it, just like any blessed kid. There was something precious unholy in the air that night. I ran back into my bedroom, and shut and locked the door. Then I sat on the bed all night, and listened to the dismal thudding of a door up the corridor. The sound seemed to echo through all the house.

"Daylight came at last, and I washed and dressed. The door had not slammed for about an hour, and I was getting back my nerve again. I felt ashamed of myself; though, in some ways it was silly; for when you're meddling with that sort of thing, your nerve is bound to go, sometimes. And you just have to sit quiet and call yourself a coward until daylight. Sometimes it is more than just cowardice, I fancy. I believe at times it is Something warning you, and fighting *for* you. But, all the same, I always feel mean and miserable, after a time like that.

"When the day came properly, I opened my door, and, keeping my revolver handy, went quietly along the passage. I had to pass the head of the stairs, along the way, and who should I see coming up, but the old butler, carrying a cup of coffee. He had merely tucked his nightshirt into his trousers, and he had an old pair of carpet slippers on.

" 'Hullo, Peter!' I said, feeling suddenly cheerful; for I was as touched, until I had finished my examination. This, I must have spent a full hour over, and then I let Peter straighten up the bed; after which we went out, and I locked the door; for the room was getting on my nerves.

"I had a short walk, and then breakfast; after which I felt more my own man, and so returned to the Grey Room, and, with Peter's help, and one of the maids, I had everything taken out of the room, except the bed—even the very pictures. I examined the walls, floor and ceiling then, with probe, hammer and magnifying glass; but found nothing suspicious. And I can assure you, I began to realise, in very truth, that some incredible thing had been loose in the room during the past night. I sealed up everything again, and went out, locking and sealing the door, as before.

"After dinner, Peter and I unpacked some of my stuff, and I fixed up my camera and flashlight opposite to the door of the Grey Room, with a string from the trigger of the flashlight to the door. Then, you see, if the door were really opened, the flashlight would blare out, and there would be, possibly, a very queer picture to examine in the morning. The last thing I did, before leaving, was to uncap the lens; and after that I went off to my bedroom, and to bed; for I intended to be up at midnight; and to ensure this, I set my little alarm to call me; also I left my candle burning.

"The clock woke me at twelve, and I got up and into my dressing-gown and slippers. I shoved my revolver into my right side-pocket, and opened my door. Then, I lit my dark-room lamp, and withdrew the slide, so that it would give a clear light. I carried it up the corridor, about thirty feet, and put it down on the floor, with the open side away from me, so that it would show me anything that might approach along the dark passage. Then I went back, and sat in the doorway of my room, with my revolver handy, staring up the passage towards the place where I knew my camera stood outside the door of the Grey Room.

"I should think I had watched for about an hour and a half, when, suddenly, I heard a faint noise, away up the corridor. I was immediately conscious of a queer prickling sensation about the back of my head, and my hands began to sweat a little. The following instant, the whole end of the passage flicked into sight in the abrupt glare of the flashlight. There came the succeeding darkness, and I peered nervously up the corridor, listening tensely, and trying to find what lay beyond the faint glow of my dark-lamp, which now seemed ridiculously dim by contrast with the tremendous blaze of the flash-powder . . . . And then, as I stooped forward, staring and listening, there came the crashing thud of the door of the Grey Room. The sound seemed to fill the whole of the large corridor, and go echoing hollowly through the house. I tell you, I felt horrible—as if my bones were water. Simply beastly. Jove! how I did stare, and how I listened. And then it came again—thud! thud! thud!—and then a silence that was almost worse than the noise of the door; for I kept fancying that some awful thing was stealing upon me along the corridor. And then, suddenly, my lamp was put out, and I could not see a yard before me. I realised all at once that I was doing a very silly thing, sitting there, and I jumped up. Even as I did so, I *thought* I heard a sound in the passage, and quite *near* me. I made one backward spring into my room, and slammed and locked the door. I sat on my bed, and stared at the door. I had my revolver in my hand; but it seemed an abominably useless thing. I felt that there was something the other side of that door. For some unknown reason I *knew* it was pressed up against the door, and it was soft. That was just what I thought. Most extraordinary thing to think.

"Presently I got hold of myself a bit, and marked out a pentacle hurriedly with chalk on the polished floor; and there I sat in it almost until dawn. And all the time, away up the corridor, the door of the Grey Room thudded at solemn and horrid intervals. It was a miserable, brutal night.

"When the day began to break, the thudding of the door came gradually to an end, and, at last, I got hold of my courage, and went along the corridor, in the half light, to cap the lens of my camera. I can tell you, it took some doing; but if I had not done so my photograph would have been spoilt, and I was tremendously keen to save it. I got back to my room, and then set-to and rubbed out the five-pointed star in which I had been sitting.

"Half an hour later there was a tap at my door. It was Peter with my coffee. When I had drunk it, we both went along to the Grey Room. As we went, I had a look at the seals on the other doors; but they were untouched. The seal on the door of the Grey Room was broken, as also was the string from the trigger of the flashlight; but the card over the keyhole was still there. I ripped it off, and opened the door. Nothing unusual was to be seen until we came to the bed; then I saw that, as on the previous day, the bedclothes had been torn off,

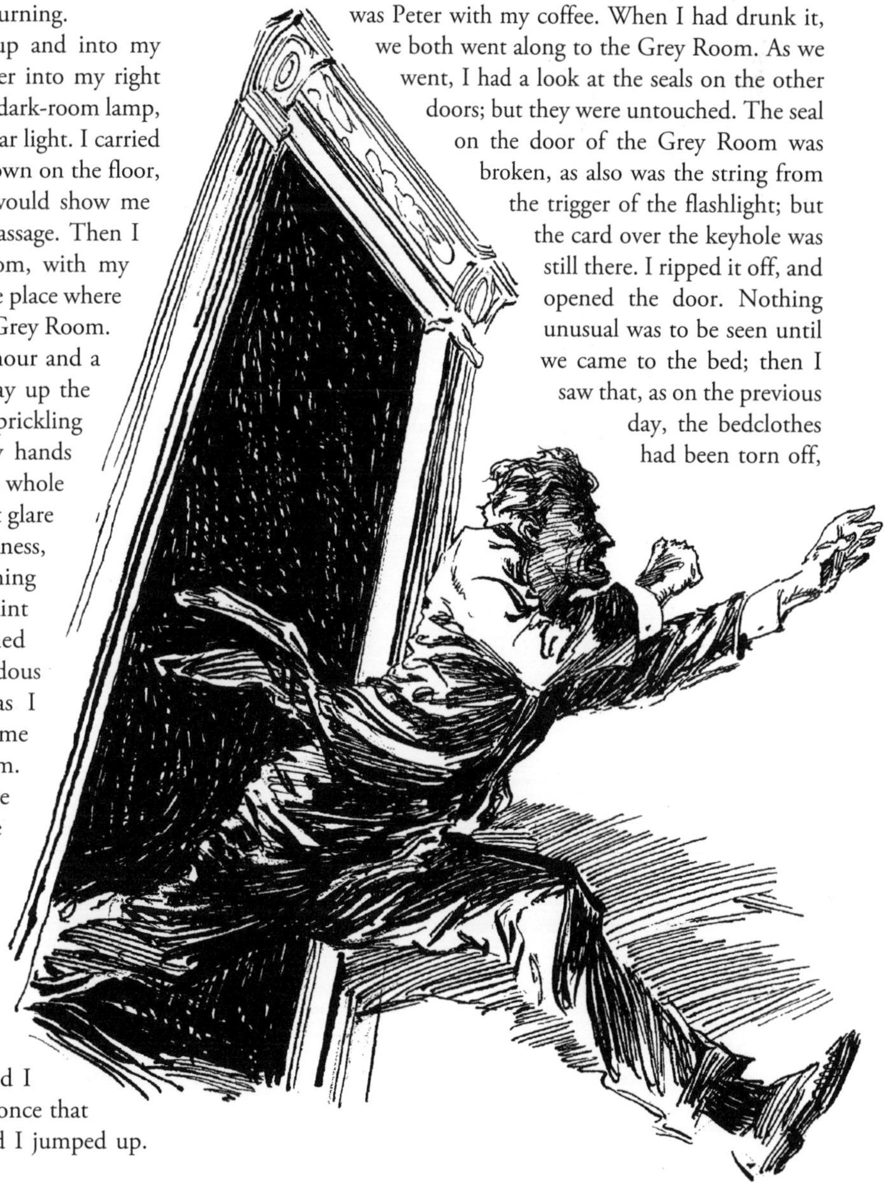

"After breakfast, I developed the negative; but it showed only the door of the Grey Room, half opened. Then I left the house, as I wanted to get certain matters and implements that might be necessary to life; perhaps to the spirit; for I intended to spend the coming night in the Grey Room.

"I got back in a cab, about half-past five, with my apparatus, and this, Peter and I carried up to the Grey Room, where I piled it carefully in the centre of the floor. When everything was in the room, including a cat which I had brought, I locked and sealed the door, and went towards the bedroom, telling Peter I should not be down for dinner. He said, 'Yes, sir,' and went downstairs, thinking that I was going to turn in, which was what I wanted him to believe, as I knew he would have worried both me and himself, if he had known what I intended.

"But I merely got my camera and flashlight from my bedroom, and hurried back to the Grey Room. I locked and sealed myself in, and set to work, for I had a lot to do before it got dark.

"First, I cleared away all the ribbons across the floor; then I carried the cat—still fastened in its basket—over towards the far wall, and left it. I returned then to the centre of the room, and measured out a space twenty-one feet in diameter, which I swept with a 'broom of hyssop.' About this, I drew a circle of chalk, taking care never to step over the circle. Beyond this I smudged, with a bunch of garlic, a broad belt right around the chalked circle, and when this was complete, I took from among my stores in the centre a small jar of a certain water. I broke away the parchment, and withdrew the stopper. Then, dipping my left forefinger in the little jar, I went round the circle again, making upon the floor, just within the line of chalk, the Second Sign of the Saaamaaa Ritual, and joining each Sign most carefully with the left-handed crescent. I can tell you, I felt easier when this was done, and the 'water circle' complete. Then, I unpacked some more of the stuff that I had brought, and placed a lighted candle in the 'valley' of each Crescent. After that, I drew a Pentacle, so that each of the five points of the defensive star touched the chalk circle. In the five points of the star I placed five portions of the bread, each wrapped in linen, and in the five 'vales', five opened jars of the water I had used to make the 'water circle.' And now I had my first protective barrier complete.

"Now, anyone, except you who know something of my methods of investigation, might consider all this a piece of useless and foolish superstition; but you all remember the Black Veil case, in which I believe my life was saved by a very similar form of protection, whilst Aster, who sneered at it, and would not come inside, died. I got the idea from the Sigsand MS., written, so far as I can make out, in the 14th century. At first, naturally, I imagined it was just an expression of the superstition of his time; and it was not until a year later that it occurred to me to test his 'Defense,' which I did, as I've just said, in that horrible Black Veil business. You know how *that* turned out. Later, I used it several times, and always I came through safe, until that Moving Fur case. It was only a partial 'Defense' therefore, and I nearly died in the pentacle. After that I came across Professor Garder's 'Experiments with a Medium.' When they surrounded the Medium with a current of a certain number of vibrations, in vacuum, he lost his power—almost as if it cut him off from the Immaterial. That made me think a lot; and that is how I came to make the Electric Pentacle, which is a most marvellous 'Defense'

and hurled into the left-hand corner, exactly where I had seen them before. I felt very queer; but I did not forget to look at all the seals, only to find that not one had been broken.

"Then I turned and looked at old Peter, and he looked at me, nodding his head.

" 'Let's get out of here!' I said. 'It's no place for any living human to enter, without proper protection.

"We went out then, and I locked and sealed the door, again.

against certain manifestations. I used the shape of the defensive star for this protection, because I have, personally, no doubt at all but that there is some extraordinary virtue in the old magic figure. Curious thing for a Twentieth Century man to admit, is it not? But, then, as you all know, I never did, and never will, allow myself to be blinded by the little cheap laughter. I ask questions, and keep my eyes open!

"In this last case I had little doubt that I had run up against a supernatural monster, and I meant to take every possible care; for the danger is abominable.

"I turned-to now to fit the Electric Pentacle, setting it so that each of its 'points' and 'vales' coincided exactly with the 'points' and 'vales' of the drawn pentagram upon the floor. Then I connected up the battery, and the next instant the pale blue glare from the intertwining vacuum tubes shone out.

"I glanced about me then, with something of a sigh of relief, and realised suddenly that the dusk was upon me, for the window was grey and unfriendly. Then round at the big, empty room, over the double barrier of electric and candle light. I had an abrupt, extraordinary sense of weirdness thrust upon me—in the air, you know; as it were, a sense of something inhuman impending. The room was full of the stench of bruised garlic, a smell I hate.

"I turned now to the camera, and saw that it and the flashlight were in order. Then I tested my

revolver, carefully; though I had little thought that it would be needed. Yet, to what extent materialisation of an ab-natural creature is possible, given favourable conditions, no one can say; and I had no idea what horrible thing I was going to see, or feel the presence of. I might, in the end, have to fight with a materialised monster. I did not know, and could only be prepared. You see, I never forgot that three other people had been strangled in the bed close to me, and the fierce slamming of the door I had heard myself. I had no doubt that I was investigating a dangerous and ugly case.

"By this time, the night had come; though the room was very light with the burning candles; and I found myself glancing

behind me, constantly, and then all round the room. It was nervy work waiting for that thing to come. Then, suddenly, I was aware of a little, cold wind sweeping over me, coming from behind. I gave one great nerve-thrill, and a prickly feeling went all over the back of my head. Then I hove myself round with a sort of stiff jerk, and stared straight against that queer wind. It seemed to come from the corner of the room to the left of the bed—the place where both times I had found the heap of tossed bedclothes. Yet, I could see nothing unusual; no opening—nothing! . . .

"Abruptly, I was aware that the candles were all a-flicker in that unnatural wind . . . . I believe I just squatted there and stared in a horribly frightened, wooden way for some minutes. I shall never be able to let you know how disgustingly horrible it was sitting in that vile, cold wind! And then—flick! flick! flick!—all the candles round the outer barrier went out; and there was I, locked and sealed in that room, and with no light beyond the weakish blue glare of the Electric Pentacle.

"A time of abominable tenseness passed, and still that wind blew upon me; and then, suddenly, I knew that something stirred in the corner to the left of the bed. I was made conscious of it, rather by some inward, unused sense than by either sight or sound; for the pale, short-radius glare of the Pentacle gave but a very poor light for seeing by. Yet, as I stared, something began slowly to grow upon my sight—a moving shadow, a little darker than the surrounding shadows. I lost the thing amid the vagueness, and for a moment or two I glanced swiftly from side to side, with a fresh, new sense of impending danger. Then my attention was directed to the bed. All the coverings were being drawn steadily off, with a hateful, stealthy sort of motion. I heard the slow, dragging slither of the clothes; but I could see nothing of the thing that pulled. I was aware in a funny, subconscious, introspective fashion that the 'creep' had come upon me; yet that I was cooler mentally than I had been for some minutes; sufficiently so to feel that my hands were sweating coldly, and to shift my revolver, half-consciously, whilst I rubbed my right hand dry upon my knee; though never, for an instant, taking my gaze or my attention from those moving clothes.

"The faint noises from the bed ceased once, and there was a most intense silence, with only the sound of the blood beating in my head. Yet, immediately afterwards, I heard again the slurring of the bedclothes being dragged off the bed. In the midst of my nervous tension I remembered the camera, and reached round for it; but without looking away from the bed. And then, you know, all in a moment, the whole of the bed coverings were torn off with extraordinary violence, and I heard the flump they made as they were hurled into the corner.

"There was a time of absolute quietness then for perhaps a couple of minutes; and you can imagine how horrible I felt. The bedclothes had been thrown with such savageness! And, then again, the brutal unnaturalness of the thing that had just been done before me!

"Abruptly, over by the door, I heard a faint noise—a sort of crickling sound, and then a pitter or two upon the floor. A great nervous thrill swept over me, seeming to run up my spine and over the back of my head; for the seal that secured the door had just been broken. Something was there. I could not see the door; at least, I mean to say that it was impossible to say how much I actually saw, and how much my imagination supplied. I made it out, only as a continuation of the grey walls . . . . And then it seemed to me that something dark and indistinct moved and wavered there among the shadows.

"Abruptly, I was aware that the door was opening, and with an effort I reached again for my camera; but before I could aim it the door was slammed with a terrific crash that filled the whole room with a sort of hollow thunder. I jumped, like a frightened child. There seemed such a power behind the noise; as though a vast, wanton Force were 'out.' Can you understand?

"The door was not touched again; but, directly afterwards, I heard the basket, in which the cat lay, creak. I tell you, I fairly pringled all along my back. I knew that I was going to learn definitely whether whatever was abroad was dangerous to Life. From the cat there rose suddenly a hideous caterwaul, that ceased abruptly; and then—too late—I snapped off the flashlight. In the great glare, I saw that the basket had been overturned, and the lid was wrenched open, with the cat lying half in, and half out upon the floor. I saw nothing else, but I was full of the knowledge that I was in the presence of some Being or Thing that had power to destroy.

"During the next two or three minutes, there was an odd, noticeable quietness in the room, and you must remember I was half-blinded, for the time, because of the flashlight; so that the whole place seemed to be pitchy dark just beyond the shine of the Pentacle. I tell you it was most horrible. I just knelt there in the star, and whirled round, trying to see whether anything was coming at me.

"My power of sight came gradually, and I got a little hold of myself; and abruptly I saw the thing I was looking for, close to the 'water circle.' It was big and indistinct, and wavered curiously, as though the shadow of a vast spider hung suspended in the air, just beyond the barrier. It passed swiftly round the circle, and seemed to probe ever towards me; but only to draw back with extraordinary jerky movements, as might a living person if they touched the hot bar of a grate.

"Round and round it moved, and round and round I turned. Then, just opposite to one of the 'vales' in the pentacles, it seemed to pause, as though preliminary to a tremendous effort. It retired almost beyond the glow of the vacuum light, and then came straight towards me, appearing to gather form and solidity as it came. There seemed a vast, malign determination behind the movement, that must succeed. I was on my knees, and I jerked back, falling on to my left hand and hip, in a wild endeavour to get back from the advancing thing. With my right hand I was grabbing madly for my revolver, which I had let slip. The brutal thing came with one great sweep straight over the garlic and the 'water circle,' almost to the vale of the pentacle. I believe I yelled. Then, just as suddenly as it had swept over, it seemed to be hurled back by some mighty, invisible force.

"It must have been some moments before I realised that I was safe; and then I got myself together in the middle of the pentacles, feeling horribly gone and shaken, and glancing round and round the barrier; but the thing had vanished. Yet, I had learnt something, for I knew now that the Grey Room was haunted by a monstrous hand.

"Suddenly, as I crouched there, I saw what had so nearly given the monster an opening through the barrier. In my movements within the pentacle I must have touched one of the jars of water; for just where the thing had made its attack the jar that guarded the 'deep' of the 'vale' had been moved to one side, and this had left one of the 'five doorways' unguarded. I put it back, quickly, and felt almost safe again, for I had found the cause, and the 'Defense' was still good. And I began to hope again that I should see the morning come in. When I saw that thing so nearly succeed, I had an awful, weak, overwhelming feeling that the 'barriers' could never bring me safe through the night against such a Force. You can understand?

"For a long time I could not see the hand; but, presently, I thought I saw, once or twice, an odd wavering, over among the shadows near the door. A little later, as though in a sudden fit of

malignant rage, the dead body of the cat was picked up, and beaten with dull, sickening blows against the solid floor. That made me feel rather queer.

"A minute afterwards, the door was opened and slammed twice with tremendous force. The next instant the thing made one swift, vicious dart at me, from out of the shadows. Instinctively, I started sideways from it, and so plucked my hand from upon the Electric Pentacle, where—for a wickedly careless moment—I had placed it. The monster was hurled off from the neighbourhood of the pentacles; though—owing to my inconceivable foolishness— it had been enabled for a second time to pass the outer barriers. I can tell you, I shook for a time, with sheer funk. I moved right to the centre of the pentacles again, and knelt there, making myself as small and compact as possible.

"As I knelt, there came to me presently, a vague wonder at the two 'accidents' which had so nearly allowed the brute to get at me. Was I being *influenced* to unconscious voluntary actions that endangered me? The thought took hold of me, and I watched my every movement. Abruptly, I stretched a tired leg, and knocked over one of the jars of water. Some was spilled; but, because of my suspicious watchfulness, I had it upright and back within the vale while yet some of the water remained. Even as I did so, the vast, black, half-materialised hand beat up at me out of the shadows, and seemed to leap almost into my face; so nearly did it approach; but for the third time it was thrown back by some altogether enormous, over-mastering force. Yet, apart from the dazed fright in which it left me, I had for a moment that feeling of spiritual sickness, as if some delicate, beautiful, inward grace had suffered, which is felt only upon the too near approach of the ab-human, and is more dreadful, in a strange way, than any physical pain that can be suffered. I knew by this more of the extent and closeness of the danger; and for a long time I was simply cowed by the butt-headed brutality of that Force upon my spirit. I can put it no other way.

"I knelt again in the centre of the pentacles, watching myself with more fear, almost, than the monster; for I knew now that, unless I guarded myself from every sudden impulse that came to me, I might simply work my own destruction. Do you see how horrible it all was?

"I spent the rest of the night in a haze of sick fright, and so tense that I could not make a single movement naturally. I was in such fear that any desire for action that came to me might be prompted by the Influence that I knew was at work on me. And outside of the barrier that ghastly thing went round and round, grabbing and grabbing in the air at me. Twice more was the body of the dead cat molested. The second time, I heard every bone in its body scrunch and crack. And all the time the horrible wind was blowing upon me from the corner of the room to the left of the bed.

"Then, just as the first touch of dawn came into the sky, that unnatural wind ceased, in a single moment; and I could see no sign of the hand. The dawn came slowly, and presently the wan light filled all the room, and made the pale glare of the Electric Pentacle look more unearthly. Yet, it was not until the day had fully come, that I made any attempt to leave the barrier, for I did not know but that there was some method abroad, in the sudden stopping of that wind, to entice me from the pentacles.

"At last, when the dawn was strong and bright, I took one last look round, and ran for the door. I got it unlocked, in a nervous and clumsy fashion, then locked it hurriedly, and went to my bedroom, where I lay on the bed, and tried to steady my nerves. Peter came, presently, with the coffee, and when I had drunk it, I told him I meant to have a sleep, as I had been up all night. He took the tray, and went out quietly; and after I had locked my door I turned in properly, and at last got to sleep.

"I woke about midday, and after some lunch, went up to the Grey Room. I switched off the current from the Pentacle, which I had left on in my hurry; also, I removed the body of the cat. You can understand I did not want anyone to see the poor brute. After that, I made a very careful search of the corner where the bedclothes had been thrown. I made several holes, and probed, and found nothing. Then it occurred to me to try with my instrument under the skirting. I did so, and heard my wire ring on metal. I turned the hook end that way, and fished for the thing. At the second go, I got it. It was a small object, and I took it to the window. I found it to be a curious ring, made of some greying material. The curious thing about it was that it was made in the form of a pentagon; that is, the same shape as the inside of the

"It was whilst I stood there, looking at the ring, that I got an idea. Supposing that it were, in a way, a doorway—you see what I mean? A sort of gap in the world-hedge. It was a queer idea, I know, and probably was not my own, but came to me from the Outside. You see, the wind had come from that part of the room where the ring lay. I thought a lot about it. Then the shape—the inside of a pentacle. It had no 'mounts,' and without mounts, as the Sigsand MS. has it:—'Thee mownts wych are thee Five Hills of safetie. To lack is to gyve pow'r to thee daemon; and surlie to fayvor the Evill Thynge.' You see,

magic pentacle, but without the 'mounts,' which form the points of the defensive star. It was free from all chasing or engraving.

"You will understand that I was excited, when I tell you that I felt sure I held in my hand the famous Luck Ring of the Anderson family; which, indeed, was of all things the one most intimately connected with the history of the haunting. This ring was handed on from father to son through generations, and always—in obedience to some ancient family tradition—each son had to promise never to wear the ring. The ring, I may say, was brought home by one of the Crusaders, under very peculiar circumstances; but the story is too long to go into here.

"It appears that young Sir Hulbert, an ancestor of Anderson's, made a bet, in drink, you know, that he would wear the ring that night. He did so, and in the morning his wife and child were found strangled in the bed, in the very room in which I stood. Many people, it would seem, thought young Sir Hulbert was guilty of having done the thing in drunken anger; and he, in an attempt to prove his innocence, slept a second night in the room. He also was strangled. Since then, as you may imagine, no one has ever spent a night in the Grey Room, until I did so. The ring had been lost so long, that it had become almost a myth; and it was most extraordinary to stand there, with the actual thing in my hand, as you can understand.

the very shape of the ring was significant; and I determined to test it.

"I unmade the pentacle, for it must be made afresh *and around* the one to be protected. Then I went out and locked the door; after which I left the house, to get certain matters, for neither 'yarbs nor fyre nor water' must be used a second time. I returned about seven-thirty, and as soon as the things I had brought had been carried up to the Grey Room, I dismissed Peter for the night, just as I had done the evening before. When he had gone downstairs, I let myself into the room, and locked and sealed the door. I went to the place in the centre of the room where all the stuff had been packed, and set to work with all my speed to construct a barrier about me and the ring.

"I do not remember whether I explained it to you. But I had reasoned that, if the ring were in any way a 'medium of admission,' and it were enclosed with me in the Electric Pentacle, it would be, to express it loosely, insulated. Do you see? The Force, which had visible expression as a Hand, would have to stay beyond the Barrier which separates the Ab from the Normal; for the 'gateway' would be removed from accessibility.

"As I was saying, I worked with all my speed to get the barrier completed about me and the ring, for it was already later than I cared to be in that room 'unprotected.' Also, I had a feeling that there would be a vast effort made that night to regain the use of the ring. For I had the strongest conviction that the ring was a necessity to materialisation. You will see whether I was right.

"I completed the barriers in about an hour, and you can imagine something of the relief I felt when I saw the pale glare of the Electric Pentacle once more all about me. From then, onwards, for about two hours, I sat quietly, facing the corner from which the wind came. About eleven o'clock a queer knowledge came that something was near to me; yet nothing happened for a whole hour after that. Then, suddenly, I felt the cold, queer wind begin to blow upon me. To my astonishment, it seemed now to come from behind me, and I whipped round, with a hideous quake of fear. The wind met me in the face. It was blowing up from the floor close to me. I stared down, in a sickening maze of new frights. What on earth had I done now! The ring was there, close beside me, where I had put it. Suddenly, as I stared, bewildered, I was aware that there was something queer about the ring—funny shadowy movements and convolutions. I looked at them, stupidly. And then, abruptly, I knew that the wind was blowing up at me from the ring. A queer indistinct smoke became visible to me, seeming to pour upwards through the ring, and mix with the moving shadows. Suddenly, I realised that I was in more than any mortal danger; for the convoluting shadows about the ring were taking shape, and the death-hand was forming *within* the Pentacle. My Goodness! do you realise it! I had brought the 'gateway' into the pentacles, and the brute was coming through—pouring into the material world, as gas might pour out from the mouth of a pipe.

"I should think that I knelt for a moment in a sort of stunned fright. Then, with a mad, awkward movement, I snatched at the ring, intending to hurl it out of the Pentacle. Yet it eluded me, as though some invisible, living thing jerked it hither and thither. At last, I gripped it; yet, in the same instant, it was torn from my grasp with incredible and brutal force. A great, black shadow covered it, and rose into the air, and came at me. I saw that it was the Hand, vast and nearly perfect in form. I gave one crazy yell, and jumped over the Pentacle and the ring of burning candles, and ran

despairingly for the door. I fumbled idiotically and ineffectually with the key, and all the time I stared, with a fear that was like insanity, towards the Barriers. The hand was plunging towards me; yet, even as it had been unable to pass into the Pentacle when the ring was without, so, now that the ring was within, it had no power to pass out. The monster was chained, as surely as any beast would be, were chains riveted upon it.

"Even then, I got a flash of this knowledge; but I was too utterly shaken with fright, to reason; and the instant I managed to get the key turned, I sprang into the passage, and slammed the door with a crash. I locked it, and got to my room somehow; for I was trembling so that I could hardly stand, as you can imagine. I locked myself in, and managed to get the candle lit; then I lay down on my bed, and kept quiet for an hour or two, and so I got steadied.

"I got a little sleep, later; but woke when Peter brought my coffee. When I had drunk it I felt altogether better, and took the old man along with me whilst I had a look into the Grey Room. I opened the door, and peeped in. The candles were still burning, wan against the daylight; and behind them was the pale, glowing star of the Electric Pentacle. And there, in the middle, was the ring . . . the gateway of the monster, lying demure and ordinary.

"Nothing in the room was touched, and I knew that the brute had never managed to cross the Pentacles. Then I went out, and locked the door.

"After a sleep of some hours, I left the house. I returned in the afternoon in a cab. I had with me an oxy-hydrogen jet, and two cylinders, containing the gases. I carried the things into the Grey Room, and there, in the centre of the Electric Pentacle, I erected the little furnace. Five minutes later the Luck Ring, once the 'luck,' but now the 'bane,' of the Anderson family, was no more than a little solid splash of hot metal."

Carnacki felt in his pocket, and pulled out something wrapped in tissue paper. He passed it to me. I opened it, and found a small circle of greyish metal, something like lead, only harder and rather brighter.

"Well?" I asked, at length, after examining it and handing it round to the others. "Did that stop the haunting?"

Carnacki nodded. "Yes," he said. "I slept three nights in the Grey Room, before I left. Old Peter nearly fainted when he knew that I meant to; but by the third night he seemed to realise that the house was just safe and ordinary. And, you know, I believe, in his heart, he hardly approved."

Carnacki stood up and began to shake hands. "Out you go!" he said, genially. And, presently, we went, pondering, to our various homes.

THE END

A TROPICAL HORROR

By William Hope Hodgson

WE ARE A HUNDRED AND thirty days out from Melbourne, and for three weeks we have lain in this sweltering calm.

It is midnight, and our watch on deck until four a.m. I go out and sit on the hatch. A minute later Joky, our youngest 'prentice, joins me for a chatter. Many are the hours we have sat thus and talked in the night watches; though, to be sure, it is Joky who does the talking. I am content to smoke and listen, giving an occasional grunt at seasons to show that I am attentive.

Joky has been silent for some time, his head bent in meditation. Suddenly he looks up, evidently with the intention of making some remark. As he does so, I see his face stiffen with a nameless horror. He crouches back, his eyes staring past me at some unseen fear. Then his mouth opens. He gives forth a strangulated cry and topples backward off the hatch, striking his head against the deck. Fearing I know not what, I turn to look.

Great Heavens! Rising above the bulwarks, seen plainly in the bright moonlight, is a vast slobbering mouth a fathom across. From the huge dripping lips hang great tentacles. As I look, the Thing comes further over the rail. It is rising, rising, higher and higher. There are no eyes visible; only that fearful slobbering mouth set on the tremendous trunk-like neck; which, even as I watch, is curling inboard with the stealthy celerity of an enormous eel. Over it comes in vast heaving folds. Will it never end? The ship gives a slow, sullen roll to starboard as she feels the weight. Then the tail, a broad, flat-shaped mass, slips over the teak rail and falls with a loud slump on to the deck.

For a few seconds the hideous creature lies heaped in writhing, slimy coils. Then, with quick, darting movements, the monstrous head travels along the deck. Close by the mainmast stand the harness casks, and alongside of these a freshly opened cask of salt beef with the top loosely replaced. The smell of the meat seems to attract the monster, and I can hear it sniffing with a vast indrawing of breath. Then those lips open, displaying four huge fangs; there

is a quick forward motion of the head, a sudden crashing, crunching sound, and beef and barrel have disappeared. The noise brings one of the ordinary seamen out of the fo'cas'le. Coming into the night, he can see nothing for a moment. Then, as he gets further aft, he *sees*, and with horrified cries rushes forward. Too late! From the mouth of the Thing there flashes forth a long, broad blade of glistening white, set with fierce teeth. I avert my eyes, but cannot shut out the sickening "Glut! Glut!" that follows.

The man on the "look-out," attracted by the disturbance, has witnessed the tragedy, and flies for refuge into the fo'cas'le, flinging to the heavy iron door after him.

The carpenter and sailmaker come running out from the half-deck in their drawers. Seeing the awful Thing, they rush aft to the cabins with shouts of fear. The second mate, after one glance over the break of the poop, runs down the companion-way with the helmsman after him. I can hear them barring the scuttle, and abruptly I realize that I am on the main deck alone.

So far I have forgotten my own danger. The past few minutes seem like a portion of an awful dream. Now, however, I comprehend my position and, shaking off the horror that has held me, turn to seek safety. As I do so my eyes fall upon Joky, lying huddled and senseless with fright where he has fallen. I cannot leave him there. Close by stands the empty half-deck—a little steel-built house with iron doors. The lee one is hooked open. Once inside and I am safe.

Up to the present the Thing has seemed to be unconscious of my presence. Now, however, the huge barrel-like head sways in my direction; then comes a muffled bellow, and the great tongue flickers in and out as the brute turns and swirls aft to meet me. I know there is not a moment to lose, and, picking up the helpless lad, I make a run for the open door. It is only distant a few yards, but that awful shape is coming down the deck to me in great wreathing coils. I reach the house and tumble in with my burden; then out on deck again to unhook and close the door. Even as I do so something white curls round the end of the house. With a bound I am inside and the door is shut and bolted. Through the thick glass of the ports I see the Thing sweep round the house, in vain search for me.

Joky has not moved yet; so, kneeling down, I loosen his shirt collar and sprinkle some water from the breaker over his face. While I am doing this I hear Morgan shout something; then comes a great shriek of terror, and again that sickening "Glut! Glut!"

Joky stirs uneasily, rubs his eyes, and sits up suddenly.

"Was that Morgan shouting—?" He breaks off with a cry. "Where are we? I have had such awful dreams!"

At this instant there is a sound of running footsteps on the deck and I hear Morgan's voice at the door.

"Tom, open—!"

He stops abruptly and gives an awful cry of despair. Then I hear him rush forward. Through the porthole I see him spring into the fore rigging and scramble madly aloft. Something steals up after him. It shows white in the moonlight. It wraps itself around his right ankle. Morgan stops dead, plucks out his sheath-knife and hacks fiercely at the fiendish Thing. It lets go, and in a second he is over the top and running for dear life up the t'gallant rigging.

A time of quietness follows, and presently I see that the day is breaking. Not a sound can be heard save the heavy gasping breathing of the Thing. As the sun rises higher the creature stretches itself out along the deck and seems to enjoy the warmth. Still no sound, either from the men forward or the officers aft. I can only suppose that they are afraid of attracting its attention. Yet, a little later, I hear the report of a pistol away aft, and looking out I see the serpent raise its huge head as though listening. As it does so I get a good view of the fore part, and in the daylight see what the night has hidden.

There, right about the mouth, is a pair of little pig-eyes, that seem to twinkle with a diabolical intelligence. It is swaying its head slowly from side to side; then, without warning, it turns quickly and looks right in through the port. I dodge out of sight; but not soon enough. It has seen me, and brings its great mouth up against the glass.

I hold my breath. My God! If it breaks the glass! I cower, horrified. From the direction of the port there comes a loud, harsh, scraping sound. I shiver. Then I remember that there are little iron doors to shut over the ports in bad weather. Without a moment's waste of time I rise to my feet and slam to the door over the port. Then I go round to the others and do the same. We are now in darkness, and I tell Joky in a whisper to light the lamp, which, after some fumbling, he does.

About an hour before midnight I fall asleep. I am awakened suddenly some hours later by a scream of agony and the rattle of a water-dipper. There is a slight scuffling sound; then that soul-revolting "Glut! Glut!"

I guess what has happened. One of the men forrard has slipped out of the fo'cas'le to try and get a little water. Evidently he has trusted to the darkness to hide his movements. Poor beggar! He has paid for his attempt with his life!

After this I cannot sleep, though the rest of the night passes quietly enough. Towards morning I doze a bit, but wake every few minutes with a start. Joky is sleeping peacefully; indeed, he seems worn out with the terrible strain of the past twenty-four hours. About eight a.m. I call him, and we make a light breakfast off the ship's biscuit and water. Of the latter happily we have a good supply. Joky seems more himself, and starts to talk a little—

iron port-covers first and have a look out. Joky argues, but I am immovable. He becomes excited. I believe the youngster is light-headed. Then, as I turn to unscrew one of the after-covers, Joky makes a dash at the door. Before he can undo the bolts I have him, and after a short struggle lead him back to the table. Even as I endeavor to quieten him there comes at the starboard door—the door that Joky has tried to open—a sharp, loud sniff, sniff, followed immediately by a thunderous grunting howl and a foul stench of putrid breath sweeps in under the door. A great trembling takes me, and were it not for the carpenter's tool-chest I should fall. Joky turns very white and is violently sick, after which he is seized by a hopeless fit of sobbing.

Hour after hour passes, and, weary to death, I lie down on the chest upon which I have been sitting, and try to rest.

It must be about half-past two in the morning, after a somewhat longer doze, that I am suddenly awakened by a most tremendous uproar away forrard—men's voices shrieking, cursing, praying; but in spite of the terror expressed, so weak and feeble; while in the midst, and at times broken off short with that hellishly suggestive "Glut! Glut!" is the unearthly bellowing of the Thing. Fear incarnate seizes me, and I can only fall on my knees and pray. Too well I know what is happening.

Joky has slept through it all, and I am thankful.

Presently, under the door there steals a narrow riband of light, and I know that the day has broken on the second morning of our imprisonment. I let Joky sleep on. I will let him have peace while he may. Time passes, but I take little notice. The Thing is quiet, probably sleeping. About midday I eat a little biscuit and drink some of the water. Joky still sleeps. It is best so.

A sound breaks the stillness. The ship gives a slight heave, and I know that once more the Thing is awake. Round the deck it moves, causing the ship to roll perceptibly. Once it goes forrard—I fancy to again explore the fo'cas'le. Evidently it finds nothing, for it returns almost immediately. It pauses a moment at the house, then goes on further aft. Up aloft, somewhere in the fore-rigging, there rings out a peal of wild laughter, though sounding very faint and far away. The Horror stops suddenly. I listen intently, but hear nothing save a sharp creaking beyond the after end of the house, as though a strain had come upon the main rigging.

A minute later I hear a cry aloft, followed almost instantly by a loud crash on deck that seems to shake the ship. I wait in anxious fear. What is happening? The minutes pass slowly. Then comes another frightened shout. It ceases suddenly. The suspense has become terrible, and I am no longer able to bear it. Very cautiously I open one of the after port-covers and peep out to see a fearful sight. There, with its tail upon the deck and its vast body curled round the mainmast, is the monster, its head above the topsail yard, and its great claw-armed tentacle waving in the air. It is the first proper sight that I have had of the Thing. Good Heavens! It must weigh a hundred tons! Knowing that I shall have time, I open the port itself, then crane my head out and look up. There on the extreme end of the lower topsail yard I see one of the able seamen. Even down here I note the staring horror of his face. At this

possibly somewhat louder than is safe; for, as he chatters on, wondering how it will end, there comes a tremendous blow against the side of the house, making it ring again. After this Joky is very silent. As we sit there I cannot but wonder what all the rest are doing, and how the poor beggars forrard are faring, cooped up without water, as the tragedy of the night has proved.

Towards noon I hear a loud bang, followed by a terrific bellowing. Then comes a great smashing of woodwork, and the cries of men in pain. Vainly I ask myself what has happened. I begin to reason. By the sound of the report it was evidently something much heavier than a rifle or pistol, and judging from the mad roaring of the Thing, the shot must have done some execution. On thinking it over further, I become convinced that by some means those aft have got hold of the small signal cannon we carry, and though I know that some have been hurt, perhaps killed, yet a feeling of exultation seizes me as I listen to the roars of the Thing, and realize that it is badly wounded, perhaps mortally. After a while, however, the bellowing dies away, and only an occasional roar, denoting more of anger than aught else, is heard.

Presently I become aware, by the ship's canting over to starboard, that the creature has gone over to that side, and a great hope springs up within me that possibly it has had enough of us and is going over the rail into the sea. For a time all is silent and my hope grows stronger. I lean across and nudge Joky, who is sleeping with his head on the table. He starts up sharply with a loud cry.

"Hush!" I whisper hoarsely. "I'm not certain, but I do believe it's gone."

Joky's face brightens wonderfully, and he questions me eagerly. We wait another hour or so, with hope ever rising. Our confidence is returning fast. Not a sound can we hear, not even the breathing of the Beast. I get out some biscuits, and Joky, after rummaging in the locker, produces a small piece of pork and a bottle of ship's vinegar. We fall to with a relish. After our long abstinence from food the meal acts on us like wine, and what must Joky do but insist on opening the door, to make sure the Thing has gone. This I will not allow, telling him that at least it will be safer to open the

How will it end? Oh! how will it end?

After a while Joky wakes up. He is very restless, yet though he has eaten nothing during the day I cannot get him to touch anything.

Night draws on. We are too weary—too dispirited to talk. I lie down, but not to sleep . . . Time passes.

A ventilator rattles violently somewhere on the maindeck, and there sounds constantly that slurring, gritty noise. Later I hear a cat's agonized howl, and then again all is quiet. Some time after comes a great splash alongside. Then, for some hours all is silent as the grave. Occasionally I sit up on the chest and listen, yet never a whisper of noise comes to me. There is an absolute silence, even the monotonous creak of the gear has died away entirely, and at last a real hope is springing up within me. That splash, this silence—surely I am justified in hoping. I do not wake Joky this time. I will prove first for myself that all is safe. Still I wait. I will run no unnecessary risks. After a time I creep to the after-port and listen; but there is no sound. I put up my hand and feel at the screw, then again I hesitate, yet not for long. Noiselessly I begin to unscrew the fastening of the heavy shield. It swings loose on its hinge, and I pull it back and peer out. My heart is beating madly. Everything seems strangely dark outside. Perhaps the moon has gone behind a cloud. Suddenly a beam of moonlight enters through the port, and goes as quickly. I stare out. Something moves. Again the light streams in, and now I seem to be looking into a great cavern, at the bottom of which quivers and curls something palely white.

moment he sees me and gives a weak, hoarse cry for help. I can do nothing for him. As I look the great tongue shoots out and licks him off the yard, much as might a dog a fly off the window-pane.

Higher still, but happily out of reach, are two more of the men. As far as I can judge they are lashed to the mast above the royal yard. The Thing attempts to reach them, but after a futile effort it ceases, and starts to slide down, coil on coil, to the deck. While doing this I notice a great gaping wound on its body some twenty feet above the tail.

I drop my gaze from aloft and look aft. The cabin door is torn from its hinges, and the bulkhead—which, unlike the half-deck, is of teak wood—is partly broken down. With a shudder I realize the cause of those cries after the cannon shot. Turning I screw my head round and try to see the foremast, but cannot. The sun, I notice, is low, and the night is near. Then I draw in my head and fasten up both port and cover.

My heart seems to stand still! It is the Horror! I start back and seize the iron port-flap to slam it to. As I do so, something strikes the glass like a steam ram, shatters it to atoms, and flicks past me into the berth. I scream and spring away. The port is quite filled with it. The lamp shows it dimly. It is curling and twisting here and there. It is as thick as a tree, and covered with a smooth slimy skin. At the end is a great claw, like a lobster's, only a thousand times larger. I cower down into the farthest corner . . . It has broken the tool-chest to pieces with one click of those frightful mandibles. Joky has crawled under a bunk. The Thing sweeps round in my direction. I feel a drop of sweat trickle slowly down my face—it tastes salty. Nearer comes that awful death . . . Crash! I roll over backwards. It has crushed the water breaker against which I leant, and I am rolling in the water across the floor. The claw drives up, then down, with a quick uncertain movement, striking the deck a dull, heavy blow, a foot from my head. Joky

gives a little gasp of horror. Slowly the Thing rises and starts feeling its way round the berth. It plunges into a bunk and pulls out a bolster, nips it in half and drops it, then moves on. It is feeling along the deck. As it does so it comes across a half of the bolster. It seems to toy with it, then picks it up and takes it out through the port.

A wave of putrid air fills the berth. There is a grating sound, and something enters the port again—something white and tapering and set with teeth. Hither and thither it curls, rasping over the bunks, ceiling, and deck, with a noise like that of a great saw at work. Twice it flickers above my head, and I close my eyes. Then off it goes again. It sounds now on the opposite side of the berth and nearer to Joky. Suddenly the harsh, raspy noise becomes muffled, as though the teeth were passing across some soft substance. Joky gives a horrid little scream, that breaks off into a bubbling, whistling sound. I open my eyes. The tip of the vast tongue is curled tightly round something that drips, then is quickly withdrawn, allowing the moonbeams to steal again into the berth. I rise to my feet. Looking round, I note in a mechanical sort of way the wrecked state of the berth—the shattered chests, dismantled bunks, and something else—

"Joky!" I cry, and tingle all over.

There is that awful Thing again at the port. I glance round for a weapon. I will revenge Joky. Ah! there, right under the lamp, where the wreck of the carpenter's chest strews the floor, lies a small hatchet. I spring forward and seize it. It is small, but so keen—so keen! I feel its razor edge lovingly. Then I am back at the port. I stand to one side, and raise my weapon. The great tongue is feeling its way to those fearsome remains. It reaches them. As it does so, with a scream of "Joky! Joky!" I strike savagely again and again, gasping as I strike; once more, and the monstrous mass falls to the deck, writhing like a hideous eel. A vast, warm flood rushes in through the porthole. There is a sound of breaking steel and an enormous bellowing. A singing comes in my ears and grows louder—louder. Then the berth grows indistinct and suddenly dark.

Extract from the steamship *Hispaniola*:
June 24.—Lat.—N. Long.—W. 11 a.m.—Sighted four-masted barque about four points on the port bow, flying signal

of distress. Ran down to her and sent a boat aboard. She proved to be the *Glen Doon*, homeward bound from Melbourne to London. Found things in a terrible state. Decks covered with blood and slime. Steel deck-house stove in. Broke open door and discovered youth of about nineteen in last stage of inanition, also part remains of boy about fourteen years of age. There was a great quantity of blood in the place, and a huge curled-up mass of whitish flesh, weighing about half a ton, one end of which appeared to have been hacked through with a sharp instrument. Found forecastle door open and hanging from one hinge. Doorway bulged, as though something had been forced through. Went inside. Terrible state of affairs, blood everywhere, broken chests, smashed bunks, but no men nor remains. Went aft again and found youth showing signs of recovery. When he came round, gave the name of Thompson. Said they had been attacked by a huge serpent—thought it must have been sea-serpent. He was too weak to say much, but told us there were some men up the mainmast. Sent a hand aloft, who reported them lashed to the royal mast, and quite dead. Went aft to the cabin. Here we found the bulkhead smashed to pieces, and the cabin door lying on the deck near the afterhatch. Found body of captain down lazarette, but no officers. Noticed among the wreckage part of the carriage of a small cannon. Came aboard again.

Have sent the second mate with six men to work her into port. Thompson is with us. He has written out his version of the affair. We certainly consider that the state of the ship, as we found her, bears out in every respect his story.

(Signed)

William Norton
Master

Tom Briggs
1st Mate

MOTHER OF TOADS

by
Clark
Ashton
Smith

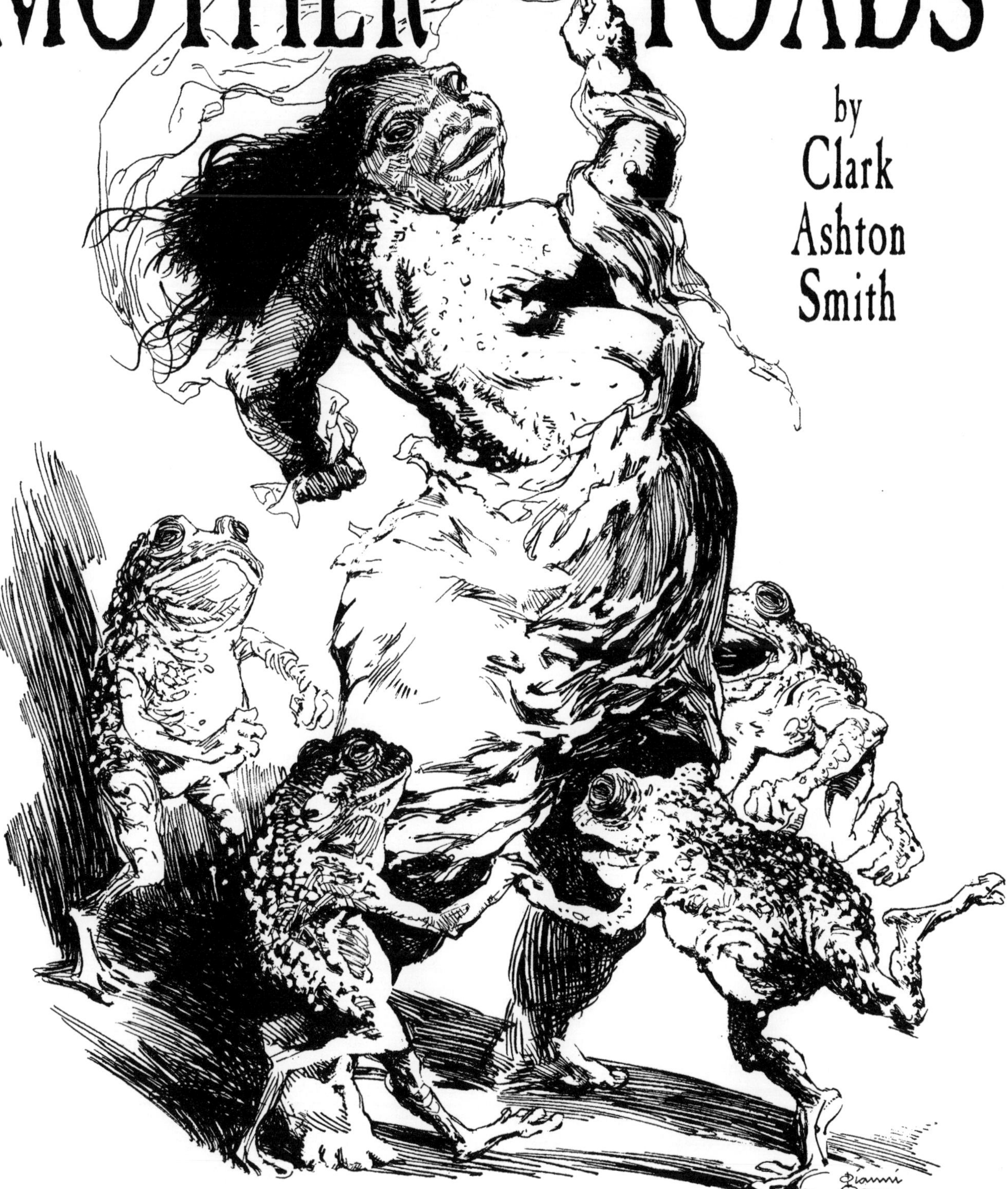

"WHY MUST YOU ALWAYS HURRY away, my little one?"

The voice of Mère Antoinette, the witch, was an amorous croaking. She ogled Pierre, the apothecary's young apprentice, with eyes full-orbed and unblinking as those of a toad. The folds beneath her chin swelled like the throat of some great batrachian. Her huge breasts, pale as frog-bellies, bulged from her torn gown as she leaned toward him.

He gave no answer, and she came closer, till he saw in the hollow of those breasts a moisture glistening like the dew of marshes . . . like the slime of some amphibian . . . a moisture that seemed always to linger there.

Her voice, raucously coaxing, persisted. "Stay awhile tonight, my pretty orphan. No one will miss you in the village. And your master will not mind." She pressed against him with shuddering folds of fat. With her short, flat fingers, which gave almost the appearance of being webbed, she seized his hand and drew it to her bosom.

Pierre wrenched the hand away and drew back discreetly. Repelled, rather than abashed, he averted his eyes. The witch was more than twice his age, and her charms were too uncouth and unsavory to tempt him for an instant. Also, her repute was such as to have nullified the attractions of a younger and fairer sorceress. Her witchcraft had made her feared among the peasantry of that remote province, where belief in spells and philters was still common. The people of Averoigne called her *La Mère des Crapauds*, Mother of Toads, a name given for more than one reason. Toads swarmed innumerably about her hut; they were said to be her familiars, and dark tales were told concerning their relationship to the

sorceress, and the duties they performed at her bidding. Such tales were all the more readily believed because of those batrachian features that had always been remarked in her aspect.

The youth disliked her, even as he disliked the sluggish, abnormally large toads on which he had sometimes trodden in the dusk, upon the path between her hut and the village of Les Hiboux. He could hear some of these creatures croaking now; and it seemed, weirdly, that they uttered half-articulate echoes of the witch's words.

It would be dark soon, he reflected. The path along the marshes was not pleasant by night, and he felt doubly anxious to depart. Still without replying to Mère Antoinette's invitation, he reached for the black triangular vial she had set before him on her greasy table. The vial contained a philter of curious potency which his master, Alain le Dindon, had sent him to procure. Le Dindon, the village apothecary, was wont to deal surreptitiously in certain dubious medicaments supplied by the witch, and Pierre had often gone on such errands to her osier-hidden hut.

The old apothecary, whose humor was rough and ribald, had sometimes rallied Pierre concerning Mère Antoinette's preference for him. "Some night, my lad, you will remain with her," he had said. "Be careful, or the big toad will crush you." Remembering this gibe, the boy flushed angrily as he turned to go.

"Stay," insisted Mère Antoinette. "The fog is cold on the marshes; and it thickens apace. I knew that you were coming, and I have mulled for you a goodly measure of the red wine of Ximes."

She removed the lid from an earthen pitcher and poured its steaming contents into a large cup. The purplish-red wine creamed delectably, and an odor of hot, delicious spices filled the hut, overpowering the less agreeable odors from the simmering cauldron, the half-dried newts, vipers, bat-wings, and evil, nauseous herbs hanging on the walls, and the reek of the black candles of pitch and corpse-tallow that burned always, by noon or night, in that murky interior.

"I'll drink it," said Pierre, a little grudgingly. "That is, if it contains nothing of your own concoction."

" 'Tis naught but sound wine, four seasons old, with spices of Arabia," the sorceress croaked ingratiatingly. " 'Twill warm your stomach . . . and . . . " She added something inaudible as Pierre accepted the cup.

Before drinking, he inhaled the fumes of the beverage with some caution but was reassured by its pleasant smell. Surely it was innocent of any drug, any philter brewed by the witch: for, to his knowledge, her preparations were all evil-smelling.

Still, as if warned by some premonition, he hesitated. Then he remembered that the sunset air was indeed chill, that mists had gathered furtively behind him as he came to Mère Antoinette's dwelling. The wine would fortify him for the dismal return walk to Les Hiboux. He quaffed it quickly and set down the cup.

"Truly, it is good wine," he declared. "But I must go now."

Even as he spoke, he felt in his stomach and veins the spreading warmth of the alcohol, of the spices . . . of something more ardent than these. It seemed that his voice was unreal and strange, falling as if from a height above him. The warmth grew, mounting within him like a golden flame fed by magic oils. His blood, a seething torrent, poured tumultuously and more tumultuously through his members.

There was a deep soft thundering in his ears, a rosy dazzlement in his eyes. Somehow the hut appeared to expand, to change luminously about him. He hardly recognized its squalid furnishings, its litter of baleful oddments, on which a torrid splendor was shed by the black candles, tipped with ruddy fire, that towered and swelled gigantically into the soft gloom. His blood burned as with the throbbing flame of the candles.

It came to him, for an instant, that all this was a questionable enchantment, a glamor wrought by the witch's wine. Fear was upon him and he wished to flee. Then, close beside him, he saw Mère Antoinette.

Briefly he marvelled at the change that had befallen her. Then fear and wonder were alike forgotten, together with his old repulsion. He knew why the magic warmth mounted ever higher and hotter within him; why his flesh glowed like the ruddy tapers.

The soiled skirt she had worn lay at her feet, and she stood naked as Lilith, the first witch. The lumpish limbs and body had grown voluptuous; the pale, thick-lipped mouth enticed him with a promise of ampler kisses than other mouths could yield. The pits of her short round arms, the concave of her ponderously drooping breasts, the heavy creases and swollen rondures of flanks and thighs, all were fraught with luxurious allurement.

"Do you like me now, my little one?" she questioned.

This time he did not draw away but met her with hot, questing hands when she pressed heavily against him. Her limbs were cool and moist; her breasts yielded like the turf-mounds above a bog. Her body was white and wholly hairless; but here and there he found curious roughnesses . . . like those on the skin of a toad . . . that somehow sharpened his desire instead of repelling it.

She was so huge that his fingers barely joined behind her. His two hands, together, were equal only to the cupping of a single breast. But the wine had filled his blood with a philterous ardor.

She led him to her couch beside the hearth where a great cauldron boiled mysteriously, sending up its fumes in strange-twining coils that suggested vague and obscene figures. The couch was rude and bare. But the flesh of the sorceress was like deep, luxurious cushions . . .

Pierre awoke in the ashy dawn, when the tall, black tapers had dwindled down and had melted limply in their sockets. Sick and confused, he sought vainly to remember where he was or what he had done. Then, turning a little, he saw beside him on the couch a thing that was like some impossible monster of ill dreams; a toadlike form, large as a fat woman. Its limbs were somehow like a woman's arms and legs.

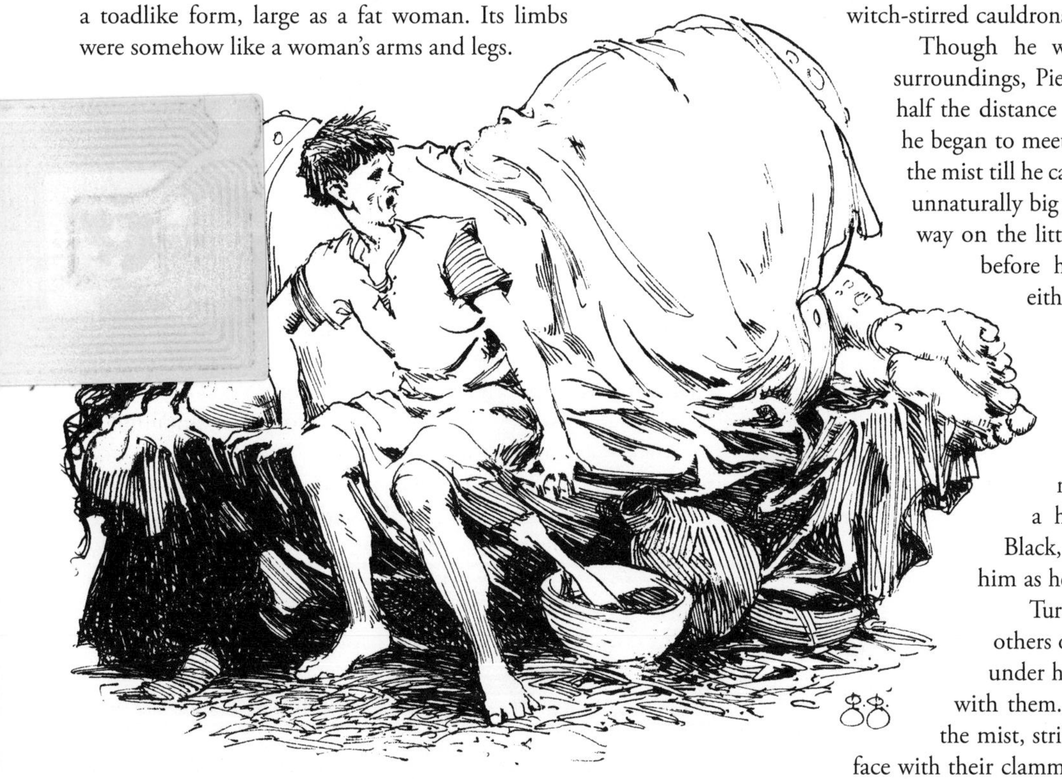

Its pale, warty body pressed and bulged against him, and he felt the rounded softness of something that resembled a breast.

Nausea rose within him as memory of that delirious night returned. Most foully he had been beguiled by the witch, and had succumbed to her evil enchantments.

It seemed that an incubus smothered him, weighing upon all his limbs and body. He shut his eyes, that he might no longer behold the loathsome thing that was Mère Antoinette in her true semblance. Slowly, with prodigious effort, he drew himself away from the crushing nightmare shape. It did not stir or appear to waken; and he slid quickly from the couch.

Again, compelled by a noisome fascination, he peered at the thing on the couch—and saw only the gross form of Mère Antoinette. Perhaps his impression of a great toad beside him had been but an illusion, a half-dream that lingered after slumber. He lost something of his nightmarish horror, but his gorge still rose in a sick disgust, remembering the lewdness to which he had yielded.

Fearing that the witch might awaken at any moment and seek to detain him, he stole noiselessly from the hut. It was broad daylight, but a cold, hueless mist lay everywhere, shrouding the reedy marshes, and hanging like a ghostly curtain on the path he must follow to Les Hiboux. Moving and seething always, the mist seemed to reach toward him with intercepting fingers as he started homeward. He shivered at its touch, he bowed his head and drew his cloak closer around him.

Thicker and thicker the mist swirled, coiling, writhing endlessly, as if to bar Pierre's progress. He could discern the twisting, narrow path for only a few paces in advance. It was hard to find the familiar landmarks, hard to recognize the osiers and willows that loomed suddenly before him like gray phantoms and faded again into the white nothingness as he went onward. Never had he seen such fog: it was like the blinding, stifling fumes of a thousand witch-stirred cauldrons.

Though he was not altogether sure of his surroundings, Pierre thought that he had covered half the distance to the village. Then, all at once, he began to meet the toads. They were hidden by the mist till he came close upon them. Misshapen, unnaturally big and bloated, they squatted in his way on the little footpath or hopped sluggishly before him from the pallid gloom on either hand.

Several struck against his feet with a horrible and heavy flopping. He stepped unaware upon one of them, and slipped in the squashy noisesomeness it had made, barely saving himself from a headlong fall on the bog's rim. Black, miry water gloomed close beside him as he staggered there.

Turning to regain his path, he crushed others of the toads to an abhorrent pulp under his feet. The marshy soil was alive with them. They flopped against him from the mist, striking his legs, his bosom, his very face with their clammy bodies. They rose up by scores like a devil-driven legion. It seemed that there was a malignance, an evil purpose in their movements, in the buffeting of their violent impact. He could make no progress on the swarming path, but lurched to and fro, slipping blindly, and shielding his face with lifted hands. He felt an eery consternation, an eldrich horror.

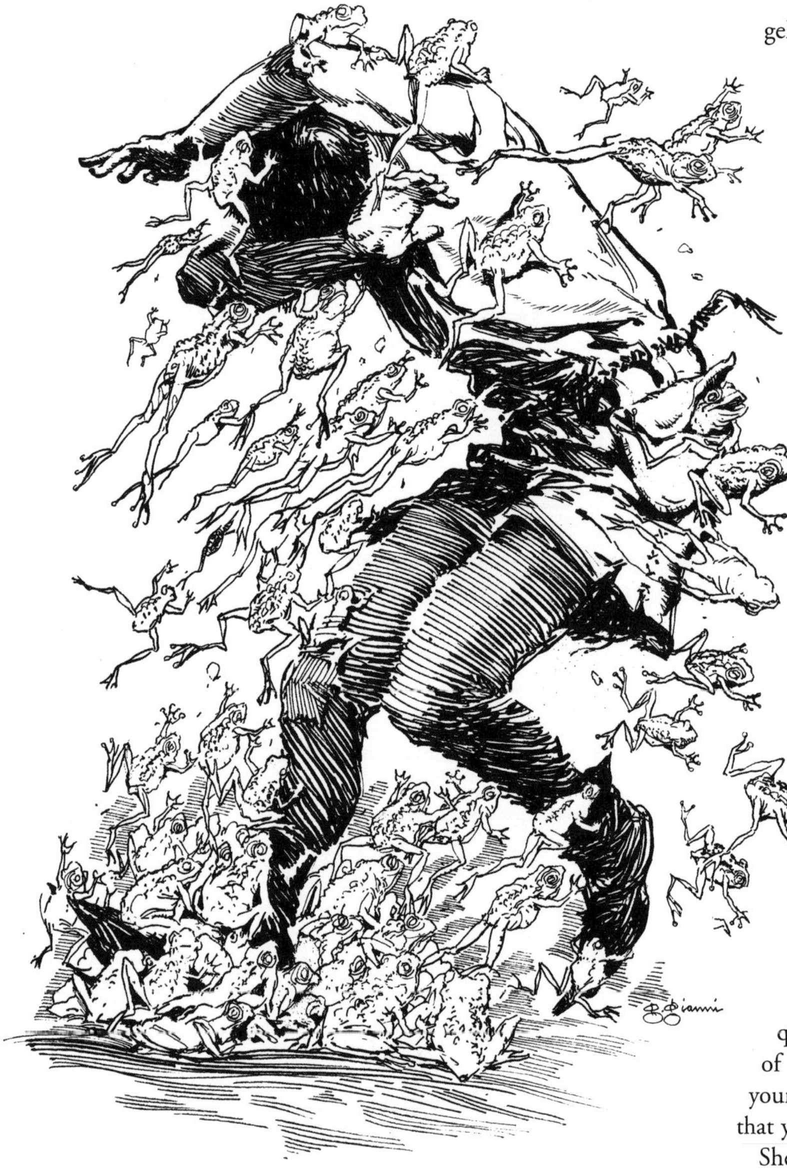

It was as if the nightmare of his awakening in the witch's hut had somehow returned upon him.

The toads came always from the direction of Les Hiboux, as if to drive him back toward Mère Antoinette's dwelling. They bounded against him like a monstrous hail, like missiles flung by unseen demons. The ground was covered by them, the air was filled with their hurtling bodies. Once, he nearly went down beneath them.

Their number seemed to increase, they pelted him in a noxious storm. He gave way before them, his courage broke, and he started to run at random, without knowing that he had left the safe path. Losing all thought of direction in his frantic desire to escape from those impossible myriads, he plunged on amid the dim reeds and sedges, over ground that quivered gelatinously beneath him. Always at his heels he heard the soft, heavy flopping of the toads; and sometimes they rose up like a sudden wall to bar his way and turn him aside. More than once, they drove him back from the verge of hidden quagmires into which he would otherwise have fallen. It was as if they were herding him deliberately and concertedly to a destined goal.

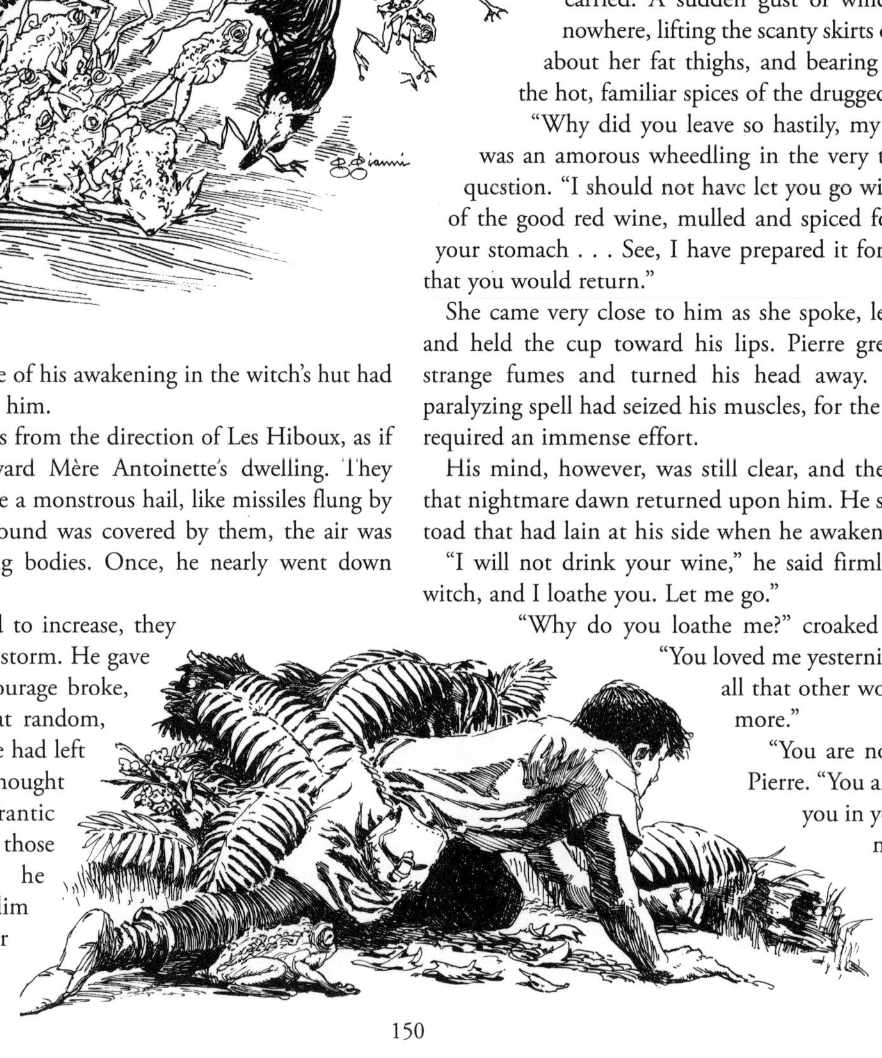

Now, like the lifting of a dense curtain, the mist rolled away, and Pierre saw before him in a golden dazzle of morning sunshine the green, thick-growing osiers that surrounded Mère Antoinette's hut. The toads had all disappeared, though he could have sworn that hundreds of them were hopping close about him an instant previously. With a feeling of helpless fright and panic, he knew that he was still within the witch's toils; that the toads were indeed her familiars, as so many people believed them to be. They had prevented his escape, and had brought him back to the foul creature . . . whether woman, batrachian, or both . . . who was known as The Mother of Toads.

Pierre's sensations were those of one who sinks momently deeper into some black and bottomless quicksand. He saw the witch emerge from the hut and come toward him. Her thick fingers, with pale folds of skin between them like the beginnings of a web, were stretched and flattened on the steaming cup that she carried. A sudden gust of wind arose as if from nowhere, lifting the scanty skirts of Mère Antoinette about her fat thighs, and bearing to Pierre's nostrils the hot, familiar spices of the drugged wine.

"Why did you leave so hastily, my little one?" There was an amorous wheedling in the very tone of the witch's question. "I should not have let you go without another cup of the good red wine, mulled and spiced for the warming of your stomach . . . See, I have prepared it for you . . . knowing that you would return."

She came very close to him as she spoke, leering and sidling, and held the cup toward his lips. Pierre grew dizzy with the strange fumes and turned his head away. It seemed that a paralyzing spell had seized his muscles, for the simple movement required an immense effort.

His mind, however, was still clear, and the sick revulsion of that nightmare dawn returned upon him. He saw again the great toad that had lain at his side when he awakened.

"I will not drink your wine," he said firmly. "You are a foul witch, and I loathe you. Let me go."

"Why do you loathe me?" croaked Mère Antoinette. "You loved me yesternight. I can give you all that other women give . . . and more."

"You are not a woman," said Pierre. "You are a big toad. I saw you in your true shape this morning. I'd rather drown in the marsh-waters than sleep with you again."

An indescribable change came upon the sorceress before Pierre had finished speaking. The leer slid from her thick and pallid features, leaving them blankly inhuman for an instant. Then her eyes bulged and goggled horribly, and her whole body appeared to swell as if inflated with venom.

"Go, then!" she spat with a guttural virulence. "But you will soon wish that you had stayed . . ."

The queer paralysis had lifted from Pierre's muscles. It was as if the injunction of the angry witch had served to revoke an insidious, half-woven spell. With no parting glance or word, Pierre turned from her and fled with long, hasty steps, almost running, on the path to Les Hiboux.

He had gone little more than a hundred paces when the fog began to return. It coiled shoreward in vast volumes from the marshes, it poured like smoke from the very ground at his feet. Almost instantly, the sun dimmed to a wan silver disk and disappeared. The blue heavens were lost in the pale and seething voidness overhead. The path before Pierre was blotted out till he seemed to walk on the sheer rim of a white abyss that moved with him as he went.

Like the clammy arms of specters, with death-chill fingers that clutched and caressed, the weird mists drew closer still about Pierre. They thickened in his nostrils and throat, they dripped in a heavy dew from his garments. They choked him with the fetor of rank waters and putrescent ooze . . . and a stench as of liquefying corpses that had risen somewhere to the surface amid the fen.

Then, from the blank whiteness, the toads assailed Pierre in a surging, solid wave that towered above his head and swept him from the dim path with the force of falling seas as it descended. He went down, splashing and floundering, into water that swarmed with the numberless batrachians. Thick slime was in his mouth and nose as he struggled to regain his footing. The water, however, was only knee-deep, and the bottom, though slippery and oozy, supported him with little yielding when he stood erect.

He discerned indistinctly through the mist the nearby margin from which he had fallen. But his steps were weirdly and horribly hampered by the toad-seething waters when he strove to reach it. Inch by inch, with a hopeless panic deepening upon him, he fought toward the solid shore. The toads leaped and tumbled about him with a dizzying eddylike motion. They swirled like a viscid undertow around his feet and shins. They swept and swelled in great loathsome undulations against his retarded knees.

However, he made slow and painful progress, till his outstretched fingers could almost grasp the wiry sedges that trailed from the low bank. Then, from that mist-bound shore, there fell and broke upon him a second deluge of those demoniac toads; and Pierre was borne helplessly backward into the filthy waters.

Held down by the piling and crawling masses, and drowning in nauseous darkness at the thick-oozed bottom, he clawed feebly at his assailants. For a moment, ere oblivion came, his fingers found among them the outlines of a monstrous form that was somehow toadlike . . . but large and heavy as a fat woman. At the last, it seemed to him that two enormous breasts were crushed closely down upon his face.

THE END

151

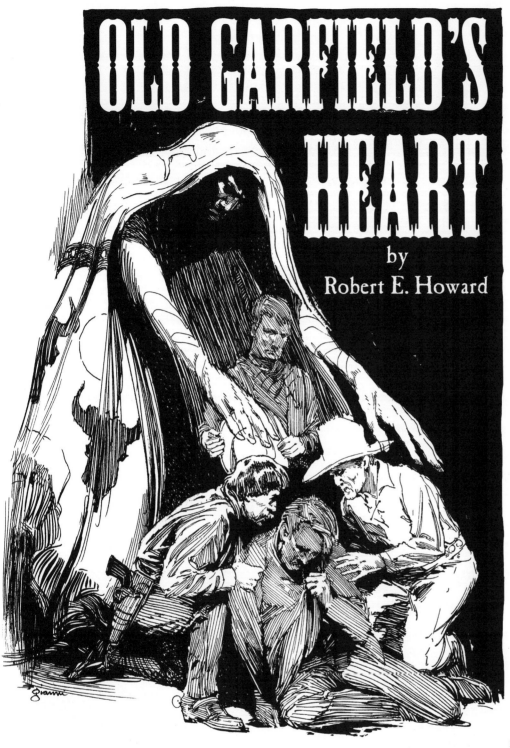

OLD GARFIELD'S HEART

by Robert E. Howard

My grandfather sucked his pipe noisily, and watched the heat lightning playing away off up in the hills; then he said: "You think old Jim's the biggest liar in this county, don't you?"

"He tells some pretty tall tales," I admitted. "Some of the things he claimed he took part in, must have happened before he was born."

"I came from Tennessee to Texas in 1870," my grandfather said abruptly. "I saw this town of Lost Knob grow up from nothin'. There wasn't even a log-hut store here when I came. But old Jim Garfield was here, livin' in the same place he lives now, only then it was a log cabin. He don't look a day older now than he did the first time I saw him."

"You never mentioned that before," I said in some surprise.

"I knew you'd put it down to an old man's maunderin's," he answered. "Old Jim was the first white man to settle in this country. He built his cabin a good fifty miles west of the frontier. God knows how he done it, for these hills swarmed with Comanches then.

"I remember the first time I ever saw him. Even then everybody called him 'old Jim.'

"I remember him tellin' me the same tales he's told you—how he was at the battle of San Jacinto when he was a youngster, and how he'd rode with Ewen Cameron and Jack Hayes. Only I believe him, and you don't."

"That was so long ago—"
I protested.

"The last Indian raid through this country was in 1874," said my grandfather, engrossed in his own reminiscences. "I was in on that fight, and so was old Jim. I saw him knock old Yellow Tail off his mustang at seven hundred yards with a buffalo rifle.

"But before that I was with him in a fight up near the head of Locust Creek. A band of Comanches came down Mesquital, lootin' and burnin', rode through the hills and started back up Locust Creek, and a scout of us were hot on their heels. We ran on to them just at sundown in a mesquite flat. We killed seven of them, and the rest skinned out through the brush on foot. But three of our boys were killed, and Jim Garfield got a thrust in the breast with a lance.

"It was an awful wound. He lay like a dead man, and it seemed

I WAS SITTING ON THE PORCH when my grandfather hobbled out and sank down on his favorite chair with the cushioned seat, and began to stuff tobacco in his old corncob-pipe.

"I thought you'd be goin' to the dance," he said.

"I'm waiting for Doc Blaine," I answered. "I'm going over to old man Garfield's with him."

My grandfather sucked at his pipe awhile before he spoke again.

"Old Jim purty bad off?"

"Doc says he hasn't a chance."

"Who's takin' care of him?"

"Joe Braxton—against Garfield's wishes. But somebody had to stay with him."

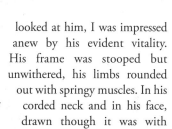

sure nobody could live after a wound like that. But an old Indian came out of the brush, and when we aimed our guns at him, he made the peace sign and spoke to us in Spanish. I don't know why the boys didn't shoot him in his tracks, because our blood was heated with the fightin' and killin', but somethin' about him made us hold our fire. He said he wasn't a Comanche, but was an old friend of Garfield's, and wanted to help him. He asked us to carry Jim into a clump of mesquite, and leave him alone with him, and to this day I don't know why we did, but we did. It was an awful time—the wounded moanin' and callin' for water, the starin' corpses strewn about the camp, night comin' on, and no way of knowin' that the Indians wouldn't return when dark fell.

"We made camp right there, because the horses were fagged out, and we watched all night, but the Comanches didn't come back. I don't know what went on out in the mesquite where Jim Garfield's body lay, because I never saw that strange Indian again, but durin' the night I kept hearin' a weird moanin' that wasn't made by the dyin' men, and an owl hooted from midnight till dawn.

"And at sunrise Jim Garfield came walkin' out of the mesquite, pale and haggard, but alive, and already the wound in his breast had closed and begun to heal. And since then he's never mentioned that wound, nor that fight, nor the strange Indian who came and went so mysteriously. And he hasn't aged a bit; he looks now just like he did then—a man of about fifty."

In the silence that followed, a car began to purr down the road, and twin shafts of light cut through the dusk.

"That's Doc Blaine," I said. "When I come back I'll tell you how Garfield is."

Doc Blaine was prompt with his predictions as we drove the three miles of post-oak covered hills that lay between Lost Knob and the Garfield farm.

"I'll be surprised to find him alive," he said, "smashed up like he is. A man his age ought to have more sense than to try to break a young horse."

"He doesn't look so old," I remarked.

"I'll be fifty, my next birthday," answered Doc Blaine. "I've known him all my life, and he must have been at least fifty the first time I ever saw him. His looks are deceiving."

Old Garfield's dwelling-place was reminiscent of the past. The boards of the low squat house had never known paint. Orchard fence and corrals were built of rails.

Old Jim lay on his rude bed, tended crudely but efficiently by the man Doc Blaine had hired over the old man's protests. As I looked at him, I was impressed anew by his evident vitality. His frame was stooped but unwithered, his limbs rounded out with springy muscles. In his corded neck and in his face, drawn though it was with suffering, was apparent an innate virility. His eyes, though partly glazed with pain, burned with the same unquenchable element.

"He's been ravin'," said Joe Braxton stolidly.

"First white man in this country," muttered old Jim, becoming intelligible. "Hills no white man ever set foot in before. Gettin' too old. Have to settle down. Can't move on like I used to. Settle down here. Good country before it filled up with cow-men and squatters. Wish Ewen Cameron could see this country. The Mexicans shot him. Damn 'em!"

Doc Blaine shook his head. "He's all smashed up inside. He won't live till daylight."

Garfield unexpectedly lifted his head and looked at us with clear eyes.

"Wrong, Doc," he wheezed, his breath whistling with pain. "I'll live. What's broken bones and twisted guts? Nothin'! It's the heart that counts. Long as the heart keeps pumpin', a man can't die. My heart's sound. Listen to it! Feel of it!"

He groped painfully for Doc Blaine's wrist, dragged his hand to his bosom and held it there, staring up into the doctor's face with avid intensity.

"Regular dynamo, ain't it?" he gasped. "Stronger'n a gasoline engine!"

Blaine beckoned me. "Lay your hand here," he said, placing my hand on the old man's bare breast. "He does have a remarkable heart action."

I noted, in the light of the coal-oil lamp, a great livid scar in the gaunt arching breast—such a scar as might be made by a flint-headed spear. I laid my hand directly on this scar, and an exclamation escaped my lips.

Under my hand old Jim Garfield's heart pulsed, but its throb was like no other heart action I have ever observed. Its power was astounding; his ribs vibrated to its steady throb. It felt more like the vibrating of a dynamo than the action of a human organ. I could

153

feel its amazing vitality radiating from his breast, stealing up into my hand and up my arm, until my own heart seemed to speed up in response.

"I can't die," old Jim gasped. "Not so long as my heart's in my breast. Only a bullet through the brain can kill me. And even then I wouldn't be rightly dead, as long as my heart beats in my breast. Yet it ain't rightly mine, either. It belongs to Ghost Man, the Lipan chief. It was the heart of a god the Lipans worshipped before the Comanches drove 'em out of their native hills.

"I knew Ghost Man down on the Rio Grande, when I was with Ewen Cameron. I saved his life from the Mexicans once. He tied the string of ghost wampum between him and me—the wampum no man but me and him can see or feel. He came when he knowed I needed him, in that fight up on the headwaters of Locust Creek, when I got this scar.

"I was dead as a man can be. My heart was sliced in two, like the heart of a butchered beef steer.

"All night Ghost Man did magic, callin' my ghost back from spirit-land. I remember that flight, a little. It was dark, and gray-like, and I drifted through gray mists and heard the dead wailin' past me in the mist. But Ghost Man brought me back.

"He took out what was left of my mortal heart, and put the heart of the god in my bosom. But it's his, and when I'm through with it, he'll come for it. It's kept me alive and strong for the lifetime of a man. Age can't touch me.

What do I care if these fools around here call me an old liar? What I know, I know. But hark'ee!"

His fingers became claws, clamping fiercely on Doc Blaine's wrist. His old eyes, old yet strangely young, burned fierce as those of an eagle under his bushy brows.

"If by some mischance I *should* die, now or later, promise me this! Cut into my bosom and take out the heart Ghost Man lent me so long ago! It's his. And as long as it beats in my body, my spirit'll be tied to that body, though my head be crushed like an egg underfoot! A livin' thing in a rottin' body! Promise!"

"All right, I promise," replied Doc Blaine, to humor him, and old Jim Garfield sank back with a whistling sigh of relief.

※ ※

He did not die that night, nor the next, nor the next. I well remember the next day, because it was that day that I had the fight with Jack Kirby.

People will take a good deal from a bully, rather than to spill blood. Because nobody had gone to the trouble of killing him, Kirby thought the whole countryside was afraid of him.

He had bought a steer from my father, and when my father went to collect for it, Kirby told him that he had paid the money to me—which was a lie. I went looking for Kirby, and came upon him in a bootleg joint, boasting of his toughness, and telling the crowd that he was going to beat me up and make me say that he had paid me the money, and that I had stuck it into my own pocket. When I heard him say that, I saw red, and ran in on him with a stockman's knife, and cut him across the face, and in the neck, side, breast and belly, and the only thing that saved his life was the fact that the crowd pulled me off.

There was a preliminary hearing, and I was indicted on a charge of assault, and my trial was set for the following term of court Kirby was as tough-fibered as a post-oak country bully ought to be, and he recovered, swearing vengeance, for he was vain of his looks, though God knows why, and I had permanently impaired them.

And while Jack Kirby was recovering, old man Garfield recovered too, to the amazement of everybody, especially Doc Blaine.

I well remember the night Doc Blaine took me again out to old Jim Garfield's farm. I was in Shifty Corlan's joint, trying to drink enough of the slop he called beer to get a kick out of it, when Doc Blaine came in and persuaded me to go with him.

As we drove along the winding old road in Doc's car, I asked: "Why are you insistent that I go with you this particular night? This isn't a professional call, is it?"

"No," he said. "You couldn't kill old Jim with a post-oak maul. He's completely recovered from injuries that ought to have killed

"None, Doc," said Garfield, pulling at his pipe. "It was gospel truth. Ghost Man, the Lipan priest of the Gods of Night, replaced my dead, torn heart with one from somethin' he worshipped. I ain't sure myself just what that somethin' is—somethin' from away back and a long way off, he said. But bein' a god, it can do without its heart for awhile. But when I die—if I ever get my head smashed so my consciousness is destroyed—the heart must be given back to Ghost Man."

"You mean you were in earnest about cutting out your heart?" demanded Doc Blaine.

"It has to be," answered old Garfield. "A livin' thing in a dead thing is opposed to nat'er. That's what Ghost Man said."

"Who the devil *was* Ghost Man?"

"I told you. A witch-doctor of the Lipans, who dwelt in this country before the Comanches came down from the Staked Plains and drove 'em south across the Rio Grande. I was a friend to 'em. I reckon Ghost Man is the only one left alive."

"Alive? Now?"

"I dunno," confessed old Jim. "I dunno whether he's alive or dead. I dunno whether he was alive when he came to me after the fight on Locust Creek, or even if he was alive when I knowed him in the southern country. Alive as we understand life, I mean."

"What balderdash is this?" demanded Doc Blaine uneasily, and I felt a slight stirring in my hair. Outside was stillness, and the stars, and the black shadows of the post-oak woods. The lamp cast old Garfield's shadow grotesquely on the wall, so that it did not at all resemble that of a human, and his words were strange as words heard in a nightmare.

"I knowed you wouldn't understand," said old Jim. "I don't understand myself, and I ain't got the words to explain them things I feel and know without understandin'. The Lipans were kin to the Apaches, and the Apaches learnt curious things from the Pueblos. Ghost Man *was*—that's all I can say—alive or dead, I don't know, but he *was*. What's more, he *is*."

"Is it you or me that's crazy?" asked Doc Blaine.

"Well," said old Jim, "I'll tell you this much—Ghost Man knew Coronado."

"Crazy as a loon!" murmured Doc Blaine. Then he lifted his head. "What's that?"

"Horse turning in from the road," I said. "Sounds like it stopped."

an ox. To tell the truth, Jack Kirby is in Lost Knob, swearing he'll shoot you on sight."

"Well, for God's sake!" I exclaimed angrily. "Now everybody'll think I left town because I was afraid of him. Turn around and take me back, damn it!"

"Be reasonable," said Doc. "Everybody knows you're not afraid of Kirby. Nobody's afraid of him now. His bluff's broken, and that's why he's so wild against you. But you can't afford to have any more trouble with him now, and your trial only a short time off."

I laughed and said: "Well, if he's looking for me hard enough, he can find me as easily at old Garfield's as in town, because Shifty Corlan heard you say where we were going. And Shifty's hated me ever since I skinned him in that horse-swap last fall. He'll tell Kirby where I went."

"I never thought of that," said Doc Blaine, worried.

"Hell, forget it," I advised. "Kirby hasn't got guts enough to do anything but blow."

But I was mistaken. Puncture a bully's vanity and you touch his one vital spot.

Old Jim had not gone to bed when we got there. He was sitting in the room opening on to his sagging porch, the room which was at once living-room and bedroom, smoking his old cob pipe and trying to read a newspaper by the light of his coal-oil lamp. All the windows and doors were wide open for the coolness, and the insects which swarmed in and fluttered around the lamp didn't seem to bother him.

We sat down and discussed the weather—which isn't so inane as one might suppose, in a country where men's livelihood depends on sun and rain, and is at the mercy of wind and drouth. The talk drifted into other kindred channels, and after some time, Doc Blaine bluntly spoke of something that hung in his mind.

"Jim," he said, "that night I thought you were dying, you babbled a lot of stuff about your heart, and an Indian who lent you his. How much of that was delirium?"

I stepped to the door, like a fool, and stood etched in the light behind me. I got a glimpse of a shadowy bulk I knew to be a man on a horse; then Doc Blaine yelled: "Look out!" and threw himself against me, knocking us both sprawling. At the same instant I heard the smashing report of a rifle, and old Garfield grunted and fell heavily.

"Jack Kirby!" screamed Doc Blaine.

"He's killed Jim!"

I scrambled up, hearing the clatter of retreating hoofs, snatched old Jim's shotgun from the wall, rushed recklessly out on to the sagging porch and let go both barrels at the fleeing shape, dim in

the starlight. The charge was too light to kill at that range, but the bird-shot stung the horse and maddened him. He swerved, crashed headlong through a rail fence and charged across the orchard, and a peach tree limb knocked his rider out of the saddle. He never moved after he hit the ground. I ran out there and looked down at him. It was Jack Kirby, right enough, and his neck was broken like a rotten branch.

I let him lie, and ran back to the house. Doc Blaine had stretched old Garfield out on a bench he'd dragged in from the porch, and Doc's face was whiter than I'd ever seen it. Old Jim was a ghastly sight; he had been shot with an old-fashioned .45-70, and at that range the heavy ball had literally torn off the top of his head. His features were masked with blood and brains. He had been directly behind me, poor old devil, and he had stopped the slug meant for me.

Doc Blaine was trembling, though he was anything but a stranger to such sights.

"Would you pronounce him dead?" he asked.

"That's for you to say," I answered. "But even a fool could tell that he's dead."

"He *is* dead," said Doc Blaine in a strained unnatural voice. "Rigor mortis is already setting in. But feel his heart!"

I did, and cried out. The flesh was already cold and clammy; but beneath it that mysterious heart still hammered steadily away, like a dynamo in a deserted house. No blood coursed through those veins; yet the heart pounded, pounded, pounded, like the pulse of Eternity.

"A living thing in a dead thing," whispered Doc Blaine, cold sweat on his face. "This is opposed to nature. I am going to keep the promise I made him. I'll assume full responsibility. This is too monstrous to ignore."

Our implements were a butcher-knife and a hack-saw. Outside only the still stars looked down on the black post-oak shadows and the dead man that lay in the orchard. Inside, the old lamp flickered, making strange shadows move and shiver and cringe in the corners, and glistened on the blood on the floor, and the red-dabbled figure on the bench. The only sound inside was the crunch of the saw-edge in bone; outside an owl began to hoot weirdly.

Doc Blaine thrust a red-stained hand into the aperture he had made, and drew out a red, pulsing object that caught the lamplight. With a choked cry he recoiled, and the thing slipped from his fingers and fell on the table. And I too cried out involuntarily. For it did not fall with a soft meaty thud, as a piece of flesh should fall. It *thumped* hard on the table.

Impelled by an irresistible urge, I bent and gingerly picked up old Garfield's heart. The feel of it was brittle, unyielding, like steel or stone, but smoother than either. In size and shape it was the duplicate of a human heart, but it was slick and smooth, and its crimson surface reflected the lamplight like a jewel more lambent than any ruby; and in my hand it still throbbed mightily, sending vibratory radiations of energy up my arm until my own heart seemed swelling and bursting in response. It was cosmic *power*, beyond my comprehension, concentrated into the likeness of a human heart.

The thought came to me that here was a dynamo of life, the nearest approach to immortality that is possible for the destructible human body, the materialization of a cosmic secret more wonderful than the fabulous fountain sought for by Ponce de Leon. My soul was drawn into that unterrestrial gleam, and I suddenly wished passionately that it hammered and thundered in my own bosom in place of my paltry heart of tissue and muscle.

Doc Blaine ejaculated incoherently. I wheeled.

The noise of his coming had been no greater than the whispering of a night wind through the corn. There in the doorway he stood, tall, dark, inscrutable—an Indian warrior, in the paint, war bonnet, breech-clout and moccasins of an elder age. His dark eyes burned like fires gleaming deep under fathomless black lakes. Silently he extended his hand, and I dropped Jim Garfield's heart into it. Then without a word he turned and stalked into the night. But when Doc Blaine and I rushed out into the yard an instant later, there was no sign of any human being. He had vanished like a phantom of the night, and only something that looked like an owl was flying, dwindling from sight, into the rising moon.

THE END

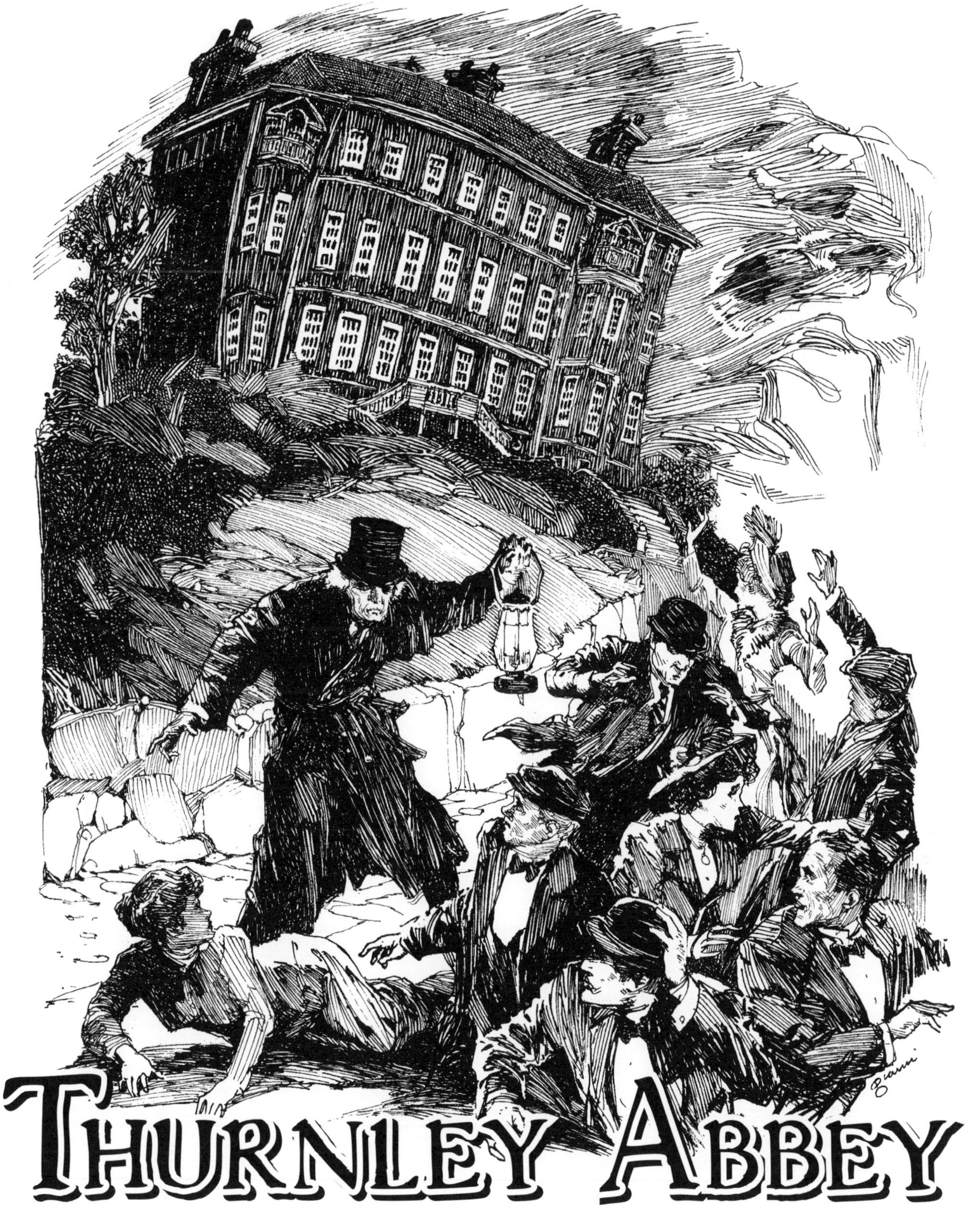

THURNLEY ABBEY

by Perceval Landon

THREE YEARS AGO I WAS on my way out to the East, and as an extra day in London was of some importance, I took the Friday evening mail-train to Brindisi instead of the usual Thursday morning Marseilles express. Many people shrink from the long, forty-eight-hour train journey through Europe, and the subsequent rush across the Mediterranean on the nineteen-knot *Isis* or *Osiris*; but there is really very little discomfort on either the train or the mail-boat, and unless there is actually nothing for me to do, I always like to save the extra day and a half in London. This time—it was early in the shipping season, probably about the beginning of September—there were few passengers, and I had a compartment to myself in the P. & O. Indian Express all the way from Calais. The journey was just like any other. We slept after luncheon; we dawdled the afternoon away with yellow-backed novels; sometimes we exchanged platitudes in the smoking room, and it was there that I met Alastair Colvin.

Colvin was a man of middle height, with a resolute, well-cut jaw; his hair was turning grey; his moustache was sun whitened, but otherwise he was clean-shaven—obviously a gentleman, and obviously also a preoccupied man. He had no great wit. When spoken to, he made the usual remarks in the right way, and I dare say he refrained from banalities only because he spoke less than the rest of us.

Of course this did not seem to me to be of any importance. Most travelers by train become a trifle infirm of purpose after thirty-six hours' rattling. But Colvin's restless way I noticed in somewhat marked contrast with the man's personal importance and dignity, especially ill suited to his finely made large hand with strong, broad, regular nails and its few lines. As I looked at his hand I noticed a long, deep, and recent scar of ragged shape. However, it is absurd to pretend that I thought anything was unusual. I went off at five o'clock on Sunday afternoon to sleep away the hour or two that had still to be got through before we arrived at Brindisi.

Once there, we few passengers transhipped our hand baggage, verified our berths—there were only a score of us in all—and then, after an aimless ramble of half an hour in Brindisi, we returned to dinner at the Hotel International, not wholly surprised that the town had been the death of Virgil. After dinner I was looking with awe at a trellis overgrown with blue vines, when Colvin moved across the room to my table. He picked up *Il Secolo*, but almost immediately gave up the pretence of reading it. He turned squarely to me and said:

"Would you do me a favour?"

One doesn't do favours to stray acquaintances on Continental expresses without knowing something more of them than I knew of Colvin. But I smiled in a noncommittal way, and asked him what he wanted. I wasn't wrong in part of my estimate of him; he said bluntly:

"Will you let me sleep in your cabin on the *Osiris*?" And he coloured a little as he said it.

Now, there is nothing more tiresome than having to put up with a stable companion at sea, and I asked him rather pointedly:

"Surely there is room for all of us?" I thought that perhaps he had been partnered off with some mangy Levantine, and wanted to escape from him at all hazards.

Colvin, still somewhat confused, said, "Yes, I am in a cabin by myself. But you would do me the greatest favour if you would allow me to share yours."

This was all very well, but, besides the fact that I always sleep better when alone, there had been some recent thefts onboard English liners, and I hesitated, frank and honest and self-conscious

as Colvin was. Just then the mail-train came in with a clatter and a rush of escaping steam, and I asked him to see me again about it on the boat when we started. He answered me curtly—I suppose he saw the mistrust in my manner—"I am a member of White's." I smiled to myself as he said it, but I remembered in a moment that the man—if he were really what he claimed to be, and I make no doubt that he was—must have been sorely put to it before he urged that fact as a guarantee of his respectability to a total stranger at a Brindisi hotel.

That evening, as we cleared the red and green harbor lights of Brindisi, Colvin explained. This is his story in his own words.

"When I was traveling in India some years ago, I made the acquaintance of a youngish man in the Woods and Forests. We camped out together for a week, and I found him a pleasant companion. John Broughton was a light-hearted soul when off duty, but a steady and capable man in any of the small emergencies that continually arise in that department. He was liked and trusted by the natives, and though a trifle over-pleased with himself when he escaped to civilization at Simla or Calcutta, Broughton's future was well assured in government service, when a fair-sized estate was unexpectedly left to him, and he joyfully shook the dust of the Indian plains from his feet and returned to England. For five years he drifted about London. I saw him now and then. We dined together about every eighteen months, and I could trace pretty exactly the gradual sickening of Broughton with a merely idle life. At last he told me that he had decided to marry and settle down at his place, Thurnley Abbey, which had long been empty. He spoke about looking after the property and standing for his constituency in the usual way. Vivien Wilde, his fiancée, had, I suppose, begun to take him in hand.

"Among other things, I asked him about Thurnley Abbey. He confessed that he hardly knew the place. The last tenant, a man called Clarke, had lived in one wing for fifteen years and seen no one. He had been a miser and a hermit. It was the rarest thing for a light to be seen at the Abbey after dark. Only the barest necessities of life were ordered, and the tenant himself received them at the side door. His one half-caste manservant, after a month's stay in the house, had abruptly left without warning, and had returned to the Southern States. One thing Broughton

any time I liked? I, of course, said I would, and equally, of course, intended to do nothing of the sort without a definite invitation.

"The house was put in thorough repair, though not a stick of the old furniture and tapestry was removed. Floors and ceilings were relaid; the roof was made watertight again, and the dust of half a century was scoured out. It was called an Abbey, though as a matter of fact it had been only the infirmary of the long-vanished Abbey of Clouster some five miles away. The larger part of the building remained as it had been in pre-Reformation days, but a wing had been added in Jacobean times, and that part of the house had been kept in something like repair by Mr. Clarke. He had, in both the ground and first floors, set heavy timber doors, strongly barred with iron, in the passage between the earlier and the Jacobean parts of the house, and had entirely neglected the former. So there had been a good deal of work to be done.

"Broughton, whom I saw in London two or three times about this period, made a deal of fun over the positive refusal of the workmen to remain after sundown. Even after electric light had been put into every room, nothing would induce them to remain, though, as Broughton observed, electric light was death on ghosts. The legend of the Abbey's ghosts had gone far and wide, and the men would take no risks. They went home in batches of five and six, and even during the daylight hours there was an inordinate amount of talking between one another, if either happened to be out of sight of his companion. On the whole, though nothing of any sort had been conjured up even by their heated imaginations during their five months' work upon the Abbey, the belief in the ghosts was rather strengthened than otherwise because of the men's confessed nervousness, and local tradition declared itself in favor of the ghost of an immured nun.

" 'Good old nun!' said Broughton.

"I asked him whether in general he believed in the possibility of ghosts, and, rather to my surprise, he said that he couldn't say he entirely disbelieved in them. A man in India had told him one morning in camp that he believed that his mother was dead in England, as her vision had come to his tent the night before. He had not been alarmed, but had said nothing, and the figure vanished again. As a matter of fact, the next possible dak-walla brought on a telegram announcing the mother's death. 'There the thing was,' said Broughton. But at Thurnley he was practical enough. He roundly cursed the idiotic selfishness of Clarke, whose silly antics had caused all the inconvenience. At the same time, he couldn't refuse to sympathize to some extent with the ignorant workmen. 'My own idea,' said he, 'is that if a ghost ever does come in one's way, one ought to speak to it.'

"I agreed. Little as I knew of the ghost world and its conventions, I had always remembered that a spook was honor bound to wait to be spoken to. It didn't seem much to do, and I felt that the sound of one's own voice would at any rate reassure oneself as to one's wakefulness. But there are few ghosts outside Europe—few, that is, that a white man can see—and I had never been troubled with any. However, as I have said, I told Broughton that I agreed.

"So the wedding took place, and I went to it in a tall hat which I bought for the occasion, and the new Mrs. Broughton smiled very nicely at me afterwards. As it had to happen, I took the Orient Express that evening and was not in England again for nearly six months. Just before I came back, I got a letter from Broughton. He asked if I could see him in London or come to

complained bitterly about: Clarke had wilfully spread the rumor among the villagers that the Abbey was haunted, and had even condescended to play childish tricks with spirit-lamps and salt in order to scare trespassers away at night. He had been detected in the act of this tomfoolery, but the story spread, and no one, said Broughton, would venture near the house except in broad daylight. The hauntedness of Thurnley Abbey was now, he said with a grin, part of the gospel of the countryside, but he and his young wife were going to change all that. Would I propose myself

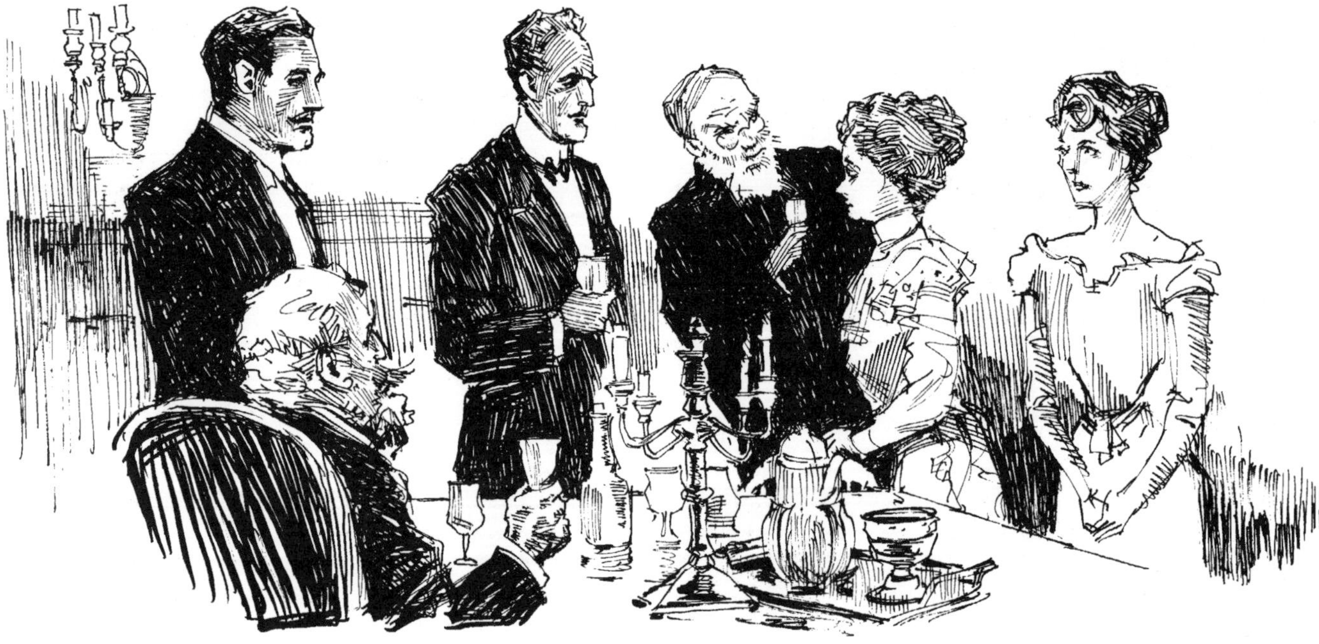

Thurnley, as he thought I should be better able to help him than anyone else he knew. I had nothing to do, so after dealing with some small accumulation of business during my absence, I packed a kit-bag and departed to Euston. I was met by Broughton's great limousine at Thurnley Road station, and after a drive of nearly seven miles, I could see the Abbey across a wide pasturage.

"Broughton had seen me coming from afar, and walked across from his other guests to welcome me. There was no doubt that the man was altered, gravely altered. He was nervous and fidgety, and I found him looking at me only when my eye was off him. I naturally asked him what he wanted of me. I told him I would do anything I could, but that I couldn't conceive what he lacked that I could provide. He said with a lusterless smile that there was, however, something, and that he would tell me the following morning. It struck me that he was somehow ashamed of himself, and perhaps ashamed of the part he was asking me to play. However, I dismissed the subject from my mind and went up to dress in my palatial room.

"It was a very large low room with oak beams projecting from the white ceiling. Every inch of the walls, including the doors, was covered with tapestry, and a remarkably fine Italian fourpost bedstead, heavily draped, added to the darkness and dignity of the place. All the furniture was old, well made, and dark. Underfoot there was a plain green pile carpet, the only new thing about the room except the electric-light fittings and the jugs and basins. Even the looking glass on the dressing table was an old pyramidal Venetian glass set in a heavy repoussé frame of tarnished silver.

"After a few minutes' cleaning up, I went downstairs. Nothing much happened at dinner. The people were very much like those of the garden party. A young woman next to me seemed anxious to know what was being read in London. As she was far more familiar than I with the most recent magazines and literary supplements, I found salvation in being myself instructed in the tendencies of modern fiction. She was a cheerless soul, yet nothing could have been less creepy than the glitter of silver and glass, and the subdued lights and cackle of conversation all around the dinner table.

"After the ladies had gone I found myself talking to the rural dean. He was a thin, earnest man, who at once turned the conversation to old Clarke's buffooneries. But, he said, Mr. Broughton had introduced such a new and cheerful spirit, not only into the Abbey, but, he might say, into the whole neighbourhood,

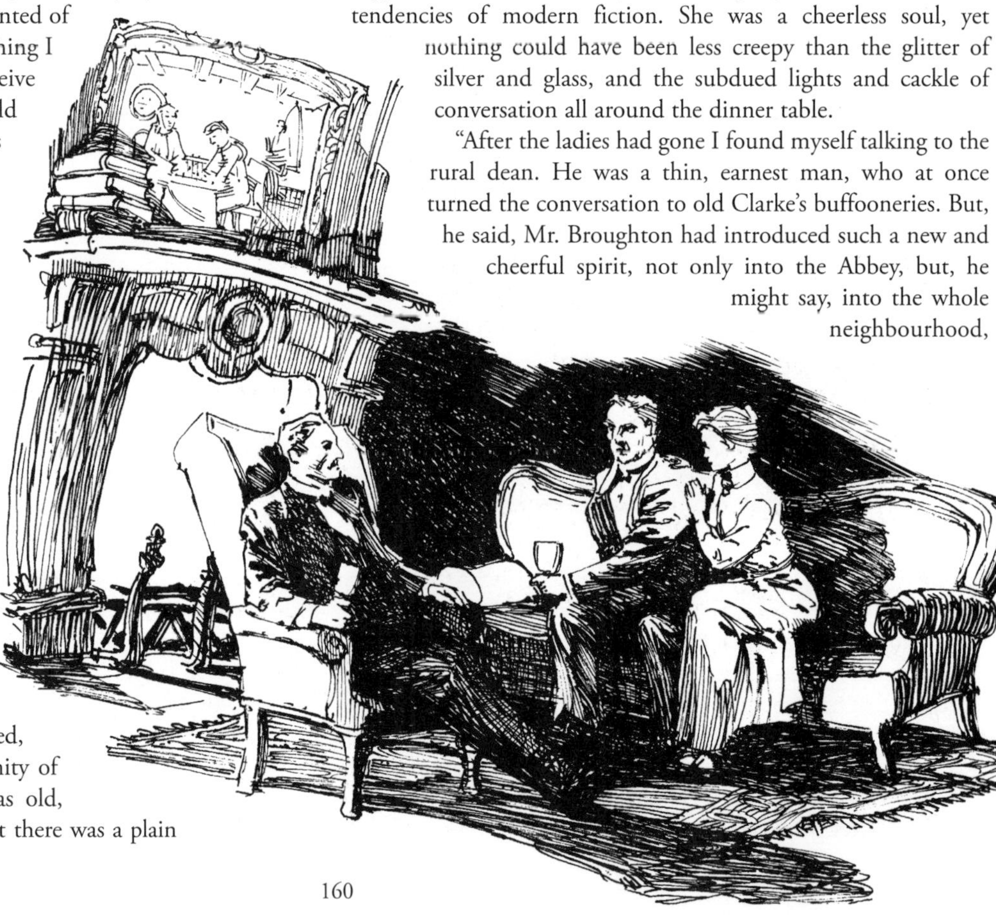

that he had great hopes that the ignorant superstitions of the past were henceforth destined to oblivion. Thereupon his other neighbour, a portly gentleman of independent means and position, audibly remarked, 'Amen,' which damped the rural dean, and we talked of partridges past, partridges present, and pheasants to come. At the other end of the table Broughton sat with a couple of his friends, red-faced hunting men. Once I noticed that they were discussing me, but I paid no attention to it at the time. I remembered it a few hours later.

"By eleven all the guests were gone, and Broughton, his wife, and I were alone together under the fine plaster ceiling of the Jacobean drawing room. Mrs. Broughton talked about one or two of the neighbours, and then, with a smile, said that she knew I would excuse her, shook hands with me, and went off to bed. I am not very good at analyzing things, but I felt that she talked a little uncomfortably and with a suspicion of effort, smiled rather conventionally, and was obviously glad to go. These things seem trifling enough to repeat, but I had the faint feeling that everything was not quite square. Under the circumstances, this was enough to set me wondering what on earth the service could be that I was to render—wondering also whether the whole business were not some ill-advised jest in order to make me come down from London for a mere shooting party.

"Broughton said little after she had gone. But he was evidently laboring to bring the conversation around to the so-called haunting of the Abbey. As soon as I saw this, of course I asked him directly about it. He then seemed at once to lose interest in the matter. There was no doubt about it: Broughton was somehow a changed man, and to my mind he had changed in no way for the better. Mrs. Broughton seemed no sufficient cause. He was clearly very fond of her, and she of him. I reminded him that he was going to tell me what I could do for him in the morning, pleaded my journey, lit a candle, and went upstairs with him. At the end of the passage leading into the old house he grinned weakly and said, 'Mind, if you see a ghost, do talk to it; you said you would.' He stood irresolutely a moment and then turned away. At the door of his dressing room he paused once more: 'I'm here,' he called out, 'if you should want anything. Good night,' and he shut the door.

"I went along the passage to my room, undressed, switched on a lamp beside my bed, read a few pages of *The Jungle Book*, and

then, more than ready for sleep, turned the light off and went fast asleep.

"Three hours later I woke up. There was not a breath of wind outside. There was not even a flicker of light from the fireplace. As I lay there, an ash tinkled slightly as it cooled, but there was hardly a gleam of the dullest red in the grate. An owl cried among the silent Spanish chestnuts on the slope outside. I idly reviewed the events of the day, hoping that I should fall off to sleep again before I reached dinner. But at the end I seemed as wakeful as ever. There was no help for it. I must read my *Jungle Book* again till I felt ready to go off, so I fumbled for the pear at the end of the cord that hung down inside the bed, and I switched on the bedside lamp. The sudden glory dazzled me for a moment. I felt under my pillow for my book with half-shut eyes. Then, growing used to the light, I happened to look down to the foot of my bed.

"I can never tell you really what happened then. Nothing I could ever confess in the most abject words could even faintly picture to you what I felt. I know that my heart stopped dead, and my throat shut automatically. In one instinctive movement I crouched back up against the headboards of the bed, staring at the horror. The movement set my heart going again, and the sweat dripped from every pore. I am not a particularly religious man, but I had always believed that God would never allow any supernatural appearance to present itself to man in such a guise and in such circumstances that harm, either bodily or mental, could result to him. I can only tell you that at the moment both my life and my reason rocked unsteadily on their seats."

The other *Osiris* passengers had gone to bed. Only Colvin and I remained leaning over the starboard railing, which rattled uneasily now and then under the fierce vibration of the over-engined mail-boat. Far over, there were the lights of a few fishing-smacks riding out the night, and a great rush of white combing and seething water fell out and away from us overside.

At last Colvin went on:

"Leaning over the foot of my bed, looking at me, was a figure swathed in a rotten and tattered veiling. This shroud passed over the head, but left both eyes and the right side of the face bare. It then followed the line of the arm down to where the hand grasped the bed end. The face was not entirely that of a skull, though the eyes and the flesh of the face were totally gone. There was a thin, dry skin drawn tightly over the features, and there was some skin

left on the hand. One wisp of hair crossed the forehead. It was perfectly still. I looked at it, and it looked at me, and my brains turned dry and hot in my head. I had still got the pear of the electric lamp in my hand, and I played idly with it; only I dared not turn the light out again. I shut my eyes, only to open them in a hideous terror the same second. The thing had not moved. My heart was thumping, and the sweat cooled me as it evaporated. Another cinder tinkled in the grate, and a panel creaked in the wall.

"My reason failed me. For twenty minutes, or twenty seconds, I was able to think of nothing else but this awful figure, till there came, hurtling through the empty channels of my senses, the remembrances that Broughton and his friends had discussed with me furtively at dinner. The dim possibility of it being a hoax stole gratefully into my unhappy mind, and once there, pluck came creeping back along a thousand tiny veins. My first sensation was one of blind unreasoning thankfulness that my brain was going to stand the trial. I am not a timid man, but the best of us needs some human handle to steady him in time of extremity, and in this faint but growing hope that it might be only a brutal hoax, I found the fulcrum that I needed. At last I moved.

"How I managed to do it I cannot tell you, but with one spring toward the foot of the bed I got within arm's length and struck out one fearful blow with my fist at the thing. It crumbled under it, and my hand was cut to the bone. With a sickening revulsion after my terror, I dropped half-fainting across the end of the bed. So it was merely a foul trick after all. No doubt the trick had been played many a time before: no doubt Broughton and his friends had had some large bet among themselves as to what I should do when I discovered the gruesome thing. From my state of abject terror I found myself transported into an insensate anger. I shouted curses upon Broughton. I dived rather than climbed over the bed-end of the sofa. I tore at the robed skeleton—how well the whole thing had been carried out, I thought—I broke the skull against the floor, and stamped upon its dry bones. I flung the head away under the bed, and rent the brittle bones of the trunk in pieces. I snapped the thin thigh bones across my knee, and flung them in different directions. The shin bones I set up against a stool and broke with my heel. I raged like a berserker against the loathly thing, and stripped the ribs from the backbone and slung the breastbone against the cupboard. My fury increased as the work of destruction went on. I tore the frail rotten veil into twenty

pieces, and the dust went up over everything, over the clean blotting paper and the silver inkstand. At last my work was done. There was but a raffle of broken bones and strips of parchment and crumbling wool. Then, picking up a piece of the skull—it was the cheek and temple bone of the right side, I remember—I opened the door and went down the passage to Broughton's dressing room. I remember still how my sweat-dripping pajamas clung to me as I walked. At the door I kicked and entered.

"Broughton was in bed. He had already turned the light on and seemed shrunken and horrified. For a moment he could hardly pull himself together. Then I spoke. I don't know what I said. I know only that from a heart full and over full with hatred and contempt, spurred on by shame of my own recent cowardice, I let my tongue run on. He answered nothing. I was amazed at my own fluency. My hair still clung lankly to my wet temples, my hand was bleeding profusely, and I must have looked a strange sight. Broughton huddled himself at the head of the bed just as I had. Still he made no answer, no defense. He seemed preoccupied with something besides my reproaches, and once or twice moistened his lips with his tongue. He could say nothing, though he moved his hands now and then, just as a baby who cannot speak moves its hands.

"At last the door into Mrs. Broughton's rooms opened and she came in, white and terrified. 'What is it? What is it? Oh, in God's name! What is it?' she cried again and again, and then she went up to her husband and sat on the bed in her night-dress, and the two faced me. I told her what the matter was. I spared her husband not a word for her presence there. Yet he seemed hardly to understand. I told the pair that I had spoiled their cowardly joke for them. Broughton looked up.

" 'I have smashed the foul thing into a hundred pieces,' I said. Broughton licked his lips again and his mouth worked. 'By God!' I shouted, 'it would serve you right if I thrashed you within an inch of your life. I will take care that not a decent man or woman of my acquaintance ever speaks to you again. And there,' I added, throwing the broken piece of the skull upon the floor beside his bed, 'there is a souvenir for you, of your damned work tonight!'

"Broughton saw the bone, and in a moment it was his turn to frighten me. He squealed like a hare caught in a trap. He screamed and screamed till Mrs. Broughton, almost as bewildered as myself, held on to him and coaxed him like a child to be quiet. But Broughton—and as he moved I thought that ten minutes ago I perhaps looked as terribly ill as he did—thrust her from him, and scrambled out of bed on to the floor, and, still screaming, put out his hand to the bone. It had blood on it from my

hand. He paid no attention to me whatever. In truth I said nothing. This was a new turn indeed to the horrors of the evening. He rose from the floor with the bone in his hand and stood silent. He seemed to be listening. 'Time, time, perhaps,' he muttered, and almost at the same moment fell at full length on the carpet, cutting his head against the fender. The bone flew from his hand and came to rest near the door. I picked Broughton up, haggard and broken, with blood over his face. He whispered hoarsely and quickly, 'Listen, listen!' We listened.

"After ten seconds' utter quiet, I seemed to hear something. I could not be sure, but at last there was no doubt. There was a quiet sound as one moving along the passage. Little regular steps came toward us over the hard oak flooring. Broughton moved to where his wife sat, white and speechless, on the bed, and pressed her face into his shoulder.

"Then—the last thing that I could see as he turned the light out—he fell forward with his own head pressed into the pillow of the bed. Something in their company, something in their cowardice, helped me, and I faced the open doorway of the room, which was outlined fairly clearly against the dimly lit passage. I put out one hand and touched Mrs. Broughton's shoulder in the darkness, but at the last moment I too failed. I sank on my knees and put my face in the bed. Only we all heard. The footsteps came to the door and there they stopped. The piece of bone was lying a yard inside the door. There was a rustle of moving stuff, and the thing was in the room. Mrs. Broughton was silent: I could hear

Broughton's voice praying, muffled in the pillow. I was cursing my own cowardice. Then the steps moved out again on the oak boards of the passage, and I heard the sounds dying away. In a flash of remorse I went to the door and looked out. At the end of the corridor I thought I saw something that moved away. A moment later the passage was empty. I stood with my forehead against the jamb of the door almost physically sick.

" 'You can turn the light on,' I said, and there was an answering flare. There was no bone at my feet. Mrs. Broughton had fainted. Broughton was almost useless, and it took me ten minutes to bring her to. Broughton only said one thing worth remembering. For the most part he went on muttering prayers. But I was glad afterwards to recollect that he had said that thing. He said in a colourless voice, half as a question, half as a reproach, 'You didn't speak to her.'

"We spent the remainder of the night together. Mrs. Broughton actually fell off into a kind of sleep before dawn, but she suffered so horribly in her dreams that I shook her into consciousness again. Never was dawn so long in coming. Three or four times Broughton spoke to himself. Mrs. Broughton would then just tighten her hold on his arm, but she could say nothing. As for me, I can honestly say that I grew worse as the hours passed and the light strengthened. The two violent reactions had battered down my steadiness of view, and I felt that the foundations of my life had been built upon the sand. I said nothing, and after binding up my hand with a towel, I did not move. It was better so. They helped me and I helped them, and we all three knew that our reason had gone very near to ruin that night. At last, when the light came in pretty strongly, and the birds outside were chattering and singing, we felt that we must do something. Yet we never moved. You might have thought that we should particularly dislike being found as we were by the servants, yet nothing of that kind mattered a straw, and an overpowering listlessness bound us as we sat, until Chapman, Broughton's man, actually knocked and opened the door. None of us moved. Broughton, speaking hardly and stiffly, said, 'Chapman, you can come back in five minutes.' Chapman was a discreet man, but it would have made no difference to us if he had carried his news to the 'room' at once.

"We looked at each other and I said I must go back. I meant to wait outside till Chapman returned. I simply dared not re-enter my bedroom alone. Broughton roused himself and said that he would come with me. Mrs. Broughton agreed to remain in her own room for five minutes if the blinds were drawn up and all the doors left open.

"So Broughton and I, leaning stiffly one against the other, went down to my room. By the morning light that filtered past the blinds we could see our way, and I released the blinds. There was nothing wrong with the room from end to end, except smears of my own blood on the end of the bed, on the sofa, and on the carpet where I had torn the thing to pieces."

Colvin had finished his story. There was nothing to say. Seven bells stuttered out from the fo'c'sle, and the answering cry wailed through the darkness. I took him downstairs.

"Of course I am much better now, but it is a kindness of you to let me sleep in your cabin."

THE END

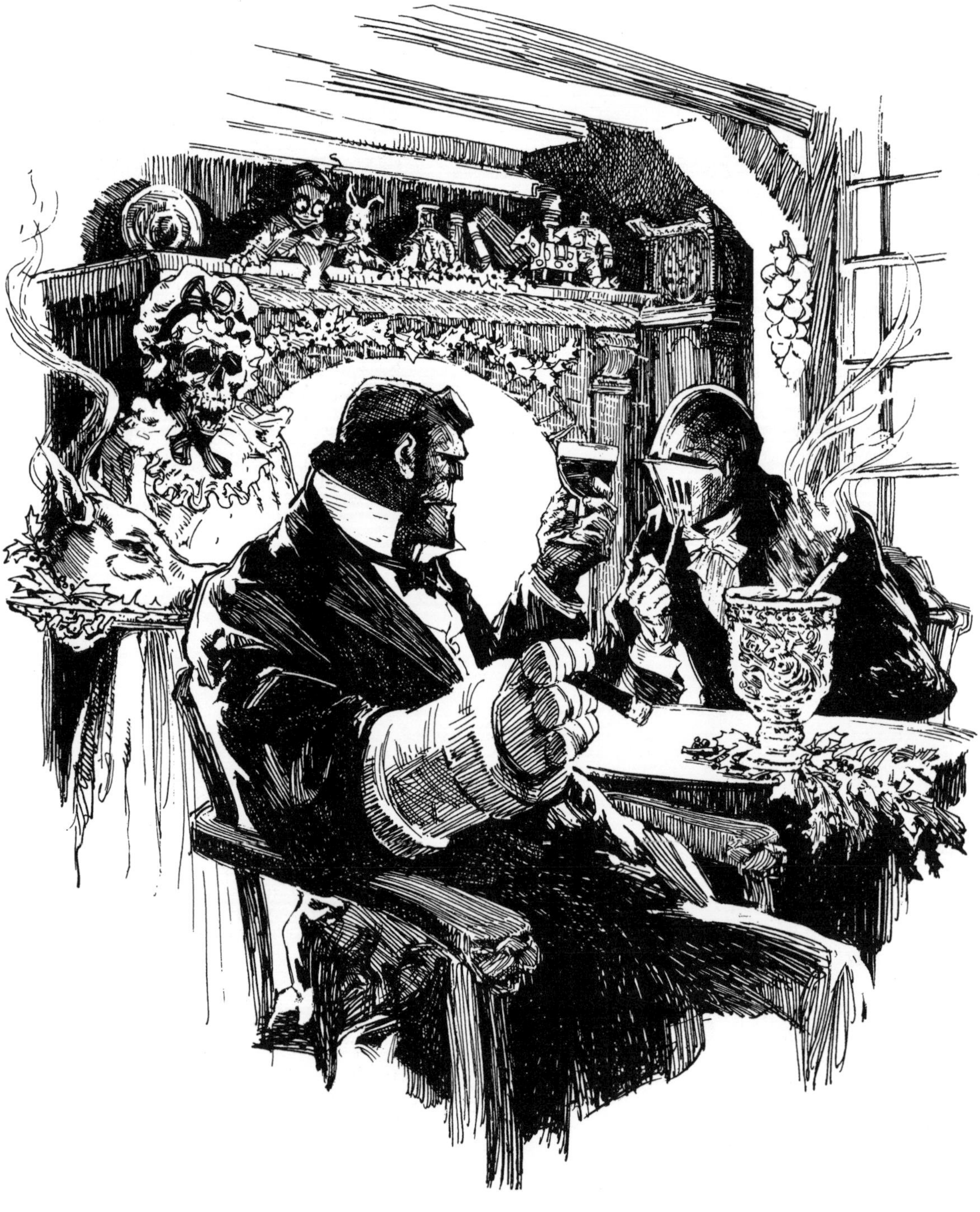

GARY GIANNI's *MonsterMen* stories originally appeared as a backup feature in Mike Mignola's *Hellboy* comics. Gianni began his career as an illustrator for Chicago newspapers and as a courtroom artist. In comics, his work includes *The Shadow*, *Indiana Jones*, *Tarzan*, *Tom Strong*, and *Twenty-Thousand Leagues Under the Sea*, and in 1997 he and Archie Goodwin received an Eisner for their Batman story "Heroes."

He has also illustrated a number of books featuring Robert E. Howard's Conan, Bran Mak Morn, and Solomon Kane. More recently he illustrated Michael Chabon's *Gentlemen of the Road* and Ray Bradbury's *Nefertiti-Tut Express*.

Gianni drew the syndicated newspaper comic strip *Prince Valiant* from 2004 to 2012.

RECOMMENDED DARK HORSE READING

steve niles
CRIMINAL MACABRE
the cal mcdonald mysteries
OMNIBUS
VOLUME 1

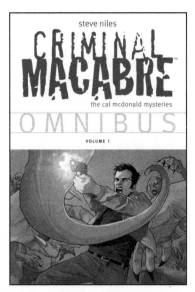

CRIMINAL MACABRE OMNIBUS VOLUME 1

Steve Niles, Kelley Jones, Ben Templesmith

Pill-popping, alcoholic reprobate Cal McDonald is the only line of defense between Los Angeles and a growing horde of zombies, vampires, possessed muscle cars, mad scientists, werewolves, and much more weirdness!

$24.99 | 978-1-59582-746-3

HELLBOY
VOLUME 1
SEED of DESTRUCTION
WAKE THE DEVIL
MIKE MIGNOLA
WITH JOHN BYRNE

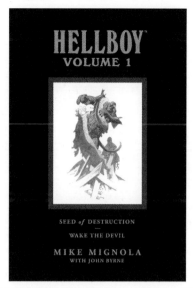

HELLBOY LIBRARY EDITION VOLUME 1: SEED OF DESTRUCTION AND WAKE THE DEVIL

Mike Mignola, John Byrne

Sized at a generous 9 x 12 inches, and handsomely bound to match *The Art of Hellboy*, each volume contains two complete story arcs—the equivalent of two full trade paperbacks. Each volume of the *Hellboy Library Edition* also includes extensive supplemental materials, including previously unreleased sketches and designs.

$49.99 | 978-1-59307-910-9

BEASTS of BURDEN
ANIMAL RITES
EVAN DORKIN JILL THOMPSON

BEASTS OF BURDEN: ANIMAL RITES

Evan Dorkin, Jill Thompson

Welcome to Burden Hill—a picturesque little town adorned with white picket fences and green, green grass, home to a unique team of paranormal investigators. Beneath this shiny exterior, Burden Hill harbors dark and sinister secrets, and it's up to a heroic gang of dogs—and one cat—to protect the town from the evil forces at work.

$19.99 | 978-1-59582-513-1

CREEPY
VOLUME ONE
COLLECTING CREEPY 1-5
WEIRD AND HAUNTING TALES OF FRIGHT!
DARK HORSE ARCHIVES

CREEPY ARCHIVES VOLUME 1

Frank Frazetta, Alex Toth, Al Williamson, and more!

Prepare for a horrifying adventure into the darkest corners of comics history. Dark Horse Comics further corners the market on high-quality horror storytelling with one of the most anticipated releases of the decade, a hardcover archive collection of legendary *Creepy* magazine.

$49.99 | 978-1-59307-973-4

AVAILABLE AT YOUR LOCAL COMICS SHOP OR BOOKSTORE

To find a comics shop in your area, call 1-888-266-4226.

For more information or to order direct, visit DarkHorse.com or call 1-800-862-0052 • Mon.–Fri. 9 A.M. to 5 P.M. Pacific Time.

Prices and availability subject to change without notice.

RECOMMENDED DARK HORSE READING

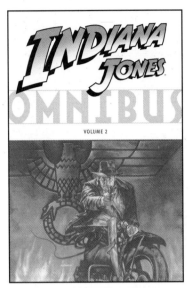

INDIANA JONES OMNIBUS: THE FURTHER ADVENTURES VOLUME 2

Gary Gianni, David Mazzucchelli, Herb Trimpe, and more!

Clouds of war gather ominously over Europe . . . The Great Depression grips the world . . . But one globetrotting archaeologist's thirst for adventure and discovery remains undaunted by his times in *Indiana Jones: The Further Adventures*!

$24.99 | 978-1-59582-336-6

THE ESCAPISTS

Brian K. Vaughan, Michael Chabon, Steve Rolston, Philip Bond, and more!

Inspired by Michael Chabon's Pulitzer Prize–winning novel *The Amazing Adventures of Kavalier and Clay*, this is Vaughan's love letter to his chosen medium, a story about what it takes to start out with nothing, and end up with a comic so hot a major corporation wants to steal it from you!

$14.99 | 978-1-59582-361-8

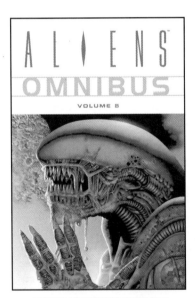

ALIENS OMNIBUS VOLUME 5

Gary Gianni, John Arcudi, Richard Corben, and more!

Living with the Alien has become a fact of life—and death—as mankind expands throughout the galaxy. And no matter how each encounter with the deadly xenomorphs inevitably leads to disaster, man's hubris and greed just as inevitably fuel the desire to try to unlock the secrets of the demonic beasts' biology or bring the creatures under control as tools to build an even more monstrous future.

$24.99 | 978-1-59307-991-8

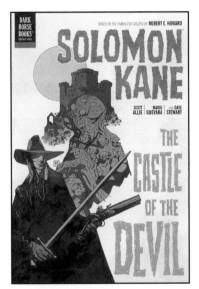

SOLOMON KANE VOLUME 1: THE CASTLE OF THE DEVIL

Scott Allie, Mario Guevara, Mike Mignola

When Solomon Kane stumbles upon the body of a boy hanged from a rickety gallows, he goes after the man responsible—a baron feared by the peasants from miles around. Something far worse than the devilish baron or the terrible, intelligent wolf that prowls the woods lies hidden in the ruined monastery beneath the baron's castle, where a devil-worshiping priest died in chains centuries ago.

$15.99 | 978-1-59582-282-6

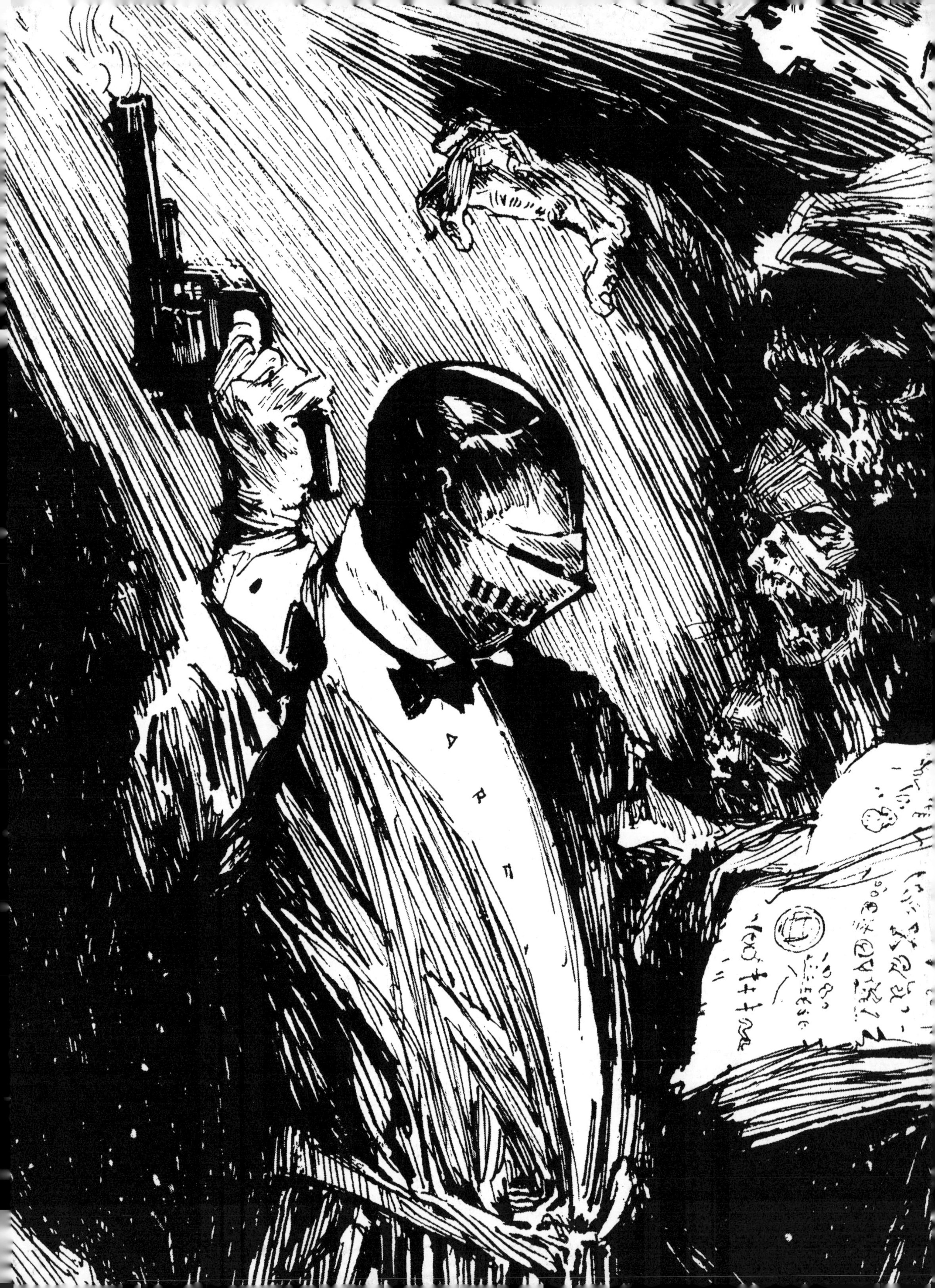